FINAL REPORT: PROJECT NO. 7-1220
CONTRACT NO. OEC-1-7-071220-5115 (095)

LIBRARY MATERIALS IN SERVICE TO THE ADULT NEW READER

HELEN HUGUENOR LYMAN

University of Wisconsin—Madison
Library School
Madison, Wisconsin

AMERICAN LIBRARY ASSOCIATION

Chicago

1973

Library of Congress Cataloging in Publication Data

Lyman, Helen H   1910-
   Library materials in service to the adult new
reader.

   At head of title: Final report: project no. 7-1220,
contract no. OEC-1-7-071220-5115   (095)
   Bibliography: p.
   1. Libraries and new literates. I. Title.
Z716.45.L93   1973   025.5'4   72-11668
ISBN 0-8389-0147-6   (1973)

The research reported herein was performed pursuant to a
contract with the Office of Education, U.S. Department of
Health, Education and Welfare. Contractors undertaking
such projects under Government sponsorship are encouraged
to express freely their professional judgment in the conduct
of the project. Points of view or opinions stated do not,
therefore, necessarily represent official Office of Education
position or policy.

International Standard Book Number 0-8389-0147-6 (1973)
Library of Congress Catalog Card Number 72-11668

Printed in the United States of America

CONTENTS

TABLES

Tables

Tables

Tables

Tables

Tables

Tables

Tables

Tables

xiv

Tables

FIGURES

CHARTS

Charts

FOREWORD

This report presents a comprehensive synthesis of the current research on reading of the adult new literate, the sociological context in which such reading takes place, provides significant new data from an extensive national survey of adult new readers, presents criteria for library analysis of needed materials, and links these to the national programs of adult reading instruction.

Need for this knowledge five years ago brought Helen H. Lyman to the University of Wisconsin-Madison's Library School to undertake development of this study. While public librarians serving adult new readers during this five-year period have winnowed some of the insights presented here as research findings and implications, this report provides a comprehensive framework for the practitioners' insights and has elaborated a set of criteria for evaluation of materials that will serve excellently in guiding and training library staff in the selection of materials for collections and in advisory services with the adult new reader.

Knowledgeable library practice has been an important ingredient in this study, from the earliest sessions of the Advisory Committee, which shaped the direction of the research, to the review and criticism of the criteria, which refined the format presented here. The close links with professional practice assure the value of this report for work with librarians serving adult new readers.

Helen H. Lyman has used consultant services and advice with skill, always relying on such help for what it could give but never losing sight of the adult new reader as a living entity with needs, wants, capacities and human dignity. This volume will serve as an educational resource for library educators and library supervisors seeking not only guidelines and methods, but a sound services philosophy to assure that the librarian's activities in selecting materials are indeed "in service to the adult new reader." Not only the reader profiles but the unique elaboration of the criteria around "personal roles," with stress on "attitudes and values," underscore this sensitivity to the reader as the basic criterion for the evaluation of materials.

Based on familiar library principles for selection and reading guid
ance, this report elaborates these basic principles in a style needed fo
service to this special public.

Margaret E. Monro

PREFACE

This research was initiated and carried out at the Library School of the University of Wisconsin-Madison, from July 1, 1967 through May 31, 1972. The research was supported under a contractual grant from the Bureau of Research, Office of Education, U.S. Department of Health, Education, and Welfare. The investigation which was devoted to establishing criteria for the evaluation of library materials for the adult new reader, was based on a design developed under a planning grant during the first year of the project from July 1, 1967 through June 30, 1968.

The problem investigated by the research was the development of standards for reading materials that would support the adult new reader in the exercise of his new-found skill and build the habit of regular use of the printed word. Bridging the gap between minimal literacy skills and the reading habit was proposed as essential to the purposes of the library program in helping the reader improve his basic education skills, increase his employability, and develop his potential as a citizen and gain personal satisfaction in his many adult roles. The nature of library materials best designed for this end required study in depth. The findings and conclusions derived from the research project provide basic information about the adult new reader and his reading, criteria for analysis of reading materials, and a bibliography of materials. These products of the study constitute a series of reading selection and guidance aids for use by all persons working in this area of service -- librarians, community workers, teachers, publishers, editors, and reading specialists.

The Committee on Reading Improvement for Adults, Adult Services Division of the American Library Association first had proposed such an investigation early in 1967. Subsequently the investigation was proposed by Margaret E. Monroe as a research project under the auspices of the University of Wisconsin-Madison, of which she was director.

The relevancy of this research and the urgent need for its findings increased during the project's early development. James E. Allen, when he was U.S. Commissioner of Education, made the

"right to read" a national goal for the 1970's and not only under-
scored the *ability* to read as a foundation stone for self-fulfillment
and the carrying out of the citizenship function but also identified
the *desire* to read as a necessary accompaniment to the skill if the
right to read is to be exercised. The desire to read is dependent
on anticipated rewards and satisfactions.

That bare literacy is not enough may be documented obliquely
by data in the second annual report of the National Advisory Committee
on Adult Basic Education which shows that in 1968, while 62,000
adults learned to read and write for the first time, 27,000 began
to subscribe to newspapers or magazines, 5,000 helped their children
with school assignments, and 3,500 began to use their public libraries.
There is an obvious need to increase the proportion of adult new
literates and adults developing reading skills who find reading
purposeful and pleasurable and make it a habit. National adult
basic education programs and job training programs are enabling
illiterates to take the first step; public and school librarians,
authors, and publishers support the new literate as he takes the
second step and gains independence in reading.

Thousands of adults in the expanded basic education programs
have acquired not only new literacy skills but also new awareness
that the contents of books, newspapers, broadsides, paperbacks, and
magazines may have value and relevance for their lives. The extended
and innovative services developed in public library programs have
created new channels of use and provide guidance in the use of library
reading materials by adults who were formerly not reached. New
demands and interests are developing readers among special segments
of the population (e.g., Appalachians, Blacks, Chicanos, and American Indians) who are not within the dominant culture of middle
class, highly educated adults who are traditionally the users of
libraries.

The development of criteria for the evaluation of materials
for the adult new reader was based on one major assumption: that
assisting the adult new reader as he progresses from minimal literacy
to an increasingly mature use of print is aided by the relevance of
the reading materials to his basic motivations, strong interests,

value system, life tasks, and life style. The identification and testing of these elements in relation to reading was a major focus of research. Each of the major phases of the project dealt with this problem in a unique fashion. The Materials Analysis Study, which continued throughout the research, developed criteria based on concepts drawn from sociological and anthropological studies and LMRP data and findings. The Population Study surveyed the new literate's reading preferences and habits of media use. The National Adult Programs Study explored the role of reading materials in a great variety of adult basic education and job training programs. The Indigenous Literature Study identified popular titles and areas in which additional materials found outside ordinary trade channels are needed. The research carried out by two doctoral students tested the relevance of cultural values and the context of reading materials for reading competence and the reading satisfaction of the adult new literate.

The research as a whole was directed toward the development of criteria and the identification of principles for the evaluation of reading materials for the adult new reader. These criteria and principles provide guidelines for the creation of needed materials as well as for materials selection and reading guidance by librarians and teachers. The *Materials Analysis Criteria (MAC): Standards for Measurement Checklist* will be interpreted by the handbook, *The Adult New Reader and His Reading*, which is in preparation for publication. The handbook contains background about the adult new reader and directions for the use of the MAC criteria. In addition, an annotated bibliography of materials which have been analyzed through application of the criteria has been compiled for future publication, this bibliography will provide a wide range of selected reading material for the adult new reader.

The research project was able to develop its unique characteristics and solve specific problems as they were identified. First, the project dealt with a complex problem which required a developmental approach to its research design, with revisions made as perspectives became clarified. The variety of reading materials and diversity of populations made variables difficult to control.

The evolution of different treatments for varied phases of research resulted in reasonable solutions. Second, the varied facets of the study and the developmental phases of the study required staff with different talents at different stages. Continuity was maintained by the full-time director of the project. Third, the study of the adult new reader in the ghetto or inner-city involved increasingly sensitive problems as community tensions arose.

The study was conceived and initiated in a period enveloped by crises. The civil rights revolution took place in both the South and the North. The ghetto risings which had begun in Harlem in 1964, continued in Watts in 1965, in Chicago and Cleveland in 1966, in Newark and Detroit in 1967, and in Washington, D.C. in 1968. The tensions and turmoil created a climate of hesitation and fear.

The choices of metropolitan areas for personal interviews with readers narrowed as a result of rapid changes in the cities and in the public libraries serving them. Libraries and other agencies were understandably reluctant to weaken the new reader's tentative confidence in the library or other agency for fear that he would be discouraged from continuing to use its services. This problem was overcome by acquiring the services of the National Opinion Research Center organization for the collection of the data through personal interviews. Its staff of indigenous interviewers was qualified and trained to talk with the survey sample of adult new readers gathered for the Population Study.

This study is the product of discussions and interviews including face-to-face contacts with hundreds of persons. They included: the adult readers; those close to the readers, namely, librarians and teachers; administrators of library and adult education programs; advisers and specialists in reading, sociology, adult education, and librarianship; and the professional staff and graduate students who took part in the work of the project over a period of four years.

Acknowledgments

In each phase of the study, staff members, consultants, and resource persons were gathered whose particular talents, points of view, or experience made an essential contribution to a phase of the research. The project staff, varied in its composition, contributed individually and in staff sessions to the progress of the study. Orilla Blackshear, materials analysis coordinator during the first two years of the study, brought to the project expertness in book selection, and skill in staff development. She initiated the development of the basic book collection, helped to formulate the process of its analysis, developed the first drafts of the criteria, and stimulated the productive student staff. The assistant materials analyst, Diane Wheeler Strauss, brought a fresh interest from her inner-city branch library experience, which enriched the approach to the materials analysis. Her field visits and materials studies provided valuable data and sensitive interpretation. The field studies coordinator, Shirley Hall, skillfully used her training and experience in social work as she assisted in the development of the questionnaire and the survey sample for the Population Study. She also took responsibility for the design and carrying out of the National Adult Programs Study.

During October and November of 1969, Evelyn Levy, supervisor of the Library Services Community Action Program at the Enoch Pratt Free Library, served as a consultant to the project. She made a notable contribution to the emerging form of the criteria which she helped clarify, expand, and reorganize in the light of her expertness in materials selection and her knowledge of readers.

In the second and last phase of the study, which focused on analysis of data and evaluation and selection of materials, the project benefited from the professional assistance of Mary Hickey Teloh, who served as materials analyst. She supervised the analysis of materials for adult new readers and assisted in the completion

of major aspects of the Materials Analysis Study.   Her judgment and
reliability were important assets.

Equally valuable and reliable was project specialist, Lynn
Lum, who helped in the analysis of data collected in the Population
Study and the National Adult Programs Study and who supervised the
tabulation of statistical data, a difficult and exacting task.

The contributions of the graduate students brought a unique
aspect to the study and their own studies. Their assistance is
sincerely acknowledged: bibliographic work on the professional
collection during the first half of the project, 1968-69, by Jerilyn
Dugan, Mary Hickey Teloh, Lawrence Hurlburt, Christine Moore, Bonnie
Prussin, Daniel Richards, Nancy Sternback; bibliographical work on
the Adult New Reader Collection and testing preliminary Materials
Analysis Criteria during the first half of the project, 1968-69 by Joyce
Bridge, Sandra Donovan, Mary Hickey Teloh, Bonnie Prussin, Anne Radtke,
Cheryl Sloan; the review of literature about national adult programs,
1968-69, by Yekutiel Deligdisch, Renee Adler Mansheim; 1970-71,
tabulation and analysis of data in the Population Study and National
Adult Programs Study by Lynn Lum and John Davidson; review and analysis
of research literature about Mexican Americans, 1969, Ruth Mason;
processing of data in the analysis for the Population Study, 1970-71,
by Robin Block, Nancy Foth, Marguerite Hammett, Roger Rigterink,
Valerie Warren; layout and typing of reports and tables, by Charles
Wolfe; review and analysis of indigenous literature, 1970-71, by
Emil Levenson, Beacher Wiggins; and the final testing of the Materials
Analysis Criteria and its application in the evaluation and selection
of Adult New Reader materials for the bibliography, particularly for
literature related to Black culture and interests, 1970-71, by David
Grant, Prentiss Gillepsie, Evelyn McQueen, Veronica Murrary, Beacher
Wiggins.

Two Library School graduate students at the University of
Wisconsin-Madison used project data for their doctoral studies.
Yekutiel Deligdisch investigated reading comprehension and Lawrence
Sherrill did research on value appeal in material content.

Special acknowledgment should be made of the central role
which Margaret E. Monroe played in the Project. During her direc-
torship of the Library School she initiated the project, selected
the director, and gave counsel and help on critical points in the
research. The advice and assistance of James Krikelas, a member
of the Library School faculty, was useful in the preparation of
the research design report and for budget construction.

The staff of the Wisconsin Survey Research Laboratory provided
technical assistance in the construction of the questionnaire and
of the survey sample for the Population Study, conducted pretest,
and assisted the staff in thinking through the problems faced in
obtaining the survey sample for interviews of inner-city persons
in increasingly tense community situations. The National Opinion
Research Center at the University of Chicago, which was selected
to collect the data for the Population Study, brought to the
research knowledge and experience in conducting national surveys,
familiarity with the problems of inner-city interviewing, and a
corps of trained interviewers located in the cities selected for
this study.

Librarians involved in service to adults of limited education
were generous in aiding the study. The members of the advisory committee
were diligent and creative in giving advice and constructive criticism
as the project developed. They also assisted in their respective
cities in the solution of serious problems during the field studies.
Their insight and thinking are embodied in the research design.
Special appreciation goes to the advisory committee: Meredith Bloss,
David Bradford, William F. Brazziel, Burton R. Fisher, John C. Frantz,
Muriel L. Fuller, Vernon Haubrich, Peter Hiatt, Fern Long, Bernice

MacDonald, Margaret E. Monroe, Wayne R. Otto, and Wilson B. Thiede.

William Brazziel's research experience and insights into the problems were drawn many times particularly in designing the survey of readers and guided reading studies.

Of particular help was the advice on the formulation of the criteria contributed by the materials analysis panel of specialists: Hardy R. Franklin, Harold H. Roeder, and Annie T. Reid.

Among the cooperating agencies were 13 public libraries and 25 local adult education agencies. The assistance, support, advice, and active help given by the directors and staffs of the cooperating public libraries was essential for the development of the research. The staffs of these libraries at different stages gave specific help on distinctive aspects of the study. In the beginning they supplied bibliographies of reading materials used in their materials service programs. Specialists on library staffs evaluated titles presumed to be useful to adult new readers. Library collections were offered freely for examination by the project staff. The library staff members arranged introductions to administrators of adult education programs and accompanied LMRP staff on visits. They provided support and advice when local problems arose and often were able to assist in finding solutions. The nature of the study and the social conditions produced obstacles which could never have been overcome or circumvented without the aid of the administrators in libraries and agencies.

Equally important to the study was the cooperation of the administrators and staff of the national adult education programs who, as resource persons for the Population Study, willingly and freely gave the help and advice needed to secure the survey sample of readers in Baltimore, Cleveland, Los Angeles, New York, and Philadelphia.

The 479 men and women who willingly and generously shared their personal experiences and gave their time to answer the 62 questions in the interview survey must remain anonymous. It is impossible to express my deep and sincere thanks to them directly. Without them the major findings and insights of the Population Study would not exist.

The field department of the National Opinion Research Center at the University of Chicago also deserves thanks, particularly Paul Sheatsley, Survey Research Service Director and Margaret Miller, Senior Field Supervisor, who gave personal attention and direction to the questionnaire data collection, coding, and processing. The individual supervisors and interviewers in each of the five cities carried out a difficult part of the survey with skill and understanding. They overcame many obstacles and achieved friendly cooperation for this research project.

For the National Adult Programs Study, 97 administrators and 26 teachers generously answered questionnaires anonymously. Their interest and shared knowledge was valuable. It is hoped that the findings of this study will be useful to them.

Special consultants were drawn upon for advice and council at difference stages of the research. Their contributions were of immeasurable value in helping to clarify problems and advance the progress of the investigation. Their knowledge and experience contributed to the following major aspects of the study: the design of the Materials Analysis Study profited by the council of Don Brown, Anabel Newman, and Harold Roeder. Helene Aqua advised on reading materials for persons of Spanish origin, and Lynne Skenadore on reading materials for the American Indian. Advice on the design and analysis of the data of the Population Study was given by William Brazziel, Philip Ennis, Myron Lefcowitz, Jeffrey Raffel, and Harold Roeder. At the conclusion of the investigation, most

helpful has been the editorial advice and assistance of Alice
Norton on the preparation of the final report. Her insights and
interest gave both support and encouragement which has been greatly
appreciated.

The provision of advisory support and funds under the Bureau
of Libraries and Educational Technology, U.S. Office of Education
was absolutely necessary. Such support has a vital place in the
encouragement of library research.

The University of Wisconsin-Madison provided the indispensable
physical and administrative resources. The particular support of
the University's Library School was too pervasive to be defined
specifically. The assistance of the directors, Margaret E. Monroe,
Jack A. Clarke, and Charles E. Bunge, under whom the project was
carried out, was especially helpful.

The opportunity to serve as principal investigator for this
research project was at all times fascinating and rewarding.

                                        - Helen Huguenor Lyman

Abbreviations

ALA - American Library Association

ABE - Adult Basic Education

ANR - Adult New Reader

ASD - Adult Services Division

CEP - Concentrated Employment Program

HEW - U.S. Department of Health, Education, and Welfare

H.R. plus number - Bill from the U.S. House of Representatives

I.T.A. - Initial teaching alphabet

LMRP - Library Materials Research Project

MAC - Materials Analysis Criteria

MDTA - Manpower Development and Training Act (not administration)

MUND - Model Urban Neighborhood Development

NC - New Careers

NORC - National Opinion Research Center

NYC - Neighborhood Youth Corps

OIC - Opportunities Industrialization Centers, Inc.

R - Respondent

SMSA - Standard metropolitan statistical area

UNESCO - United Nations Educational, Scientific, and Cultural
Organization

UPB - Upward Bound

WIN - Work Incentive program

PART 1   BACKGROUND OF THE LIBRARY MATERIALS RESEARCH PROJECT
         INVESTIGATION

1.   Previous Research and Studies

2.   The Problem of Adult Illiteracy

3.   Research Design for the Library Materials Research
     Project

4.   Cooperating Libraries in LMRP

5.   National Adult Programs in LMRP

1.

PREVIOUS RESEARCH AND STUDIES

Millions of adults with limited reading interests, abilities and experience live in the metropolitan and rural areas of the United States. They are to be found most frequently among the poor, disadvantaged, and undereducated population. Not all adults in this population are illiterate or ill-educated, but such circumstances increase the likelihood that they will be.

What an adult reads and how much he reads are influenced by his attitudes toward reading, reading skills, interests and needs, motivations and education, and anticipated rewards. The content of the materials, its values and subjects, reading level, organization, format, and treatment are other major influences.

Research that focuses directly on the multifaceted problem of reading materials for adults who are in the process of becoming more mature, critical readers, and the role and responsibilities of libraries in providing service of appropriate and effective materials is at a beginning stage. Information frequently has been gained through trial and error in experimental programs that have had limited successes and bitter failures. Studies about adult reading and materials in achieving purposeful and pleasurable reading experiences are almost nonexistent. Although some research has been done in the field of adult literacy, it has not focused on the adult new reader as defined for the purpose of this research project.

The assumptions, concepts, and information in this study were determined on the bases of findings from areas of relevant research in other fields. The knowledge and experience of the staff and consultants were equally important in the planning of the investigation. The review of the literature which follows includes research from the fields of librarianship, adult education, literacy, reading, sociology and anthropology, and from evaluative studies of public library adult reading programs.

Librarians, teachers, and others concerned with adult reading are wise to recognize the fact that as Bryher, the sensitive novelist observes, "Few remember that to learn to read and write is one of the great victories of life."[1]

A major source for insights and understanding has been the writings of novelists and artists, and biographies and autobiographies. Many of the choices and directions taken in this investigation are based on the life records and creative works of persons who speak directly from experience -- men and women, well known and unknown: Malcolm X, Kenneth Clark, Ralph Ellison, John Griffin, Scott Momaday, Rodolfo "Corkey" Gonzales, Maya Angelou, Dudley Randall, Harper Lee, Piri Thomas, Frantz Fanon, John Steinbeck.

Ralph Ellison describes most aptly the value reading has for him:

> The pleasure which I derive from reading had long been a necessity, and in the *act* of reading, that marvelous collaboration between the writer's artful vision and the reader's sense of life, I had become acquainted with other possible selves -- freer, more courageous and ingenuous and during the course of the narrative at least, even wise.[2]

A significant world literacy program exists, but the literature surveyed is that concerned with the United States. Because the more recent research is related more closely to the problem of functional literacy in today's society the findings from studies of the last two decades are drawn upon for the purposes of this research project. Because of the project's goals, the implications of the findings in the existing research are interpreted primarily in relation to public library service.

The discussion which follows begins by defining literacy, problems and purposes, and reviews the responses of various social agencies as well as the public library and publishers.

Literacy and Functional Literacy

What is literacy? What is illiteracy? The answer varies depending primarily on the framework within which the definition is established, the geographic location, the period in history, the United States census definition, and the literacy requirements for

4

achievement. A quarter of a century of work by the Laubachs resulted in experience and knowledge unexampled. Their great pioneer effort has reached into ninety-six countries. They have pioneered the way in writing for "new literates" and prepared lessons in 274 languages. They have had, not only priority, but dominance in the field. Their knowledge is depended upon by everyone interested in the problem of worldwide literacy.[3]

After World War II leadership moved to the United Nations which operates a world literacy program through the United Nations Educational Scientific and Cultural Organization (UNESCO). UNESCO assists nations in achieving basic literacy for their populations. UNESCO defines literacy in this way,

> A person is literate when he has acquired the essential knowledge and skills which enable him to engage in all those activities in which literacy is required for effective functioning in his group and community, and whose attainments in reading, writing and arithmetic make it possible for him to continue to use those skills toward his own and the community's development.[4]

The usual grade school equivalent for judging literacy has been the completion of the fourth or fifth grade level. This standard has been used by UNESCO, the U.S. Bureau of the Census, and the U.S. Army.

> Functionally illiterate adults are defined as those who have not completed the first four elementary grades or first four years of school. For practical purposes, a "literate" person is one who, according to the Census or other qualified agency, *can* read and write at the fourth grade level, an "illiterate" person is one who *cannot*.[5]

After half a century of research, study, and observation, reading is conceived as a complex activity and has been defined by Gray[6] as having five dimensions: perception of words, a clear

5

grasp of meaning or comprehension, thoughtful reaction, assimi-
lation or integration, and flexible rates of reading.[7]

Based on the assumption that literacy is "a necessary commodity,"
Harmon defines literacy as encompassing three stages: the conceptualization of literacy as a tool; literacy attainment, the learning
of reading and writing skills; the practical application of
these skills in activities meaningful to the learner.[8]

Robinson on his "stairway of reading literacy" places adults
who are able to read at grade levels one through four, only one
step beyond complete illiteracy. They are "barely able to contend"
with the adult reading materials available. They often regress to
complete illiteracy because of lack of use and practice.

They move from this low-level literacy to partial literacy
when they are able to read at grade levels five through six, sometimes said to be the reading level of the general public. At this
point they are able to read essential information for daily living
and working at low levels. Rapid progress is possible where there
is help for those who are capable. Regression takes place when
opportunities for extensive reading are not available. And
finally, complete literacy or highest reading level is attained
when one reads critically and with understanding.[9]

Reading Achievement

Another problem arises. Functional literacy when measured by
grade level is not equivalent with achievement. Hilliard reports
a study, done in 1962, to determine literacy levels of welfare recipients
16 years of age and over in the Woodlawn area of the city of
Chicago, Illinois. It was found that when the average achievement
levels for each reported grade completed were compared, at no grade
did the average achievement measure up to the reported grade.
Indications were that not until the completion of the 13th grade
did scores show functional literacy.

In the total sample of 680 persons, there were 6.6 percent who
completed less than five years of schooling (functional illiterates
according to grade placement), 19 percent who completed the fifth,
sixth, or seventh grade; 16.5 percent who graduated from elementary

school but went no further; 45.9 percent who started school but did not graduate; 11.6 percent who completed high school but went no further; 1.0 percent who went to college for one or more years and two recipients who attended ungraded schools. The average educational level equaled 8.8 years.

The actual achievement levels were quite different. These achievement levels as indicated by their test scores showed that 50.7 percent of the sample had achieved less than five completed school years and thus were functionally illiterate. There were 42.2 percent who scored over 6.0 but less than the maximum of 10.0 on the test, and 6.5 percent who scored the maximum, indicating that they had completed the learning of the fundamentals of reading. The average achievement equaled a score of 5.9.

As the age of the recipients increased, the educational and achievement levels decreased. As the age at leaving school increased, the educational and achievement levels also increased. This literacy gap between educational background and reading ability, which Hilliard characterized as the blackboard curtain, showed a massive under-educated population.[10]

A similar study of the East St. Louis area resulted in similar findings. Of the recipients of public aid who were tested 58.5 percent were unable to read at the fifth grade level. Although 82.1 percent had completed the fifth grade. Final conclusions drawn from both studies were that undereducation is a basic cause of dependency in this automated age and grade level cannot be used to predict socioeconomic functioning level. Such functional illiteracy prevents any vocational retraining.[11]

Literacy in the United States

In the past, the population of the United States was thought to be highly literate, with limited reading abilities being confined to the immigrants who came to the shores of the United States. With their own cultures suppressed and submerged, they were assimilated as naturalized citizens. While their children learned, they supplied manpower for the unskilled jobs which were plentiful in a developing industrial economy. Others learned in Americanization classes, used public libraries for self-education, moved upward and outward from the ghetto. The public schools and the public libraries were the agencies in which the entire population would be educated. Literacy was the result and the method for achieving educational goals. Illiteracy, it was thought, was a problem only in other countries. It was assumed that the Laubachs with their farflung literacy program, "the each one teach one" way, would bring literacy to the rest of the world.

A steady decline in illiteracy was recorded by the United States Census Bureau based on statistics of persons who could not read or write in any language.[12] Beginning in 1940 statistics were gathered by the Census Bureau with the years of schooling used to estimate the extent of literacy or illiteracy. The 1960 census figures continued to collect data on years of schooling of persons 25 years old and over and indicated that over 3 million persons were illiterate.

Figures from the 1970 census and the Office of Education show the number of persons unable to read and write in any language has decreased in the nation by 50 percent since the 1960 census. Southern totals dropped by only 25 percent leaving 950,000 completely illiterate persons. Another million are barely able to contend with written words. Like other parts of the country, especially in the northern cities, they include young and old and most of them poor. All ethnic groups are represented. They are scattered from the Rio Grande to Appalachia, from California to Maine.[13]

The proponents of the 1966 Adult Education Act established that over 23 million adult men and women in the United States had not completed eighth grade and 11 million of these has less than a sixth grade education. The Census Bureau estimates that by 1980 there will be more than 5 million persons 25 years and over with less than five years of schooling, and over 21 million with less than eight years. In spite of attempts to eradicate illiteracy, by 1985 there will be more than 800,000 persons 25 years and over with no schooling, over 3.5 million with less than five years of schooling and over 10 million with less than eight years.[14]
Laubach, in A Study of Communications to Adults of Limited Reading

Ability, estimates the dimensions of the problem to be contained in one statistic -- that 8.3 million men and women in the United States, 25 years of age and over,have less than a fifth grade education. The population in this age group totals approximately 100 million.[15]

Today an individual must be at an eighth grade literacy level to be considered functionally literate. Many adults lapse into illiteracy because they drop out of school or because they have no reading materials suited to their needs or reading skills. Many become disillusioned and are apathetic about continuing their reading.

The application of the amplified definition and broadened concept of functional literacy increases the total number of readers who are considered to have inadequate reading abilities. These readers require special materials and guidance, not only in the first stage of learning and acquiring skills, but until a degree of independence is reached. The broader concept of what constitutes functional literacy is the basis for the definition of the adult new reader in this research project on library materials. For the purposes of this research study the adult new reader is identified as follows: he is 16 years of age and over, his native language is English or he is learning English as a second language, his formal education has not extended beyond eleventh grade, his reading level is at least at an eighth grade level.

Purpose for Reading

Closely allied with the concept of literacy and reading is the purpose for reading. The attainment of skill is only a first step. Gray envisions the full attainment of the reading skills and abilities as leading to greater understanding of issues, solutions to problems, and development of richer lives.[16] Literacy is viewed by Paulo Freire as a medium for the freedom of man.[17] The common conception exists that the literacy process is the only educational method, is the source of spiritual and aesthetic enlightenment, is the way to job placement and security.

Postman finds a basic assumption to be that "educational practices are profoundly political" and promote "certain modes of thinking and behavior." He proceeds in his iconoclastic analysis to assert that all activity of reading teachers is rooted in political bias, "For to teach reading, or even to promote vigorously the teaching of reading, is to take a definite political position on how people should behave and on what they ought to value."[18]

He says that teachers promote the reading process as an essential skill. They believe that reading is neutral, prepares for vocations, opens minds to wonders, is a pleasure. Postman believes otherwise. He thinks proponents of reading promote reading for purposes of creating good consumers, obedient citizens, and perpetuating political and historical myth. In comparison with the electronic media, it is obsolete and reactionary, perpetuates ideas, and brainwashes minority groups. He proposes that the school ought to "...be problem-centered, *and* future-centered, *and* change-centered; and, as such, would be an instrument of cultural and political radicalism."[19]

Much of what Postman says about teachers applies in many ways to librarians and both need to find answers to the following questions: What is reading for? What motives are behind its promotion? How does it relate to helping adults achieve multi-media literacy? What are the goals to be? Should perhaps multi-media literacy be the goal sought with the aid of the new technology? The distinction is made more and more often between being able to read and being literate. O'Neil sees the only proper literacy as that which extends a man's control over his life and environment and allows him to continue to deal rationally and in words with his life and decisions.[20]

Would many persons be better off if it were socially acceptable for large numbers not to read? Goodman suggests, that, "conceivably, *more people might become genuinely literate if it were understood that reading is a useful art with a proper subject matter, imagination and truth -- not 'communication' of top down decisions and bad norms*."[21]

Once the functionally illiterate adult has mastered the skills of literacy, he must move into the habit of the regular use of the printed word if the objectives of the literacy program are to be fulfilled. Bridging the gap between minimal literacy skills and the reading habit is essential if the adult is to obtain from the content of the printed materials the ideas and knowledge useful in his daily life.

A major obstacle to teaching and providing reading guidance to the adult who is developing his reading skills and habits is finding appropriate and interesting materials related to the new reader's interests and needs. Publishers are only beginning to produce special materials suitable to the interests of various groups. Uncertainty exists about what is needed and the extent of that need. Teachers, reading specialists, and librarians find difficulty in selecting materials because appropriate materials have not been identified in abundance. The development of adult basic education and job training programs has increased the need for materials. These adult readers are a heterogeneous group composed of smaller, more homogeneous groups whose orientations to daily life, to reading, and to libraries differ significantly enough to require different materials within different contexts of use.[22]

The sociological and anthropological studies during the 1950's and 1960's contain significant information and concepts on poverty, the disadvantaged, and cultural deprivation. Their relation to library literacy programs and understanding of problems of materials for adults with limited reading abilities is evident in three discussions of the literature by Dalzell[23], McCrossan[24], and Stoffle[25].

Social Agencies and Literacy

Social scientists and social agencies have had a somewhat obsessive concern with poverty in the United States since Harrington's *Other America* resulted in national attention to the Americans who are often invisible, suffering, and ignored. Dalzell compares and contrasts the "landmark works" of the 1960's while relating the ideas and opinions to the library's philosophy of service. She concludes that the role of the library depends on the local situation. On the whole, libraries lack precedent, preparation, and materials to do the job. The most baffling problem is the dearth of materials, particularly for beginning readers.

McCrossan reviews research on reading of Americans in

socioeconomic group, "culturally disadvantaged" because of
nonexistent or limited economic, educational, and social opportunities in comparison with the average citizen. He concludes
the research provides no conclusive answers to causal relationships between economic-social conditions of the disadvantaged and
reading and library use.

He found some evidence that they are less skilled readers,
but that studies clearly show a large portion of our population,
adults of low socioeconomic status, make relatively little or no use
of books and libraries. He concludes that the library profession
needs to know more about readers who deviate from norms, reader
interests, provide individual reading guidance, and expend great
effort to achieve successful service.

In recognition of certain aspects of the problem adult basic
education and job training programs have been developed. The programs
have been oriented toward economic goals of increasing employment
skills, placement in jobs, and decreasing welfare aid. Major Federal
legislation during the sixties provided general basic education,
vocational training, and job placement through the following acts:
Manpower Development and Training Act of 1962, Amended 1963 and
1965; Vocational Act of 1963; Economic Opportunity Act, 1964;
Title II-B and Title V Work Experience Program, 1965; National
Science Foundation Act, 1963; Area Rehabilitation Act of 1961;
Higher Education Act of 1963; Library Services and Construction
Act, 1964; Adult Education Act of 1966.

The purpose of the Adult Education Act of 1966 was to develop
and expand basic educational programs for adults 18 years of age and
over. Amended in 1970, it was expanded to include all adults 16
years of age and over below the college level of education. Adult
basic education was defined as education for adults whose inability
to speak, read, or write the English language constitutes a substantial impairment of their ability to get or retain employment
commensurate with their real ability.[26] In 1969 adult basic education programs had a total of 484,626 students. Among 442,604,
30 percent were in beginning (1-3) grade level, 36 percent, inter-
mediate (4-6), and 34 percent advanced (7-8).[27] These three groups
indicate potential users of a wide range of library materials.

With the advent of two world wars and subsequent conflicts the problem of adult reading was further highlighted when the rejection of thousands of young men because of illiteracy or limited reading abilities stimulated the special training programs for men in the armed forces.[28,29] Remedial literacy programs were instituted which were successful within limited military purposes and conditions. In 1966, the Department of Defense revised the entrance standards for the military to accept men previously disqualified. The "New Standards" program for men, known as Project One Hundred Thousand, had among various objectives those of improving literacy, competency in reading, arithmetic, and social studies. The inadequacy of the equation of reading level with grade level was reconfirmed when the median reading ability by grade level was shown to be three to four grade levels below the mean level of school grades completed. Most men entering Project One Hundred Thousand upgraded their reading ability from the fourth grade to the sixth grade level. Eighty percent or more completed the course in a period of three to eight weeks.[30]

The concept of reading readiness, the ability to learn to read at any age, was demonstrated in World War II U.S. Army literacy programs. It no longer can be assumed that all reading abilities are ready to be tapped at the age of six. Many service men failed to read until a readiness program was instituted.[31]

The Problem of Reading Materials

One of the most significant findings in much of the research reveals the importance of using meaningful subject matter in teaching the beginning adult new reader. Six major studies which are concerned with the native-born population indicate that materials for adults have definite significant characteristics. These studies are: U.S. Army studies[32]; Norfolk State College Project[33]; Wayne County Basic Adult Education Program[34]; Missouri Adult Vocational-Literacy Materials Development Project[35]; and the Buffalo Study of Adult City-Core Illiterates[36].

A valuable analysis of each study and review of other relevant investigations is presented by Brown and Newman in the article "Research in Adult Literacy."[37] There is general agreement that the provision of reading materials with appropriate content for the adult population is imperative. All too frequently materials are inappropriate both in vocabulary and content. Utilitarian practical interests motivate adults and are necessary. Adults relate strongly to subject areas, areas, vocations, family, community, self-improvement. Modern content, recent knowledge and concepts are necessary. The desirability of adult and vocationally oriented materials is essential.

Brown and Newman found in their Buffalo study that it was necessary and desirable to develop supplementary materials both from an interest standpoint and from the need of extending the materials horizontally for the slower members of the group. Subjects of particular interest to adult city-core illiterates included: Langston Hughes' poetry, hints on careful buying, information about better jobs, selected readings from the Bible, biographical sketches, and topics of sociological interest. Readers were not interested generally in childish fantasy, humor, and animal-type stories, nor adult stories about sports, adventure, and travel. A positive relationship seemed to exist between preference for certain book titles and reading gain. The high achieving group tended to read more sophisticated materials than the low achieving group and showed greater interest in science, travel, sociological and utilitarian topics. The use of relevant adult materials combining good format with content which meets the expressed needs are essential.

Berke whose study preceded Brown and Newman's found a dispro- portionate majority of illiterate adults among the Black population because of complex causes of cultural discrimination, particularly, in education. He found specific goals to be an important motivator. Reading preferences indicated a strong rejection of children's stories and "Dick and Jane" types of materials.[38]

Strong evidence was shown for the importance of using materials specially developed for adults and the limitations imposed by inapro-

14

priate materials in the 1965 research study on basic adult education
programs conducted by the University of Detroit-Center for Continuing
Education.

The Norfolk State College Experiment, a pioneer and pilot study in the
training of hard-core unemployed, unskilled workers, is a success
story with far-reaching effects. The levels of competence in basic
language and number skills of the trainees fall into several
categories: some had never been to school or had completed less
than three grades; some had less than seven years of school; some
had high levels of schooling but low levels of competence. The
upgrading of adult literacy often suffers from lack of motivation
on the part of adults. Upgrading of technical skill levels of
adults suffers from lack of adult literacy. These two problems
were solved by the training pattern which meshed technical and
general education training. The general education core consisted
of language arts, number skills, occupational information, and
human relations coupled with assistance on daily family problems.
The gain in reading ability for the men classified as functional
illiterates was raised an average of 1.87 years. Some made gains of
three years during the six months of training. "The crowning
point of the Norfolk State experiment was the rising sense of
dignity and worth in the men."[39]

The importance of appropriate reading selections and reading
guidance is stressed by many researchers. Certainly no area
presents more significant potential for library services than in
this area of service to readers improving and expanding their skills
and interests. The adult literacy studies in Buffalo (New York),
Missouri, Wayne County (Michigan), and Cook County (Illinois),
found handicaps of inappropriate materials to be insurmountable.
In the earlier study of the U.S. Army literacy program Goldberg
recommended that any civilian adult literacy program have a follow-up
system even if only to forward reading materials to insure graduates
with some continuous stimulation to use their newly acquired skills.
Accessibility and availability of materials coupled with plentiful
opportunities for practice are essential ingredients of a complete
literacy program. The evaluators of the Chicago literacy program

15

raised other pertinent questions about the need for readily
available reference and supplementary reading, the inadvisability
of using children's materials, and the inaccuracy of standard
reading level tests.[40]

Materials clearly present a continuing problem to the profession.
Librarians increasingly are aware of the complexities of indenti-
fying, evaluating, and interpreting materials that will satisfy the
varied interests of adults who are developing their reading skills.
The problem is documented in the first study of public library
service to adult illiterates. The investigation was carried
out under the auspices of the American Library Association, Adult
Services Division, Committee on Reading Improvement for Adults. In
field trips to 15 cities literacy training was observed and the
role of the library in relation to the training was evaluated.
MacDonald found librarians participating in many ways in the various
adult educational literacy programs. The lack of effective
appropriate materials was the most critical need because inferior
or inappropriate materials often had to be resorted to by teachers
and librarians. All too frequently juvenile materials were supplied for
adults. MacDonald recommended immediate action to compile bibliographie
for easy reading materials and the testing and evaluating of materials.[4]

Several reading lists for adults beginning to read were compiled
in spite of many subject area gaps, poor formats, and inadequacies.
O'Brien noted other deficiencies - uneven quality, lack of materials
of the kind that give pleasure and satisfaction while developing
reading skills, and the dependence on juvenile materials. "The
Library and Adult Literacy," a special issue of the *Wilson Library
Bulletin*, brought together the knowledge and experience of many
experts including accounts on current methods of instruction and
types of books suitable for use. It served as a stimulus to further
developments in the public library field.[43] The reading list
"Books for Beginning Readers" and a supplement was published.[44]

It appears that, in spite of special bibliographies and various
library programs, the same problem exists six years later. Librarians
still express concern, alarm, fear in trying to develop reading
collections for literacy programs and adult illiterates. The need

for new materials and the failure to identify a broader range of materials persists. Many collections are being developed on principles expressed by Warren who is literacy librarian, responsible for the Dallas program of assembling demonstration collections of materials and sample collections specially tailored to needs and interests of teachers and readers. She points out, "it has been necessary,... to order materials largely on intuition, buttressed here and there with limited experience and standard lists developed by other libraries and agencies...[although] we have included a variety of other-than-standard materials in our beginning demonstration collection."[45]

Martin analyzes the Baltimore public library's potential for service to economically and culturally underprivileged citizens in his study based on interviews of a sample of nearly 200 house-holders in the population and a review of Enoch Pratt Free Library's history of adult service. He defines the typical disadvantaged person, whether a reader or nonreader, as one who is not born into a reading family, has a limited education, and does not partici-pate in community institutions and activities. His study data, he concludes, confirm the fact that Baltimore residents of limited cultural and educational background do not turn easily to books and libraries, although admittedly many readers break out of this statistical pattern.

Martin further concludes that librarians give first priority to the identification and analysis of reading materials for the disadvantaged   because librarians are society's experts in reading materials. He recommends a strong program with an "Opportunity Library" of special materials, informational kits, and library centers. Reading programs are handicapped by the sparsity of suitable reading materials, the emphasis in libraries on materials of a "middle class" nature, and the lack of materials which combine simplicity of reading level with maturity of content.[46]

Regardless of how the disadvantaged population is characterized, it is established through numerous studies, that either totally or in part it is a most important segment of the population for which a library service program is required. Service to this

neglected area and these persons is a key recommendation in
Martin's 1969 study of the Chicago Public Library. This study
constitutes the major survey of every aspect of public library
service to the large urban community. The research design and
data collection included an unusually wide range of approaches
-- interviews with users and staff, extensive field work and
observation study of records of all kinds, investigation of every
aspect of the functioning library.

Martin emphasizes again and again the neglect of adults in
the ghetto areas. The less educated among the black and white
population and the young and the old must be considered. Ethnic
groups are large. At the time of the study the Spanish-speaking
group comprised 4 percent of the population. It is projected
that the Black population by 1984 will constitute 50 percent of
the city, if present trends continue. He concludes materials
need to be easily accessible and flexible in kind. It is necessary
"to mobilize and intensify service" with special resources such as
a learning center, specialists on the staff, special publications,
vans with special informational materials, and publications of
utilitarian value. He further recommends a "republication office"
to take resources where simplified presentations are lacking and
prepare them in leaflet, folder, or pamphlet form for use in the
ghetto areas.[47]

Library Responses to the Problem

Changes in society and technological advances create new demands
on individuals. New social awareness, findings in sociological
and reading studies, programs in adult basic education and job
training, and the impetus given by support available from federal
and state funds have combined to influence library service in the
last decade. The response in library practice, particularly in
public and school libraries, has been the creation of new programs
and the extension of services for adults improving their reading
skills and using reading materials. Libraries have provided three
types of service: (1) the provision of materials and guidance
in their use is primary; (2) a few engage in teaching or tutoring

18

programs for illiterates; (3) others extend or initiate services to institutions and groups, as well as individuals. Programs have flourished and disappeared. Some are absorbed into regular service and readapted. From Brooklyn to Los Angeles, Kalamazoo to Corpus Christi, in Rochester, Buffalo, St. Louis, Dallas, Northport, Oakland, Baltimore, and Philadelphia special programs exist. A few of the major programs have had a research or evaluative component.

The Fader experiment with young men in an institutional and school settings, through the fusion of program development and research evaluation in questions of teaching literacy in public schools, brought new ideas and changes. Fader's saturation and diffusion concepts succeeded where the rigid educational system failed. The focus on creating a learning situation with relevant reading throughout the curricula, the use of newspapers, magazines, pamphlets, paperbacks, with the freedom of choice, with access to guidance, resulted in young men reading at a level of literacy previously unapproached. Fader proved that modification of attitude toward reading and writing would lead to changes in performance and to greater skill. He let books speak for themselves and showed that content in print media can be meaningful in the lives of young men.[48]

Hiatt, in his study based on interviews with adults of eighth grade education or less at two urban branch libraries found an important factor in the use of the public library by readers of limited education to be the continued adaptation of the materials which make the collection an integral part of services. Collections must be kept up to date and constantly matched to the needs of their changing neighborhoods. Collections are selected with close attention to content in relation to new trends, new interests, readable books for adult students, individual selections to meet individual needs and interests, and special foreign-language materials.[49,50]

The Reading Improvement Program, initiated at the Brooklyn Public Library in 1955 as an experimental research program, was designed to discover whether a free program to improve the reading ability of adults might be effectively carried on in a library setting with the collaboration of a local college.[51] This goal was demonstrated successfully and a manual was developed to assist librarians in carrying on the program.

The Reading Improvement program became primarily a group developmental reading course for college graduates who were good readers mainly interested in improving reading speed and comprehension. Remedial reading groups were few because only a few of the applicants were at second or fourth grade level. Gradually more and more functional illiterates, defined as persons reading at less than the sixth grade level, were given more time individually and in groups.[52,53]

Keller who worked in the program from the beginning is convinced that counseling and guidance are inseparable from remedial teaching. His accumulated knowledge about materials and readers' problems constitutes a unique contribution. He uses, in particular, workbooks, dictionaries, series of remedial readers, simplified classics, Science Research Associates materials and the Initial Teaching Alphabet (i.t.a.) system. The resources of the library collection are drawn upon constantly. Keller concludes that the volume of reading is important because it exposes the reader to an endless repetition of hundreds of words, gives him practice, arouses enjoyment and appreciation of reading. He believes that nothing helps overcome the regression common to poor readers better than this type of extended reading.[54]

Brooklyn's unique program extending over a period of more than fifteen years with a dedicated and experienced readers' adviser has tested an administrative pattern and philosophy and methods of teaching applicable to more advanced readers. Its goal of demonstrating the possibility that libraries throughout the country might initiate reading improvement programs with college or university assistance, has not resulted in other programs. It is also unclear whether the findings based chiefly on reading improvement of the more advanced reader group are common to the remedial reading group.

The Reading Center's Program at the Cleveland (Ohio) Public Library served the disadvantaged population and specifically the functionally illiterate or limited reader in the Cleveland community. Three Reading Centers assisted 500 Clevelanders to read better and provided materials for the Board of Education Adult Basic Education classes. In this experimental program adults were tutored. Barensfield, director of the project, in his review of it emphasizes the fact that "the functional illiterate -- or, if you prefer, the limited, disadvantaged, reluctant, semi-literate, poor, or nonreader -- represents no one level of attainment or nonattainment but a whole spectrum of abilities and disabilities." The Cleveland Public Library evaluated and tested materials and published bibliographies. Although the teaching of adults was successful, this part of the program was not continued.[55]

In Baltimore the Enoch Pratt Free Library, in continuing its traditional patterns of service but modifying to meet other needs, built a library service component into the Community Action program. This allowed the library to reach into the most deprived areas of the city, integrating service with community branches, and later integrating similar service into a new reorganization plan. Paperback racks and library room collections were placed throughout the neighborhood centers. The library's most successful efforts in working with adults have been in practical ways. Easy reading materials, largely job and skill oriented, are used in cooperation with the city's adult basic education program. Books and reading must be relevant to immediate concerns. Black literature and black authors were popular.[56]

The Neighborhood Center Program of the New Haven Public Library is based on the premise that the library has a unique service in diffusion of knowledge through materials, personnel, and methods. The experimental demonstration project explored new ways of bringing books and other media of communication to bear upon individual and community needs for increased skills in communication and life enrichment. There is no trace of paternalism or doing good which is discernable in some other reports. It includes no philosophy of lifting up the masses.[57]

The function and purpose defined for the library will be carried out and reflected in the kind of multimedia material assembled. Bloss, director at New Haven, conceives of the library as a change-agent, a community cultural center, as well as data bank and literature depository. Such an idea is powerful enough to change the type of collections traditionally found in libraries. This philosophy of community librarianship requires a belief in diffusion of knowledge and in the power of ideas. Bloss asks who is disadvantaged? A misleading dangerous term. Possibly it is the librarians and the libraries that are disadvantaged. Perhaps because they fail to know what is in the communication collection.[58]

Purpose and practice at New Haven has proved successful in one critical area, demonstration and extended service has been continued with local support. People understand that "the centers in New Haven are not branch libraries with programs for the disadvantaged added on as something extra, but are centers for people to pursue their own interests in a reasonably free and open setting with some help from library personnel."[59]

The public library programs for the disadvantaged in New York state at Buffalo, Rochester, and Syracuse are major sources for information and insights on materials for persons in the ghetto areas of cities. Clift, in his study of these programs, reports many facts about materials. The titles of the Buffalo and Erie County *Blacklists* indicate areas of interest to Blacks: the origin of the Negro, Mother Africa, Black Slavery, Contributions of Black People, Roots of Blackness in America, Black Power and Black Nationalism, Plays and Poems, Novels and Short Stories.[60] Clift recommends larger collections of paperbacks and magazines. Materials should reflect local interests and needs in subject areas on economic and vocational improvement, consumer education, health, family life, black heritage, community resources information, and foreign languages.[61]

The Measurement of Readability

The difficulty of measuring accurately readability levels of materials and reading achievement levels of readers has become evident. The problem becomes paramount and demands solutions as soon as further research can find the answer. A lack of reliability and validity of the present measures or formulas is recognized. Although rejected by some, at the same time widespread use is made of the formulas. A complete summary of readability research and its implications is Klare's *The Measurement of Readability*.[62]

Criteria for evaluation of reading materials is a major problem. Several attempts have been made to develop criteria both for instructional and supplementary reading materials. Otto and Ford developed a "yes/no" checklist of 50 items concerning materials, e.g., materials have adult appearance, are programmed, present citizenship or civic responsibility content, have attractive layout design.[63]

Barnes and Hendrickson established criteria for evaluation of materials for use with individuals learning to read. Some of the criteria of items included: publishers use level, standardized readability formula place, classification in terms of basic or supplementary use, format and content appeal, and special features. They found that the materials were being used in basic education programs at three levels to which they arbitrarily assigned approximate grade levels: initial instruction (grade one through three); expansion of reading skills (grades four through six); and broad development of reading skills (grades seven and over). They concluded that there is no one ideal material. Instructional materials with high degree of adult interest are available at the same time there is great need for materials produced by teachers to fit individual needs.[64]

Responses in Publishing

Publishing trends show a shift from the general reader interests to special interests. The tastemakers are no longer confined to the major and semi-major publishing firms. Special groups, particularly ethnic ones, are influencing the change. Established firms, possibly overly concerned with profits and consolidation, fearful or unknowing of new subject interests, have lost leadership.[65]

A new freedom and unprecedented technological developments have made it possible for groups, even individuals, to publish easily. Local and underground publishers are publishing books, leaflets, newspapers. Small specialized publishing houses are emerging, which represent the black population, Chicanos, and American Indians. The approaches and policies of these publishers, as well as their first publications, give hope that the desperate need for authentic ethnic materials will be met. They promise to change a situation in which they feel their cultures are misrepresented; where misinformation is customary; and where peoples are degraded. Trade publishers and librarians also are finding new authors and identifying interests that lead them to new publishing ventures.[66]

These wider sources of materials and potential readers will furnish new materials and bring new users to library programs. Librarians in turn must find new criteria for analysis and evaluation of materials. Racism, biases, and misconceptions are perpetuated in many books. Librarians contribute to this situation through ignorance, insensitivity, and imposition of personal values. All writings must be scrutinized to assure that library collections have authentic material, and all librarians must analyze materials in detail to give honest appraisals and informed objective reading guidance.

Ironically the focus on literacy is at a time when many social scientists, librarians, and educators think that in a time of multi-electronic communication reading belongs to another age. Supporters of reading are thought by some critics to be engaged in political activity scarcely worthy of political morality. Others look to the decades of the seventies in which complete literacy will be achieved through the Right to Read nation-wide program.

Attempts to raise the standards of literacy are complicated as the concept of literacy broadens. What does illiteracy mean? What is the purpose of reading? How can literacy enable persons to control their own self-development and gain educational and personal satisfaction?

The problem which this project is attempting to solve is one no one in the library field seems as yet to have solved. The problem is appraising reading content and levels in materials accurately and matching the print material to that of the reader's abilities, skills, and interests. There is recognition that literacy requires more highly developed skills and abilities, various ways of measurement, and other measures than schooling or intuition. A growing literature of research and evaluation is found in related fields of reading, linguistics, literacy, social sciences, and librarianship.

A growing segment of librarians are aware for the first time of responsibility to persons with limited reading abilities. No longer does certainty exist that libraries are simply for those who come in to read or to borrow print materials. At the same time there exists a continuation of historical concern that public libraries serve young people and adults with less advantages. Recognition of the need for reading materials to meet interests and needs of a population defined in a variety of ways as disadvantaged, deprived, functionally illiterate, dropouts, nonreaders, and unreached, hopefully will lead to improved service.

In general, changes in materials service seem to be in large urban libraries with histories of serving and reaching new groups in the community. The efforts of socially conscious, dedicated librarians played a particularly strong role. A trend to coordinate library materials service with other programs in adult education and job training frequently results in dependency on the cooperating agencies' programs.

Certain themes run throughout the studies and social consciousness of researchers the failure of school systems; the technological changes that eradicate skills and jobs; the direct relation between poverty, welfare, and illiteracy; the urgent need for the appropriate materials essential to effective library service, and the major problem of setting the issue within the proper perspective in a society where electronic communication is pervasive.

Although little is truly different or revolutionary, the response to everyday pressures and change has resulted in willingness to extend materials service, to find new sources of materials, to create materials, and to bring them to readers. Only an intensive effort by librarians throughout the next decade can even begin to solve the problem of reading materials for adults of limited reading abilities.

Librarians must ask for evidence of the value of materials. Are they what they purport to be? Will libraries stock the unknown, the revolutionary, the different, the ethnic materials, the materials to span the range of reading interests at all reading levels. The philosophical commitments, the assumptions and concepts librarians accept will determine the nature of their reading collections. The future promises to libraries and librarians the opportunity of enabling adults to become mature independent users of print in a way that truly satisfies their interests and needs.

Notes

1. Bryher [Ellerman, Winifred], *The Heart to Artemis: A Writer's Memoirs* (New York: Harcourt, Brace and World, Inc., 1962), p. 14.

2. Ralph Ellison, *Shadow and Act* (New York: The New American Library, Inc., 1966), pp. xvii-xviii.

3. Frank C. Laubach and Robert S. Laubach, *Toward World Literacy: The Each One Teach One Way* (New York: Syracuse University Press, 1960).

4. Peter du Sautoy, *The Planning and Organization of Adult Literacy Programmes in Africa,* (Manuals on Adult and Youth Education, No. 4) (Paris: UNESCO, 1966), p. 17.

5. Betty Arnett Ward, *Literacy and Basic Elementary Education for Adults: a Selected Annotated Bibliography,* U.S. Department of Health, Education and Welfare, OE-13017, Bulletin, 1961, No. 19 (Washington, D.C.: U.S. Government Printing Office, 1961), p. 9.

6. William S. Gray, "How Well Do Adults Read?" in *Adult Reading,* The Fifty-Fifth Yearbook of the National Society for the Study of Education, Part II, ed. Nelson B. Henry (Chicago: University of Chicago Press, 1956), pp. 33-34.

7. Helen M. Robinson, "Major Aspects of Reading," in *Reading: Seventy-Five Years of Progress,* Proceedings of the Annual Conference on Reading at the University of Chicago, 1966, ed. H. Alan Robinson (Chicago: University of Chicago Press, 1966), pp. 22-32.

8. David Harmon, "Illiteracy: An Overview," *Harvard Educational Review* 40, no. 2 (May 1970): 226-243.

9. H. Alan Robinson, "Libraries: Active Agents in Adult Reading Improvement," *ALA Bulletin* 57 (May 1963): 416-420.

10. Raymond M. Hilliard, *The Blackboard Curtain: A Study to Determine the Literacy Level of Able-Bodied Persons Receiving Public Assistance* (Chicago: Cook County Department of Public Aid, 1962), pp. 91-93.

11. Raymond M. Hilliard, *First, They Must Read: A Study to Determine the Literacy Level of Able-Bodied Persons Receiving Public Assistance in East St. Louis, Illinois* (Chicago: Cook County Department of Public Aid, 1964), p. 11.

12. Irwin Isenberg, ed., *The Drive Against Illiteracy* (The Reference Shelf, vol. 36, no. 5) (New York: H.W. Wilson Co., 1964).

13. James T. Wooten, "Illiteracy is Persisting in South As It Drops Sharply Elsewhere," *New York Times,* 19 July 1971, pp. 1,15.

14. U.S. Bureau of the Census, *Statistical Abstract of the United States* (Washington, D.C.: U.S. Department of Commerce), p. 110.

15. Robert S. Laubach, *A Study of Communications to Adults of Limited Reading Ability by Specially Written Materials* (Ph.D diss., Graduate School of Education, General, Syracuse University), (Ann Arbor, Mich.: University Microfilms, 1963), p. 1.

16. Gray, "How Well Do Adults Read?" p. 34.

17. Paulo Freire, "The Adult Lieracy Process As Cultural Action for Freedom," *Harvard Educational Review* 40, no. 2 (May 1970): 205-225.

18. Neil Postman, "The Politics of Reading," *Harvard Educational Review* 40, no. 2 (May 1970): 244.

19. *Ibid.*, 40: no. 2: 251.

20. Wayne O'Neil, "Properly Literate," *Harvard Educational Review* 40, no. 2 (May 1970): 260-263.

21. Paul Goodman, "The Universal Trap," in *The School Dropout*, ed. Daniel Schreiber (Washington, D.C.: Project School Dropouts, National Education Association, 1964), p. 48.

22. Helen H. Lyman, *Library Materials in Service to the Adult New Reader, Phase I, The Planning Year, Final Report* (Madison, Wis.: University of Wisconsin, Library School, 1969, Educational Resources Information Center, ED-024436).

23. Anne M. Dalzell, "The Role of the Public Library in Serving the Culturally Deprived: a Bibliographic Essay," (Unpublished M.S. diss. prepared for the School of Library Science of the Catholic University of America, 1966).

24. John McCrossan, *The Reading of the Culturally Disadvantaged* (Occasional Papers, no. 80.), (Urbana: University of Illinois Graduate School of Library Science, Oct. 1966).

25. Carla J. Stoffle, "Public Library Service to the Disadvantaged: A Comprehensive Annotated Bibliography, 1964-1968," (1969: reprint ed., New York: R.R. Bowker Co., 1969).

26. Adult Education Act of 1966, Title II--*Adult Education in Amendments to the Elementary and Secondary School Act of 1966*, Public Law 89-750. Amended April 1970, Public Law 91-230, p. 39.

27. National Center for Educational Statistics, *Adult Basic Education Program Statistics: Students and Data, July 1, 1968-June 30, 1969*, (U.S. Department of Health, Education and Welfare, Office of Education HE5-213: 13037). (Washington, D.C.: U.S. Government Printing Office, 1970). p. 18.

28. Samuel Goldberg, *Army Training of Illiterates in World War II* (New York: Bureau of Publications, Teachers College, Columbia University, 1951).

29. Eli Ginzberg and Douglas W. Bray, *The Uneducated* (New York: Columbia University, 1953).

30. Office Secretary of Defense - Assistant Secretary of Defense, *Project One Hundred Thousand: Characteristics and Performance of "New Standards" Men* (Washington, D.C.: Office Secretary of Defense, Dec. 1969).

31. Helen M. Robinson, "Development of Reading Skills," *Elementary School Journal* 58 (Feb. 1958) : 270.

32. Goldberg, *Army Training of Illiterates in World War II.*

33. Lyman B. Brooks, "The Norfolk State College Experiment in Training and Hard-Core Unemployed." *Phi Delta Kappan* 64 (Nov. 1964): 111-116.

34. Gerald Clark et al., *Research Report on Basic Adult Education Program* (Sponsored by Wayne County Bureau of Social Aid Work Experience Project) (Detroit, Mich.: University of Detroit--Center for Continuing Education, Oct. 1965).

35. H.W. Heding et al., *Missouri Adult Vocational--Literacy Material Development Project* Columbia, Missouri: University of Missouri, 1967), (U.S.O.E. Project no. 034-65).

36. Don A. Brown and Anabel P. Newman, *A Literacy Program for Adult City-Core Illiterates*:..., Final Report Project No. 6-1136 (U.S. Department of Health, Education and Welfare, Office of Education Bureau of Research, Educational Resources Information Center, ED 026619, 1968).

37. Don A. Brown and Anabel P. Newman, "Research in Adult Literacy," *Journal of Reading Behavior* 2, no. 1 (Winter 1970): 19-46.

38. Norman Daniel Berke, *An Investigation of Adult Negro Illiteracy:
Prediction of Reading Achievement and Description of Educational
Characteristics of a Sample City Core Adult Negro Illiterates*
(Ph.D diss., State University of New York at Buffalo) (Ann Arbor,
Mich.: University Microfilms, 1967).

39. Brooks, "The Norfolk State College Experiment in Training
the Hard-Core Unemployed," p. 116.

40. Ann Hayes et al., *An Investigation of Materials and Methods
for the Introductory Stage of Adult Literacy Education* (Illinois:
State Office for the Supt. Public Instruction, 1967, Educational
Resources Information Center, ED 014629).

41. Bernice MacDonald, "Libraries and Literacy Activities," *Wilson
Library Bulletin* 40 (Sept. 1965): 48-50.

42. Bernice MacDonald, *Literacy Activities in Public Libraries*
(Chicago: American Library Association, 1966).

43. "The Library and Adult Literacy," *Wilson Library Bulletin* 40
(Sept. 1965): 40-83.

44. "Books for Adults Beginning to Read," *Wilson Library Bulletin*
40 (Sept. 1965): 67-70, 41 (Sept. 1966): 1-4.

45. Margaret Warren, "The Literacy Librarian: Case Studies of
Experiments in Dallas," *Wilson Library Bulletin* 45 (Nov. 1970):
280.

46. Lowell A. Martin, *Baltimore Reaches Out: Library Service to
the Disadvantaged* (Deiches Fund Studies of Library Service, No. 3.)
(Baltimore, Maryland: Enoch Pratt Free Library, June, 1967).

47. Lowell A. Martin et al., *Library Response to Urban Change: a Study of the Chicago Public Library* (Chicago: American Library Association, 1969), pp. 1-13, 39-42.

48. Daniel N. Fader and Elton B. McNeil, *Hooked on Books: Program and Proof* (New York: Berkley, 1968).

49. Peter Hiatt, *Public Library Branch Services for Adults of Low Education* (Ph.D diss. Graduate School Rutgers, the State University, New Brunswick, New Jersey) (Ann Arbor, Mich.: University Microfilms, 1963).

50. "Urban Public Library Services for Adults of Low Education," *The Library Quarterly* 35 (Apr. 1965): 81-96.

51. Max Siegal, "Adult Reading Improvement: A Five-Year Report," *Reading Teacher* 15 (Jan. 1962): 246-253.

52. Richard L. Keller, *Manual of the Reading Improvement Program: Brooklyn College--Brooklyn Public Library, 1955-1960* (Brooklyn, N.Y.: Brooklyn Public Library, 1960).

53. Richard L. Keller, "Reading Faster and Better: A Report on the Reading Improvement Program of the Brooklyn Public Library," *ALA Bulletin* 56 (Dec. 1962): 1019-1021.

54. Richard L. Keller, "How the Brooklyn Public Library Helps the Functional Illiterate," *American Library Association, Adult Services Division Newsletter* 56 (Fall 1967): 5-8, 13.

55. Thomas E. Barensfeld, "The Limited Adult Reader: an Account of the Cleveland Public Library's Reading Centers Program...," *Library Journal* 92 (Sept. 15, 1967): 3004-3007.

56. Evelyn Levy, "Library Service in the Inner City," *Wilson Library Bulletin* 41 (Jan. 1967): 471-477.

57. Meredith Bloss, "Take a Giant Step: New Haven Library Center's First Year Report," *Library Journal* 91 (Jan. 15, 1966): 323-326.

58. Meredith Bloss, "Public Library Service to Disadvantaged Adults," in *Public Library Service to the Disadvantaged: Proceedings of an Institute, December 7th and 8th, 1967)* (Atlanta, Georgia: Division of Librarianship, Emory University, 1969), pp. 23-31.

59. "Happiness in New Haven: Neighborhood Centers Win," *Library Journal* 95 (June 15, 1970): 2216.

60. Virgil A. Clift, *A Study of Library Services for the Disadvantaged in Buffalo, Rochester, and Syracuse* (New York: The Center for Field Research and School Services, School of Education, New York University, June 1969).

61. *Ibid.*, pp. 138-145.

62. George R. Klare, *The Measurement of Readability* (Ames, Iowa, Iowa State University Press, 1963).

63. Wayne Otto and David Ford, *Teaching Adults to Read* (Boston: Houghton Mifflin, 1967).

64. Robert R. Barnes and Andrew Hendrickson, *A Review and Appraisal of Adult Literacy Materials and Programs*, Cooperative Research Project No. G-029 (Columbus, Ohio: Ohio State University, College of Education, Center for Adult Education, 1965).

65. Bradford Chambers, "Book Publishing: A Racist Club?" *Publishers' Weekly* 199 (Feb. 1, 1971): 40-44.

66. Bradford Chambers, "Why Minority Publishing: New Voices Are Heard," *Publishers' Weekly* 199 (Mar. 15, 1971): 35-50.

2.

THE PROBLEM OF ADULT ILLITERACY

The Extent of the Problem

The problem of achieving functional literacy for adults in the United States is of awesome dimensions. The corollary problem of providing reading materials and reading guidance for adults with limited reading ability and experience is a major concern in public library service during this latter half of the twentieth century. The proponents of the Federal Adult Education Act of 1966 established that over 23 million adult men and women in the United States have not completed eighth grade, and over 11 million of these have less than a sixth grade education. In 1968 at the time this research project was designed the U.S. Census Bureau estimated that by 1980 there would be five million persons 25 years and over with less than five years of schooling. They are found in every city and county and on almost every social and economic level. Some are technically high school graduates. In 1969 the census of the population, in which a literate person is assumed to be one who has completed six or more years of school, revealed that illiteracy had decreased but had not been eradicated.[1]

Compared with a century ago, the rate of illiteracy has declined to one-twentieth of its previous level. In 1870 one out of every five persons 10 years and over was illiterate, that is, unable to read and write. The 1969 census shows that one out of every 100 persons 14 years and over is so handicapped. During the decade of the 1960's illiteracy was reduced by half.

The census figures show that illiteracy rates are related to educational attainment, age, sex, and race. With each increase in educational attainment, as measured by years of school completed, there is a decrease in the illiteracy rate (table 1).

Table 1   Percent Illiterate of Persons 14 Years Old and Over, by Years
           of School Completed and Sex: November 1969 (civilian noninsti-
           tutional population)[2]

Years of School Completed	Both Sexes	Male	Female
Total	1.0	1.1	1.0
No school years	57.4	57.0	58.3
1 year	46.6	48.4	45.8
2 years	21.8	21.3	21.6
3 years	10.9	12.5	9.0
4 years	4.5	3.6	5.4
5 years	2.3	3.1	1.4

A significant factor in the decline in the proportion of persons with little or no schooling was the replacement of older
persons who generally had less education with younger persons who
generally had more. Thus, a larger proportion of illiterates is
concentrated in the oldest group who are 65 years old and over.
They constitute about 45 percent of all illiterates (table 2).

The number of illiterate men in the population, 708,000 is
approximately the same as the number of illiterate women,
727,000. The percentage of men and women in each age group is
shown in the following chart 1   .[4]

Table 2   Percent Distribution of Illiterate Persons 14 Years Old and
           Over, by Age and Sex: 1969 and 1959 (civilian noninstitu-
           tional population)3

Age and Sex	1969	1959
Both Sexes		
Total, illiterate	100.0	100.0
14 to 24 years	6.8	5.5
25 to 44 years	16.5	22.0
45 to 64 years	31.3	35.5
65 years and over	45.4	37.1
Male		
Total, illiterate	100.0	100.0
14 to 24 years	8.6	6.8
25 to 44 years	16.7	24.5
45 to 64 years	36.3	37.0
65 years and over	38.4	31.7
Female		
Total, illiterate	100.0	100.0
14 to 24 years	5.1	3.9
25 to 44 years	16.6	18.6
45 to 64 years	26.3	33.5
65 years and over	52.0	44.1

Chart 1   Age Distribution of Illiterate Men and Women: November 1969

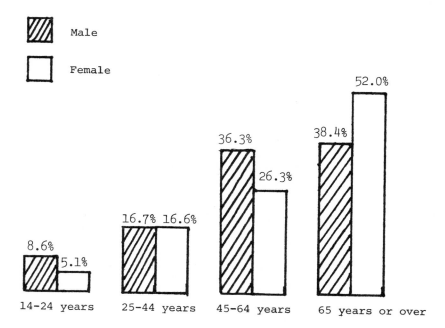

A comparison of illiteracy rates by race shows that among white persons 14 years old and over, about 891,000, or 1 percent, are unable to read and write. The illiteracy rate is approximately the same for both white men and white women. Among Negroes of this age, about 4 percent of the men and about 3 percent of the women are illiterate.

The illiterate white men and women are more likely not to have completed any years of school than are illiterate Negro men and women. Among illiterate white men, 60 percent have completed no years of school as compared with 39 percent of the illiterate Negro men. Among illiterate white women, 70 percent have completed no years of school as compared with 53 percent of the illiterate Negro women (table 3).

Table 3   Percent Distribution of Illiterate Persons 14 Years Old
and Over, by Years of School Completed, Race and Sex:
1969 and 1959 (civilian noninstitutional population)[5]

Years of School Completed and Race	1969		1959	
	Male	Female	Male	Female
White				
Total, illiterate	100.0	100.0	100.0	100.0
No school years	60.2	70.4	53.2	68.6
1 year	8.0	5.2	11.4	7.8
2 years	10.2	10.9	13.8	8.3
3 years	13.7	7.1	12.1	9.9
4 years	4.1	5.0	6.9	2.9
5 years	3.7	1.3	2.6	2.4
Negro*				
Total, illiterate	100.0	100.0	100.0	100.0
No school years	39.0	52.6	44.3	53.7
1 year	18.4	18.4	20.5	17.0
2 years	17.0	8.3	17.3	10.9
3 years	13.5	9.6	11.4	14.1
4 years	5.3	7.5	5.0	3.2
5 years	6.7	3.5	1.6	1.1

* Negro and other races in 1959.

These figures fail to indicate the extent of the illiteracy problem. As the review of the literature in this report shows, the census figures for literacy are misleading because they appear to underestimate greatly the number of persons functionally illiterate. The Laubach study estimated that approximately 100 million men and women, 25 years of age and over have less than a fifth grade education. In 1969 the Office of Education estimated that 3.6 million adults were enrolled part-time in public or private schools below the college level either to complete their high school educations, or to gain basic literacy.[6]

In late 1969 when James E. Allen was the U.S. Commissioner of Education he conceived the Right to Read program to help solve some serious contemporary problems. Allen pointed out at that time that nationwide, one out of four students has significant reading deficiencies. In large city schools, up to half the students read below expectation. About half of the unemployed youths between 16 and 21 years of age are functionally illiterate. Three-quarters of the juvenile offenders in New York City are retarded two or more years in reading. Functional illiteracy raises a barrier to success that for many young adults produces the misery of a life marked by poverty, unemployment, alienation, and in many cases crime.

Another aspect of the problem, particularly in relation to the younger adult population, is the problem posed by the refusal to read or rejection of reading. Fader, on the basis of his findings in his new approach to literacy, concludes that "The functional illiterate may be able to read; he simply cannot or *will not* read well enough for written language to bring him either pleasure or profit."[7] Fader's experiment in education combines wisdom and compassion with knowledge and competence in a highly successful and risky literacy venture. He says, "The difference between *cannot* and *will not* is difficult to perceive and even more difficult to act upon. It is the difference, for instance, between teaching literacy and teaching the pleasures of literacy."[8]

H. Alan Robinson identifies various stages in reading development in his stairway of reading literacy (appendix 1

Stairway of (Reading) Literacy). The adult who is developing his reading abilities and habits must not only have the opportunity and desire to read to the full limits of his capability, but also the means. The adult who is completely illiterate, unable to read or write English at all, is at the beginning stage. He needs instruction and guidance. Unlike the child, he may draw upon the experiences of his entire lifetime. The adult reader with a low level of literacy, at grade levels 1-4, is barely able to contend with adult reading material. He often reverts to complete illiteracy because of lack of use of reading skills. The adult reader who achieves partial literacy is able to read at grade levels 5-6. At this point he is able to read information essential for daily living and for working at unskilled levels. Where there is help for those who are capable, rapid progress is possible.

The adult reader who achieves the next step is at a stage of variable literacy. He is able to read many kinds of materials at a variety of levels. Reading guidance will help the reader improve his reading skills and find effective materials that meet his special interests and needs.[9]

The adult reader achieves complete literacy when he is able to read critically, to evaluate what he reads, and to use the concepts gained to help understand further reading. He becomes a discriminating, independent reader. Such achievement is the goal both for the reader and the librarian.

Today an individual must be at an eighth grade level to be considered functionally literate. Many adults lapse into illiteracy immediately on leaving school. Reading materials of interest to them and appropriate to their reading capacities and abilities are nonexistent or inaccessible. Many see little or no reward or value in reading. They are potential participants for continuing education. Today the one in five adults who are continuing to learn through adult education programs inevitably use reading materials.

When the adult who is functionally illiterate has mastered the skills of literacy, he must develop the habit of the regular use of the printed word if the objectives of the literacy program are to be achieved. It is essential that the adult bridge the gap between minimal literacy skills and complete literacy if he is to obtain from the content of print materials the information and ideas useful and pleasurable for his daily life. Only when he becomes a mature reader can he gain independence and freedom of choice in reading.

A major obstacle in teaching the functionally illiterate adult to read and in encouraging him to continue reading, is the finding of appropriate and interesting materials related to the reader's needs. Publishers have been slow to produce these materials because of uncertainty about what is needed and the extent of that need. Teachers, reading specialists, and librarians find it difficult to select material because a sufficient variety of appropriate materials have not been identified. The lack of materials constitutes a further handicap.

The inability of the functionally illiterate adult to realize his personal potential and to make his contribution to society constitutes a deprivation for the individual and a loss to society with resultant drain on its resources. Sociologists, legislators, and educators recognized this problem, and initiated adult education and job training programs to help solve it. Similarly, librarians, teachers, and others in the fields of reading, education, and community services initiated programs to serve these adults. These efforts have had partial success in identifying the interests and needs of the adults with limited reading skills and experience. They have been able to identify a limited amount of material for use by them. The literature of librarianship, as has been noted previously in this report, documents the desperate need for appropriate and effective reading materials.

The majority of readers with problems of functional illiteracy come from the disadvantaged population. They are likely to have low incomes and cultural deprivations. They may be identified both in urban and rural areas. They are among the recent immigrants to the cities, the migrant population, the ghetto youths, and such minority ethnic groups as American Indians, Blacks, Chicanos, and Puerto Ricans. Not all adults in these groups are

41

illiterate or ill-educated, but their circumstances increase the likelihood that they will be. Robert Lampman reports that "The leading characteristic which distinguishes the poor from the non-poor population is limited educational attainment."[10]

It would seem that adult new readers are a heterogeneous group composed of smaller, more homogeneous groups whose orientations to daily life, to reading, and to libraries differ significantly enough to require different reading materials and in different contexts for use of these materials. Numbers of studies of culturally disadvantaged groups exist. Unfortunately these studies have not distinguished the unique characteristics of that segment of the culturally deprived population within the broader cultural group that chooses to become readers.

Major Questions

Major questions about the reader and materials have been asked which are subsidiary to the general one of how to evaluate reading materials to meet the interests and needs of the adult reader who is developing his reading experience and skills. These questions center around several major categories which relate to information about the materials and about the reader.

Questions about reading materials for the adult reader include: What are the nature and uses of reading materials used by adult new readers? What types of materials are of interest? Are their subjects and types of material of common appeal? Are there specific characteristics of materials which have special appeal to groups, for example, age, ethnic? Are existing materials adequate and appropriate to needs, interests, and reading abilities of adults? What factors are important in evaluating reading materials? What types of materials are needed?

Questions about the adult new reader include: What are the basic social characteristics? What use does he make of his free time? What are his uses of the communication media? What are his reading interests and needs? What relations exist between social characteristics and his reading activity? What are the patterns of reading behaviors? How does he perceive his reading? What are the developmental reading patterns? What are the current activating influences in reading behavior? What are the reasons for reading? Who reads what and why?

These questions are classified into six major categories: background of readers, their reading history, current interests and attitudes, current reading behavior, current general or media level communications behaviors, specific reading interests, needs and opinions.

1. U.S. Bureau of the Census, *Current Population Reports*, Series p-20, no. 217, "Illiteracy in the United States: November 1969, "U.S. Government Printing Office, Washington, D.C., 1971, p.5. Illiteracy is defined, "In 1969, as in past censuses and surveys, persons who were reported as not able both to read and to write a simple message either in English or any other language were classified as illiterate. Thus, illiterates include persons who are able to read but not write. Persons who formerly knew how to read and write but who were unable to do so at the time of the survey because of mental or physical impairment, such as blindness, are classified as literate. In the 1969 literacy survey, respondents were asked (1) if the person could read and write the language now usually spoken in his home; (2) if the person could read and write English, if some other language than English was now usually spoken in his home; and (3) if the person could read and write the language spoken in his home when he was a child, if some language other than English had been spoken."

2. *Ibid.*, p. 1.

3. *Ibid.*, p. 2.

4. *Ibid.*, p. 3.

5. *Ibid.*, p. 4.

6. William K. Stevens, "September Means Back-to-School Time for Adults, As Well As Children." *New York Times*, 25 September 1971, p. L-48.

7. Daniel Fader, *The Naked Children,* (New York: Macmillan, 1971), p. 29.

8. *Ibid.,* pp. 211-12.

9. H. Alan Robinson, "Libraries: Active Agents in Adult Reading Improvement," *ALA Bulletin,* 47 (May 1963).

10. Robert J. Lampman, *Population Change and Poverty Reduction, 1947-1975,* (Madison: University of Wisconsin, Institute for Poverty Research, 1966).

3.

RESEARCH DESIGN FOR THE LIBRARY MATERIALS RESEARCH PROJECT

Background

The research plan for the development of evaluative criteria for reading materials for the adult new reader was designed during the first year of this study. The final plan for the research was based on the findings in relevant research literature, many conferences with specialists, the deliberations of the advisory committee, and final staff decisions. The staff surveyed findings of research in the fields of sociology, anthropology, and adult education, as well as library science and current practice in public library service to the disadvantaged population in various cities. A study of the major aspects of the research problem resulted in a more precise definition of the problem itself, the adoption of basic assumptions, the establishment of objectives, scope, and research methods to be used in the collection and analysis of the data, and the recognition of possible results.

An advisory committee was appointed at the beginning of the planning year. Members included experienced, practicing librarians responsible for services to adults who are developing reading habits and skills in inner city public libraries and research-oriented specialists in the fields. of adult reading, adult education, sociology, psychology, and library adult services. They combined to provide highly professional and technical advice and counsel in developing proposals for the research design.

Committee members examined staff proposals and working papers critically and discussed problems and procedures in detail during meetings held in Madison on November 6-7, 1967, on December 11, 1967, on March 14-15, 1968, and on September 29, 1969. During the planning year they advised on issues, answered questions, and assisted in the development of research methods.

Committee members helped to formulate the major focus and scope of the study, pointed out biases and problems inherent in such an investigation, advised on the role and selection of the cooperating public libraries, devised alternative ways to accomplish the original plan, and suggested methods for dissemination of the project's findings

The committee helped develop a plan for the production of an audiovisual report through film, slides, videotape and cassettes to supplement the printed research reports. The university faculty members on the committee played an important role in advising on research materials and procedures. Each person, speaking from the point of view of his field, scrutinized concepts and principles. They helped to clarify the technical problems related to the survey of the adult new reader.

In September 1969, midpoint in the investigation, the research design was reevaluated and changes were made to meet new situations. At this time the committee considered tentative materials analysis criteria, discussed obstacles and problems in the survey of readers, and advised on necessary procedural changes. Ultimately, the director, as the principal investigator, is responsible for the interpretation of the committee's advice, for incorporating it into the research design, and, finally, for carrying out the design.

Scope and Limitations

The Library Materials Research Project has investigated a problem on which no previous research has been done. The LMRP's major concern has been the establishment of criteria for the evaluation of library materials in the context of use. The variables in any reading situation are multiple. Important factors include: the reader's motivation, the environment, the educational agency's services, the teacher, and the librarian, as well as the reading materials.

The reader's motivation is thought by some to be dominant. Studies of reading improvement programs emphasize that the real success of these programs depends on the individual reader's desire to improve the content and quality of his reading.[1] Limitations set on this research project have excluded direct study of these variables. Although the selected aspects of adult library use are investigated, it should be remembered that the Library Materials Research Project is not a study of adult use of the public library.

The lack of documented facts from previous studies makes this inquiry into library reading materials for adults achieving functional literacy more complex. It is difficult, even impossible, to define the problem narrowly and precisely. In attempting to define hypotheses, it was found again and again that only assumptions could be made. Consequently, the problem statement is based not on a theoretical framework derived directly from related research, but instead on the study of existing programs of service, the experience of practicing librarians and the research staff, relevant data in sociology and education, and frequently on intuition and conjecture. Nevertheless, in the analysis of data from the survey of readers, hypotheses based on the data could be applied to specific aspects of the problem.

Assumptions

The basic assumptions underlying the study are -

1. the progress of the adult new reader from minimal literacy to an increasingly mature use of print is aided by the relevance of materials to his basic motivations, strong interests, value system, life style, roles and tasks;

2. the continued reading of materials by the adult new reader serves as a reinforcement in the development of basic reading skills and as a source of general information, enrichment, broader understanding, aesthetic pleasure, and immediate goal satisfaction;

3. the more that can be known about the adult new reader, his characteristics and reading behavior, the more effective can be the reading guidance service to him;

4. the standards for selection of reading materials, as they are commonly used by librarians, are inadequate for the analysis and evaluation of material for the adult new reader.

48

Definitions

In designing the study, the three major elements needed a precise definition which could set the necessary limits to their use in this research: the adult new reader, reading materials, and national programs.

The *adult new reader* is identified in terms of four characteristics:

- he is 16 years of age or over;
- his native language is English, or he is learning English as a second language;
- his formal education has not extended beyond grade 11;
- his reading level does not exceed that of the eighth grade.

Reading materials are those print materials that serve broad reading purposes, that place emphasis primarily on the substantive content rather than the development of reading skills, and that either have been prepared specifically for the adult new reader or are adaptable to his level of use and interests.

National adult programs are those educational programs suitable for the adult new literate that stress adult basic education and job training and that may involve some study aspects which will use print materials or stimulate their use in independent reading.

Objectives

The main objectives of the research have been to -

1. identify and evaluate the reading materials being produced for and used by the adult new reader after the first stage of literacy to an eighth grade reading level; that is, bridging the gap from literacy skills to independent reading habits;

2. identify the kinds of reading materials suited to the variety of categories of adult new readers;

3. develop criteria for the creation and evaluation of materials for the adult new reader;

4. identify the implications relating to the materials retail
market and the potential demand for these materials.

Secondary objectives which have been essential for achieving the
primary research objectives and which also were carried out during the
four year period are -

1. the development during the planning year, July 1, 1967 to
April 1, 1968, of a research plan designed to accomplish
the primary objective of the study of library materials for
the adult new reader;

2. the identification and collection of materials that have
proved useful or are thought to be useful in serving the
adult new reader;

3. the development of research and testing procedures for the
continuing revision of the materials analysis criteria;

4. the objective examination of the adult new reader collection
of materials by application of the various revisions of the
criteria;

5. the identification of the variables that describe the
characteristics of the adult new reader and the situations
that determine his reading interests and needs in order to
relate the criteria for materials to his context of use;

6. the identification of the characteristics of locally-produced
indigenous materials created by individuals and special ethnic
groups and the incorporation of findings into the criteria;

7. the application of the final criteria developed through
this investigation to the analysis of a range of reading
materials for generating a selective, annotated bibliography
of reading materials for the adult new reader;

8. the preparation of a handbook to summarize findings from
the LMRP research and for guidance in use of the criteria, and

9. an investigation of the usefulness of materials for the adult new reader which had been identified and evaluated in the other four studies in this research project, through an experimental study.

The primary results of the research as envisioned in the design have been -

1. criteria for the evaluation and creation of reading materials with a handbook to serve as a guide to the use of the criteria, and to provide background information for understanding the adult new reader;

2. a selective annotated bibliography of reading materials evaluated by criteria which have been developed by the research project for use by the adult new reader;

3. final summary reports on the research design and on the entire study;

4. reports on various and specific aspects of the findings.

In summary several important elements are assumed. The adult must not only have the opportunity and desire to read to the full limits of his capability, but also the means and the knowledge of the content and character of the reading materials potentially of interest and accessible to him. The problem of guidance and support for the adult new reader's use of reading materials is related to two current limitations: (1) the difficulty, and frequently failure, of relating the reading materials to realistic situations and interests in the normal life patterns of adult new readers; and (2) the lack of appropriate reading materials because they do not exist, are inaccessible, or unknown. The library profession's concern in this area which is delineated in the literature, is understandable because the library is a natural supplier of such reading materials in the everyday reading situation. The public, school, and college or university all have a responsibility for service

Concepts

A close interrelationship exists between the gathering of data about the two major elements of the problem - reading materials and the adult new reader. The general research design has been developed so that data bearing on both these elements, the reader and the materials aspects of the problem, have been served. This rationale is evident in the major phases into which the study is structured: the content analysis of existing materials; a survey of the adult new reader in a universe drawn from participants and students in selected public library programs and local adult literacy and job training programs; a study of reading materials within the context of use in national adult basic education and job training programs; and the analysis and testing of indigenous literature for any special relevance to bridging the gap between reading skills and continuing use of print materials. Each study focuses on either reader or material, and whenever possible investigates the relationships between them.

This plan for the investigation has provided procedures based on this rationale. The adult new reader himself is a most important source for the identification and evaluation of reading materials useful or potenially useful to him. The librarian, the teacher, and others who are closest to the reader or may influence his reading are important secondary sources of information. The qualitative and quantitative analyses of reading materials being used in various contexts provide a source for determining criteria to be used in measuring library reading materials for specific purposes by the adult user in definable reading situations. A bibliography of reading materials for the adult new reader will be selected on the basis of criteria analysis and findings about readers' use of material.

The several concepts which serve as a foundation for the research design relate to adult literacy, life styles, value systems,

purposes for reading, context of use, and content analysis. On
the basis of population statistics and published findings in sociological and educational studies it was decided that adult literacy
or functional literacy in twentieth century society requires a
reading achievement level of eighth grade, and formal educational
level of eleventh grade. Even these customary measurements frequently prove meaningless and inadequate. As stated previously
in this report, it was decided that the total population of adult
new readers might be characterized primarily as disadvantaged or
deprived persons, with low incomes and limited formal education.
At the same time, it is recognized that not all such persons are
illiterate, ill-educated, poor; but such circumstances increase
the likelihood that they will be. They may have limited experience with reading materials.

The basic assumptions and concepts upon which the investigation was built are studies in the fields of sociology, anthropology, and education. The investigation has drawn upon knowledge
gained from experience and information which is accumulated in
library.practice. Librarians have described their experiences
for the benefit of others. Consequently, the programs are initiated by relatively few libraries. Others follow with imitative
programs. It appears that the original source of an idea is the
source for philosophical and conceptual framework.[2,3,4]

Practice and experiment as reported in the Hiatt and Drennan
account of a panel discussion show dedication, disagreement, and
confusion in library service to the functionally illiterate.
Problems in the area of materials are approached frequently through
trial and error. Librarians with experience in this area of service subscribe to the belief "that the public library has an ob-
ligation and an opportunity to be of great service as a vehicle
for social change; as a place where people may, as they have in
times past, find the wherewithal and the encouragement for

53

intelligent self-realization; for participation in a humane and civilized society."[5]

The concept of developmental tasks as set forth by Havighurst has influenced each part of the study.[6] This concept has been incorporated into questions relating to the use of reading materials in the context of employment, adult study, home life, and leisure time activities. The evaluation of materials in the context of various adult roles in society is a basic part of the criteria for the analysis of material. Although Havighurst's developmental tasks relating to work, citizenship, homemaking, parenthood, civic responsibility, and church seem ordered and sequential, individuals follow an individual development and have their own rates and time of facing problems. The patterns of human development are rarely in progressive stages as they seem to be when classified into categories. The responsibilities and expectations of adult life and the developmental tasks inherent in them are found at various ages and frequently overlap. The rigidity of the classification and its suitability for middle= class society in the 1930's and 1940's make it less applicable to the segment of the population included in the LMRP investigation.[7,8]

American life today is characterized by a diversity of life styles. Sociologists and anthropologists present a variety of theories and disagreements. Life styles overlap and frequently reflect ways of life in transition. Life style is related to such contingencies as sex, age, occupation, accessible family resources, marital status, parental status, and ethnic background. What may be more important is that the concept of change is inherent in the life cycle. Hannerz, in his study of Washington, D.C. ghetto culture, suggests four main life styles: mainstreaming, swingers, street families, and streetcorner men. He finds that drifting between life styles is evident in the ghetto life and that relation to the dominant mainstream norms and culture

54

must be taken into account.[9]

The personal system of an individual influences both his perception of others and his behavior toward them. Within the personal system is the individual's storehouse of facts, concepts, and generalizations about the world - his values, feelings, and sentiments about this cognitive structure. This construct is applicable to printed materials which are products of individuals or groups. The appeal of the content of the material and the identification of values and attitudes in the material are vital to library reading materials service.

The methodological approach has been developmental and not entirely sequential insofar as an attempt has been made to get communication in various ways. In the process, it has been possible to discover patterns and meanings and to relate each phase of the investigation to the other phases. What has been learned in one study has been channeled into developing the others by moving back and forth among the four studies. The result has been the incorporation of information about readers and materials into the construction of instruments for data collection, suggestions for categories in the criteria for materials analysis based on new insights, and the selection of materials for adult new readers based on appeal identified from readers' opinions.

The structure of the project provides two major approaches to constructing and testing the criteria for evaluating materials - the continuous revision of the criteria in the light of findings from each phase of the research, and the application of the criteria as finally revised to a selected group of materials for adult new readers for the purpose of generating a bibliography.

Content analysis has been applied as a research technique to identify and evaluate four major aspects found in the reading materials, that is, adult roles, subject areas, attitudes and values, and intellectual challenge and style in structure and development. The use of content analysis as a technique in the LMRP

investigation is not to be confused with the use of content analy-

sis as developed by Berelson and others. Content analysis in

Berelson's definition is "a technique for the objective, system-

atic, and quantitative description of the manifest content of

communication."[10] The analysis of content in LMRP is objective,

systematic, and evaluative, but does not follow the kind of quan-

titative description used by Berelson.

Reading materials contain resources in facts and knowledge

which the adult uses because of instrumental values which relate

to his adult responsibilities in home, job, club, and continuing

education. Such contexts stimulate the use of reading materials.

Reading materials are equally important for pleasure and personal

satisfaction in extending experience and understanding.

Life situations generate the use of facts, knowledge, and

wisdom contained in reading materials which are a part of library

resources. This concept has been a guiding principle for various

parts of this research project in the attempt to explore use or

potential use in relation to the context of daily life situations

of the adult new reader and in particular in the context of nation-

al adult education programs.

Significant social values are shared by different social

strata. Concrete knowledge and experiences of values and life

styles of many segments of the population is essential to build-

ing reading collections and service on resources that have breadth,

depth, and appeal to many persons. Librarians like anthropolo-

gists and ethnologists must free the self from preconceptions and

misconceptions inherent in one's own values and attitudes. Other-

wise, there is the danger of invidious comparisons, harsh value

judgments, and evaluation becomes "a mere exercise in provincial

comparison" against the standard of one's own way of life.[11]

Procedures

The procedures designed to achieve LMRP objectives and used for the collection of information about the reader and the materials relevant to his interests and needs are: the Materials Analysis Study; the Population Study; the National Adult Programs Study; and the study of Indigenous Literature. An experimental study, Guided Reading vs. Free Reading, which was planned to test materials in a public library service program, has been postponed due to lack of resources and time. The final report for Phase I: The Planning Year describes the LMRP research plan.[12]

Each phase of the study has had definite time periods. Various activities overlapped as data were integrated with the overall study of materials and as timing changed under exigencies of the situation. On the whole, the original schedule was maintained except for a long delay in the Population Study because of the complex negotiations necessary to contract for service for collecting and tabulating data in the survey of readers. The time periods for each phase of the study were approximately: July 1967 to April 1968, planning research design; December 1967 through June 1968, initiation of Materials Analysis Study and its continuation through 1972; 1968 through 1971, Population Study; 1969 through 1971, National Adult Programs Study; 1970 through 1971, Indigenous Literature Study; 1971 through March 1972, analysis and reporting.

The Materials Analysis Study has provided the basis for the draft of the criteria through analysis of the characteristics of existing reading materials. The construction of data-gathering instruments in the Population Study and the National Adult Programs Study has relied on the Materials Analysis Study for identification of problems to be investigated and categories of data to be sought.

The survey of readers, the Population Study, has been developed: to identify general and unique characteristics of a segment of the population who are thought to be disadvantaged and deprived, and who choose to be readers; to identify within this adult new reader group any special groups and their special reading interests. Major categories of information about these readers who are participants in reading and adult educational programs include: background characteristics; environmental elements influencing reading; the context of readers' use of print as contrasted with their use of other media; reasons for the use of materials; influences on reading; patterns of reading development; self-perception of reading; and readers' attitudes and opinions about reading. The information provided new insights for the criteria and suggestions for the bibliography.

The National Adult Programs Study has explored the nature, use, and inadequacies of reading materials in the context of adult basic education and job training programs. Teachers and administrators reported the use of materials, and materials needed in the program. These data indicate specific types of materials used, reveal gaps, and contribute to the conceptualization of the criteria.

The Indigenous Literature Study has added further dimension to the LMRP investigation through analysis of these materials by pointing out areas of subject interests and types of materials. It has distinguished attitudes and values in the material. It has helped to confirm categories in the Materials Analysis Criteria.

Special studies of the indigenous literature were undertaken. These studies focused on a primary concern of analysis of indigenous literature's effectiveness in assisting the reader to build the desire to read, once he has the basic literacy skills. One of these studies, "Measurement of the Affective Reading Responses of Black and Puerto Rican Readers,"[13] focused on the relative satisfaction which the adult new reader expresses with values and themes of the indigenous literature of his own cultural group, as contrasted with those of other cultural backgrounds. Another study, "The Reading Comprehension of Adult New Readers in Relation to Their Ethnic

Backgrounds,"[14] focused on the relative competence in reading which the adult new reader demonstrates in using the indigenous literature of his own cultural group as contrasted with the literature of other curtural groups.

Randomization and stratification has been used in drawing the sample for the survey of readers and in the study of national adult programs. Some control has been achieved by drawing respondents from adult classes and reading programs. The self-selection factor obviously is involved because the respondent is not only initially self-selected into the class or program, but also finally decides to participate in supplying information. This is characteristically true throughout the project in data-collection procedures whether in relation to gaining information from readers, teachers, or librarians.

Sources of Data Collection

The sources of data for the Library Materials Research Project cover a wide range. The methods of data collection, the survey samples, the data-gathering instruments, their development and use are described in some detail in parts of this report concerned primarily with the individual studies. In general, the primary sources include -

1. selected research findings in areas of social urban problems, poverty, adult reading, literacy, and library service to the disadvantaged;

2. recorded experiences of librarians;

3. published and unpublished documents and reports of national adult programs;

4. statistics of the U.S. Bureau of Census and federal adult basic education and job training programs;

5. personal interviews based on a questionnaire in a sample survey of adult new readers;

6. responses to mail questionnaires eliciting information from librarians, teachers, and administrators in relevant adult education, job training, and library reading programs;

7. the examination and identification of reading materials for the LMRP analysis in library reading development collections, inner-city and university book stores, and bibliographies published by public libraries and adult education agencies;

8. the knowledge and insights gained in analysis of materials and testing of criteria for analysis;

9. special knowledge and experience of the LMRP staff;

10. consultations about reading materials and their use with librarians, community workers, and administrators in personal interviews and by telephone and correspondence;

11. field visit surveys of cooperating public libraries and adult education agency programs.

The intensive review and study of literature, analysis of materials and data necessary in this investigation has been balanced by continuous contact with the field and practitioners. The LMRP Field Trips, figure 2 , shows the major field visits made by the LMRP staff.

During the entire study, close and continuous contact was maintained with the specialist staffs of the cooperating public libraries and the adult education agencies served by the public library collections. Project staff visited 14 public libraries in Baltimore, Boston, Brooklyn, Buffalo, Cleveland, Los Angeles, Madison, Menominee County (Wis.), Milwaukee, New Haven, New York, Norfolk, Philadelphia, and Prince Georges County (Md.). The materials analysts, the field study coordinator, and the director interviewed staff members responsible for this special area of adult service. Staff members included library directors, supervisors, reading specialists, and community coordinators as well as administrators and teachers in the adult education programs. Project staff interviewed more than a hundred persons. They examined reading development collections in cooperating public libraries in Boston, Buffalo, Los Angeles, New Haven, New York, Philadelphia, and Prince Georges County. The information gained augmented information obtained in the Survey of Reading Materials evaluated by specialists in selected libraries, and in the two special studies - Population Study, and National Adult Programs Study. These significant data, collected through the personal interviews, observations, examination and discussion of materials, have become an integral part of the Materials Analysis Study.

Data Analysis

The types of analysis and presentation of data have varied depending upon the kind of information collected through the separate studies, the purposes for which the data are intended, and their use in the development of the LMRP investigation.

Data analysis has included: preliminary analysis of information in various pretest situations, descriptive statistical analysis ex post facto frequency distributions, averages, correlations, cross tabulations of data, comparison of frequencies and percentages, interrelations between two to three variables, evaluative scales, and content analysis of the reading materials.

Special instruments of analysis have been constructed for use in the research. The Reading Activity Index and Reader Profile have been used in the Population Study. The MAC Checklist has been applied in the analysis of reading materials for the adult new reader in the Materials Analysis Study. In addition, three standard reading formulas, Flesch, Fry, and Gunning, have been applied to obtain readability levels.

Some preliminary analysis of data was made possible by the pretesting of the structured questionnaires which were major instruments for data collection. Revision and changes were based on concrete facts gained in the pretest analysis. More precoding was made possible on the basis of the answers in these tests, and consequently greater efficiency in the coding and processing of the information was possible. An unanticipated result of the Population Study preliminary analysis was the discovery of the feasibility of developing biographical profiles of each reader.

Categorization of data collected through responses to open-ended questions has been carried out in all phases of the LMRP investigation. The classification of responses to open-ended questions and the establishment of code intervals for other responses was completed with the summary data at hand. General categories have been based on tabulations and classification for such data as: individual reading of newspapers, magazines, and books; reasons for reading; problems in reading; social characteristics of age, schooling, residency in a locality, employment, participation in adult programs; family and individual incomes. A similar classification has been made in the analysis of the subjective opinions expressed by librarians, teachers, and readers in personal interviews and in mail questionnaires, about specific types of reading, problem areas in reading, reading interests, and lack of reading materials.

The analysis of independent variables in the Population Study and National Adult Programs Study has been of an ex post facto nature. The independent variables such as age, sex, race, education, participation in adult education classes and programs, have occurred. It is necessary to study them in retrospect for their possible relation to and effects upon the pattern of the reading development and the individual reader's opinions of materials used, and current reading behavior.

The statistical measurement of variables is mainly through frequency distribution of answers in the responses to each question. This analysis, based on computerized marginals, includes percentages, means, medians, ranges, and subsets. It is presented in tabular form, graphs, bar charts, histograms, cross partitions, and evaluative scales. All percentages have been rounded to the whole number. These descriptive statistics are compared and analyzed further in cross tabulations for interrelations between independent variables and observations of dependent variables. Although chi-square (x^2) analysis has been done, the data are not presented. Coefficient correlations, contingency tables, factorial and psychometric analyses are areas for further analysis.

Data collected in the National Programs Study have been handcoded and tabulated. Descriptive statistics of data include frequency counts of the precoded data, percentages, means, medians, and ranges. Subjective data expressed in administrators' and teachers' opinions about reading materials and participants' interests and needs have been interpreted subjectively.

The computerized analysis of data was carried out by the National Opinion Research Center (NORC), University of Chicago, and the University of Wisconsin Computer Center (UWCC). NORC coded, classified, and tabulated marginals and frequency distribution responses to each question in the LMRP Population Study Questionnaire. The further computerized analysis of the data was carried out through services of the University of Wisconsin Computer Center and the Data and Computation Center (DACC). The UWCC UNIVAC 1108, general purpose, solid-state binary computer was used. DACC has provided programming service based on specifications provided by the LMRP staff. The UWCC STATJOB system of statistical programs developed for use on the 1108 computer has been used for statistical analysis: descriptive statistics and correlations, cross tabulations and chi-square contingency table analysis, and recoded and reformated data sets.

Two instruments for analysis of reading behavior of each respondent interviewed in the Population Study have been developed: the Reading Activity Index and the Reader Profile. The problem of validity and acceptability of literacy tests and grade levels in schools to categorize the adult new reader forced the identification of an alternative set of categories. The solution has been to establish the index of reading activity at four levels ranging from least active, somewhat active, active, to very active, which are based on the several variables in the reader's use of newspapers, magazines, comic books, and books. This Reading Activity Index results in evaluation of reading behavior by quantitative score and reading activity level. The Fortran (Formula Translation) program for analyzing data on the computer has been used for establishing the categorization of the adult new reader and the reader profile. The profiles of readers in biographical essay form, showing life-time patterns of reading with personal data, add dimension and depth to the statistical figures insofar as they humanize and individualize the aggregate statistical facts.

The reading materials, trade publications, and indigenous literature have been analyzed primarily through the application of structured criteria for evaluation. The final instrument for the content analysis of materials is the MAC Checklist - Materials Analysis Criteria Standards for Measurement - developed during the LMRP study. The MAC Checklist has been used to analyze the reading materials for the selective, annotated bibliography for adult new readers. Two parallel analyses have been carried on: the analysis of the materials and the analysis and continuing revision of the criteria in the light of findings in the LMRP studies. Two standard readability formulas, the Flesch Reading Ease and the Gunning Fog Index, and two recently developed formulas, the McLaughlin Smog and the Fry Graph for Estimating Readability, were tested for use in analyzing the readability levels of materials.

Notes

1. Bernice MacDonald and Faye Simkin, *Adult Reading Improvement* (ASD Guide to the Literature of Adult Services, No. 2) (Chicago: American Library Association, 1967).

2. Evelyn Levy, "Library Service in the Inner City," *Wilson Library Bulletin* 41 (January 1967): 471-78.

3. Meredith Bloss, "Take a Giant Step: New Haven Library Center's First Year Report," *Library Journal* 91 (January 15, 1966): 323-26.

4. John C. Frantz, "Big City Libraries: Strategy and Tactics for Change," *Library Journal* 93 (May 15, 1968): 1968-70.

5. Peter Hiatt and Henry Drennan, *Public Library Service for the Functionally Illiterate: a Survey of Practice* (Chicago: American Library Association, 1967): pp. 66-67.

6. Robert J. Havighurst, *Developmental Tasks and Education* (New York: McKay, 1952).

7. Robert J. Havighurst and Betty Orr, *Adult Education and Adult Needs* and *Supplement, 1960: Adult Education for Our Time* by Robert J. Havighurst (Chicago: Center for the Study of Liberal Education for Adults, 1956).

8. Clemmont E. Vontress, "Adult Life Styles: Implications for Education," *Adult Leadership* (May 1970): 11-12, 25-28.

9. Ulf Hannerz, *Soulside: Inquiries into Ghetto Culture and Community* (New York: Columbia University Press, 1969).

10.   Bernard Berelson, *Content Analysis in Communication Research* (Glencoe, Ill.: The Free Press, 1952): p. 18.

11.   Charles A. Valentine, *Culture & Poverty: Critique & Counter= Proposals* (Chicago: University of Chicago Press, 1969).

12.   Helen Huguenor Lyman, *Library Materials in Service to the Adult New Reader, Phase I: The Planning Year, Final Report* (Library School, University of Wisconsin-Madison, October 1968) (ERIC number ED02-4436).

13.   Laurence L. Sherrill, "Measurement of the Affective Reading Responses of Black and Puerto Rican Readers" (Ph.D. dissertation, University of Wisconsin-Madison, in preparation).

14.   Yekutiel Deligdisch, "The Reading Comprehension of Adult New Readers in Relation to Their Ethnic Backgrounds" (Ph.D. dissertation, University of Wisconsin-Madison, 1971).

4.

COOPERATING PUBLIC LIBRARIES IN LMRP

The cooperating public libraries have been an indispensable element in the development of the LMRP study. They have been a major resource for each phase of the study. Their staffs contributed concrete assistance, advice, active support to the research effort, and what is equally important, encouragement. Each cooperating library has responded to the interests and needs of individuals and special groups among adult new readers. These libraries had, in common, characteristics necessary to cooperation with the study. These factors include -

1. public service programs which are innovative and distinctive;

2. an adequate representation of adult new readers;

3. resources within the library to serve the disadvantaged adult in the ghetto;

4. special collections which provided the library's community with broader exposure to printed sources of information and knowledge;

5. the willingness to support research;

6. the means to work cooperatively within the LMRP fact-finding techniques;

7. a coordinated program of materials service to a substantive program of one or more adult education agencies.

The geographical coverage is as reasonable as possible within the limitations of the public libraries' ability to meet the demands of the study. During the period of the study, changes which took place within the libraries and communities necessitated adaptations and adjustments within the research design. The public libraries and adult education agencies cooperating with the research were willing to be a part of the research, contribute to it, incorporate extra tasks entailed by cooperation, support the objectives of the researchers and make available the advice and assistance of their experienced staffs.

Public libraries cooperating with the Materials Analysis Study include -

1. Boston (Mass.) Public Library

2. Brooklyn (N.Y.) Public Library

3. Buffalo and Erie County (N.Y.) Public Library

4. Carnegie Library of Pittsburgh (Pa.)

5. Cleveland (Ohio) Public Library

6. Enoch Pratt Free Library (Baltimore, Md.)

7. The Free Library of Philadelphia (Pa.)

8. Los Angeles Public Library (Calif.)

9. Madison (Wis.) Public Library

10. Milwaukee (Wis.) Public Library

11. New Haven (Conn.) Public Library

12. The New York (N.Y.) Public Library

13. Prince Georges County (Md.) Memorial Library

Six public libraries cooperated with the Population Study. Milwaukee Public Library and Cleveland Public Library participated in the pretest of the Population Study questionnaire. The survey sample of readers interviewed in the Population Study was drawn from participants in programs in five cities - Baltimore, Cleveland, Los Angeles, New York, and Philadelphia - where materials resources of the public libraries were coordinated through direct service to the local adult basic education and job training programs. The libraries had developed strong reading collections and reading development programs for persons who were adult new readers as defined in the context of this study.

The Norfolk (Va.) Public Library contributed to the planning of the Guided Reading vs. Free Reading Study which has been postponed.

5.

NATIONAL ADULT PROGRAMS IN LMRP

The national adult programs which are an integral part of the
Library Materials Research Project investigation are all engaged
in adult basic education and job training. LMRP gathered data
about both the programs' participants in their roles as readers
and also about the nature and use of reading materials within the
context of these programs.

As a preliminary to planning and conducting this research,
it was necessary to search for and analyze extensive data about
approximately 36 programs, both at the national and local levels.
The following brief descriptions contain background information
about the programs that eventually were selected for study in various phases of the LMRP research. The following 11 programs had
particular continuity and permanence. Capsule reports are derived
from more extensive data about these and the other national
programs.[1]

Adult Basic Education (ABE)

The Adult Basic Education program, authorized by the Federal
Adult Education Act of 1966, makes funds available to State education agencies to implement approved State ABE plans. A State
agency then provides funds for local public school systems to operate ABE programs. Under certain conditions, a nonprofit agency
may be funded by a State to handle a local ABE program.

The ABE program is administered by the Office of Education,
U.S. Department of Health, Education, and Welfare, which usually
provides 90 percent of the funds, with the State providing the
other 10 percent.

The ABE program also includes a teacher training institute
and an experimental demonstration projects program.

The program focuses on the educational limitations of adults,

16 years of age and over, who have less than eight years of formal schooling, and may include those with more than eight years of schooling, but with a basic skills performance of less than eighth grade achievement level.

Concentrated Employment Program (CEP)

The Concentrated Employment Program is a manpower training program aimed at the needs of those in areas of hard core unemployment. Working through locally established community programs and centers, CEP staff members undertake a variety of activities such as recruitment, orientation, counseling, job coaching, and basic education. Medical care and day-care services are provided. Some programs offer work experiences and vocational training. CEP is an agency of the U.S. Department of Labor and usually operates through a community action agency such as Neighborhood Youth Corps, Operation Mainstream, or Community Action Agency. The sponsoring agency provides funding. The U.S. Department of Labor grants planning funds to the local CEP sponsor.

Participation in CEP is open to local area residents who are under 22 or over 45 years of age, and who are unemployed, underemployed, school dropouts, members of minority groups, or physically handicapped. By September 1968, CEP staff had screened 118,000 participants and had placed 38,000 of these in jobs.

Job Corps

The Job Corps is a residential program serving youths from underprivileged backgrounds. Its mission is to help school dropouts, the unemployed, and the undereducated learn to be self= sufficient, productive, and participating citizens. The program is based on the assumption that young people from a poverty environment need to escape from that environment in order to make the best use of their training and instruction.

The Job Corps operates Civilian Conservation Centers for youths which are located on Federal lands such as National Parks and Forests, men's and women's centers near urban communities. These centers provide education up to high school equivalency and skill training in 11 basic vocational clusters.

The Civilian Conservation Centers are operated by the U.S. Department of Agriculture and the U.S. Department of Interior. The centers provide basic education, vocational skills, and conservation work. The urban centers are established and operated under contract with private agencies such as private firms, educational or social service agencies, or universities. The contractor is the sole administrator. Instruction concentrates on intensive specialized vocational training.

The Job Corps legally is open to anyone 16 through 21 years of age who is a U.S. citizen. In practice, applicants are screened according to neighborhood conditions, family income, and prospects for completing education and for finding work. Recruitment is conducted among youths in high-poverty urban and rural areas.

Laubach Literacy, Inc.

The Laubach Literacy program, founded in the 1920's by Frank Laubach, has as its basic principle and method "each one teach one." Its goal is to achieve world-wide literacy. Literacy programs reach into 96 countries and include 274 languages. The program has 30 centers in the United States which provide instruction in English conversation, reading, and writing up to the fifth grade level.

Well known as the "each one teach one" program, the Laubach program is privately endowed and nonprofit. Volunteer teachers come chiefly from the program itself, and a learner is strongly encouraged to tutor someone else, not only to spread the learning,

71

but also to strengthen his own skill and enthusiasm. The one-to-
one relationship is promoted, although others may observe during
the instruction period which is held in comfortable surroundings
such as a center, home, church, or school.

The organization develops and refines the methods and materials, and produces alphabet charts and various publications. In
the United States a weekly journal is issued on two levels of
English and one of Spanish.

Tutors are trained in the Laubach method during a nine-hour
institute which stresses the building of confidence and the early
achievement of success. Laubach has developed what he calls
"easy-to-read, easy-to-teach" techniques using phonetic approaches.
The shape of each letter, using the Roman alphabet, is associated
with an object which begins with that sound. The program reports
success with 50 percent of the participants.

Manpower Development and Training Act (MDTA)

The Manpower Development and Training Act program offers
occupational training to the unemployed and underemployed who
cannot reasonably be expected to obtain full time jobs without
training. Although MDTA organizations and programs vary, all
revolve around the needs of the trainees. The two basic categories of training are institutional training and on-the-job
training.

Institutional training refers to manpower training that
occurs at Manpower Training Skills Centers. These centers are
either self-contained facilities which are open full time, or
part-time training centers which operate in schools on an after=
hours, part-time basis. From 1963 through 1968, one million
persons were enrolled in the program. In 1968 basic education
represented 27 percent of the training.

The U.S. Department of Health, Education, and Welfare and

the U.S. Department of Labor jointly sponsor the training program. The Department of Labor recruits, selects, and refers candidates for training and determines their training needs. The department also places trainees in jobs after they have completed their training. HEW provides the training through State education agencies or other organizations.

The Federal government finances these training programs although the State government is obligated to contribute 10 percent of the cost. All states now have MDTA programs in operation. In the selection of candidates, priorities are given to the unemployed, persons working part-time or below their skill capacity, persons out of work because of automation, disadvantaged youths age 16 through 22 who are out of school and in need of job training, and persons who are to be trained in skills needed by the community or State.

The purpose of on-the-job training is to extend job skills and knowledge to unemployed and underemployed persons whose employment is threatened by technology and automation. On-the-job training is defined as the actual performance of work duties in any occupation under the supervision and guidance of a trained worker or instructor.

The MDTA solicits bids for on-the-job training programs from business firms, labor organizations, government agencies, community organizations, or other public and private agencies. In exchange for training enrollees and the prospect of employing them permanently, the sponsor receives funds for job instructors' fees, training materials, and instructional supplies. In 1968 the program had 125,000 enrollees.

A participant must be certified as disadvantaged by a local employment services office. Each trainee receives the hourly minimum wage during his training, and is subject to dismissal by his employer like a regular employee.

Neighborhood Youth Corps (NYC)

The purpose of the Neighborhood Youth Corps is to provide adequate education for job retention by participating youths. The first of the NYC's three major parts provides part-time employment for high school youths from low-income families so the participants can remain in school. Secondly, the program provides full time work for dropouts of high school age, and encourages them to return to school. Finally, NYC offers a summer employment program which places youths in constructive, paid jobs and is widely regarded.

The NYC, which was authorized by the Federal Economic Opportunity Act of 1964, is administered by the Manpower Administration. The Department of Labor provides training funds but wages are paid to the worker by his employer.

Participation in the NYC is open to in-school youths 14 through 21 years of age, and to out-of-school youths 16 through 21. In 1968 the year-round program included 200,000 youths, of which 160,000 were out of school. An additional 364,000 young people took part in the summer program.

New Careers (NC)

The New Careers program has two major objectives--to relieve shortages of professional personnel in human service activities, and to meet the need of the unemployed and underemployed for meaningful jobs with career-ladder possibilities.

New Careers was created by an amendment to the Economic Opportunity Act of 1966. Originally in the Office of Economic Opportunity, New Careers was moved to the Department of Labor in 1967.

The program is open to men and women 18 years of age or older who are poor or unemployed. Only 10 percent of the participants in the program may be 18 through 21. State and local government agencies and local private organizations engaged in public service

74

activities may sponsor projects. Participants work in preprofes-
sional and paraprofessional positions which offer opportunities
for advancement in the fields of health, education, welfare, public safety, recreation, and neighborhood development. Agencies
apply for enrollees and must guarantee permanent employment after
training.

Opportunities Industrialization Centers, Inc. (OIC)

Opportunities Industrialization Centers provide a program of
self-help and self-motivation in which training is given for jobs
which are readily available locally. Job training programs are
developed to fit both the skills of the graduates and the needs
of the employers.

The Reverend Leon H. Sullivan started the program in Philadelphia in 1962. By 1968, 65 centers had been opened across the
country. Although each center has independence in its operation,
a national OIC Institute offers advice, technical assistance, and
help in finding financial aid. OIC is an independent agency
which accepts some funds from the Federal government and other
public and private agencies. The government, however, has no
administrative control over the program.

The program recruits widely and applications far exceed the
number of spaces available. Applicants take aptitude tests,
verbal and non-verbal skills tests, and an occupational survey
test.

Upward Bound (UPB)

Upward Bound is a national, precollege program for under=
achieving high school students from low-income families. The
program, which began in 1965, is funded under a contract from the
Office of Economic Opportunity. The program seeks to compensate

youths for economic, cultural, and educational deficiencies while preparing them to perform in college. The students are given special instruction during a summer program between the junior and senior year of high school, supportive tutoring during the senior year, and, if necessary, another summer session before entering college.

The Office of Economic Opportunity extends Upward Bound grants to colleges and universities, high schools, two-year colleges, and Community Action agencies. Generally, a college or university that receives a grant cooperates with local high schools in setting up the program.

Participants are students in their second or third year of high school, whose families have incomes below the poverty line. Selection is generally made through the high school, either by teachers, counselors, or principals, or through an interview with Upward Bound staff. A student himself may apply to the school for consideration.

Retention of Upward Bound students by colleges is high. Of the graduates of the program, 80 percent have attended college, and 54 percent have earned degrees.

Vocational Education

The Vocational Education Act of 1963 greatly expanded Federal aid to vocational education by increasing both the number and variety of students. Before 1963 the Federal aid was limited to specific occupational categories, but this Act provides for the use of funds to prepare people for employment in all occupations that require less than four years of college.

The Special Needs Program and Work-Study Program, both programs of vocational education aid, are primarily for the disadvantaged youth of urban ghetto areas. The 1968 amendments to the Vocational Education Act strengthened these programs which are designed to help the hard-to-reach and the hard-to-teach.

Persons with "special needs" are defined as those with academic, socioeconomic, mental, or physical handicaps that prevent them from succeeding in the usual vocational education programs. The Federal government allocates funds for Vocational Education which are matched in part by State and local funds.

The Work-Study Program provides part-time work to youths who are unable to afford schooling and would otherwise not be able to begin or continue vocational training. The Federal government finances 75 percent of this program and the states contribute 25 percent. Grant allotments are based on the relative number of persons in a state who are 15 through 21 years of age, which are the ages of participants.

Work Incentive Program (WIN)

The Work Incentive Program provides for welfare recipients who are covered by Aid to Families of Dependent Children. The purpose of the program is to give these recipients basic and vocational training in order to allow them to get off welfare and into permanent jobs.

The U.S. Department of Labor and the U.S. Department of Health, Education, and Welfare administer WIN through the State employment services. WIN replaced the Work Experience and Training Program under a 1967 amendment to the Social Security Act. The WIN budget for 1969 was $118 million, and the program had 100,000 enrollees. Participants and services are divided into three categories: job placement and follow-up services for those ready to take jobs, basic education and skill training for those who need training to compete for jobs, and special work projects for those who are not prepared for training in special work projects.

Participants must be 16 years of age or older, and receiving Aid to Families of Dependent Children. State welfare boards make referrals. While enrolled, participants receive day-care service and wages, in addition to their welfare allowances.

Notes

1. General references for national adult programs represent a selection from the many documents and publications both local and national that have been used in the Library Materials Research Project.

Greenleigh Associates, Inc. A Report to the Committee on Administration of Training Programs. *Opening the Doors: Job Training Programs.* Part One: *Recommendations and Summary Findings.* Part Two: *Text and Tables.* Washington, D.C.: Government Printing Office, 1968.

Laubach, Frank C. and Laubach, Robert S. *Toward World Literacy; The Each One Teach One Way.* Syracuse, N.Y.: Syracuse University Press, 1960.

Sullivan, Leon H. "Self-Help and Motivation for the Under-Privileged." *Adult Leadership,* 16 (February, 1968).

U.S. Congress. *Economic Opportunity Act of 1964.* Public Law 88-452.

U.S. Congress. *Economic Opportunity Amendments of 1966.* Public Law 89-794.

U.S. Congress. *Economic Opportunity Amendments of 1967.* Public Law 90-222, Title I, Sec. 123, part a.

U.S. Congress. *Elementary and Secondary Education Amendments of 1966.* Public Law 80-750, Title III, *Adult Education Act of 1966.*

U.S. Congress. *Manpower Development and Training Act of 1962.* Public Law 87-415, Title II-A, *On-the-Job Training;* Title II-B, *Institutional Training;* Title II-C, *Redevelopment Areas.*

U.S. Congress. *Manpower Development and Training Act Amendments.* Public Law 90-636, 90-248 (1968).

U.S. Congress. *Social Security Ammendments of 1967.* Public Law 90-248, 1968.

U.S. Congress. *Vocational Education Act of 1963*. Public Law
88-210, H.R. 4955.

U.S. Department of Labor. *Manpower Report of the President*. 1969.

U.S. Department of Labor. Manpower Administration. *Manpower Development and Training Act of 1962, As Amended* (42 U.S.C.
2571-2620).

U.S. Office of Economic Opportunity. *Catalog of Federal Assistance
Programs*. Washington, D.C.: Government Printing Office, 1967.

U.S. Office of Economic Opportunity. *Catalog of Federal Domestic
Assistance*. Washington, D.C.: Government Printing Office,
1969.

U.S. Office of Economic Opportunity. *As the Seed is Sown, 4th
Annual Report* [fiscal year 1968]. Washington, D.C.: Government Printing Office, 1969.

PART 2 SURVEY OF ADULT NEW READERS - POPULATION STUDY

6.

THE STUDY

Introduction

The survey of readers is the phase of the investigation designated as the Population Study in the Library Materials Research Project. The reader himself is the source of information. The study is concerned with determining the parameters of the adult new reader group. The characteristics of this group are described on the basis of the survey sample of adults actively engaged in improving job skills, studying in adult basic education, improving reading skills and abilities. The data about adult new readers, their reading behavior and attitudes, use of the communication media, and their interests and needs for which reading materials are used, were collected through personal interviews by skilled interviewers. The data-gathering instrument was a specially constructed questionnaire.

No previous research investigates the problem of the adult new reader and his reading. For purposes of this study, as previously noted, adults are defined as 16 years of age and over; whose native language is English or who are learning English as a second language; whose formal education is limited; and who are able to read from beginning to eighth grade level. It is assumed further, that an eighth grade level of reading achievement may be equated with eleventh grade level of formal schooling. These adults are primarily among low income, deprived population in inner-city areas. A large number may be found among minority groups of the U.S. population. The universe is limited to adult readers who have been participants in four types of programs: adult basic education, library reading development, job training, and high school equivalency. They do not constitute a sample drawn by random selection from the total population. The population has been sampled according to the proportional representation in a stratified sample of adult programs.

The major categories of information about these adults and their reading are -

1. background characteristics which include personal characteristics of sex, race, cultural and national orientation, language, age, and residency; educational characteristics related to years of schooling and continuing education; socioeconomic characteristics, that is, employment of time, occupation, income; and specific social characteristics regarding activities in the use of free and leisure time;

2. current general or media level communication behavior in the use of television, radio, and printed materials - newspapers, magazines, comic books, and books;

3. use of reading materials in relation to general and specific interests and needs in daily life activities and tasks such as job, home, club, and adult classes;

4. specific reading interests reported in relation to subject areas, type of literature, and specific titles, and opinions of what is read;

5. attitudes and influences toward reading, such as reasons for reading and self-perception of reading;

6. developmental patterns of reading or reading history;

7. reading activity patterns.

Conclusions which can be drawn about the adult new reader and his reading from these major categories of information concern the elements in the environment connected with reading behavior - his attitudes toward the communication media, levels of achievement in literacy or education, the reading materials related to the objectives, needs, and interests of his life. Significant findings are used in determining evaluative principles and criteria and the selection of a bibliography for adult new readers.

Past studies in adult reading have reported that the major correlates of reading and library use are the education of readers and accessibility of reading resources.[1,2,3] Doubt persists concerning the reliability of conclusions carried out in the context of the traditional educational system attuned to white, middle-class population. Reading materials of appeal to this segment of the population are less likely to be of interest or value to adults with other life styles and in different situations.

The fields of sociology, anthropology, and education have produced in recent years facts and concepts that could be drawn upon in designing the research plan. Poverty in the United States has been a major concern of sociologists during the 1950's and 1960's. Harrington perhaps more than any other writer demonstrated the extent of poverty among millions of Americans living in the United States. His emphasis on the invisibility of the poor in an affluent society made visible this part of the society. He stimulated the attention of government and social agencies to the economic and educational problems inherent in a life of poverty.[4]

Much of the prior research in poverty and studies of urban poor emphasize the apathy, the poverty, the anomie, the invisibility of Americans so situated. A set of life situations, conditioned by continuously low income, results in an alienation from society because of limited alternatives or comparative simplification of the experience world, a helplessness, deprivation, and insecurity at the mercy of life's unpredictability. Illiteracy and lack of education generate handicaps that perpetuate poverty and hopelessness. Despite a general picture of isolation and powerlessness, research on goals and values supports the notion that in several ways the poor have some of the same goals and values as other Americans. They want comforts, better jobs, education for their children, security, escape from precarious everyday living, health care, decent housing.[5] Valentine points out

85

that significant cultural values are shared by different social strata.[6] The culture of poverty theories are questioned by many researchers, and recently in a series of thoughtful essays edited by Leacock.[7]

Although the data are incontrovertible, many of the conclusions and interpretations raised more questions than they answered. Moynihan's report on the condition of the negro family led to a literature of controversy.[8] Many researchers point out the inadequacies of the culture of poverty theories. Although the insights gained from sociological studies and research have been essential to the development of the LMRP research, consideration has been given to various conflicting theories. The confusion and plethora of studies about the disadvantaged and poverty has made it impossible to depend upon or understand clearly the conflicting ideas or to relate them directly to the LMRP research. An attempt has been made to maintain a neutral attitude regarding certain characteristics, especially in regard to negative absolutes of problems stated to be exclusive to disadvantaged persons. Broken families, low income, problems of drugs, alcoholism, credit buying, behavioral problems with young adults, violence, alienation permeate all of society today. The generalizations applied to entire minority groups frequently are biased.

The rising expectations of individuals and groups among large segments of the population - the Blacks, Chicanos, Indians - have led to militant demands and changes. At the same time, the meaning of poverty and discrimination is expressed throughout the literature. What it means to grow up poor in the United States is told by researchers close to youth and in young persons' own words in the collection by Gottlieb and Heinsohn.[9]

The values which the individual realizes from his reading have been formulated in various ways by researchers. They are classified as instrumental, reinforcement, aesthetic, prestige, respite, personal security, social security. These values have been considered in the formulation of questions asked of respondents in the survey of readers. [10,11,12]

The goals, attitudes, and values of adult new readers are not defined easily. Today, attitudes toward values and life styles are in a state of flux for almost all segments of society. This ambivalence toward values and life goals and the fluctuation of attitudes toward them which may range from total acceptance to total rejection makes almost impossible the setting of the immediate concerns, interests, and needs of the adult new reader within a general framework. Categorical statements of the acceptance or rejection of the values of stability, security, self-realization, violence, order, education, work - to name but a few - by the adult new reader are unrealistic. The LMRP survey of readers does not attempt to collect information about these complex matters. It does attempt, as will be evident in the other studies, to identify values and attitudes expressed in the material analyzed.

Being disadvantaged implies a comparison with a standard of being advantaged. It can mean economically impoverished, culturally deprived, or culturally different. It can include an unfavorable environment, physical handicaps, language obstacles, and expectations and values different from the norm. Who is to judge? What is the measure? Standards frequently used are: amount and type of education, amount of income, status of the individual or the group to which he belongs, housing conditions, and value of possessions.

Actually, the terms "disadvantaged," "underprivileged," and "deprived" themselves often raise doubts and hostilities. Their use seems to be patronizing and presumptuous. The user often fails completely to recognize the potential of the so-called disadvantaged person or group. Among the country's various deprived groups, usually minority groups, are the American Indians, Appalachians, Mexican Americans or Chicanos and Puerto Ricans who are Spanish speaking, and the Blacks. Others include the white urban poor, the rural disadvantaged, and the ghetto populations, all of whom have deprivations and needs for services yet to be explored. The numbers of persons involved and the many differences among the deprived groups present complexities and opportunities for libraries.

The single most significant factor in serving the disadvantaged person and groups may be the respect and understanding between the library user or potential user, the individual or community, and the library personnel. It is imperative to know and appreciate the life styles, cultural beliefs and values, motivations, desires, interests, and aspirations of various groups.[13]

THE SURVEY SAMPLE

The survey of readers in the project's supportive special study, the Population Study, was carried out in five cities with the cooperation of the following public libraries: Enoch Pratt Free Library, Baltimore (Md.), Cleveland Public Library, Cleveland, (Ohio), Los Angeles Public Library, Los Angeles (Calif.), Brooklyn Public Library and The New York Public Library, New York (N.Y.), and The Free Library of Philadelphia, Philadelphia (Pa.). Only large metropolitan areas are represented because these libraries, at the time of the study, had responded to the needs of special groups and individuals among the adult new readers. The six libraries represented agreed to cooperate in the survey and to fill the minimal research requirements of the project. These requirements alsc made it impossible to include cooperating libraries in communities in the South or the Southwest areas of the country. Nor are small cities, towns, or rural country represented. The inclusion of rural areas would have widened the study's already large geographic area to an unmanageable point. Budgetary considerations also influenced the decisions not to use a national sample of the population and not to have a representative control group. These geographic biases were accepted. The representation of different sections of the country made possible a cross section of segments of the population, Puerto Ricans in New York City, Mexican Americans in Los Angeles, Blacks in all five cities. The adult programs included in the samples are representative of the various national programs requiring reading materials and are found in each of the five cities.

Changes in circumstances and events which occurred during the planning period and the initial development of this study reduced the original number of eight potential cooperating public libraries to six. Some library programs providing reading improvement programs and materials for adult new readers became casualties because of losses in staff and funds. In one library some staff members developed reservations about the objectives and methodology of the research project. Although local fears and tensions in relation to services in ghetto areas grew as a result of the increased tensions and disturbances of the time, in general such obstacles were overcome. At one critical time, for example, when negotiations in New York failed in the effort to find the necessary sample of readers through the New York and Brooklyn public libraries, the Work Incentive Program rescued the project.

The area in each city represented in the survey was determined by the location of the population served by the cooperating public library and by the national adult programs cooperating in the survey. These libraries had established programs providing materials and reading guidance for adults who were developing reading competence and experience. These libraries also had organized substantive programs and provided materials in cooperation with and in support of other agencies which provided programs in adult basic education and job training. Of necessity, the sample was selected from available programs where adult new readers could be found.

On the advice of the advisory committee and because of budgetary considerations an average of 100 persons were to be interviewed in each city or a total of approximately 500 persons. In anticipation of interview losses because of mobility, language difficulties, unavailability, refusals, and program restrictions, approximately 150 persons were to be selected in each city. A major issue revolved around not only the statistically appropriate number but also what the attitudes of the potential respondent would be at a time of social tension. Librarians and adult educators closest to the participants who felt assured that a reservoir of goodwill toward the library would gain cooperation and friendliness were proved correct. The final decisions on whether or not to open the channel of access to the reader or student was made by local administrators and accepted by the research staff.

The primary sampling units included only programs which had been established on a continuing basis for at least two years. The sample of individual readers was drawn from among readers and students who were participating at the time of the survey or had participated within the preceding year in adult basic education, job training, high school equivalency, or library reading development programs. In these programs they were developing and improving

various skills. The men and women surveyed did meet the requirements for designation as adult new readers. These requirements
were: they were 16 years of age and over; English was either their
native language or they were learning English as a second language;
and their formal education had not extended beyone the 11th grade.
It should be reemphasized that the sample was not drawn randomly
from the population of the United States in a statistical sense.
Above all, the persons surveyed were able to read. How typical
they were of adult new readers is not known.

In each city, the desired sampling process involved four steps
beginning with the estimation of the total number of participants
in each program, and ending with the final completed interviews -

1. estimating the total number of participants in each program
   from which respondents were to be selected;

2. selecting a proportionate stratified random sample of
   persons from the programs;

3. contacting through the interviewers the proportionate
   stratified sample;

4. granting an interview through self-selection by the respondents, who in the end decided whether or not to
   participate.

Through this procedure the sample was selected by taking sub-
samples proportional to the size of the significant programs in the
subdivisions of the universe. These subdivisions are adult basic
education, job training, and public library reading development
(table 4, b).

The adult new reader as a variable is considered to be relatively homogeneous within each stratum and to be heterogeneous
between strata. Different levels of reading skills and abilities
are represented. The procedure used in selecting the programs in
each city depended on the available records from which names of
students or library users and their addresses could be obtained.

When the agency was unable to release participants' names without their permission, an initial random sample was drawn from the complete list. The agency then obtained consent for interviewing. The proportionate stratified random sample then was selected from this latter list of names. In one instance when these methods failed, the interviewers were directed to approach students who were not drawn using this sampling procedure.

The size of each subsample or program was determined by the total number of persons who were enrolled in each program during the preceding six months, or were currently enrolled. The diverse sources for the sample of adult readers resulted in disproportionate representation which made it impossible to combine all names from the subdivisions of programs for the random sample. To correct such disproportionate representation, the number of names selected randomly from each program was based on the total number of adult new readers being served by all programs in that city.

The use of proportionate representation in drawing the sample is illustrated in the sample for Cleveland where nine programs provided the sources for names. The current enrollment of adult new readers in these nine programs totaled 2,541. The total was divided by 150, which was the size of the sample to be drawn for interviews in the city, to reveal that the proportionate sample should represent one out of 17 of the total number. The number in each of the nine programs was then divided by this number. For example, the Adult Basic Education Program, which had an enrollment of 1,653, is represented by 98 persons in the random sample to be interviewed. The Work-Study Program, with an enrollment of 332, is represented by 20 persons (table 4, e). Each of the other programs has its proportionate share in the sample (table 4, d,f, g,h).

In two pretests of the interview questionnaire, the samples of readers were drawn by the same methods and with equal care. The pretests made it possible to evaluate the interview instrument and the procedures for interviewing as well as the respondents' attitudes toward questions and the interview process.

During the survey, because the major problem was the inability to interview all cases in the original sample, a second random sample was selected by using the same probability sampling procedures. New names were added to the sample for interviews in Los Angeles, New York, and Philadelphia.

In the final list adult new readers from each program stratum totaled 8,720 which yielded the proportionate sample of 874 persons. In the final samples a total of 66 percent of the persons are from adult basic education programs, 26 percent from job training, and eight percent from public library reading programs. Among the five cities, by far the greatest number are identified as being in adult basic education programs - over 90 percent of the sample in New York and Philadelphia, two-thirds in Cleveland, and one= third in Baltimore and Los Angeles (table 4, a,b).

Only Baltimore and New York samples include persons identified as participating in public library development programs. In Cleveland, Los Angeles, and Philadelphia reading development programs in each library were focused directly on supplying reading materials to the program, not the individual. Consequently, the respondent might not be aware of the service. The interviewer was not able to determine every program involved in serving the reader.

This sample total includes the additional 124 names added by the second sample to the original estimated total of 750 (150 for each city) which proved to be insufficient. This estimate had been based on projections based on the pretest in Cleveland which yielded 63 percent completion. The rate for completed interviews in the survey was 55 percent. The reasons for the failure to complete interviews and thus not maintain the pretest completion rate in all five cities has several explanations (table 4, i-j).

Baltimore and Cleveland had the largest number of completed interviews, with 77 and 63 percent respectively. In these cities the sample of students was drawn from current, up-to-date records. In Baltimore an additional advantage was that students could be interviewed in school or at home. In Los Angeles and Philadelphia interviewers met with less success because circumstances made it impossible to use lists as up-to-date. The population in these cities appeared to be more mobile and forwarding addresses were unknown. In a few instances no addresses existed, and in some instances even the buildings had been demolished.

Prior to the interviewing, it was thought that it would be relatively easy to complete 100 interviews in New York because two or three interviewers would be able to contact persons in the original samples on the days classes were scheduled. This procedure proved unsuccessful because of the informality and irregular class attendance. Only the persistent efforts by the interviewers and the interviewing of individuals not in the random samples made it possible to carry out the recorded interviews.

The findings in the Population Study are based on the data collected in the 479 completed interviews which comprised 55 percent of the total sample of 874 persons (table 4,a).

Respondents' reports on their participation in adult education classes and programs shows that 82 percent were attending classes and only 18 percent not. As is to be expected, by far the majority are in adult basic education programs, 58 percent, about one-third in high school equivalency and 57 percent in job training, while 13 percent identified public library reading development programs (table 4,c).

In spite of the imperfections in the sample and data collection, the findings are sound and interpretable as will be seen in the analysis and tentative conclusions in other parts of the report.

a.   LMRP Population Study Sample

ity	Number of Program Partici- pants	Original Stratified Random Sample	Proportionate Stratified Sample	Interviews Completed	Percent of Interviews Completed
altimore	2236	150	150 - 5 = 145	112	77
leveland	2541	150	150 - 2 = 148	93	63
os Angeles	905	150	150 + 60 = 210	92	44
ew York	790	150	150 + 65 = 215	105	47
hiladelphia	2248	150	150 + 6 = 156	77	45
Total	8720	750	750 + 124 = 874	479	55

b.   Final Sample for LMRP Population Study, by Type of Program and City *(expressed in percent)*

ty	Type of Program			
	Adult Basic Education	Job Training	Public Library Read- ing Development	Total
altimore	31 *(45)*	28 *(40)*	41 *(60)*	16 *(145)*
leveland	66 *(98)*	34 *(50)*	0 *(0)*	17 *(148)*
os Angeles	38 *(80)*	60 *(130)*	0 *(0)*	24 *(210)*
ew York	94 *(203)*	0 *(0)*	6 *(12)*	25 *(215)*
iladelphia	91 *(142)*	9 *(14)*	0 *(0)*	18 *(156)*
Total	66 *(568)*	26 *(234)*	8 *(72)*	100 *(874)*

Table 4 Sample for LMRP Population Study (continued)

c. Participation in Adult Education Classes or Programs As Reported by Respondents *(expressed in percent)*

Respondents Who Attend Classes or Programs	82 *(394)*	
Adult Basic Education		58 *(227)*
Job Training		57 *(225)*
High School Equivalency		30 *(119)*
Public Library Reading Development		13 *(50)*
Respondents Who Do Not Attend Classes or Programs	18 *(85)*	
Total	100 *(479)*	

Table 4   Sample for LMRP Population Study (continued)

d. Baltimore, Maryland Local Programs	Period Used (months)	Total Participation in Program	Original Stratified Sample	Proportionate Stratified Sample
Adult Basic Education				
Baltimore Public Schools Neighborhood Study Groups (MUND) and Work Incentive Program	7/68 - 12/68	150	9	9
Howard Adult Education Center		120	8	8
Adult Education Regular Evening School Classes		480	33	28
Job Training				
Concentrated Employment Program	7/68 - 12/68	200	14	14
Manpower Development and Training	7/68 - 12/68	300	20	20
Opportunities Industrialization Center	6/68 - 11/68	94	6	6
Public Library Reading Development				
Enoch Pratt Free Library Community Action Center Libraries	6/68 - 11/68	263	18	18
Broadway Branch Library	8/68 - 1/69	46	3	3
Hollins Payson Branch Library	8/68 - 1/69	103	7	7
Penn. Branch Library	8/68 - 1/69	198	13	13
Light St. Branch Library	11/68 - 4/69	32	2	2
Summer Concentration Employment Program Library Program	Summer/69	250	17	17
Total		2236	150	145

Interviews Completed = 112 (77%)

97

Table 4   Sample for LMRP Population Study (continued)

e. Cleveland, Ohio Local Programs*	Period Used (months)	Total Par- ticipation in Program	Original Stratified Sample	Proporti ate Stra fied Sam
Adult Basic Education				
Division of Adult Education	9/68 - 2/69	1653	98	98
Project Libros (ABE)	1/69 - 7/69	200	12	12
Job Training				
AIM/JOBS	12/68 - 5/69	72	4	4
Cleveland College Training Center New Careers	1/69 - 6/69	50	3	3
Manpower Training Center	10/68 - 3/69	85	5	5
Opportunities Industriali- zation Center	12/68 - 5/69	40	2	2
Project PEACE Skill Center	2/69 - 7/69	55	3	1
Woodland Job Center	12/68 - 5/69	54	3	3
Work-Study Program	1/69 - 6/69	332	20	20
Total		2541	150	148

Interviews Completed = 93 (63%)

*Cooperating Library: The Cleveland Public Library provides materials
 for the above programs

98

f. Los Angeles, Calif. Local Programs	Period Used (months)	Total Participation in Programs	Original Stratified Sample	Proportion-ate Stratified Sample
ult Basic Education				
Jefferson Community Adult School	1/69 - 6/69	40	6	6 + 2
Lincoln Community Adult School	1/69 - 6/69	42	7	7 + 10
Manual Arts Comm. Adult School	1/69 - 6/69	102	17	17
Venice Community Adult School	1/69 - 6/69	166	27	27 + 11
b Training				
Bookmobile Services* to MDTA Programs Watts Skill Center	5/69 - 10/69	555	90	75 + 32
Community Skill Center	1/69 - 6/69			15 + 5
Teen Posts	------------	unknown	3	3
Total		905	150	150 + 60* = 210

Interviews Completed = 92 (44%)

ooperating Library: Los Angeles Public Library

umber of participants added to original sample for participants
ho could not be contacted

Table 4 Sample for LMRP Population Study (continued)

g. New York, New York Local Programs	Period Used (months)	Total Participation in Program	Original Stratified Sample	Proportionate Stratified Sampl
Adult Basic Education				
Neighborhood House	2/69 - 7/69	8	1	1
Work Incentive Program	6/69 - 11/69	718	137	137 + 65
Public Library Reading Development				
Reader Development Program, Brooklyn	1/69 - 6/69	64	12	12
Total		790	150	150 + 65* =

Interviews Completed = 105 (47%)

h. Philadelphia, Pa. Local Programs	Period Used (months)	Total Participation in Programs	Original Stratified Sample	Proportionate Stratified Sampl
Adult Basic Education				
Operation Alphabet	9/68 - 2/69	1657	125	136 + 6
Job Training				
Antonini Center	9/68 - 2/69	41	3	3
Opportunities Industrialization Center	9/68 - 2/69	550	22	11
Total		2248	150	150 + 6* =

Interviews Completed = 77 (45%)

* Number of participants added to original sample for participants who could not be contacted

Table 4   Sample for LMRP Population Study (continued)

i. Reasons for Not Completing Interviews (New York reported separately)	Baltimore	Cleveland	Los Angeles	Philadelphia
Unable to locate	18	16	65	44
No such address	4	8	15	7
Moved out of area	2	12	4	1
Temporarily not available (in hospital, out of town, in jail, etc.)	0	0	5	1
Not home (4 or more calls)	4	2	11	10
Did not keep 3 or more appointments	1	0	4	2
Refused	3	4	10	10
Interviewer failure to make follow-up calls (1 call only)	1	0	0	1
Did not speak English	0	11	1	1
Deaf mute	0	1	0	0
Mental reasons (senile, emotionally disturbed)	0	1	1	1
Deceased	0	0	2	1
Total	33	55	118	79

Table 4   Sample for LMRP Population Study (continued)

j. Reasons for Not Completing Interviews (New York)

Not in school - (4 or more attempts made)	51
Haven't attended class for some time (per instructor)	31
Officially dropped out of class	10
Instructor had no record of person ever being enrolled in class	5
Changed class or program - no record of enrollment in another class	5
Completed class	3
Class cancelled	3
Illness - not attending class	2
Total	110

Questionnaire Development

The final questionnaire for the LMRP survey of readers resulted from continuing revision based on consultations and testing
of the content and forms developed primarily by the director,
field studies coordinator, and LMRP staff (appendix 3 Library
Materials Research Project Population Study Questionnaire). The
first versions of the questionnaire were developed in consultation
with personnel at the Wisconsin Survey Research Laboratory, and the
staffs of the cooperating public libraries and selected adult education agencies. Changes were made after special consultations
with reading specialists and advisory committee members. In the
final analysis, only the LMRP staff were able to construct the
interview questions to fit the LMRP objectives.

The nature of each question was determined in relation to the
assumptions, goals, and concepts of the LMRP investigation. In
several instances the questions were planned to gather data which
might be compared with earlier literacy studies reviewed in Part I
of this report and such reading studies as those reported by Berelson, Ennis, and others. The questions are stated simply and directly. The categories used were established by careful research
and testing. The units of enumeration were defined precisely and
tested. The questions are programmed in sequence to lead from
possibly more known to less familiar aspects, for example, newspapers, magazines, comic books, books. The difficult series of
questions about specific titles are separated from each other.

An examination of the questionnaire best shows the continuity
and sequence of questions. The opening question relates to the
familiar communication medium of television because the largest
percentage of respondents was expected to be able to answer affirm-
atively. Studies show that the low income population is as likely
to have at least one television set as is the general population.
It is one source of communication used by 97 percent of the

population. It was felt that the ability to answer positively
about specific programs watched would enhance the chances of the
respondent being at ease immediately, as well as supply minimal
information about use of the medium. As a result interest would
be aroused and rapport established. The television programs were
selected for specific mention on the basis of: Nielsen ratings
of the top ten programs as listed in *Variety;* staff knowledge and
observation; revision in the light of pretest answers by respondents; and updated to current status of programs in the fall of
1969 at the time the field study began.

Book titles were selected on the basis of findings from the
Materials Analysis Study. The points considered in the selection
of the 24 titles included: subject appeal, accessibility based
on the public libraries' own bibliographies, reading grade level,
high and low interest levels, cultural significance, age group
appeal, and a title that is self-explanatory.

The majority of questions relate to reading behavior, interests, and opinions of the adult new reader. Questions are asked
about the mass communication media for purposes of comparison.
Questions about the use of print materials relate to the use of
reading materials in daily activities, the reader's perception of
his ability and the amount of reading he has done, and his pattern
of reading development from childhood to the present. In addition,
a number of questions are asked about sociological facts and attri-
butes of the individual. Only basic information thought to be
essential to the analysis of data and of a neutral nature concerning sex, age, race-ethnic background, education, continuing adult
education, occupation, and income has been obtained.

The problem of obtaining readers' opinions about individual
titles and use of books has been difficult because of the diversity
of reading interests and lack of previous research knowledge. It
seemed essential to gain some information about interest or potential

interest from the reader's point of view, and to depend on his ability to recall and to distinguish values.

An initial pretest in Milwaukee was carried out by the field staff of the Wisconsin Survey Research Laboratory. Revisions based on this test were made in the questions. When the services of the National Opinion Research Center (NORC), University of Chicago, were secured the format was revised, coded for computer programming, and tested a second time in Cleveland by NORC. The LMRP director, NORC director, and NORC senior field supervisor made changes and were able to precode several open-ended questions based on knowledge gained in this pretest. Most of the questions permitted free responses which could be noted by the interviewer. The pretesting and pilot studies were significant not only in perfecting and refining the questionnaire for interviews, but supplied actual data which were used in other phases of the study. The immediate value was in the use in development of the criteria for analysis of materials in identifying titles, subject interests, attitudes, and opinions.

The concern for construction of objective questions that would influence answers least, and the problem of terms and phrases in reading being different was matched by concern that respondents be interviewed in a permissive atmosphere by skilled, trained interviewers. In order to minimize problems of differences, it was essential that interviewers have the same ethnic or racial background, and be residents of the community. It also was necessary in some instances that interviewers be able to speak the Spanish language. However, interviews were conducted only in English. Of overriding concern was the protection of privacy of each individual and that the anonymity and confidentiality of answers be assured.

The collection of data was carried out by the Survey Research Service of the National Opinion Research Center. Interviews of

respondents were conducted in each city by the NORC staff of local,
trained interviewers who were guided by experienced supervisors.
NORC then coded, tabulated, and processed the data. Interviews
were conducted from October 1969 to February 1970. Holiday periods
and losses in the sample accounted for delays.

The completion rate of interviews is too low to allow for
uncritical generalizations of the national population. The findings
are limited to the universe of adult readers interviewed. The
significance of the data may lie primarily in what has been learned
about the adult new readers at the time of the study. At this
period in their lives, they are readers with varying degrees of
reading activity. The clientele of the agencies and programs
from which the sample of readers is drawn are in urbanized areas.

To summarize, the data obtained in this survey of readers
measures: basic and specific social characteristics and activities; factual information and past behavior in relation to reading
interests, needs, values, and attitudes; and to a limited extent
psychological variables in relation to attitudes toward reading,
self-evaluation and self-perception of the individual's reading.

Five Cities in the LMRP Population Study

The five cities - Baltimore, Cleveland, Los Angeles, New York, and Philadelphia - in the LMRP Population Study are central cities in the Standard Metropolitan Statistical Areas (SMSA) which are defined by the Bureau of the Census as a county or group of contiguous counties which contain at least one city of 50,000 inhabitants or more, or "twin cities" with a combined population of at least 50,000. An SMSA also may include counties contiguous to the city because of social and economic ties.

In general, over two-thirds of the United States population are metropolitan residents. The distribution of the Black and white population in these metropolitan areas shows a correlation similar to the proportion of the general population.[14] However, a larger percentage of the Black population live in the central cities. In all regions except the South, over 90 percent of the Black population live in metropolitan areas. Of the Black residents in the northern, central, and western metropolitan areas, over 80 percent live in the central city (chart 2).[15]

Another characteristic of the SMSA's central cities is that in most cities the educational attainment for the population in the central city is slightly less than for the population outside the central city. A comparison of the amount of formal education between the Black and white populations in the central city also shows that the Black population has about one-half a grade less schooling than the white population (table 5).[16]

The median family income for the total population of the United States is $9,433. In the metropolitan areas, the family income is slightly higher than in non-metropolitan areas. The comparison of the median incomes between the Black and white populations in the metropolitan areas shows that the median income of the Black family is $3,000 less than the median income, $10,694 of the white family. In the central city, both Black and white populations have a slightly smaller family income, $6,837 and $9,789 respectively.[17]

The setting and background for the Population Study is indicated through the following brief review of a few characteristics of each city and the programs in the public libraries cooperating with the LMRP investigation.

Baltimore: The population of Baltimore, which is the seventh largest city in the United States, is 939,000 according to the 1970 census. Of this total population, 46.4 percent are Black residents.[18] The median number of school years completed for the entire city is 10.1 years.[19] The income for 28.8 percent of the population is under $3,000 per year.[20]

In 1965 the Baltimore City Health Department estimated the population of the Inner City Action Area to be 198,165 persons. Of the families in this area, 33.5 percent earned less than $3,000 per year and 60 percent of the individuals 25 years of age and over had completed less than eight years of formal education.

The Enoch Pratt Free Library in Baltimore contributed support and advice for the LMRP study. This library is one of the strong municipal libraries in the United States. The Pratt Free Library has a long tradition of serving non-readers in low-income areas. The staff of the library foresaw early in the 1950's the problems of the inner city which manifested themselves in the 1960's.[21] The branch libraries in the library system played a part in local renewal programs for low-income areas of the city. In the summer of 1965 the Pratt Free Library began its participation in the Community Action Program of Baltimore. In this program, the Library worked with and through other social agencies in contact with the disadvantaged population, operating Community Action Centers for one purpose "to bring the library to the people."[22] Library service and materials were taken to the community in a variety of ways. Library collections which consisted primarily of paperback books were set up in these centers. Professional librarians and many aides from the inner city area staffed the program. This successful program received national recognition and became an example for other public libraries in the country.[23]

Cleveland. With a total population of 876,000 Cleveland ranks as the tenth largest city in the United States. The median school years completed for city inhabitants in 1969 was 10.5 years. The family income for 25.6 percent of the population was under $3,000 per year.

The Cleveland Public Library's Adult Education Department initiated four programs specially designed for the functionally illiterate adult. These programs included: Reading Centers Program, Books/Jobs Pilot Project, Project Libros, and the Afro-American History and Culture Project. All of these programs were funded through the U.S. Library Services and Construction Act. The purpose of the Reading Centers Program was first, to help functionally illiterate adults to read, and second, to prove that a library could perform the task of teaching reading. The Books/Jobs Project was initiated to help people who "need information and skills in order to get and hold jobs." The Cleveland Public Library is the regional center for books, pamphlets, and audiovisual aids for the Project. Lending collections and racks of free materials are placed in job training centers, outreach offices, and other social agencies in Cuyahoga County. Special ethnic and indigenous materials are provided by Project Libros for the Spanish-speaking population and by the Afro-American History and Culture Project for the Black community.[24,25]

Los Angeles. During the last decade, Los Angeles has grown rapidly and now ranks second in the United States with a total population of 2,479,000 inhabitants. The central Los Angeles area is inhabited by persons who have low income, poor housing, and family

problems. According to the latest U.S. Census, the median school
years completed by residents of the city is 12.6 years. The family income for 26.6 percent of the residents is under $3,000 per
year.

A special study in 1965 stated that "one of every eight persons in metropolitan Los Angeles can be classified as 'functionally
illiterate.' More than 30,000 of these individuals have not had
any educational experience at all." A rapidly growing adult basic
education program was established in 1965 to provide educational
opportunities for this population.[26] The Los Angeles Public Library, with the help of funds provided by the federal government,
developed a program to reach readers and non-readers in the Los
Angeles central city area. In three inner city areas - Central
Region, Lincoln Heights, and Venice - the staff of the public
library made contacts with community organizations. Special collections of book and audiovisual materials considered of significant interest to the residents of the community were established.
Emphasis was placed on Bookmobile Service in which recordings and
films were an important part. Library staff members cooperated
with adult educators to provide materials and set up special programs for adult students. Public library staff cooperated with
ministers in the areas and provided special service and paperback
collections for church members.

New York. The largest metropolitan area in the United States,
New York has the largest central city, with a total population of
7,782,000 inhabitants. The median years of schooling completed
for the entire city is 12.0 years. The family income for 24.7
percent of the population is under $3,000 per year.

The New York metropolitan area contains several library systems that have progressive programs serving inner city residents.[27]
The LMRP survey sample from New York was obtained through the

cooperation of the Brooklyn Public Library Reader Development Program and the city-wide Work Incentive Program (WIN). The Reading Development Program conducted by the Brooklyn Public Library offers remedial and developmental reading instruction. This program has been serving adults since 1955. In the late 1960's the focus of the reading program has been to help functionally illiterate adults improve their reading.[28] The Work Incentive Program provides basic education, vocational and skill training, and placement and follow-up supportive services for adults in need of permanent jobs. In an emergency situation for the drawing of the LMRP survey sample in New York, this program helped the project complete the New York sample.

Philadelphia. With a population of 2,003,000, Philadelphia ranks as the fourth largest city in the United States. The median years of schooling completed for residents of Philadelphia is 11.1 years. The family income for 27.4 percent of the population is under $3,000 per year.

The Free Library of Philadelphia has been active in extending its services into the inner city. There are six branches in low-income areas - Columbia Avenue, Southward, Germantown, Kensington, West Philadelphia, and Kingsessing. The populations of these areas are characterized by low income and low educational attainment. Inhabitants of the six areas served by the branch libraries are predominantly Black or of Italian origin. The Kensington Branch serves a Puerto Rican Spanish-speaking population. Germantown and Kingsessing, when judged from educational and income levels, appear to be more prosperous than the other four areas served by the branch libraries.[29]

The Free Library of Philadelphia has "reached out to the citizens of the inner city area, through the Reader Development Program." This program which was initiated in June, 1967, was based on the premise that the public library not only should but must be prepared to serve *all* the people. The broad objectives of the Reader Development Program are: to make available materials that will meet the vocational, cultural, and recreational needs of those adults and young adults whose reading level is eighth grade or below; to provide and encourage the use of meaningful library materials for those adults and young adults who do not read; and to instill in children a love of reading and books. The Free Library, in this innovative program, loans materials to organizations and individuals. The program publishes a newsletter, *Pivot,* to inform library patrons and participants in adult education classes or programs about reading and audiovisual materials available in the Reader Development Program's collections.[30]

Chart 2   Five Cities in the LMRP Population Study, by Black
           Population in the SMSA Central City

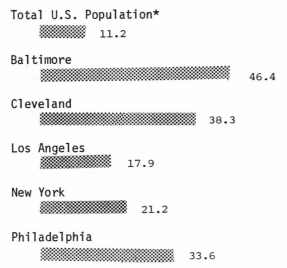

Total U.S. Population*
        11.2

Baltimore
        46.4

Cleveland
        38.3

Los Angeles
        17.9

New York
        21.2

Philadelphia
        33.6

* U.S. Bureau of the Census, *Supplementary Report,* Series PC (S1)-2,
  "Negro Population in Selected Places and Selected Countries,"
  U.S. Government Printing Office, Washington, D.C., 1971.

Table 5   Median Years of School Completed in the Central City
           and LMRP Population Study

Median Years

	Median Years
U.S. Population*	12.2
LMRP	10.2
Baltimore	10.1
White	10.7
Black	9.4
LMRP	10.0
Cleveland	10.5
White	10.7
Black	10.3
LMRP	9.7
Los Angeles	12.5
White	12.6
Black	12.2
LMRP	11.3
New York	12.0
White	12.1
Black	11.3
LMRP	9.9
Philadelphia	11.1
White	11.3
Black	10.7
LMRP	10.5

*   U.S. Bureau of the Census

Notes

1. Bernard Berelson, *The Library's Public* (New York: Columbia University Press, 1949).

2. Philip H. Ennis, *Adult Book Reading in the United States* (Chicago: National Opinion Research Center, University of Chicago, Report no. 105, September, 1965).

3. Jan Hajda, *An American Paradox: People and Books in a Metropolis* (Ph.D. dissertation, University of Chicago, 1963).

4. Michael Harrington, *The Other America: Poverty in the United States* (Baltimore, Md.: Penguin, 1963).

5. Lola M. Irelan, ed., *Low-Income Life Styles* (U.S. Department of Health, Education, and Welfare, Welfare Administration, Division of Research, Publication no. 14, Washington, D.C., 1968).

6. Charles A. Valentine, *Culture & Poverty: Critique & Counter= Proposals* (Chicago: University of Chicago Press, 1969).

7. Eleanor Burke Leacock, ed., *The Culture of Poverty: a Critique* (New York: Simon and Schuster, 1971).

8. Lee Rainwater and William L. Yancey, *The Moynihan Report and the Politics of Controversy* (Cambridge, Mass.: Massachusetts Institute of Technology Press, 1967).

9. David Gottlieb and Anne Lienhard Heinsohn, *America's Other Youth: Growing Up Poor* (Englewood Cliffs, N.J.: Prentice-Hall, 1971).

10. Douglas Waples, Bernard Berelson, and Franklyn R. Bradshaw, *What Reading Does to People* (Chicago: University of Chicago Press, 1940).

11. Wilbur Schramm, "Why Adults Read," in *Adult Reading* (Fifty= fifth Yearbook of the National Society for the Study of Education, Chicago: University of Chicago Press, 1956): pp. 79-81.

12. Bradley S. Greenberg and Brenda Dervin, *Mass Communication Among the Urban Poor* (Report no. 5, Project CUP: Communication Among the Urban Poor, Department of Communication) (Michigan State University, Mimeograph. March 1969).

13. Helen Huguenor Lyman, "Introduction, Library Programs and Services to the Disadvantaged," *Library Trends* 20, No. 2 (October 1971): 188, 193.

14. U.S. Bureau of the Census, *Statistical Abstract of the United States, 1971* (Washington, D.C.: U.S. Government Printing Office, 1971): p. 18.

15. U.S. Bureau of the Census, *Special Studies*, Series P-23, No.38, "The Social and Economic Status of Negroes in the United States," U.S. Government Printing Office, Washington, D.C., 1971, p.14.

16. U.S. Bureau of the Census, *Population Characteristics,* Series D-20, No. 219, "Educational Attainment in 30 Selected Standard Metropolitan Statistical Areas: 1969," U.S. Government Printing Office, Washington, D.C., 1971.

17. U.S. Bureau of the Census, *Statistical Abstract, 1971.*

18. Population statistics for the five cities are from U.S. Bureau of the Census, *Statistical Abstract, 1970,* pp. 18,19.

19. Educational attainment statistics for the five cities are from U.S. Bureau of the Census, "Educational Attainment: 1969."

20. U.S. Bureau of the Census, *Statistical Abstract, 1970,* pp. 845, 859.

21. Lowell A. Martin, *Baltimore Reaches Out: Library Service to the Disadvantaged* (Baltimore, Md.: Enoch Pratt Free Library, June 1967): p. 9.

22. Enoch Pratt Free Library, Report for the Year July, 1967-June, 1968, p. 3.

23. Evelyn Levy, "Library Service in the Inner City," *Wilson Library Bulletin* 41 (January 1967): 471-78.

24. Cleveland Public Library, *Adult Education Department Annual Report, 1968,* p. 6.

25. Cleveland Public Library, Afro-American History and Culture Project, *Narrative Report,* January 1969: pp. 1-4.

26. Memorandum, Dr. T. Stanley Warburton to Hunter Fitzgerald, May 25, 1966, Los Angeles City School Districts. Division of College and Adult Education, *Adult Basic Education Program EOA.*

27.   Charlotte B. Winsor, *Study of Four Library Programs for Disadvantaged Persons*; Conducted by Bank Street College of Education (Albany, N.Y.:   State Education Department, Division of Library Development, 1968).

28.   Richard L. Keller, "How the Brooklyn Public Library Helps the Functionally Illiterate," American Library Association, *Adult Services Division Newsletter*, Fall, 1967, pp. 5-8,13.

29.   Free Library of Philadelphia, *Branch Library Information Population Characteristics*, pp. 2-4.

30.   John A. Axam, *The Free Library of Philadelphia Reader Development Program Report for the Period June 12, 1967 - June 30, 1968*, pp. 2-3.

7

SOCIAL CHARACTERISTICS OF THE ADULT NEW READER

The survey of adults undertaken in this phase of the research yields revealing information which characterizes the adult new readers as defined in the LMRP research. The adults interviewed were participants in adult basic education, job training, and public library reading programs in the five cities of Baltimore, Cleveland, Los Angeles, New York, and Philadelphia. The total number of respondents is 479. The characteristics are classified under four general areas:

1. Personal characteristics. Sex, race, cultural and national orientation, language(s) spoken, language first learned, age, and years lived in present locality.

2. Educational characteristics. Amount of formal education, location of grammar school, location of high school, and participation in adult classes and programs.

3. Socioeconomic characteristics. Employment of time, occupation in current employment, family income, and individual income.

4. Specific social characteristics. Special aspects of the major social characteristics and activities of readers.

5. Specific educational characteristics.

(1) Personal Characteristics (table 6)

(a) Sex. Among the 479 reader respondents interviewed, less than one-third are men (31 percent), while 69 percent are women.

(b) Race. Among the respondents, three-fourths (74 percent) were identified by the interviewers as Black, while one-fourth were reported as white (26 percent).

(c) Cultural and National Orientation. As is to be expected in the light of the figures on race, the dominant place of origin is Africa, which 44 percent of the respondents identified as the country from which most of their ancestors came. The United States is the place of origin for 19 percent, and Puerto Rico for 8 percent. Mexico, Central and South America, and the Caribbean area are places of origin for over 5 percent. The European countries, the British Commonwealth, and Ireland are countries of origin for over 12 percent.

(d) Language(s) Spoken. Nearly all readers speak English and one-fourth also speak a second language.

(e) Language first learned. Spanish is the second language most frequently spoken (16 percent), and Spanish was the first language learned by 11 percent.

(f) Age. The majority of readers are in the younger age groups, under the age of 35 (54 percent) and under the age of 45 (75 percent). Nearly one-fourth are in the 15 to 24 age group, and an equal percentage are over forty-five. The median age is 33.7 years.

(g) Years Lived in Present Locality. Two-thirds of the readers have come from outside localities, yet one-third have lived all their lives in the same city. Nearly a third (32 percent) have lived from six to 20 years in the same city. Eleven percent have lived a short time, one to five years in the present locality. The median period of residence is 24 years.

2) Educational Characteristics (table 7)

(a) Formal education. In terms of formal education, that is, last year completed in school, adult new readers have attended school an average of 10.2 years. The majority (62 percent) have completed between seven and 11 years of school. Nearly 20 percent have less than sixth grade schooling and an equal number have completed high school.

(b) Location of grammar school. Among the respondents who have not lived in the city all their lives, only 3 percent have gone to suburban schools. One-fourth have attended small town or

city schools and 20 percent, schools in large cities, while
10 percent have attended country schools and 9 percent schools
in medium-sized cities.

(c) Location of high school. More than 50 percent of the
respondents have attended high school. Thirty-seven percent
have gone to a school other than those in their present
locality, 18 percent have attended schools in large cities,
17 percent in small towns and medium-sized cities, and 2 percent
in the country or suburban areas.

(d) Participation in adult classes and programs. The major
adult education programs in which readers have participated
are: adult basic education (58 percent), high school equivalency
(30 percent), Work Incentive Program (19 percent), and Manpower
Development and Training (16 percent). Thirteen percent have
participated in public library reading development programs.
Adult basic education may include the Laubach program which is
not identifiable in this study as a separate program.

(3) Socioeconomic Characteristics (table 8)

(a) Employment of time. More than half (52 percent) of the
readers are in the labor force, with 39 percent in full-time
jobs and 7 percent looking for work. One-fourth are in school
and 19 percent are keeping house.

(b) Occupations of currently employed. Those respondents who
are currently employed (45 percent) are classified in general
areas: white collar (12 percent), clerical (16 percent),
craft (18 percent), blue collar (18 percent), and service (36
percent). Occupations engaged in by respondents are listed
in table

(c) Family income. The median family income of the adult
reader is $5,009 a year. Nineteen percent have annual incomes
of less than $3,000, 59 percent less than $6,000, and about
12 percent, $10,000 or more. Although the range of incomes is
great among the respondents, they are relatively low in comparison with the general population figures. The median income

120

of families in the United States was $9,870 in 1970, according to estimates by the Bureau of the Census, Department of Commerce. In 1970 the median income of families of Negroes and other races was $6,520. The poverty threshold for a nonfarm family of four was $3,968. The median income deficit for poor families was about $1,100.[1]

(d) Individual income. The median individual income is $3,449 a year. Nearly 40 percent (37 percent) receive less than $3,000 a year and 71 percent less than $6,000. A significant percentage (15 percent) did not answer this question.

Table 6   Personal Characteristics of Adult New Reader *(expressed in percent)*

---

a. Sex *

Male	31 *(148)*
Female	69 *(331)*
Total	100 *(479)*

b. Race **

White	26 *(123)*
Black	74 *(353)*
Other	∷ *(3)*
Total	100 *(479)*

∷ The percentage is equal to less than 1%

* Respondent's sex was noted under "Interviewer Remarks, D."

** Respondent's race was noted under "Interviewer Remarks, C."

Table 6   Personal Characteristics of Adult New Reader *(expressed in percent)*

c.   Cultural and National Orientation of Adult New Reader*

England, Scotland, Wales, Canada, Australia	2 *(10)*
Ireland	2 *(10)*
Germany, Austria, Switzerland	1 *(7)*
Scandinavia	0 *(0)*
Italy	2 *(8)*
France, Belgium	⁑ *(3)*
Poland	1 *(5)*
Russia, other Eastern European countries	4 *(17)*
Spain, Portugal	⁑ *(3)*
Africa	44 *(211)*
Mexico, Central America	2 *(12)*
Puerto Rico	8 *(39)*
Cuba, West Indies, Caribbean area	3 *(13)*
South America	⁑ *(3)*
China, Taiwan, Orient	⁑ *(2)*
Other	4 *(17)*
United States	19 *(90)*
Don't know	3 *(12)*
No answer	4 *(17)*
Total	100 *(479)*

* Question 42: *From what country did most of your ancestors originally come?*

⁑ The percentage is equal to less than 1%

Table 6   Personal Characteristics of Adult New Reader *(expressed in percent)*

d.   Language(s) Spoken by
     Adult New Reader*

English	75 *(361)*
Spanish only	⁑ *(1)*
Other only	⁑ *(1)*
English & Spanish	15 *(71)*
English & Other	9 *(39)*
English, Spanish, & Other	1 *(5)*
No answer	⁑ *(1)*
Total	100 *(479)*

e.   Language First Learned
     by Adult New Reader
     Who Speaks More Than
     One Language**

English	8 *(37)*
Spanish	11 *(52)*
Other	5 *(25)*
No answer	⁑ *(2)*
Total	24 *(116)*

⁑ The percentage is equal to less than 1%

* Question 43:   *What languages do you speak?*

** Question 43A: (If R speaks more than one language) *Which of these languages did you first learn to speak?*

Table 6 Personal Characteristics of Adult New Reader *(expressed in percent)*

f. Age in Years*

16 - 24	23 *(111)*
25 - 34	31 *(148)*
35 - 44	21 *(101)*
45 - 54	14 *(66)*
55 - 64	7 *(31)*
65 and over	4 *(20)*
No answer	∷ *(2)*
Total	100 *(479)*

Median = 33.7 years

∷ The percentage is equal to less than 1%

* Question 35: *What is your age now?*

Table 6   Personal Characteristics of Adult New Reader *(expressed in percent)*

g.   Years Respondent Has Lived
     in Present Locality*

1 or less	2 *(11)*
2 - 5	9 *(44)*
6 - 10	11 *(51)*
11 - 15	10 *(48)*
16 - 20	11 *(54)*
21 - 25	9 *(42)*
26 - 30	8 *(39)*
31 - 40	3 *(14)*
41 - 50	4 *(19)*
51 - 66	1 *(3)*
All one's life	32 *(154)*
Total	100 *(479)*

Median = 24 years

* Question 39:   *How long have you lived in this city?*

Table 7 Education of the Adult New Reader *(expressed in percent)*

a. Amount of Formal
    Education: Last Year
    Completed in School*

0 - 4	6 *(31)*
5 - 6	10 *(47)*
7 - 9	30 *(146)*
10 - 11	32 *(151)*
12	17 *(82)*
13 or more	4 *(17)*
No answer	1 *(5)*
Total	100 *(479)*

Median = 10.2

* Question 34: *What is the last year you completed in school?*

126

Table 7 Education of the Adult New Reader *(expressed in percent)*

b. Location of Grammar School*

Small town/city (under 25,000)	24 *(116)*
Large city (100,000 or more)	20 *(94)*
Country	10 *(49)*
Medium size city (25,000-100,000)	9 *(45)*
Suburb of a large city	3 *(15)*
No answer	1 *(6)*
Total who went to grammar school in locale other than present residence	67 *(325)*

c. Location of High School**

Large city (100,000 or more)	18 *(87)*
Small town/city (under 25,000)	10 *(50)*
Medium size city (25,000-100,000)	7 *(31)*
Country	1 *(5)*
Suburb	1 *(5)*
Didn't go to high school	28 *(136)*
No answer	2 *(11)*
Total who went to high school in locale other than present residence	67 *(325)*

Base   479

* Question 40B: *Was that* [grammar school] *in the country, a small town or city, medium size city, suburb of a large city, or large city?*

** Question 41B: *Was that* [high school] *in the country, a small town or city, medium size city, suburb of a large city, or large city?*

Table 7 Education of the Adult New Reader *(expressed in percent)*

d. Participation in Adult
   Classes or Programs*

Adult Basic Education	58 *(227)*
High School Equivalency Program	30 *(119)*
Work Incentive Program	19 *(72)*
Manpower Development and Training	16 *(64)*
Public Library Programs or Reading Development Programs	13 *(50)*
Concentrated Employment Program	8 *(29)*
Opportunities Industrialization Centers	6 *(19)*
Neighborhood Youth Corps	5 *(16)*
Job Corps	4 *(12)*
New Careers	2 *(8)*
Programs sponsored by private industry	1 *(4)*
Upward Bound	⋇ *(1)*
Laubach Literacy Program	0 *(0)*
Special Impact	0 *(0)*
Other	9 *(35)*

Base = 394

⋇ The percentage is equal to less than 1%

* Question 28A: *What were these classes or programs* [attended within the last year]?

128

Table 8 Socioeconomic Characteristics of Adult New Reader *(expressed in percent)*

a. Employment of Time*

Working Force	52 *(249)*
Working Full-time (35 hrs. or more)	39 *(187)*
Working Part-time	6 *(28)*
With a job but not at work because of temporary illness, vacation, strike, etc.	$\times$ *(3)*
Unemployed (looking for work)	7 *(31)*
Not in the Working Force	47 *(226)*
Retired	3 *(14)*
Keeping House	19 *(92)*
In School	25 *(120)*
Other	1 *(4)*
Total	100 *(479)*

$\times$ The percentage is equal to less than 1%

* Question 24: *How do you spend most of your time...working full-time, part-time, looking for work, (going to school,) (keeping house,) or what?*

129

Table 8   Socioeconomic Characteristics of Adult New Reader *(expressed in percent)*

b.   Occupation in Current Employment
     (Based on Question 24A)

White Collar	12 *(27)*
Clerical	16 *(34)*
Craft	18 *(39)*
Blue Collar	18 *(40)*
Service	36 *(79)*
Total respondents who are currently employed	100 *(218)*

c.   Total Family Income*

$ 1 - 2,999	19 *(90)*
3,000 - 5,999	40 *(191)*
6,000 - 9,999	19 *(93)*
10,000 and over	13 *(61)*
No answer	9 *(44)*
Total	100 *(479)*

Median = 5,009

* Question 62: *What was your total family income for the last twelve months, from all sources such as wages, social security, or other payments?* (In some instances the interviewer estimated income.)

Table 8 Socioeconomic Characteristics of Adult New Reader (expressed in percent)

d. Total Individual Income*

$ 0 - 2,999	37 (179)
3,000 - 5,999	34 (160)
6,000 - 9,999	11 (51)
10,000 and over	3 (16)
No answer	15 (73)
Total	100 (479)

Median = $3,449

* Question 63: *What was your own total individual income for the last twelve months, from all sources such as wages, social security, or other payments?* (In some instances the interviewer estimated income.)

(4) Specific Social Characteristics

Further analysis of the basic characteristics of the respondents interviewed in the survey distinguishes specific characteristics which describe in more detail adult new readers. These characteristics include: race and sex, cultural and national origin, language spoken, age, education and continuing education, locality, occupations, income, and free and leisure time activities.

Race and Sex. Among the Black adults there are proportionately three times as many women as men, while among whites, the ratio of men to women is one-to-one (table 9). Participants in adult basic education and high school equivalency programs are distributed in similar proportion. White men and women are on a one-to-

131

one basis, while five times as many Black women as men are in high
school equivalency programs. The participants in library development programs include more women, both Black and white, than men.
While the proportion of participants in adult basic education is
similar, the proportions of Black and white participants in employment oriented programs are radically different. Over 50 percent
of Black men and women participate in an employment oriented program. On the other hand, white men and women have low percentages
of participation, 24 and 30 percent respectively (table 10 and chart
3).

Cultural and National Origin. The places from which respondents'
ancestors came originally, are identified in 13 general categories.
Admittedly, this information is extremely limited, but it is of
interest and has relevance. By far the greatest number of respondents are of African origin. The United States, although it is not
included in the 13 categories, is identified by 19 percent of the
respondents as the place from which their ancestors originally
came. It appears that this group includes primarily Black
respondents, with representatives from the white, American Indian,
and Mexican American respondents in the survey sample. It is to be
noted that 11 percent of the respondents identified the Caribbean
area as place of origin, which includes Puerto Rico, Cuba, and the
West Indies; and another two percent reported Central and South
America. A total of 12 percent reported their place of origin as
Eastern and Western Europe and the British Isles (tables 6c and 11

Language Spoken. As is to be expected, the English language is
common to everyone. One-fourth of the respondents indicated having
a second language, with 16 percent having Spanish as a second language. Of the respondents who speak a second language, 45 percent
have Spanish as their first language (tables 12 and 13).

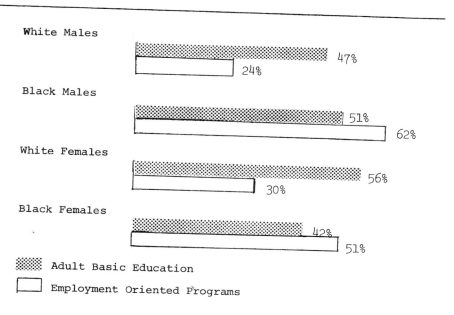

White Males
47%
24%

Black Males
51%
62%

White Females
56%
30%

Black Females
42%
51%

░░░ Adult Basic Education

☐ Employment Oriented Programs

Age. The median age among respondents is 33.7 years, which is nearly ten years older than the average reported among participants in programs surveyed in the LMRP National Adult Programs Study. Over half of the respondents in the survey of readers are between 16 and 34 years of age, the other 46 percent include a much wider range of ages, being between 35 and 65 and over years of age. While differences in age among men and women of both races do not vary in any major sense, it should be noted that women, both Black and white, are older than the men. The highest proportion, 33 percent, of the youngest group who are between 16 and 24 years of age, is to be found among Black males. The largest proportion of the younger adult groups, who are between 24 and 34 years of age, is to be found among white females, while in the middle adult group, who are between 35 and 54 years of age, the largest proportion is found among the Black females (table 14).

Table 9   Distribution of Males and Females among White and Black
           Respondents *(expressed in percent)*

	Male	Female	Total
White	13 *(62)*	13 *(61)*	26 *(123)*
Black	18 *(84)*	56 *(269)*	74 *(353)*
Other	∺ *(2)*	∺ *(1)*	∺ *(3)*
	31 *(148)*	69 *(331)*	100 *(479)*

∺ The percentage is equal to less than 1%

Residence in Present Locality. Respondents had lived in the present
locality or residence, generally, for a longer rather than a shorter
time. Only 11 percent had lived in the city less than six years,
while 32 percent had lived in the same city all their lives, and
another third had lived in the same city between 6 and 20 years
(table 15).

Occupations. In order to identify major activities engaged in
by adult new readers, respondents were asked, "How do you spend
most of your time?" The largest number, 39 percent, are employed
full-time, and another 6 percent are working part-time, while 7
percent are looking for work, making a total of 52 percent of the
respondents in the work force. School and keeping house occupied
the time of 25 percent and 18 percent, respectively. A few persons
are retired, 13 percent (table 16).

Among those adults, 45 percent, who are employed full or part=
time, over a third are engaged in service occupations. One-third
are in blue-collar and crafts, and another third in clerical and
white-collar occupations (table 17).

134

Within these broad areas of use of time - working, going to school, keeping house, looking for work, and retirement - variations may be identified. Of those men and women who make up the work force the highest percentage employed, 66 percent, are among white males; the lowest number, 26 percent, are among white females. Among Black females, 41 percent are currently employed and 23 percent are keeping house. On the other hand, among the white females, the greater number, 42 percent are keeping house. Over half of the Black males are employed. Twice as many Black males as white are unemployed. The percentage of unemployed Black and white women is almost equal (chart 4). Comparing the three out of ten women who keep house, the Black women are somewhat younger and have more formal education than the white women (table 18).

The kind of work done by the respondents is varied and diverse. The occupations are classified in table 19 . The service and

---

Chart 4 Employment of Time, by Race and Sex

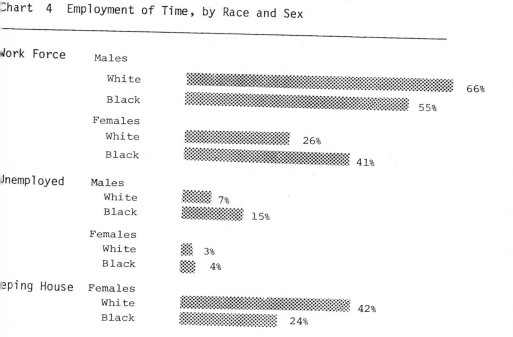

Work Force	Males	
	White	66%
	Black	55%
	Females	
	White	26%
	Black	41%
Unemployed	Males	
	White	7%
	Black	15%
	Females	
	White	3%
	Black	4%
Keeping House	Females	
	White	42%
	Black	24%

Adult Basic Education

	White	Black	
Male	13 *(29)*	20 *(43)*	33 *(72)*
Female	15 *(34)*	52 *(114)*	67 *(148)*
	28 *(63)*	72 *(157)*	100 *(220)*

High School Equivalency Program

	White	Black	
Male	19 *(21)*	10 *(12)*	29 *(33)*
Female	19 *(22)*	52 *(61)*	71 *(83)*
	38 *(43)*	62 *(73)*	100 *(116)*

Public Library Programs

	White	Black	
Male	4 *(2)*	17 *(8)*	21 *(10)*
Female	17 *(8)*	62 *(31)*	79 *(39)*
	21 *(10)*	79 *(39)*	100 *(49)*

clerical classifications are engaged in by more persons; fewer are
in professional and business and manufacturing occupations. The
kinds of jobs reported by the unemployed or retired persons follow
a similar pattern (table 20).

Perhaps of more significance are the responses of the 60 percent who expressed expectations in the kind of work they had considered getting into. It is to be noted that six out of ten persons are interested in changing or moving into clerical, professional, and service positions. Some may aspire to advancement, others
to entering new lines of work. Of special interest are the types
of work represented in these classifications which are indicative
of the variety of aspirations. Various occupations are reported which do not appear among the current occupations. In the
professional and technical group such occupations as accountants,
athletes, authors, clergymen, professors, musicians, medical and
dental technicians are represented. Within clerical occupations
new interests are reported, for example, clerical library attendants and assistants and mail carriers. It may be concluded that
career and vocational guidance and counseling materials as well as
information about job opportunities, curricula-related collections,
special subject emphasis, are areas of immediate interest and
potential use (tables 21 and 22).

Free and Leisure Time Activities. Of particular importance in
the provision of public library service are the major interests
and needs of adults. The main occupational concerns, present
and future, and their use of other time defined as free or leisure time activities, must be known or projected if materials
relevant to those interests and generated by those activities
are to be selected, made accessible, and used. It is within
this framework that as full a range of activities as possible
was explored through specific questions and answers about

occupations, free time activities, and previous schooling and participation in continuing education.

Adult new readers have many interests. Activities other than their main occupations range from visiting friends and relatives to practicing judo or karate, from going to church and the movies to participating in activities at a neighborhood center and the Y or YW. Respondents were asked about things that they had done or places they had gone to during the last six months or when they had free time (tables 23 and 24). A list of possible activities was suggested. The suggested list includes various activities that may be engaged in at relatively little or no cost. Two important activities among things done during the last six months by the largest number of respondents are visiting with friends and relatives and reading a book or magazine, reported by 83 and 82 percent, respectively, of the respondents. Four other major activities are engaged in by three-fourths of the respondents: driving or walking around town, listening to records, going to church, synagogue, mosque, and going to the movies. Playing cards, bingo or other games are enjoyed by 47 percent, and 32 percent play pool, baseball, or go bowling. A large number, 65 percent, go to the park or a zoo, while half that many, 32 percent, go to museums, concerts, exhibits. Even though they are urban dwellers, 8 percent go fishing. Among the women, 60 percent crochet, knit or sew. Other social entertainment is found by 40 to 50 percent of the respondents in going to dances and to a bar, cocktail lounge, or tavern.

Some differences are apparent between the activities of older and younger persons, between men and women, and between the races. Young people tend to go to dances, the movies, and a pool hall or bowling alley to a greater degree than older people. Older people attend church, synagogue, mosque more often than do young people and this activity increases proportionately with age. Other

138

activities such as going to the park or a zoo or to the neighborhood center do not differ significantly with regard to age (table
25   ).   Men go to the pool hall or bowling alley, a bar, cocktail
lounge, or tavern more often than women do, while women attend a church,
synagogue, mosque, the neighborhood center, and the park or a zoo
more often than men.   Attendance at movies and dances does not
differ significantly among men and women (table   26).   Black
respondents participate to a greater degree than white respondents
in all activities listed except going to the park or a zoo, in
which participation is about the same.   The greatest differences
between the two groups are shown in the substantially greater participation by Blacks in the activities of church, synagogue, mosque
and in going to the movies, dances, and bars (table 27   ).

Sports are of interest to a large majority of the readers.
Watching sports is enjoyed by 80 percent of the respondents, of
whom 42 percent enjoy it a great deal.   Over half of the newspaper
readers read about sports and 16 percent of them would miss it
most in the newspaper.   Sports news interests more men than women.
Appeal is particularly to adults between 35 and 54 years of age
and to those in the youngest group, 16 to 24.   Sports magazines
are read by 14 percent.   They are second among the magazines that
would be missed most by magazine readers (tables 28, 83, 85,
101, and 102).

Membership in clubs, societies, and organizations is held by
four out of ten of the adult new readers.   Nearly one-third of
these are labor union members, one-fourth belong to a religious
group.   Between 10 and 14 percent of the respondents also are members of neighborhood improvement associations, Parent-Teacher Associations, and other parent groups.   Membership in a fraternal organization or lodge and in a civil rights group is reported by
11 percent.   Less than 10 percent report membership in other
organizations, that is, a sports or hobby club, nationality group,

veterans and political organizations. Among these members, 36 percent have held an office in their organization (tables 29, 30 , 31).

Among the 13 purposes or activities which respondents reported in their use of the public library within the past six months is that of borrowing books, reported by nearly two-thirds of the 414 public library users; one-fifth of these users went to the library to ask for some information or to read a book. Between 10 and 20 percent of the respondents engaged in special activities, that is, a library tour, magazine or newspaper reading, a lecture or movie program, or viewed an exhibit. A third of the respondents took advantage of the library to take children there, while 8 percent met friends there (tables 32 and 33). Use of the public library varied little between men and women, races, age, and income groups. A high percentage of respondents, between 90 and 98 percent, participated in continuing education programs. As might be expected, respondents with the least formal education, less than five years of schooling, and those rated as least active readers by the Reading Activity Index reported least use of the public library (table 34).

Households and Incomes. The number of persons living in a household varied considerably. Table 35 shows the range from one to 13, but the majority of respondents were in households with between two and five persons. Although no comparison has been made between incomes and size of household, the median family income of $5,009 and individual income of $3,449 suggest the financial limitations of a majority of the respondents.

Specific Social Characteristics of the LMRP Respondents in Five Cities. The five cities of the LMRP Population Study, Baltimore, Cleveland, Los Angeles, New York, and Philadelphia, were selected on the basis of the programs which the metropolitan public libraries made available to adult new readers. The following summary describes some of the similarities and differences in the social components of the cities in the LMRP survey which are shown in charts 5 to 12 .

In all of the five cities, nearly two-thirds of the respondents are Black. Philadelphia has the highest percentage of Black respondents, 94 percent. Women are in the great majority in all of the cities except Los Angeles where men and women have nearly equal representation. The youngest sample of adult new readers is in Los Angeles, with a median age of 29.1 years, while the oldest sample is in Cleveland, with the median age of 36.6 years. It is to be noted that one-fourth of the respondents in Cleveland are over 55 years of age. Cleveland has the lowest median number of years of formal schooling, 9.7, while Los Angeles has the highest median, 11.3 years. Nearly two-thirds of the respondents in Baltimore, Cleveland, and Los Angeles are employed. Although Los Angeles has one of the higher percentage rates of employment, it has the highest rate of unemployment, 19 percent. New York's employment rate is the lowest among the five cities, but New York's percentage rate of respondents in school is the highest, 64 percent. Philadelphia, where the sample of respondents is 83 percent women, has the highest rate of respondents keeping house, 49 percent. The lowest median family income is found in Philadelphia, $3,899. The highest median family incomes are in Los Angeles and Baltimore, where over two-thirds of the respondents are employed. With the exception of Baltimore, approximately 20 percent of the sample in the other four cities have a family income considerably less than $3,000 a year. In contrast, the family income of approximately

20 percent of the respondents in Baltimore, Cleveland, and Los Angeles is $10,000 and over. In Cleveland where the sample has a higher percentage of older persons, and in Philadelphia where the sample is predominantly female the median individual income is less than $3,000. The highest median individual income, $3,659, is found in New York City.

Table 11 Area of Cultural and National Origin (Based on Question 42) *(expressed in percent)*

Africa	44
United States	19
Caribbean area	11
British Isles and Western Europe	7
Eastern Europe	5
Central and South America	2
Far East	⁛
Other	4
Don't know and No answer	7

⁛ The percentage is equal to less than 1%

Chart 5 LMRP Respondents in Five Cities, by Race

```
         0    10    20    30    40    50    60    70    80    90
```

Balti-
more
White   ▒▒▒▒ 13%
Black   ▒▒▒▒▒▒▒▒▒▒▒▒▒▒▒▒▒▒▒▒▒▒▒▒▒▒▒▒▒▒▒▒▒▒▒▒ 87%
Other   ▌ 0%

Cleve-
land
White   ▒▒▒▒▒▒▒▒▒▒▒▒▒ 38%
Black   ▒▒▒▒▒▒▒▒▒▒▒▒▒▒▒▒▒▒▒▒▒ 60%
Other   ▒ 2%

Los
Angeles
White   ▒▒▒▒▒▒▒▒▒▒▒ 32%
Black   ▒▒▒▒▒▒▒▒▒▒▒▒▒▒▒▒▒▒▒▒▒▒ 67%
Other   ▒ 1%

New
York
White   ▒▒▒▒▒▒▒▒▒▒▒▒ 37%
Black   ▒▒▒▒▒▒▒▒▒▒▒▒▒▒▒▒▒▒▒▒▒ 63%
Other   ▌ 0%

Phila-
del-
phia
White   ▒▒ 6%
Black   ▒▒▒▒▒▒▒▒▒▒▒▒▒▒▒▒▒▒▒▒▒▒▒▒▒▒▒▒▒▒▒▒▒▒▒▒▒▒ 94%
Other   ▌ 0%

Chart 6 LMRP Respondents in Five Cities, by Sex

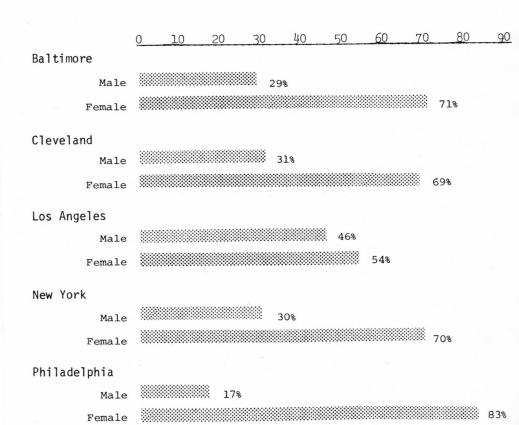

```
            0    10   20   30   40   50   60   70   80   90
Baltimore
    Male    ▓▓▓▓▓▓▓▓▓▓▓ 29%
  Female    ▓▓▓▓▓▓▓▓▓▓▓▓▓▓▓▓▓▓▓▓▓▓▓▓▓▓▓ 71%

Cleveland
    Male    ▓▓▓▓▓▓▓▓▓▓▓▓ 31%
  Female    ▓▓▓▓▓▓▓▓▓▓▓▓▓▓▓▓▓▓▓▓▓▓▓▓▓▓ 69%

Los Angeles
    Male    ▓▓▓▓▓▓▓▓▓▓▓▓▓▓▓▓▓ 46%
  Female    ▓▓▓▓▓▓▓▓▓▓▓▓▓▓▓▓▓▓▓▓ 54%

New York
    Male    ▓▓▓▓▓▓▓▓▓▓▓ 30%
  Female    ▓▓▓▓▓▓▓▓▓▓▓▓▓▓▓▓▓▓▓▓▓▓▓▓▓▓ 70%

Philadelphia
    Male    ▓▓▓▓▓▓ 17%
  Female    ▓▓▓▓▓▓▓▓▓▓▓▓▓▓▓▓▓▓▓▓▓▓▓▓▓▓▓▓▓▓▓ 83%
```

Chart 6a LMRP Respondents in Five Cities, by Reading Activity
         Rating

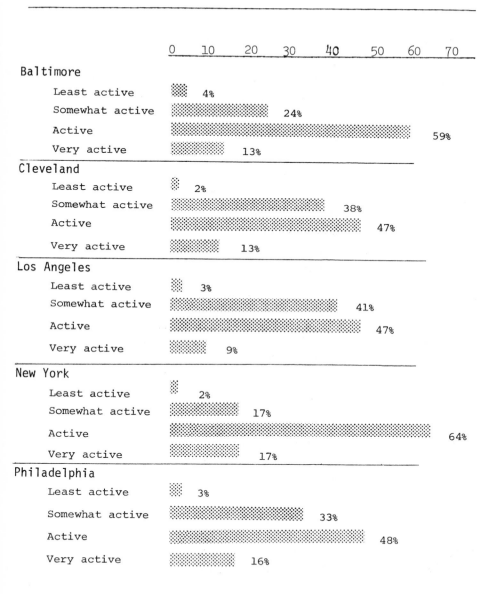

	0	10	20	30	40	50	60	70

Baltimore
  Least active — 4%
  Somewhat active — 24%
  Active — 59%
  Very active — 13%

Cleveland
  Least active — 2%
  Somewhat active — 38%
  Active — 47%
  Very active — 13%

Los Angeles
  Least active — 3%
  Somewhat active — 41%
  Active — 47%
  Very active — 9%

New York
  Least active — 2%
  Somewhat active — 17%
  Active — 64%
  Very active — 17%

Philadelphia
  Least active — 3%
  Somewhat active — 33%
  Active — 48%
  Very active — 16%

Chart 7 LMRP Respondents in Five Cities, by Age

		Median Age
Baltimore	16 - 24 34%	31.4 years
	25 - 34 25%	
	35 - 44 18%	
	45 - 54 18%	
	55 - 64 3%	
	65 + 2%	
Cleveland	16 - 24 23%	36.6
	25 - 34 25%	
	35 - 44 10%	
	45 - 54 16%	
	55 - 64 12%	
	65 + 14%	
Los Angeles	16 - 24 27%	29.1
	25 - 34 30%	
	35 - 44 16%	
	45 - 54 17%	
	55 - 64 8%	
	65 + 2%	
New York	16 - 24 17%	32.9
	25 - 34 41%	
	35 - 44 33%	
	45 - 54 8%	
	55 - 64 1%	
	65 + 0%	
Phila-delphia*	16 - 24 10%	35.7
	25 - 34 35%	
	35 - 44 29%	
	45 - 54 9%	
	55 - 64 10%	
	65 + 4%	

*No response was made by 3%.

Table 12 Languages Spoken by Adult New Reader *(expressed in percent)*

Question 43: *What languages do you speak?*

English	99 *(476)*
Spanish	16 *(77)*
Other	9 *(45)*
English only	75 *(361)*
Spanish only	⁑ *(1)*
Other only	⁑ *(1)*
English & Spanish	15 *(71)*
English & other	9 *(39)*
English, Spanish, & other	1 *(5)*
No answer	⁑ *(1)*
Total	100 *(479)*

⁑ The percentage is equal to less than 1%

Table 13 Language First Spoken *(expressed in percent)*

Question 43A: *Which of these languages did you first learn to speak?*

Language	
English	32 *(37)*
Spanish	45 *(52)*
Other	21 *(25)*
No answer	2 *(2)*
Total	100 *(116)*

Table 14 Age Distribution for Whites and Blacks of Both Sexes *(expressed in percent)*

Age	Male		Female	
	White	Black	White	Black
16 - 24	27 *(17)*	33 *(28)*	20 *(12)*	20 *(53)*
25 - 34	36 *(22)*	23 *(19)*	39 *(24)*	31 *(83)*
35 - 54	32 *(20)*	33 *(28)*	28 *(17)*	38 *(100)*
55 +	5 *(3)*	11 *(9)*	13 *(8)*	11 *(31)*
Total	100 *(62)*	100 *(84)*	100 *(61)*	100 *(264)**

* This total does not include five who did not answer.

Chart 8   LMRP Respondents in Five Cities, by Education

		Median Years Completed

Baltimore

0-4	4%	10
5-6	7%	
7-9	38%	
10-11	29%	
12	16%	
13 or more	5%	

Cleve-land

0-4	15%	9.7
5-6	13%	
7-9	24%	
10-11	16%	
12	25%	
13 or more	6%	

Los Angeles

0-4	5%	11.3
5-6	12%	
7-9	16%	
10-11	38%	
12	24%	
13 or more	3%	

New York

0-4	3%	9.9
5-6	9%	
7-9	42%	
10-11	36%	
12	9%	
13 or more	0%	

Phila-delphia

0-4	6%	10.5
5-6	8%	
7-9	29%	
10-11	40%	
12	13%	
13 or more	4%	

Table 15 Years Respondent Has Lived in Present Locality *(expressed in percent)*

Question 39: *How long have you lived in this city?*

Residence in Years	
1 or less	2 *(11)*
2 - 5	9 *(44)*
6 - 10	11 *(51)*
11 - 15	10 *(48)*
16 - 20	11 *(54)*
21 - 25	9 *(42)*
26 - 30	8 *(39)*
31 - 40	3 *(14)*
41 - 50	4 *(19)*
51 - 66	⊠ *(3)*
All one's life	32 *(154)*
Total	100 *(479)*

⊠ The percentage is equal to less than 1%

Table 16 Employment of Time by Adult New Reader *(expressed in percent)*

Question 24: *How do you spend most of your time . . . working full time, part time, looking for work, (going to school), (keeping house), or what?*

Employment of Time	
Working full time	39 *(187)*
In school	25 *(120)*
Keeping house	19 *(92)*
Unemployed (looking for work)	7 *(31)*
Working part time	6 *(28)*
Retired	3 *(14)*
Other (specify)	1 *(4)*
With a job but not at work because of temporary illness, vacation, strike, etc.	:: *(3)*
Total	100 *(479)*

:: The percentage is equal to less than 1%

Table 17 Current Employment of Adult New Reader According to Occupation Classification *(expressed in percent)*

Occupation Classification (Based on Question 24A)	Total *(479)*	Currently Employed *(218)*
White Collar	6 *(27)*	12 *(27)*
Clerical	7 *(34)*	16 *(34)*
Craft	8 *(39)*	18 *(39)*
Blue Collar	8 *(40)*	18 *(40)*
Service	16 *(79)*	36 *(79)*
Totals	45 *(218)*	100 *(218)*

Chart 9   LMRP Respondents in Five Cities, by Employment of Time

| | | 0 | 10 | 20 | 30 | 40 | 50 | 60 | 70 |

Total Sample
- Currently working — 46%
- Unemployed — 6%
- Retired — 3%
- Keeping house — 19%
- In school — 25%

Balti-more
- Currently working — 68%
- Unemployed — 3%
- Retired — 3%
- Keeping house — 6%
- In school — 20%

Cleve-land
- Currently working — 62%
- Unemployed — 1%
- Retired — 5%
- Keeping house — 19%
- In school — 13%

Los Ange-les
- Currently working — 65%
- Unemployed — 19%
- Retired — 1%
- Keeping house — 6%
- In school — 9%

New York
- Currently working — 5%
- Unemployed — 7%
- Retired — 1%
- Keeping house — 23%
- In school — 64%

Phila-del-phia
- Currently working — 29%
- Unemployed — 4%
- Retired — 5%
- Keeping house — 49%
- In school — 13%

Chart 10 LMRP Respondents in Five Cities, by Occupation

```
                       0    10    20    30    40    50    60    70
Balti-
more     White Collar  ▒▒▒▒▒ 10%
(68%)*   Clerical       ▒▒▒ 7%
         Craft          ▒▒▒ 6%
         Blue Collar    ▒▒▒▒▒▒▒ 16%
         Service        ▒▒▒▒▒▒▒▒▒▒▒▒▒ 29%
Cleve-
land     White Collar  ▒▒▒ 6%
(62%)    Clerical       ▒▒▒▒▒▒ 12%
         Craft          ▒▒▒▒▒▒▒▒ 18%
         Blue Collar    ▒▒▒ 6%
         Service        ▒▒▒▒▒▒▒▒▒ 20%
Los
Ange-    White Collar  ▒▒▒▒▒ 9%
les      Clerical       ▒▒▒▒▒ 9%
(63%)    Craft          ▒▒▒▒▒▒ 13%
         Blue Collar    ▒▒▒▒▒▒▒ 14%
         Service        ▒▒▒▒▒▒▒▒ 18%
New
York     White Collar  ▌ 1%
(5%)     Clerical       ▌ 1%
         Craft          ▌ 1%
         Blue Collar    | 0%
         Service        ▒ 2%
Phila-
del-     White Collar  ▒ 3%
phia     Clerical       ▒▒▒▒ 8%
(29%)    Craft          ▒ 3%
         Blue Collar    ▒▒ 5%
         Service        ▒▒▒▒▒ 10%
```

*Percent currently employed. Percentages in table are based
on total sample by city rather than the total of currently
employed.

Chart 11 LMRP Respondents in Five Cities, by Family Income

Family Income								Median Income
	0	10	20	30	40	50	60	70

Baltimore $6,779

$ 0 - 2,999	6%
3,000 - 5,999	31%
6,000 - 9,999	32%
10,000 and over	20%

Cleveland   5,549

0 - 2,999	20%
3,000 - 5,999	33%
6,000 - 9,999	24%
10,000 and over	19%

Los Angeles   6,919

0 - 2,999	22%
3,000 - 5,999	20%
6,000 - 9,999	24%
10,000 and over	18%

New York   4,139

0 - 2,999	19%
3,000 - 5,999	65%
6,000 - 9,000	4%
10,000 and over	1%

Philadelphia   3,899

0 - 2,999	32%
3,000 - 5,999	51%
6,000 - 9,000	12%
10,000 and over	4%

Chart 12 LMRP Respondents in Five Cities, by Individual Income

Individual Income

Median Income

Individual Income		Percent	Median Income
Baltimore	0	0%	$3,131
	1 - 2,999	27%	
	3,000 - 5,999	39%	
	6,000 - 9,999	17%	
	10,000 or more	5%	
Cleveland	0	1%	2,731
	1 - 2,999	42%	
	3,000 - 5,999	20%	
	6,000 - 9,999	11%	
	10,000 or more	7%	
Los Angeles	0	3%	3,269
	1 - 2,999	35%	
	3,000 - 5,999	24%	
	6,000 - 9,999	17%	
	10,000 or more	1%	
New York	0	5%	3,659
	1 - 2,999	24%	
	3,000 - 5,999	45%	
	6,000 - 9,999	1%	
	10,000 or more	2%	
Philadelphia	0	13%	2,581
	1 - 2,999	43%%	
	3 - 5,999	36%	
	6,000 - 9,999	7%	
	10,000 or more	1%	

Table 18 Women Who Keep House, by Race, Age (under 35 and over 35), and Amount of Formal Education (less than 10 years and more than 10 years)

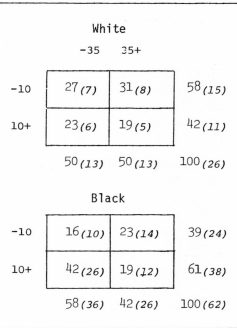

White

	-35	35+	
-10	27 (7)	31 (8)	58 (15)
10+	23 (6)	19 (5)	42 (11)
	50 (13)	50 (13)	100 (26)

Black

	-35	35+	
-10	16 (10)	23 (14)	39 (24)
10+	42 (26)	19 (12)	61 (38)
	58 (36)	42 (26)	100 (62)

Table 19 Occupation in Current Employment* *(expressed in percent)*

Question 24A: If currently employed: *What kind of work do you do?*

Professional and Business: 5 *(24)*

    Aeronautical and metallurgical engineers, nurses,
social and welfare workers, teachers, professional,
technical and kindred workers, inspectors, local
and state public administrators, insurance and real
estate, other industries (hotel, motel, theater, etc.)

* The occupational classification is based on the usual 9 part
census gross classification of the U.S. Census classification
(1950). "n.e.c." means *not elsewhere classified.*

Clerical and Sales: 7 *(32)*

Agents, bank tellers, office machine operators,
shipping and receiving clerks, stenographers, typists,
secretaries, telephone operators, clerical and kindred
workers, insurance agents and brokers, salesmen and
salesclerks

Craftsmen, Foremen, and Kindred Workers: 5 *(21)*

Boilermakers, masons and tile setters, carpenters,
crane and derrickmen, linemen and servicemen, machinists, mechanics and repairmen, millers, plumbers, shoe-
makers and repairers, tailors and tailoresses, tool-
makers and dyemakers and setters, upholsterers

Operative and Kindred Workers: 4 *(20)*

Apprentice carpenter, auto service and parking attendants, delivery and route men, dressmakers and
seamstresses (except factory), metal filers, grinders,
and polishers, furnacemen, smeltermen and pourers,
laundry and dry cleaning operatives, photographic
process workers, taxi drivers and chauffeurs, truck
and tractor drivers, welders and flame-cutters

Manufacturing - Durable Goods: 5 *(24)*

Operative and kindred workers (n.e.c.), taxicab
drivers and chauffeurs (n.e.c.), miscellaneous wood
products, furniture and fixtures, glass and glass
products, cement, concrete, and plaster products,
metal industries, blast furnaces and steelworks, other
primary metal industries, office and store machines
and devices, miscellaneous machinery, electrical
machinery, equipment and supplies, transportation
equipment, aircraft and parts, professional and
photographic equipment and watches, other manufacturing
industries, motor vehicles and equipment.

Manufacturing - Non-durable Goods: 3 *(16)*

   Food and kindred products, meat products, canning and
   preserving fruits, vegetables and seafood, confec-
   tionery and related products, apparel and acces-
   sories, miscellaneous fabricated textiles products,
   drugs and medicines, footwear, paper and allied
   products, not specified manufacturing industries

Service Workers: 14 *(70)*

   Private household workers (including baby sitters),
   hospital and other institutional attendants, professional and personal service attendants (n.e.c.) charwomen and cleaners, cooks, counter and fountain
   workers, housekeepers and stewards, janitors and
   sextons, policemen and detectives, practical nurses,
   waiters and waitresses, service workers (n.e.c.)

Laborers: 2 *(8)*

   Garage laborers, car washers and greasers

   _____

                                                               45 *(218)*

_____

Table 20 Former Occupation (if unemployed or retired)
_____

   Question 24F: *What kind of work did you do on your last job?*
_____

   Professional and Business:

       Dietician, professional, technical and kindred workers (n.e.c)
       other (including not reported)

   Clerical and Kindred Workers:

       Secretaries and typists, clerical

                                  158

Craftsmen, Foremen, and Kindred Workers:

> Linemen and servicemen, plasterers, pressmen and plate printers

Operative and Kindred Workers:

> Auto service and parking attendants, furnacemen, painters

Manufacturing, Non-durable Goods:

> Food and kindred products, apparel and accessories

Non-manufacturing Industries:

> Telecommunications and utilities and sanitary service

Service Workers:

> Private household workers, professional and personal service attendants, bartenders, cooks, elevator operators, guards, watchmen and doorkeepers, janitors, practical nurses, waiters and waitresses, service workers (n.e.c.)

Laborers

> Gardeners

Table 21 Adult New Readers Who Consider Occupations for the Future
(expressed in percent)

Question 25: *Do you ever think about getting into some (other) kind of work?*

Yes	60 *(285)*
No	37 *(178)*
No answer	3 *(16)*
Total	100 *(479)*

Table 22 Occupations Considered by Adult New Reader for the
Future *(expressed in percent)*

Question 25A: *If Yes: What type of work have you thought
about getting into?*

Professional, Technical and Kindred Workers: 28 *(79)*

    Accountants, athletes, authors, clergymen, professors
and instructors (subject unspecified), designers,
dieticians and nutritionists, mechanical and metallur-
gical engineers, foresters and conservationists,
funeral directors and embalmers, musicians and music
teachers, nurses, osteopaths, recreation and group
workers, social and welfare workers, teachers, medical
and dental technicians, other technicians, therapists
and healers

Managers, Officials, and Proprietors: 4 *(10)*

    State and local public administrators and officials,
local public administration inspectors, food and
dairy products stores and milk retailing, other
industries (hotel, theatre, barbershops...), manu-
facturers

Clerical, Sales, and Kindred Workers: 34 *(97)*

    Agents (n.e.c.), library attendants and assistants,
bank tellers, bookkeepers, cashiers, mail carriers,
office machine operators, secretaries, typists, and
stenographers, telephone operators, tickets, station
and express agents, salesmen and sales clerks for
manufacturing, wholesale trade and other

Craftsmen, Foremen, and Kindred Workers: 13 *(36)*

     Boilermakers, masons, carpenters, compositors, and
typesetters, electricians, excavating, grading and
road machinery, heat treaters, annealers and
temperers, inspectors, linemen and servicemen for
telegraph, telephone and power, machinists, mechanics
and repairmen, millers, plumbers and pipe fitters,
tool and die makers and setters, upholsterers

Operative and Kindred Workers: 3 *(8)*

     Apprentice carpenters, dressmakers and seamstresses,
furnacemen and smeltermen, laundry and dry cleaning
operators, sailors and deck hands, welders and flame
cutters, stationary firemen

Manufacturing - Durable Goods: 2 *(5)*

     Electrical machinery, equipment and supplies,
miscellaneious manufacturing industries

Non-manufacturing Industries: :: *(1)*

     Telecommunications, utilities, and sanitary service

Service Workers: 27 *(76)*

     Private household workers, hospital workers, hospital
and other attendants, professional and personal service
attendants, barbers, beauticians and manicurists,
charwomen and cleaners, cooks, counter and fountain
workers, firemen, guards, watchmen and doorkeepers,
housekeepers and stewards, janitors and sextons,
policemen and detectives, practical nurses, waiters
and waitresses, crossing watchmen and bridge tenders

Base = 285

:: The percentage is equal to less than 1%

Table 23 Use of Free Time *(expressed in percent)*

Question 2: *When you have had free time during the last six months, did you do any of these things?*

Use of Free Time	Yes	No
Visit with friends and relatives	83 *(398)*	17 *(80)*
Read a book or magazine	82 *(392)*	18 *(85)*
Drive or walk around town	72 *(347)*	27 *(130)*
Listen to records	72 *(343)*	28 *(134)*
Play cards, bingo or other games	47 *(225)*	52 *(250)*
Play pool, baseball or go bowling	32 *(155)*	67 *(318)*
Go to museums, concerts, exhibits	32 *(152)*	68 *(324)*
Go fishing	8 *(38)*	91 *(436)*
Practice judo or karate	3 *(17)*	96 *(458)*
Crochet, knit or sew *	60 *(199)*	37 *(122)*

*Base = 331 (includes women only)   Base = 479

162

Table 24 Use of Free Time *(expressed in percent)*

Question 13: *When you have some free time, do you sometimes go to...*

Free Time Activity	Yes	No
Church, synagogue, mosque	73 *(349)*	27 *(130)*
The movies	72 *(347)*	28 *(132)*
The park or a zoo	65 *(311)*	35 *(168)*
Dances	48 *(228)*	52 *(251)*
A bar, cocktail lounge, or tavern	38 *(182)*	62 *(297)*
Pool hall or bowling alley	30 *(146)*	70 *(333)*
A neighborhood center	28 *(136)*	72 *(343)*
The Y or YW	10 *(49)*	90 *(429)*

Base = 479

Table 25 Use of Free Time, by Age *(expressed in percent)*

Use of Free Time	Age					
	16-24 *(111)*	25-34 *(148)*	35-44 *(101)*	45-54 *(66)*	55-64 *(31)*	65+ *(20)*
Dances	73 *(81)*	54 *(79)*	43 *(43)*	32 *(21)*	3 *(3)*	0 *(0)*
The park or a zoo	61 *(67)*	78 *(116)*	68 *(69)*	64 *(42)*	42 *(13)*	50 *(10)*
A bar, cocktail lounge, or tavern	48 *(53)*	48 *(71)*	35 *(36)*	24 *(16)*	16 *(5)*	0 *(0)*
The movies	81 *(90)*	81 *(120)*	70 *(71)*	65 *(43)*	52 *(16)*	30 *(6)*
The Y or YW	9 *(10)*	11 *(16)*	16 *(16)*	6 *(4)*	7 *(2)*	5 *(1)*
The neighborhood center	27 *(30)*	29 *(43)*	29 *(30)*	29 *(19)*	23 *(7)*	35 *(7)*
Church, synagogue, mosque	56 *(62)*	76 *(112)*	77 *(78)*	74 *(49)*	93 *(29)*	95 *(19)*
Pool hall or bowling alley	45 *(50)*	21 *(46)*	31 *(31)*	26 *(17)*	7 *(2)*	0 *(0)*

Table 26   Use of Free Time, by Sex *(expressed in percent)*

Use of Free Time	Sex	
	Male (148)	Female (331)
Dances	50 (74)	47 (154)
The park or a zoo	61 (91)	68 (226)
A bar, cocktail lounge, or tavern	45 (67)	35 (115)
The movies	73 (108)	72 (239)
The Y or YW	13 (19)	9 (30)
A neighborhood center	23 (34)	31 (102)
Church, synagogue, mosque	61 (61)	78 (78)
Pool hall or bowling alley	48 (70)	23 (23)

Table 27 Use of Free Time, by Race *(expressed in percent)*

| | Race | |
Use of Free Time	White *(123)*	Black *(356)*
Dances	39 *(48)*	51 *(180)*
The park or a zoo	66 *(81)*	66 *(234)*
A bar, cocktail lounge, or tavern	24 *(29)*	44 *(153)*
The movies	63 *(77)*	76 *(268)*
The Y or YW	6 *(7)*	12 *(42)*
A neighborhood center	25 *(31)*	30 *(105)*
Church, synagogue, mosque	60 *(73)*	77 *(274)*
Pool hall or bowling alley	28 *(34)*	31 *(111)*

Table 28 Enjoyment of Watching Sports *(expressed in percent)*

Question 3: *How much do you enjoy watching sports? Would you say you enjoy watching sports a great deal, a little, or not at all?*

Degree of Enjoyment	
A great deal	42 *(200)*
A little	38 *(180)*
Not at all	20 *(98)*
No answer	⊠ *(1)*
Total	100 *(479)*

⊠ The percentage is equal to less than 1%

Table 29 Membership in Clubs *(expressed in percent)*

Question 27: *Are you a member of any club or group, or society or union*

Response	
Yes	40 *(192)*
No	60 *(287)*
Total	100 *(479)*

Table 30 Membership in Specific Types of Clubs and Organizations
(expressed in percent)

Question 27A: If Yes: *What clubs or organizations do you belong to?*

Type of Club or Organization	
Labor union (local of some union)	29 *(56)*
Religious group (men's club, Holy Name or Altar Rosary Society, Missionary Society)	25 *(48)*
Parent-Teacher Association	14 *(38)*
Neighborhood Improvement Association, or neighborhood club	13 *(37)*
Fraternal organization or lodge (Masons, Knights of Columbus, Elks, Eastern Star)	11 *(22)*
Civil rights group (SNCC, NAACP, CORE)	11 *(22)*
Sports or hobby club	8 *(13)*
Organization of people of the same nationality background (Sons of Italy, B'nai B'rith, Steuben Society)	7 *(12)*
Veterans organizations, (American Legion, Veterans of Foreign Wars)	6 *(11)*
Political club or organization	4 *(8)*
Other (Specify) Parents, mother	10 *(18)*
Social club	2 *(5)*
Welfare	3 *(6)*
Other	3 *(6)*

Base = 192

Table 31 Club Participation As Officer *(expressed in percent)*

Question 27B: *Within the last two years, have you been an officer of any of these clubs or organizations?*

Yes	36 *(70)*
No	64 *(122)*
Total of the Respondents who are members of a club	100 *(192)*

Table 32 Use of Public Library *(expressed in percent)*

Question 14: *Have you ever gone to a public library?*

Yes	87 *(414)*
No	13 *(64)*
No answer	⁑ *(1)*
Total	100 *(479)*

⁑ The percentage is equal to less than 1%

Table 33 Use of Public Library Services *(expressed in percent)*

Question 14A: If Yes: *Within the past six months, have you gone to a public library ...*

Activity	Yes	No
To borrow books	63 *(260)*	36 *(148)*
To ask for some information	43 *(179)*	55 *(227)*
To read a book	38 *(159)*	60 *(247)*
To study there	35 *(143)*	64 *(266)*
To take children there	30 *(125)*	67 *(279)*
To tour the library	22 *(91)*	76 *(316)*
To read a magazine	18 *(73)*	80 *(332)*
To go to a lecture or program	16 *(66)*	82 *(341)*
To see an exhibit	14 *(58)*	83 *(345)*
To read a newspaper	11 *(47)*	87 *(360)*
To see a movie	10 *(42)*	89 *(366)*
To borrow or listen to records	10 *(42)*	89 *(366)*
To meet friends	8 *(29)*	90 *(376)*

Base = 414

Table 34 Use of the Public Library by Adult New Reader *(expressed in percent)*

Question 14: *Have you ever gone to a public library?*

Basic Social Characteristics	
Sex	
Male	86 *(127)*
Female	87 *(287)*
Race	
White	83 *(101)*
Black	88 *(310)*
Age (in years)	
16 - 24	89 *(99)*
25 - 34	86 *(128)*
35 - 44	85 *(86)*
45 - 54	88 *(57)*
55 - 64	84 *(26)*
65 +	85 *(17)*
Education (last grade)	
0 - 4	77 *(24)*
5 - 6	80 *(37)*
7 - 9	89 *(130)*
10 - 11	89 *(135)*
12	84 *(69)*
13 +	88 *(15)*
Adult Education Classes or Programs	
Adult Basic Education	91 *(207)*
Employment Oriented	91 *(180)*
Youth Oriented Employment	96 *(28)*
Reading Development Program	98 *(41)*
High School Equivalency	90 *(108)*
Other	85 *(30)*

Table 34 Use of the Public Library by Adult New Reader (continued)
(expressed in percent)

Question 14: *Have you ever gone to a public library?*

Basic Social Characteristics	
Employment of Time	
Working Force	
White collar	85 *(23)*
Clerical	79 *(27)*
Craft	87 *(34)*
Blue collar	80 *(32)*
Service	90 *(70)*
Unemployed	90 *(28)*
Retired	85 *(11)*
Keeping house	86 *(79)*
School	89 *(107)*
Family Income	
$ 1 - 2,999	88 *(79)*
3,000 - 5,999	88 *(167)*
6,000 - 9,999	83 *(77)*
10,000 or more	87 *(53)*
Individual Income	
$ 0 - 2,999	88 *(158)*
3,000 - 5,999	89 *(142)*
6,000 - 9,999	78 *(40)*
10,000 or more	94 *(15)*
Adult New Reader Rating	
Very active	97 *(63)*
Active	89 *(227)*
Somewhat active	81 *(117)*
Least active	54 *(7)*

Table 35 Number of Others in Living Quarters *(expressed in percent)*

Question 64: *How many people live in this household, including yourself?*

Number of Persons	
One	10 *(49)*
Two	16 *(77)*
Three	18 *(88)*
Four	16 *(74)*
Five	14 *(67)*
Six	8 *(38)*
Seven	8 *(37)*
Eight	4 *(19)*
Nine	3 *(13)*
Ten	* *(2)*
Eleven	1 *(5)*
Twelve	* *(2)*
Thirteen	* *(1)*
No answer	2 *(7)*
Total	100 *(479)*

* The percentage is equal to less than 1%

(5) Specific Educational Characteristics

The amount of formal education, that is, the last year completed in school, for 62 percent of the respondents falls between grades 7 and 11. The median years of schooling completed is 10.2 years which is approximately two years less than the median of 12.1 years of educational attainment reported for the general population in 30 central cities census figures for 1969.[1]

Table 36 shows education correlated with sex and race. Among Black and white females, educational attainment is very similar except for a small increase in the proportion of high school graduates among white females. The educational attainment of the men in the survey shows a rather large proportion of white males having seven to nine years of schooling with a comparable decrement in proportion of those with some high school or more. The median grade achieved by white males is 9.4 years, about one grade lower than that of Black males and females, and of white females. With this exception the educational attainment of males and females differs very little.

In general, the respondents who are over age 35 have less schooling than those who are under 35 years of age (table 37). This generation gap in education is more conspicuous among the Black respondents of the study. A comparison between young Black and white respondents who are less than 35 years of age, shows that the Black respondents in the survey have had more years of schooling than the white respondents. A similar situation exists in the general population. The 1969 census report shows that a significant factor in the decline in the proportion of persons with little or no schooling is the replacement of older persons by younger persons who generally had higher levels of education.

Respondents were asked at what age they left school. The highest percentage, 46 percent, did remain in school up to 16 or 17 years of age which is usually the compulsory age for attendance.

A significant number, about one-fourth, left school at a younger age, between 12 and 15 years, and 3 percent between the ages of 8 and 11 years. Nearly one-fourth remained in school after 18 years of age (table 38). Many reasons account for respondents having to leave school. The continuity of education is affected by responsibilities of daily living and family life. It is note-worthy that 15 percent graduated, which is much less than the average for 30 central cities where 31.2 percent completed four years of high school. The foremost reason for leaving school before graduation is an economic one, that is, lack of money needed to support oneself or family. Family reasons such as mar-riage, pregnancy, family illness, and family problems also are important factors for leaving school. Circumstances in school that caused the respondents to drop out are: getting poor grades, trouble with teachers or school authorities, being expelled, and disturbances in school. Similar patterns which are shown in table 39 were found by Hilliard in his Chicago study (table 40).[2]

When reasons for leaving school are compared between Black and white, male and female respondents, no difference is found in the percentage who graduated from high school. However, a comparison of reasons for leaving school by male and female re-spondents shows a marked difference in economic and family rea-sons. The males have a higher percentage of respondents who left school to support their family and themselves. On the other hand, the females have a higher percentage of respondents who left school for family reasons such as marriage, pregnancy, and illness in the family.

Likewise, a comparison of reasons for leaving school by the race of the respondents shows differences in the same areas. Nearly one out of four white respondents left school to support a family, while one out of seven Black respondents left for the same reason. The percentage rates for leaving school because of family reasons was slightly higher for the Black respondents. It must be noted that the general pattern of reasons for leaving school does not differ radically among Black and white, male and female respondents (tables 42 and 41).

Table 36 Education, by Sex and Race *(expressed in percent)*

Amount of Formal Education: (year completed in school)	Male		Female	
	White	Black	White	Black
0 - 6	16 *(10)*	20 *(17)*	15 *(9)*	15 *(41)*
7 - 9	42 *(26)*	27 *(23)*	29 *(17)*	30 *(80)*
10 - 11	26 *(16)*	33 *(27)*	29 *(17)*	34 *(91)*
12 or more	16 *(10)*	20 *(17)*	27 *(16)*	20 *(54)*
No answer	0 *(0)*	0 *(0)*	※ *(2)*	※ *(3)*
Total	100 *(62)*	100 *(84)*	100 *(61)*	100 *(269)*
Median	9.4	10.2	10.6	10.4

※ The percentage is equal to less than 1%

176

Table 37 Educational Level Less Than 10 Years Schooling, by Sex,
Race, and Age - Under 35 (-35) and Over 35 (35+)
(expressed in percent)

Male

Education Less Than 10 Years	White		Black	
	-35	35+	-35	35+
	54 *(21)*	65 *(15)*	26 *(12)*	76 *(28)*
Total	39	23	47	37

Female

Education Less Than 10 Years	White		Black	
	-35	35+	-35	35+
	40 *(14)*	50 *(12)*	25 *(34)*	67 *(76)*
Total	36	25	136	131*

* No answer = 2

Table 38 Age When Left School *(expressed in percent)*

Question 34B: *What age were you when you left school?*

Age When Left School (in years)	
8 - 11	3 *(15)*
12 - 15	26 *(124)*
16 - 17	46 *(221)*
18	11 *(53)*
19 and over	9 *(42)*
Still attending	2 *(8)*
No answer	3 *(16)*
Total	100 *(479)*

Median = 16.9

Table 39 Reasons for Leaving School *(expressed in percent)*

Question 34C: *What reasons did you have for leaving school?*

Reasons for Leaving School	
Had to support self	18 *(85)*
Had to support family	17 *(81)*
Graduated	15 *(74)*
Pregnant	12 *(57)*
Married	11 *(52)*
Other family problems	10 *(47)*
Was getting poor grades in school	8 *(36)*
Wanted to earn extra spending money	5 *(22)*
Own illness	3 *(16)*
Trouble with teachers or school authorities	2 *(11)*
Illness in family	2 *(10)*
Expelled	1 *(5)*
Disturbances in school	1 *(5)*
Military service	1 *(5)*
Other	8 *(40)*
Tired, bored, not meaningful, didn't like	6 *(31)*

Base = 479

Table 40 Reasons for Leaving School *(expressed in percent)*

Question 34C: *What reasons did you have for leaving school?*

Reasons for Leaving School	LMRP (479)		Hilliard* (759)	
Lack of money	40		35.4	
Had to support self		18		
Had to support family		17		
Wanted extra money		5		
Graduated	15		1.2	
Pregnant	12		16.9	
Married	11		10.0	
Other family problems	10			
Poor grades	8		2.2	
School disciplinary action	4		2	
Trouble with teachers		2		
Disturbances in school		1		
Expelled		1		
Own illness	3		3.4	
Family illness	2		5.0	
Other reasons	9		10.7	
Others		8		5.3
Military service		1		
Urged to quit				3.4
Moved to other state				1.2
School said too slow				0.7
Police disciplinary action				0.1

* Raymond M. Hilliard, *First, They Must Read,* 1964, Table C-43, p.

Table 41   Reasons for Leaving School, by Race

Reasons	Race	
	White (123)	Black (353)
Was getting poor grades in school	11 (13)	7 (23)
Expelled	0 (0)	1 (5)
Trouble with teachers or school authorities	3 (4)	2 (7)
Disturbances in school	1 (1)	1 (4)
Own illness	3 (4)	4 (12)
Illness in family	1 (1)	3 (9)
Other family problems	7 (9)	11 (38)
Had to support self	17 (21)	18 (64)
Had to support family	24 (30)	14 (51)
Wanted to earn extra spending money	5 (6)	5 (16)
Military service	2 (2)	1 (3)
Married	14 (17)	10 (35)
Pregnant	1 (1)	16 (56)
Graduated	15 (18)	15 (54)

Table 42   Reasons for Leaving School, by Sex

Reasons	Sex	
	Male *(148)*	Female *(331)*
Was getting poor grades in school	11 *(16)*	7 *(20)*
Expelled	4 *(5)*	0 *(0)*
Trouble with teachers or school authorities	4 *(6)*	2 *(5)*
Disturbances in school	1 *(2)*	1 *(3)*
Own illness	3 *(4)*	4 *(12)*
Illness in family	0 *(0)*	3 *(10)*
Other family problems	10 *(14)*	10 *(33)*
Had to support self	24 *(35)*	15 *(50)*
Had to support family	29 *(44)*	11 *(37)*
Wanted to earn extra spending money	6 *(8)*	4 *(14)*
Military service	4 *(5)*	——
Married	2 *(3)*	15 *(49)*
Pregnant	——	17 *(57)*
Graduated	15 *(22)*	16 *(52)*

Although education has been interrupted, the respondents have found it possible to continue their education in the adult education programs available to them at this period in their lives. Among the respondents eight in ten or 82 percent are attending or had attended within the last year adult education classes which are primarily adult basic education, employment oriented or job training, and high school equivalency programs. The basic and general areas of education overlap with the job training in which respondents were learning work skills. Although only 10 percent of the respondents identified public library reading development programs, it should be remembered that the public library in its auxiliary capacity provides reading materials through coordinated programs. The adults in these classes and programs may or may not be aware of the source or the extent of the libraries' involvement, and consequently may not identify such service. For example, the Cleveland Public Library and the Free Library of Philadelphia channel a major part of the reading materials services directly to the adult education programs through the cooperation of the staff of the agencies (tables 43 and 44).

Participants in the adult education classes and programs as a group show few distinctive differences in relation to basic social characteristics. When participants in specific types of classes and programs are compared, differences are evident. Chart 3 shows that Black males and females participate more in the employment oriented programs. As may be expected and as a reflection of the social and economic situation, a significantly greater percentage of Black males are in employment oriented programs. Chart shows that age is a factor in the type of program in which the adult new reader chooses to continue his education. By far the greater participation in adult basic education programs is among the adults who are 45 years of age and over. In contrast, by far the greater participation in the employment oriented programs are the youngest adults who are 16 to 24 years of age. To some extent this large majority reflects the fact that the employment oriented programs are directed to young adults; but equally important is the fact that adults 45 years of age and over also participated in these employment oriented programs. It is this oldest group who are attracted by the public library reading development programs. The greater participation in these programs by the older adult may be interpreted to mean that they are more comfortable in the less formal school situation. (Chart 13)

The continuation of an interrupted education is important particularly to adult new readers who are 25 to 44 years of age. They make up an important segment of the participants in the high school equivalency programs. It would appear that the adult at this period in life finds it important to continue formal education for the purpose of acquiring the high school diploma and the accreditation it represents.

Chart 14 shows the relationships between participation in adult education classes or programs and the amount of formal education. Regardless of the number of years of schooling, adults are continuing education at various levels. The adults who have less years of schooling are continuing education primarily through adult basic education and public library reading development programs. Adults with more years of schooling, as may be expected, are continuing their education primarily through the high school equivalency and employment or job oriented programs. In contrast, many adults do not move in a graded sequence which is usually expected within the educational system. As chart 14 clearly shows, adult new readers with less than seven years of schooling and with more than 11 years had participated in all types of adult classes or programs.

Participants in adult basic education programs who are in the work force come primarily from blue-collar and service occupations;

in comparison, the participants in high school equivalency are from the white-collar and clerical occupations. Respondents from each occupational category reported participation in the various skill training programs (table 45). In these programs participants studied primarily subjects in the areas of basic communication and computational skills, 87 percent and 75 percent respectively. The subjects of American history and science are important enough to be identified separately by between a third and one-fourth of the respondents. The other major areas of study are directed to the acquisition of special skills, primarily household skills and job training in basic office and manual skills (table 46).

Some significant differences in relation to subject areas studied appear between Blacks and whites participating in adult education classes or programs. Although the subject area - English, reading, writing, spelling - engage equal percentages of partici- pants, the computational subjects - mathematics, arithmetic, book- keeping - are studied by 81 percent of the Black participants as compared to 59 percent of the white participants. American history is studied by more of the white participants than by Black parti- cipants. A higher percentage of Black participants study basic office skills - typing, filing, shorthand, business machines (table 47).

To identify which classes influenced the daily life of respond- ents, the adult classes or programs were correlated with the 65 percent of the respondents who reported that classes had changed their lives in some way. Manpower Development and Training programs had direct influence for 75 percent of the participants in the program. Adult basic education programs and the Work Incentive Program influenced the daily life of at least two-thirds of the participants in these programs. Most of the programs had at least 50 percent of the participants who reported changes taking place in their daily life because of class influences (table 48).

Of the 65 percent who found that things learned in class had caused changes in their life, two-thirds of the participants in the adult classes or programs said that they were better able to communicate with people; over half had more self-confidence and had better relations or understanding of other people; and one in three saw better job prospects (table 49). Respondents perceived these changes in four areas: better relations or understanding of other people; more self-confidence; better job prospects; and better able to communicate with people. For example, among participants who reported ways in which the public library program had affected their lives, 86 percent felt that they had better relations with other people, 79 percent gained self-confidence, 29 percent had better job prospects, and 89 percent were better able to communicate with others. The respondents' perception of changes caused by other classes focuses mainly on personal relations included in the better relations and communications categories. The slight variations are seen upon examination of table 50 .

One of the ways in which the participants' lives have changed due to adult education classes or programs was in the area of better job prospects. Over two-thirds of the participants considered getting into other types of work as shown in table 21 . When these percentages are compared with the percentage of participants who felt their lives had been changed in regard to job prospects by adult education classes or programs, it is seen that considerably fewer persons designated a change in better job prospects although much of the training was directed to job skills (table 51)

Adult education classes or programs stimulated reading outside of class for some of the participants. Although programs by no means stimulate reading for everyone, it appears that at least a majority use reading materials in the context of class or program, particularly for the high school equivalency and Work Incentive Programs (table 52).

Table 43 Attendance of Adult Education Classes or Programs *(expressed in percent)*

Question 28: *Within the last year, have you gone to any adult education classes or programs?*

Yes	82 *(394)*
No	18 *(85)*
Total	100 *(479)*

Chart 13 Participation in Adult Education Classes or Programs, by Age

Adult Basic Education

16 - 24	39%
25 - 44	57%
45 and over	79%

Employment Oriented

16 - 24	83%
25 - 44	56%
45 and over	32%

Public Library Reading Development

16 - 24	5%
25 - 44	7%
45 and over	32%

High School Equivalency

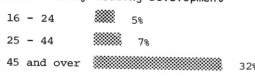

16 - 24	28%
25 - 44	36%
45 and over	16%

Table 44 Participation in Adult Education Classes or Programs
          (expressed in percent)

Question 28A: If Yes: *What were these classes or programs?*

Category	
Adult Basic Education	58 *(227)*
High School Equivalency Program	30 *(119)*
Work Incentive Program	19 *(72)*
Manpower Development and Training	16 *(64)*
Public Library Programs or Reading Development Program	13 *(50)*
Concentrated Employment Program	8 *(29)*
Opportunities Industrialization Centers	6 *(19)*
Neighborhood Youth Corps	5 *(16)*
Job Corps	4 *(12)*
New Careers	2 *(8)*
Programs sponsored by private industry	1 *(4)*
Upward Bound	⁑ *(1)*
Other	9 *(35)*

Base = 394 (Total number of respondents who attend classes

⁑ The percentage is equal to less than 1%

Chart 14 Participation in Adult Education Classes or Programs,
by Amount of Formal Education

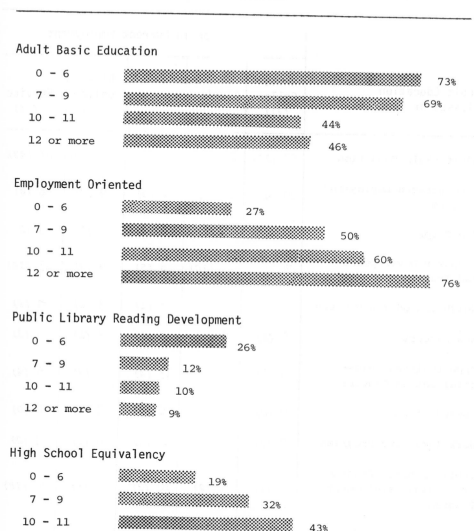

Adult Basic Education

0 - 6   73%
7 - 9   69%
10 - 11   44%
12 or more   46%

Employment Oriented

0 - 6   27%
7 - 9   50%
10 - 11   60%
12 or more   76%

Public Library Reading Development

0 - 6   26%
7 - 9   12%
10 - 11   10%
12 or more   9%

High School Equivalency

0 - 6   19%
7 - 9   32%
10 - 11   43%
12 or more   19%

Table 45 Participation in Adult Education Classes or Programs, by Occupation in Current Employment *(expressed in percent)*

Adult Education Classes or Programs	Occupation in Current Employment				
	White Collar *(21)*	Clerical *(29)*	Craft *(31)*	Blue Collar *(35)*	Service *(64)*
Adult Basic Education	52 *(11)*	24 *(7)*	55 *(17)*	86 *(30)*	67 *(43)*
Concentrated Employment Program	20 *(4)*	10 *(3)*	10 *(3)*	9 *(3)*	6 *(4)*
Job Corps	0 *(0)*	3 *(1)*	6 *(2)*	0 *(0)*	3 *(2)*
Manpower Development and Training	24 *(5)*	34 *(10)*	16 *(5)*	9 *(3)*	25 *(16)*
Neighborhood Youth Corps	5 *(1)*	3 *(1)*	3 *(1)*	3 *(1)*	3 *(2)*
New Careers	5 *(1)*	3 *(1)*	0 *(0)*	3 *(1)*	5 *(3)*
Opportunities Industrialization Centers	5 *(1)*	7 *(2)*	13 *(4)*	9 *(3)*	6 *(4)*
Upward Bound	0 *(0)*	0 *(0)*	0 *(0)*	3 *(1)*	0 *(0)*
Work Incentive Programs	9 *(2)*	3 *(1)*	10 *(3)*	6 *(2)*	3 *(2)*
Public Library Programs or Reading Development Program	5 *(1)*	7 *(2)*	10 *(3)*	9 *(3)*	28 *(18)*
Programs sponsored by private industry	0 *(0)*	3 *(1)*	3 *(1)*	0 *(0)*	0 *(0)*
High School Equivalency Program	40 *(8)*	31 *(9)*	16 *(5)*	26 *(9)*	22 *(14)*
Other	9 *(2)*	24 *(7)*	16 *(5)*	3 *(1)*	10 *(6)*

Table 46   Specific Subjects Studied by Adult New Reader *(expressed in percent)*

Question 28B: *Specifically, what have you studied in this (these) class(es)?*

Subjects Studied	
English, reading, writing, spelling	87 *(343)*
Mathematics, arithmetic, bookkeeping	75 *(294)*
American history	37 *(145)*
Science	26 *(102)*
Job training in basic office skills (typing, filing, shorthand, business machines)	15 *(58)*
Household skills (nutrition, cooking, sewing, home management)	12 *(46)*
First aid, home nursing	10 *(39)*
Job training in manual skills (welding, carpentry, machinery, electricity)	10 *(38)*
Child care, child psychology	6 *(22)*
Other	6 *(22)*

Base = 394

Table 47 Subject Areas Studied by Adult New Reader, by Race
(expressed in percent)

Subject Areas Studied	Race	
	White *(110)*	Black *(281)*
English, reading, writing, spelling	86 *(94)*	88 *(246)*
Mathematics, arithmetic, bookkeeping	59 *(65)*	81 *(228)*
Science	27 *(29)*	26 *(73)*
American history	43 *(47)*	35 *(98)*
Child care, child psychology	7 *(8)*	5 *(14)*
Household skills, (nutrition, sewing, etc.)	8 *(9)*	13 *(37)*
First aid, home nursing	6 *(7)*	11 *(32)*
Job training in basic office skills	4 *(4)*	19 *(54)*
Job training in manual skills	11 *(12)*	9 *(25)*
Other	7 *(8)*	5 *(14)*

Table 48 Influence of Classes on Life *(expressed in percent)*

Question 30: *Because of the things you learned in your class(es),*
has your life changed in any way?

Yes	65 *(256)*
No	29 *(137)*
No answer	⁑ *(1)*
Total number who attend programs	100 *(394)* **

⁑ The is equal to less than 1%

** 85 respondents do not attend any adult education classes or programs

Table 49 Ways in Which Classes Influence Life *(expressed in percent)*

Question 30A: If Yes: *In what ways has it changed?*

Change	
Better able to communicate with people (i.e., learned to read and write English, able to talk with all kinds of people)	62 *(159)*
Have more self-confidence, more mature, feel uplifted	53 *(136)*
Better relations or understanding of other people	50 *(129)*
Better job prospects	39 *(100)*
Other	5 *(13)*

Base = 256

Table 50 Adult Basic Education Classes or Programs, by Ways Adult New Reader's Life Has Changed (*expressed in percent*)

Adult Education Classes or Programs	Ways Life Has Changed			
	Better Relations	Self-Confidence	Job Prospects	Better Communicatio
Adult Basic Education (145)	54 (81)	53 (79)	39 (58)	69 (103)
Concentrated Employment Program (17)	53 (9)	59 (10)	53 (9)	47 (8)
Job Corps (6)	50 (3)	83 (5)	67 (4)	67 (4)
Manpower Development and Training (48)	44 (21)	39 (19)	57 (27)	44 (21)
Neighborhood Youth Corps (7)	57 (4)	43 (3)	71 (5)	29 (2)
New Careers (4)	50 (2)	50 (2)	50 (2)	50 (2)
Opportunities Industrialization Centers (10)	20 (2)	30 (3)	60 (6)	30 (3)
Upward Bound (1)	100 (1)	100 (1)	0 (0)	100 (1)
Work Incentive Programs (46)	48 (22)	67 (31)	35 (17)	59 (27)
Public Library Programs (29)	86 (25)	79 (23)	29 (8)	89 (26)
Programs sponsored by private industry (4)	75 (3)	100 (4)	50 (2)	75 (3)
High School Equivalency Program (70)	69 (48)	70 (49)	44 (31)	76 (53)
Other (23)	50 (12)	39 (9)	35 (8)	61 (14)

Table 51   Adult Education Classes or Programs, by Considering Other Kind of Work

Adult Education Classes or Programs	Percent Who Have Considered Other Types of Work*
Adult Basic Education	55 *(124)*
Concentrated Employment Program	62 *(18)*
Job Corps	67 *(8)*
Manpower Development and Training	61 *(39)*
Neighborhood Youth Corps	63 *(10)*
New Careers	75 *(6)*
Opportunities Indus- trialization Centers	68 *(13)*
Upward Bound	100 *(1)*
Work Incentive Programs	93 *(67)*
Public Library Programs or Reading Development Program	44 *(22)*
Programs sponsored by private industry	75 *(3)*
High School Equivalency Program	73 *(87)*
Other	51 *(18)*

* Percentages are based on the number of respondents who partici- pate in the class or program.

Table 52   Classes Stimulated Reading Outside of Classes, by Adult
Education Classes or Programs *(expressed in percent)**

Adult Education Classes or Programs	Percent Who Were Stimulated to Read Outside of Class
Adult Basic Education	53 *(120)*
Concentrated Employment Program	59 *(17)*
Job Corps	42 *(5)*
Manpower Development and Training	56 *(36)*
Neighborhood Youth Corps	50 *(8)*
New Careers	63 *(5)*
Opportunities Industrialization Centers	58 *(11)*
Upward Bound	100 *(1)*
Work Incentive Programs	61 *(44)*
Public Library Programs or Reading Development Program	52 *(26)*
Programs sponsored by private industry	50 *(2)*
High School Equivalency Program	64 *(76)*
Other	54 *(19)*

* Percentages are based on the number of respondents who participate
in the class or program (table 44).

Reading Activity of the Adult New Reader

Each adult new reader is classified according to the extent of his reading activity, as very active, active, somewhat active, least active, based on his use of newspapers, magazines, comic books, and books as reported in the Population Study interviews. Each respondent in the LMRP Population Study is assigned a score between 0 and 10 which reflects his reading activity. The score is arrived at in the following manner.

Newspapers

If a respondent does not read newspapers, he is considered least active in the particular use and assigned a score of 0. Those who do read newspapers are assigned a score between 1 and 3 which reflects their activity in reading newspapers (table 53).

Table 53 Newspaper Use - Reading Activity Score and Rating (Based on Question 4B)

Newspaper Use (Frequency of Reading)	Score	Rating	Percent of Respondents
Every day	3	Very active	47 (224)
A few times a week	2	Active	30 (146)
Once a week	1	Somewhat active	9 (40)
Sundays only	2	Active	4 (19)
Less often than that	1	Somewhat active	3 (14)
Don't read newspapers	0	Least active	7 (36)*
		Total	100 (479)

* Includes one (1) no answer to question 4B.

Magazines

Magazine reading activity is rated according to the number of types of magazines which the respondent reads (table 54).

Table 54 Magazine Use - Reading Activity Score and Rating (Based on Question 10A)

Magazine Use (Number of Types Read)	Score	Rating	Percent of Respondents
5 or more	3	Very active	14 *(65)*
3 - 4	2	Active	52 *(249)*
2 - 1	1	Somewhat active	22 *(105)*
Don't read magazines	0	Least active	12 *(60)*
		Total	100 *(479)*

Comic Books

If the respondent reads comic books, he is scored 1 - somewhat active or 0 - least active (table 55).

Table 55 Comic Books Use - Reading Activity Score and Rating (Based on Question 15)

Comic Book Use	Score	Rating	Percent of Respondents
Yes	1	Somewhat active	34 *(161)*
No	0	Least active	66 *(318)*
		Total	100 *(479)*

Books

Finally the respondent is rated and scored for his book reading activity. The scoring is based upon the number of books read within the last six months previous to the interview (table 56).

Table 56 Book Use - Reading Activity Score and Rating (Based on Question 16A)

Book Use (Number of Books Read)	Score	Rating	Percent of Respondents
10 or more	3	Very active	12 *(56)*
4 - 9	2	Active	24 *(105)*
3 - 1	1	Somewhat active	31 *(148)*
Don't read books	0	Least active	33 *(160)* *
		Total	100 *(479)*

* Includes 11 respondents who reported reading books in the last six months but did not indicate the number of books they had read.

Final Reading Activity Score

The respondent's final score is the total of his individual scores within the four areas of print material use. The scores cover the full range between 0 and 10 (table 57).

Table 57 Reading Activity of Adult New Reader *(expressed in percent)*

Reading Activity Score

0	3 *(13)*
1	4 *(18)*
2	5 *(22)*
3	9 *(45)*
4	12 *(59)*
5	18 *(85)*
6	20 *(96)*
7	15 *(75)*
8	9 *(42)*
9	4 *(20)*
10	1 *(4)*
Total	100 *(479)*

Mean = 5.4

200

Chart 15 Reading Activity of Adult New Reader

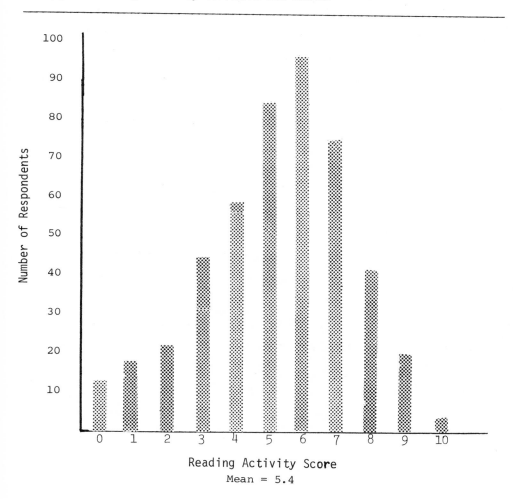

Reading Activity Score
Mean = 5.4

Each respondent's reading activity rating is determined on
the basis of his total score. A respondent with a score of zero
is classified as a least active reader. A respondent with a score
from one to four is classified as a somewhat active reader. A
respondent with a score from five to seven is an active reader.
A respondent with a score of eight to ten is a very active reader
(table 58).

Table 58   Final Reading Activity Score and Rating of the Use of
Print Materials

Final Combined Score	Rating	Percent of Respondents
0	Least active	3 *(13)*
1 - 4	Somewhat active	30 *(144)*
5 - 7	Active	53 *(257)*
8 - 10	Very active	14 *(65)*
	Total	100 *(479)*

The reading activity rating provides an index that measures
the extent of the adult new reader's reading activity by his use
of print materials, that is, newspapers, magazines, comic books,
and books. A majority of the respondents in the survey when
measured by this Reading Activity Index have a reading activity
score from 5 to 7, which places them in the active reader group.
A third of the respondents have a score from 0 to 4; most of these
are in the somewhat active group of readers; only 13 respondents
are rated with a score of zero as least active readers. Because
of the nature of the sample, the small number of least active
readers is to be expected. At the other end of the scale are the
very active readers, 14 percent, who have a reading activity
score from 8 to 10 (table 58).

The mean or average reading activity score is 5.4 which falls
within the active reader group (chart 15). Tables 59,60,61 indicate
no significant differences between men and women, or in relation
to race or age when looked at as a group. But distinctions are
evident when age and education are held constant. Table 62 shows
the activity score expressed as a mean for men and women of both
races, holding constant age and education. For example, in the

first cell there are 21 young, under 35 years of age, white male individuals who have a mean reading activity score of 3.6 which identifies them as somewhat active readers. The eight white male and nine Black older individuals, over 35 years of age, and with more formal education, have a mean reading score of 6.9 and 6.8 respectively, which rates as active readers.

Table 59   Sex, by Adult New Reader Activity Rating *(expressed in percent)*

Sex	Least Active	Somewhat Active	Active	Very Active
Female	2 *(8)*	28 *(94)*	53 *(176)*	16 *(53)*
Male	3 *(5)*	34 *(50)*	55 *(81)*	8 *(12)*

Table 60   Race, by Adult New Reader Activity Rating *(expressed in percent)*

Race	Least Active	Somewhat Active	Active	Very Active
White *(123)*	2 *(3)*	37 *(45)*	50 *(61)*	11 *(14)*
Black *(353)*	3 *(10)*	28 *(98)*	55 *(195)*	14 *(50)*
Other *(3)*	0 *(0)*	33 *(1)*	33 *(1)*	33 *(1)*

Table 61   Age, by Adult New Reader Activity Rating *(expressed in percent*

| Age | Adult New Reader Activity Rating | | | |
	Least Active (13)	Somewhat Active (144)	Active (257)	Very Active (65)
16 - 24	31 (4)	19 (28)	25 (65)	21 (14)
25 - 34	15 (2)	30 (43)	30 (78)	38 (25)
35 - 44	15 (2)	19 (28)	22 (56)	23 (15)
45 - 54	15 (2)	13 (19)	15 (37)	12 (8)
55 - 64	0 (0)	12 (17)	5 (13)	2 (1)
65+	24 (3)	6 (8)	3 (8)	2 (1)
No answer	0 (0)	1 (1)	0 (0)	2 (1)

Table 62   Mean Reading Activity Score of Males and Females of Both Races, by Age and Education

| Age | Education | Mean Reading Activity Score | | | |
| | | White | | Black | |
		Male	Female	Male	Female
Under -35	-10	3.6 (21)	3.7 (14)	4.8 (12)	5.3 (34)
	10+	4.6 (18)	5.7 (21)	5.1 (35)	6.1 (102)
Over 35+	-10	5.0 (15)	4.0 (12)	4.1 (28)	4.8 (86)
	10+	6.9 (8)	6.2 (12)	6.8 (9)	5.0 (42)

Table 63 Amount of Formal Education, by Adult New Reader Activity Rating *(expressed in percent)*

Amount of Formal Education (in years)	Adult New Reader Activity Rating			
	Least Active	Somewhat Active	Active	Very Active
0	0 *(0)*	1 *(2)*	0 *(0)*	0 *(0)*
2	8 *(1)*	2 *(3)*	׃ *(1)*	0 *(0)*
3	8 *(1)*	4 *(5)*	2 *(5)*	1 *(1)*
4	8 *(1)*	6 *(8)*	1 *(3)*	0 *(0)*
5	15 *(2)*	6 *(9)*	3 *(7)*	0 *(0)*
6	15 *(2)*	10 *(15)*	4 *(11)*	1 *(1)*
7	0 *(0)*	8 *(12)*	7 *(18)*	5 *(3)*
8	15 *(2)*	10 *(15)*	11 *(29)*	20 *(13)*
9	15 *(2)*	13 *(19)*	12 *(30)*	5 *(3)*
10	8 *(1)*	12 *(17)*	16 *(40)*	17 *(11)*
11	0 *(0)*	15 *(21)*	20 *(50)*	17 *(11)*
12	0 *(0)*	11 *(16)*	19 *(49)*	26 *(17)*
13 or more	0 *(0)*	1 *(1)*	4 *(11)*	8 *(5)*
No answer	8 *(1)*	1 *(1)*	1 *(3)*	0 *(0)*
Total	100 *(13)*	100 *(144)*	100 *(257)*	100 *(65)*

׃ The percentage is equal to less than 1%

The data in table 62 which show the mean reading activity scores of males and females of both races, by age and education are summarized in the following sign tests. Comparisons are made among the adult new readers in relation to race, sex, age, and education. When the results of all eight comparisons between Blacks and whites, with age, that is, young and old, remaining constant the younger Blacks score higher than whites for both females and males. Among the older persons, the whites score higher than Blacks.

In general, the younger Blacks score higher than younger whites with similar educational backgrounds. Among the older persons, the whites score higher than Blacks.

Blacks Score Higher than Whites

	+	=	—
Younger 4			0
Older 1			3
Total 5			3

Again, the sign test for the younger groups is distinguished from those of the older group. Among those under 35 years of age, women score higher than men, but the opposite is true for the older persons - again regardless of race or education.

Women Score Higher Than Men

	+	=	—
Younger 3	1		0
Older 1			3

Again, the sign test shows that the older persons score higher than the younger irrespective of race, sex, or education.

Older Persons Score Higher Than Younger

+	=	-
7		1

Finally, the comparison between persons with more formal education and those with fewer years of schooling shows that those persons with more education have higher activity reading scores than those with less.

Persons with More Education Score Higher Than Those with Less

+	=	-
8		0

In summary, when comparisons are made on reading activity scores in relation to race, sex, age, and education, the sign tests show: Blacks score higher than whites, women score higher than men, older persons score higher than younger, and persons with more education score higher than those with less.

Education is a correlate to reading activity which has been identified by earlier studies. These studies have shown "a close relationship between the amount of reading done in a community and its educational status, the accessibility of libraries and books, the extent of literacy, the ability of adults to read easily, the intelligence level of its citizens, and its productivity." Most reading studies confirm this conclusion and in addition determine that more education results in seeking high education levels. The circular nature in the dependent relationship between current educational system and reading may distort this finding. The cycle can be broken at any stage. The cycle can be entered at any stage.

The reading activity of adult new readers in the LMRP investigation similarly shows a relationship between the use of print materials and education. This relationship between years of schooling and reading activity ratings is shown dramatically in tables 63 and 64 . The median years completed in school is 10.2 years which may be compared with the national median of 12.2 years, with 52 percent completing between 7 and 11 years. Within the context of functional literacy as defined in this study, table 7a shows that 6 percent of the adults with less than five years of schooling are at a low level literacy at the point where continuing use of the newly acquired skill is essential to prevent loss of literacy (appendix 1 Stairway of (Reading) Literacy).

Adults who have achieved partial literacy constituted 10 percent of the respondents, with five to six years of schooling. It has been assumed in this study that at this stage of partial literacy skill the adult new reader is able to read and to use information essential to daily living and work. A critical factor in his further development is his access to appropriate materials. At this time, the right material and guidance of the librarian and teacher is crucial to his continuing improvement. The reading activity rating shows that among the rather low level literacy group, 0 to 4 years of schooling, two-thirds are less active readers (table 64). In comparison, among the respondents who have achieved partial literacy, 5 to 6 years of schooling, an active group of readers appears. The reading activity rating shows nearly 40 percent are active readers. It confirms that such readers are not only capable of making use of print materials, but do make use of them.

Adults who achieved the next stage, between 7 and 9 years of

schooling and defined in this study as variable literacy, constitute one-third of the respondents. Among these respondents, 47
percent are active readers, 13 percent are very active. This
total of nearly two-thirds of active readers contrasts sharply
with the two-thirds of less active readers among the readers with
less schooling. Adults who had completed between 10 and 11 years
of schooling, which in the context of this study is considered
close to functional literacy, constitute nearly one-fourth of the
respondents. In this group, two-thirds are active readers. At
this stage, guidance and access to effective materials that meet
individual interests and needs as well as develop further reading
skills have particular significance.

Of the adults who have completed between 12 and 13 or more
years of schooling, 80 percent are active or very active readers.
It is at this stage of literacy that the adult is able to read
with ease and critical understanding. He has established an autonomy which permits independent use of reading materials. As a
mature reader he can make productive use of a wide range and variety of materials.

It becomes possible through the use of the Reading Activity
Index to describe a pattern of current and past reading behaviors.
for each reading activity group. The individual profile of each
reader permits a more personal, human description of the individual
pattern of reading behavior. Material in the interview records
has been reorganized for a biographical record to gain coherence
and continuity. The data have been selected to describe the
readers' reading habits and media use, as well as social characteristics. It is in no way a complete picture of the life of a
reader. There is no intention of confusing statistical summaries
with culture patterns. In all cases respondents are anonymous.
Names are pseudonyms assigned to give more interest and individuality to each record. The profiles included here are representative

of various ages and social and ethnic backgrounds, and provide
examples of four types of reading activity measured by the Reading
Activity Index, that is, least active, somewhat active, active,
and very active.

The "Least Active" Readers

A person with a reading activity score of zero is a least
active reader. His score indicates that he does not read newspapers, magazines, or comic books and has not read a book within
the last six months. His inactivity does not mean that this person does not or cannot read. Among the least active readers, the
book is the type of print material most often read. Biography and
autobiography are the types of books that the least active reader
likes to read. Among the 13 least active readers, eight own books.
The least active reader's purpose of reading is primarily for
school and school work, and secondarily for relaxation and pleasure. The least active reader watches television and listens to
the radio comparatively less than the more active reader does.

Least active readers are aware of their reading problems and
of their reading activity. In reply to the question on how much
reading the respondent now does, 10 out of the 13 who score zero
on the reading activity index answered "hardly any." Answers to
questions relating to reader development reveal that as a child
the least active reader was read to only occasionally; he did not
have friends who were active readers; and he did not read books
other than school books. This reading inactivity remains through
his teenage years. Although the least active reader now has
friends who are active readers, he reads comparatively less than
his parents, his present friends, and the people with whom he
lives. Mrs. Anna Stewart, and Amos Johnson are
representative of the least active reader group.

Least active: reading score - 0. Mrs. Anna Stewart is a housewife who has lived in this city for 26 years. She is 54 years of age and her family income is less than $1500. She identifies Africa as her ancestral origin. She attended grammar school through the sixth grade in a small Mississippi town and left school then to support herself. She is now studying English, reading, writing, and spelling in a public library reading development program. Her classes have helped to improve her understanding and relations with other people, and also her communication with them.

Mrs. Stewart has read no books in the last six months, nor does she read magazines, newspapers or comic books. She has no books of her own. When she does read, she enjoys plays the most. She also reads for information, help in her school work, and to improve her English, reading ability, and vocabulary.

She has been to the library in the last six months to borrow books and attend lectures. In her free time she takes drives or walks, goes to the neighborhood center, and attends church. Mrs. Stewart watches television: news and weather, *Bonanza* or *Gunsmoke*, *Mod Squad, Mayberry RFD,* cartoons, the *Bill Cosby Show,* and *Ironside,* the last being her favorite. Her radio listening includes music - country, rock-and-roll, soul, mood, religious, and classical - news, sports, religious programs and talk shows.

She perceives herself as a poor reader who hardly reads. She feels that she has no reading problems. In her childhood and teenage years she liked to read, but her attitude in adulthood changed. Presently she likes to read a little.

Least active: reading score - 0. Amos Johnson, whose ancestral origin is Africa, and who is 74 years of age, completed the fifth grade when he left school in order to support himself. He is now a retired factory worker. Mr. Johnson attends adult basic education classes where he is studying English, reading, and spelling. These classes have helped him to understand others better, to have more self-confidence, and to communicate better with other people.

In his free time he visits his friends and relatives, fishes, takes drives or walks, goes to the park or zoo, the movies, to the neighborhood center and to church. He has been to the library in the past six months to ask for information. His favorite television programs are the sports shows and he also enjoys the news and weather, movies, *As the World Turns,* and *Dark Shadows.* On the radio he listens to music - soul, jazz, mood, religious, classical, and folk - and to sports and religious programs.

He is rated an inactive reader and perceives himself as a poor reader who hardly reads. Reading has never played an important part in his life. He is reading now to help educate himself. Of the books on the interview list, he has read the Bible, and would find *Health in the Later Years* and *Get Your Money's Worth* helpful.

The "Somewhat Active" Readers

A respondent who reads the newspapers once a week or less often than that, one or two comic books, or one to three books in the last six months will be rated as a somewhat active reader. The scores of the respondents who are rated in this category can be a combination of reading activities which will give a score of from one to four on the Reading Activity Index. The somewhat active reader reads the church bulletin or newsletter. When metropolitan daily newspapers are read, two features, news about world affairs and the advertisements, are most often read. Newspapers are read more than any other medium. When magazines are read, stories about the lives of real people, adventure, and love and romance are preferred. About one-third of the somewhat active readers had read a book within the last six months. The major sources for hearing about books are from the school and friends. The school is the main place from which books are obtained. Bookstores and friends are secondary sources. Among the somewhat active readers, 8 in 10 use public library services. About 7 in 10 own books. Short stories, biographies and autobiographies are favorite types of books.

The somewhat active reader reads to educate himself and for school work. In addition, unlike the least active reader, he also reads for enjoyment. The somewhat active reader is not only aware of his reading limitations, but also recognizes when he has begun to overcome reading problems. A similar awareness of limitations in the current amount of reading activity is evident in that 8 in 10 of the somewhat active readers measure their reading activity as some or hardly any.

In general, the childhood and teenage reading activity of the somewhat active readers shows that many did not read books outside of school, nor have friends who were active readers. As children they were read to only occasionally. The somewhat active reader reports that his reading activity is comparably less than his friends and the people with whom he lives. However, 4 in 10 perceive that they read more than their parents. Sophia Chirinos, Ivan Filsić, John Brill, and George Bonham represent the somewhat active group of readers.

Table 64   Adult New Reader Activity Rating, by Education *(expressed in percent)*

Grade	Least Active	Somewhat Active	Active	Very Active
0 - 4	9 *(3)*	58 *(18)*	29 *(9)*	3 *(1)*
5 - 6	9 *(4)*	51 *(24)*	38 *(18)*	2 *(1)*
7 - 9	3 *(4)*	32 *(46)*	52 *(77)*	13 *(19)*
10 - 11	1 *(1)*	24 *(38)*	58 *(90)*	14 *(22)*
12	0 *(0)*	19 *(16)*	59 *(49)*	21 *(15)*
13 or more	0 *(0)*	6 *(1)*	65 *(11)*	29 *(5)*

Somewhat active: reading score - 4. Sophia Chirinos is a Greek immigrant, 20 years of age. She has been in this country for two years. When she left Greece at 18, she had completed two years of high school. She is attending adult basic education classes and a library reading program to learn English. Miss Chirinos is currently employed as a seamstress in a dry cleaning company.

Although she has read no books in the last six months, Miss Chirinos would like to read *Call Them Heroes*, *People and Places*, *Selected Poems* by Langston Hughes, *Profiles in Courage*, and *Diane's New Love*. Miss Chirinos reads two Greek newspapers in addition to two metropolitan dailies. She reads Greek magazines also, as well as English ones, of which *Life* is her favorite. Miss Chirinos reads books primarily to help with her school work. She also finds that reading is relaxing and enjoyable.

In her spare time Miss Chirinos listens to records, goes fishing, knits, goes to church club meetings, dances, movies, and to a neighborhood center. She watches television and her favorite program is the *Dean Martin Show*. She listens to the radio. She uses the public library in her free time to borrow books and to study there.

She has always liked to read a lot. She is rated as a somewhat active reader. She says she has no reading problems and rates herself as a fair reader who reads a moderate amount. When she was a child, her parents read to her very often, and she had friends who read a lot. When she was a child and a teenager, she did not read anything besides her school texts. She has had no period of little reading, but at present is reading more than previously.

Somewhat active: reading score - 1. Ivan Filsic is learning
to read and write English. He has lived in this city for two
years. At 37 years of age he is attending English classes at a
neighborhood center. His reading consists only of a Yugoslavian
newspaper which he gets from Canada.

Mr. Filsic watches television: news and weather, *Bonanza,*
the *Dean Martin Show,* the movies, *Mod Squad,* and *Ironside.* Dean
Martin is his favorite. He listens to the radio: talk programs,
news, sports events, and music - jazz and folk. He likes to visit,
take drives, read, go to dances, and to his neighborhood center.
He belongs to a carpenters' labor union and reads its bulletin.
He attends church and receives its newsletter which he also reads.

Mr. Filsic has always liked to read, but his problem is to
learn English well enough to read. He says he reads for pleasure
and for information, and reads most types of literature. He
says, "I am learning to read English very well."

Somewhat active: reading score - 2. John Brill, of African
origin, 43 years of age, is a maintenance worker in a hospital.
He completed the fourth grade in a rural grammar school, leaving
school to help support his family. He is attending adult basic
education and reading development classes in order to learn to
read better.

During the last six months Mr. Brill has read two books. One
was a biography of George Washington Carver; he could not remember
the other title. He does not read magazines or comic books, but
does read a newspaper about once a week, usually the news about
politics and government. His major source for books is his classes.
Books have helped him in his school work. He owns books on Black
history. Mr. Brill is not interested in any of the books listed in
the questionnaire.

In the last six months, he has been to the library to study, ask for information, and to borrow books. He includes reading as one of his pastimes. Other are: visiting friends and relatives, listening to records, taking drives, going to the YMCA, and playing pool or bowling. *Ironside* or *Dragnet* is his favorite television program. He listens to the radio as well: music - rock-and-roll, jazz, soul, mood, religious, classical - to sports, religious programs, and talk shows.

Mr. Brill rates himself as a fair reader who hardly reads. He does not like to read at all and feels that he has not yet overcome his reading problems. "Hope I can master the art of reading. As of now I'm very slow."

Somewhat active: reading score - 2. George Bonham is 52 years of age and currently is employed as a machine operator in a steel mill, and identifies Africa as his ancestral origin. He has lived in this city all his adult years. At 16 he left school, having completed the fourth grade, to support himself. He is enrolled now in an adult basic education program, a public library program, and a high school equivalency program. He is studying basic language and mathematics, and American history. Because of his classes he has gone on to read other things and he feels that the classes have changed his life. He comments, "Read better, spelling is better, my math is better, little more educated."

By the Reading Activity Index Mr. Bonham is a somewhat active reader. He reads the newspapers once a week and also gets his union bulletin. News, sports, and advertisements are the features he usually reads. He reads no magazines, but in the last six months he has read three books, one on Black history, another on American history, and the third, he says, was "something written by John F. Kennedy." Books have helped him in "math and reading, English, spelling, how to get a better job, and how to get along with people."

Mr. Bonham owns several books on the following topics: Black history, home decoration or furnishing, reference, and religion. He sees or hears about books in school and from his friends and family. The major sources for his books are the library and his school.

He has read *Baby and Child Care* which he did not find helpful, the *Holy Bible, Autobiography of Malcolm X,* and *Profiles in Courage.* He shows an interest in reading *Letters from Vietnam, People and Places, Black Like Me,* and the Perry Mason mysteries.

In his free time Mr. Bonham likes to visit, fish, read, and play pool. He is also interested in sports. He belongs to a labor union in which he is an officer. He is a regular television viewer, and his favorite shows are on National Educational Television. He also enjoys listening to the radio: news, sports, religious and talk shows, and music - rock-and-roll, soul, jazz, and religious.

The public library is where he studies and attends classes. He has not used the other services there during the last six months.

Mr. Bonham's reading development shows that he feels he finally has overcome his reading problems. Only when he was a teenager did he not like to read. In the other periods of his life, including the present, he has always enjoyed reading. He thinks that he is a fair reader who reads a great deal. He reads for pleasure and for information. He particularly likes short stories, historical books, and scientific writings.

The "Active" and "Very Active" Readers

The active reader is a respondent who has a score of between five and seven on the Reading Activity Index. This rating is based upon an accumulation of scores he was given for his use of each type of print material. Any combination of reading activities that totals from five to seven will place a respondent in the active group. Similarly, a very active reader is one whose combined score falls between eight and ten. A respondent with a score of ten reads newspapers every day, regularly reads five to ten or more magazines, reads comic books, and within the last six months has read ten or more books. The more active readers, active and very active, watch television and listen to the radio more than the less active respondents. This increased activity is reflected in higher percentages of those who use various types of newspapers, ranging from the local neighborhood newspapers to racing forms. In general, these active and very active readers make greater use of all types of print material as well as the other communication media. They have reached a level of literacy in which they can enjoy as well as learn from reading. The more active readers have fewer reading problems than the less active ones. They recognized reading problems, and also perceived that they were able to overcome them.

In response to the question regarding the amount of reading done, the active reader indicated that he read some or a great deal. Significantly, three out of four very active readers replied a great deal. The developmental reading patterns of the more active groups are similar, except that more very active readers had friends who were also active readers.

In general, the more active a reader is, the more varied is his use of print material and other resources. This pattern of reading behavior can be traced clearly in the many tables which show the relationships between the basic social characteristics use of print material and reading development, and the Reading Activity Index (tables 59 to 64). Jill Bock, Mrs. Bertha Bissel, and Mr. Ted Reis are representative of the active reader group; and Frank Lester, Mark Appel, and Madeline Simon represent the very active reader group.

Active: reading score - 7. Jill Bock is 18 years of age and
a high school graduate. She works as a secretary in a furniture
store. She is attending night school taking courses toward certi-
fication in practical nursing. In these classes she has studied
basic language skills and nursing skills such as child care and
first aid.

In her leisure time Jill likes to visit, listen to records,
play cards, take walks or drives, read, bowl, and watch television.
She goes to movies and listens to the radio, as well. She watches
all types of television programs: variety, talk shows, comedies,
crime and mystery series, and soap operas. *Mod Squad* is her favorite program. Her radio listening includes news, talk shows, and
music - country and western, rock, soul, jazz, mood, and classical.

As an active reader, Jill reads newspapers, magazines, books
and comic books. She reads her metropolitan newspaper every day
in addition to her neighborhood paper. She reads most of the columns and features, and would miss the horoscope most if she could
not get the newspapers for a few weeks. *McCalls*, *Life* or *Look*,
fashion magazines, *True Confession*, and *Bride* are the magazines
she reads. Her favorite magazine is *True Confession*. She enjoys
romance and human interest stories in these magazines. In the past
six months Jill has read two books: *The Reader's Digest Short
Stories* and *Basic Nursing*. She got the Reader's Digest book when
she was in the hospital from a fellow patient.

Jill has read *Write Your Own Letters,* which she found very helpful. She also has read *Love and Sex in Plain Language, Profiles in
Courage,* and Perry Mason mysteries. She is interested in reading
Letters from Vietnam, Diane's New Love, Shane, the Bible, and *Life
with the Lucketts.*

Jill reads primarily for pleasure. She enjoys short stories
and novels the most. She owns self-improvement and reference books.
She feels that these books have helped her in school work and job
placement.

Jill is not interested in reading, although she liked to in her teenage years. She always has had friends who read a lot, but she feels that she reads less than any of them. She has no reading problems to overcome. Her parents read to her fairly frequently when she was a child. She rates herself as a good reader who reads some.

Active: reading score - 5. Mrs. Bertha Bissel's life has changed since she started adult basic education and reading development classes. She says, "I learned to read and write. When I started school I couldn't write; now I'm proud I can write." Mrs. Bissel, of African origin, is 64 and is a maid in a nursing school. She would like to be a nurse's aide. Before quitting school to be married at 16, she had completed the third grade.

Mrs. Bissel is an active club member. She holds an office in one of her organizations which include a religious group and a fraternal organization. She likes spectator sports. She visits and reads in her spare time, as well as watching television and listening to radio. She watches the news and weather, *Let's Make a Deal,* Johnny Carson, Dean Martin, the movies, *Mod Squad,* cartoons, *Laugh-In, As the World Turns, Ironside,* Bill Cosby (her favorite), sports events, *Mission Impossible,* and National Educational Television. On the radio, Mrs. Bissel listens to sports events and religious programs.

Mrs. Bissel has read two books in the last six months, a history of the United States and a basic education book on mathematics. She reads *Look, Ebony,* and *The Saturday Evening Post,* which is her favorite magazine. In these magazines she enjoys stories of war, crime, mystery and science fiction. She reads the newspapers every day. In addition she reads the neighborhood paper, church bulletin, union newsletter, and the *Weekly Reader.* She reads most of the features in the metropolitan paper: news of the world and civil rights, weather, sports, editorials, letters to the editor, adver-

tisements, obituaries, movie news and television news, her favorite
section.

Mrs. Bissel's major source of books is her school. During the
last six months she has been to the library to borrow a book, see
an exhibit, and to take a tour. Mrs. Bissel reads primarily for
information. She owns books on health and nutrition, reference,
religion, and cooking. She enjoys biographies the most.

Mrs. Bissell has read the Bible, and is in a Bible-reading
group. She shows interest in reading *Get Your Money's Worth*, *Write
Your Own Letters*, *Call Them Heroes*, *Letters from Vietnam*, *People
and Places*, *Profiles in Courage*, and *Up from Appalachia*.

In her later adult years, Mrs. Bissel has had a great interest
in reading. In her childhood and teenage years she had little
interest in it. She did not read material aside from school but
had friends who were active readers. Her parents read to her when
she was a child. She reads more than her parents did, and more
than the people with whom she lives. She has no reading problems
and rates herself as a fair reader who reads a good deal.

Active: reading score - 6. At age 15, after completing the
fifth grade, Mr. Ted Reis left school to support himself. Now 47,
he is enrolled in an adult basic education and a public library
program. Language skills, mathematics, and American history are
the subjects he is studying. Mr. Reis, of African origin, is a
custodian's assistant in a public school. He feels that his classes have helped him "get along better with people and my family."

Mr. Reis is an active member of his labor union, civil rights
and religious group. In his free time he enjoys walks and drives,
visiting with friends and relatives, playing games, reading, playing pool, and bowling. He watches television reagularly, with
Bonanza as his favorite program. He listens to all kinds of radio
programs and likes all types of music.

In the past year Mr. Reis has read three books. He remembers two, a biography of John F. Kennedy and one of George Washington Carver. Books have helped him in all phases of his life: relations with others, school work, self-improvement, home improvement, and job placement. Books that he owns include the subjects of child care, romance, Black history, sports, war, self-betterment, reference, and religion. His major sources of books are friends, the bookstore, newsstand, and the library. He shows an interest in all of the titles on the questionnaire list. He has read the Reader's Digest books and the Bible.

Mr. Reis reads other things also: the newspapers a few times a week, his neighborhood, church, and union newspapers. In the newspaper he reads news, stock quotations, and sports sections regularly. He reads all types of magazines and likes best *Better Homes and Gardens*.

Only in his later years has Mr. Reis begun to like reading. He now rates himself as a fair reader who reads a great deal. He reads much, and often reads aloud to his wife. He feels that he reads the same amount as his parents. When he was a child they read aloud to him frequently.

Mr. Reis has used the library extensively in the last six months. He has met friends there, borrowed books, asked for information, read a book, seen a movie, heard a lecture and records, taken a tour, and studied there.

His feelings toward reading are indicated by his statement, "I can read more books now. Before, I was not interested because the words were too difficult for me to read...It's easier than I thought."

Very active: reading score - 8. Frank Lester is a 28-year-old man whose origin is African. He is studying spelling, arithmetic, and Black history in an adult basic education program. He is employed part-time as a factory worker. He would like to be in body and fender work. Mr. Lester completed the tenth grade before he was expelled from school.

He spends his free time visiting, playing cards and other games, taking drives or walks, reading, playing pool or bowling. He enjoys going to movies and to the YMCA. He also goes to the neighborhood center and attends church. He watches television regularly: National Educational Television, news, talk shows, movies, *Black Journal,* variety shows, sports events, crime and mystery series, situation comedies, game shows, and soap operas. He likes the sports events the most. He listens to the radio frequently: news, sports events, religious programs, and talk shows. He belongs to a union.

Mr. Lester reads newspapers, magazines, and books. He read newspapers every day and the *Christian Science Monitor* as well as his club and union newsletters. He would miss the sports section of the newspaper most, and also reads his horoscope, news, advice to the lovelorn, and television news. He reads a variety of magazines: *Life, Reader's Digest, Ebony, Time, Ladies' Home Journal, Mademoiselle, True, Sports Illustrated, Photoplay, True Stories, Black Digest,* and *Mechanics Illustrated.* He enjoys *True* the most. He likes the crime and mystery stories, human interest, travel, and sports stories in these magazines. In the past six months he has read: *Blues for Mr. Charley, Message to the Black Man, How to Eat to Live,* and *The Devil's Advocate.* Mr. Lester is interested in reading *Autobiography of Malcolm X, Selected Poems* by Langston Hughes, *Black Like Me, People and Places,* the James Bond stories and Perry Mason mysteries.

Mr. Lester reads for pleasure and information. He owns books on Black history, religion, and reference. He enjoys reading novels, biographies, and historical books. His chief scource of books is the public library where he has borrowed books, asked for information, read a magazine, book, heard a lecture, taken a tour, and studied during the last six months.

As a child and teenager, Mr. Lester had no interest in reading. He read the least in his early teenage years. Now he enjoys reading and rates himself as a fair reader who reads a lot. As his parents did for him, he reads to his sister's children.

Mr. Lester heard about many of the books he has read when he was in jail. He is very concerned about ex-convicts and their life outside of prison. He says of his reading, "I read more. I want to become more affluent with my reading, to go to the library every day. I think I could be a much better reader."

Very active: reading score - 8. Mark Appel is 44 years of age. He had to leave school after completing the third grade in order to support himself. In the last year he has been attending adult basic education classes, studying basic language skills. He is a construction boilermaker who has lived in this city for 22 years.

Until about two years ago, Mr. Appel did not know how to read. He says he "...can read all the road signs now." During the last six months he has read six books. He remembers one about the moon walk and another aobut the assassination of John F. Kennedy. He sees or hears about books from friends that he now has who are active readers, from the library, and the newsstands. He has borrowed books from the library in the last six months, but he does not own any. Most of the books on the questionnaire list interested him and he has read the Reader's Digest books.

Mr. Appel reads the newspapers every day. He also reads his
neighborhood paper, and church, union, and club bulletins. The
news and sports sections he reads regularly. He reads *Life, Reader's Digest* and women's magazines to which his wife subscribes.
He enjoys stories of war, human interest, space, sports and adventure.

His reading interests are reflected in his television viewing.
He enjoys adventure, crime and mystery shows, sports, and situation
comedies. He listens to the radio: music, news, sports, and religious programs. He spends his spare time with friends and relatives, reading, playing cards, bowling, fishing, going to dances,
to movies, and to his fraternal club meetings.

Mr. Appel reads for pleasure and information, and to improve
himself. He rates himself as a fair reader now. His attitude
toward reading can be summed up by his statement, "In talking to
people, it's easier. It's helped me on jobs. It's changed me
completely around. Before, I couldn't read books, now I can."

Very Active: reading score - 10. Mrs. Madeline Simon, 25 years
of age, is a high school graduate rated as a very active reader.
She reads the newspapers every day and is mainly interested in the
news, comic strips, advertisements, advice to the lovelorn, television and movie news, and the horoscope. She would miss the horoscope most if she did not get the newspaper every day. Her magazine
reading includes those about movies, love and romance, and religious
subjects and also *Life* and *Ebony*. She enjoys stories about crime
and mystery, love, human interest, travel and adventure. She would
miss *Ebony* the most. Mrs. Simon says she has read 50 books in the
last six months, among which are *Four of a Kind* and *The Pearl*. She
also reads comic books.

Books have helped Mrs. Simon in getting a better job, raising
her children, and in homemaking. She owns books which help her in

these areas as well as ones on adventure and Black history. She
enjoys short stories, novels, and biographies, and reads primarily
for pleasure. Her sources for books are friends and the drugstore.

Mrs. Simon indicates interest in reading *Baby and Child Care,*
Getting and Holding a Job, Love and Sex in Plain Language, Letters
from Vietnam, People and Places, The Autobiography of Malcolm X,
Black Like Me, Diane's New Love, and the Perry Mason mysteries.

She spends her free time in various activities, visiting friends
and relatives, going to movies, taking drives, going to a tavern,
and reading. Mrs. Simon also watches television, her favorite program being *Mod Squad,* and listens to the radio. She listens to
music, religious, soul, and rock and roll.

Mrs. Simon read the least as a child. As a teenager, she began
to enjoy reading, and now she is reading more than at any other
period in her life. She is in an OIC program as well as an adult
basic education program. She is studying history, English, and
office skills. She rates herself as a fair reader who reads a
great deal.

Notes

1. U.S. Bureau of the Census, *Population Characteristics,* "Educational
Attainment . . . 1969."

2. Raymond M. Hilliard, *The Blackboard Curtain,* pp. 90-93.

8

NATURE AND USE OF THE COMMUNICATION MEDIA

Extensive and significant are the data about the nature and current use of the communication media as reported by the 479 respondents interviewed in Baltimore, Cleveland, Los Angeles, New York, and Philadelphia. Although the use of television and radio is included, the character and use of the mass media represented in print materials - newspapers, magazines, and books - are the chief areas of concern. What does the adult new reader view on television? What does he listen to on radio? What does he read? Where does he get what he reads? Why does he read? What are his opinions about books and reading? The findings on various aspects of these questions are shown in the tables relating to communication media.

Television. The general use of the three major communication media - television, radio and newspapers - is evident in the percentage of persons using these media. Chart 16 shows the current use. Nearly everyone, 99 percent of the LMRP respondents, usually or regularly watch television programs. This pervasive use among adult new readers is to be expected in view of a recent Harris poll which showed the almost total reach that television has achieved in American society. Ninety-six out of 100 Americans have one working television set. Among families with incomes of less than $5,000 a year, the income level for 50 percent of LMRP respondents, one in four has a color set.[1]

The fairly high percentage of viewers for the 18 television programs selected for analysis in this survey of readers indicates that respondents do a fair amount of television viewing. The general use also is high among those who listen to radio, 95 percent, and who read newspapers, 93 percent. In contrast, three other print media have a somewhat lesser number of users -

88 percent read magazines, 69 percent read books, and considerably less, 34 percent, read comic books.

Among the selected network shows in which the respondents are interested particularly, nearly half are watched usually or regularly by 50 to 90 percent, the other half are watched by 30 to 40 percent of the respondents. News and weather and movies are the most popular programs, with about eight in ten watching usually or regularly. The dramatic shows of adventure are watched by over two-thirds of the respondents - *Mod Squad, Mission Impossible, Bonanza* or *Gunsmoke, Ironside* or *Dragnet*. These dramatic shows generally are more popular than comedy, variety, or the talk show type of programming, and the former programs retain a devoted audience. The majority of viewers watch sports and the Bill Cosby show. The comedy and talk shows, *Laugh-In* or *Hee Haw*, the Dean Martin or Johnny Cash shows, *Let's Make a Deal*, cartoons, and Johnny Carson or Joey Bishop, have a considerable following.

The lower percentage of viewers for National Educational Television (NET) and *Black Journal* may reflect partially the unavailability of these channels including the need for Ultra High Frequency (UHF) sets. In many instances the distinction between a particular program on NET and the network itself is obscured. The daytime and early evening programs, *As the World Turns, Mayberry RFD,* and *Dark Shadows*, perhaps reach fewer respondents because of the time in which they are scheduled (table 65).

Mod Squad is the program liked best by the many viewers who watch it. Other programs which are liked best or would be missed most by viewers are *Mission Impossible*, news and weather, and *As the World Turns*. The majority of the programs do not elicit any strong preferences by respondents of what is liked best. This lack of preference might be interpreted to mean that the kind of program watched is of little concern. In general, the LMRP viewers' preferences seem to parallel the Harris poll's national findings.

Network news, sports, and movies rank relatively high. Crime, westerns, and situation comedies break even with audiences. Soap operas, quiz shows, and talk shows maintain small percentages of the audience who have strong preference for them (table 66).[2]

Who are the viewers who usually watch the four favorite programs - news and weather, *Mod Squad, As the World Turns,* and *Mission Impossible*? Tables 67 to 71 show interesting comparisons. News and weather has a broad range of viewers, both between Black and white respondents and between men and women, among all age groups and various educational levels. *Mod Squad* and *Mission Impossible* are viewed by men and women, but by a higher percentage of Black, younger persons and by those with more formal education, between 10 and 12 years of schooling. *As the World Turns* is watched by more Black respondents than white, by more women than men, by those over 35 years of age, and to some extent by those with less formal education. This afternoon program, often described as soap opera and thought to be viewed by women only, is watched by 15 percent of the men, and by individuals of all ages. In general, the more active readers, according to the Reading Activity Index, are more interested in all four programs.

Television may have a special use for adult new readers, particularly for the less literate. Such a use is reflected in one respondent's comment, "English is too hard to speak and read. My children speak too fast. I learn most from television."

Radio. Radio listening is an activity common to nearly everyone. Most respondents listen to the radio for news and weather and for music, while a lesser but substantial majority listen to religious programs, talk and interview programs, and sports. All types of music programs are popular. Religious music, soul music, jazz, and rock and roll have first preference. Semi-classical or mood music interest over half of the respondents. Classical, folk, and country music each have about two-fifths of the respondents who enjoy listening to these types of music (tables 72 to 75).

Chart 16 Use of Communication Media and Printed Material

Percent of
Adult New
Readers
Who:

	0	10	20	30	40	50	60	70	80	90	100

Watch
Television   99%

Listen to
Radio   95%

Read
Newspapers   93%

Read
Magazines   88%

Read
Books   69%

Read Comic
Books   34%

Based on Questions:

1A: *First, I want to read you a list of television programs. Please tell me if you usually or regularly watch any of them.*

8: *Do you ever listen to the radio?*

4: *Do you ever get a chance to read a newspaper?*

10: *Do you ever read magazines?*

16: *During the last six months, have you read any paperback or hardcover books?*

15: *Do you ever read comic books?*

Table 65 Television Programs Usually Watched *(expressed in percent)*

Question 1A: *First, I want to read you a list of television programs. Please tell me if you usually or regularly watch any of t*

Television Program	Yes	No
News and Weather	89 *(427)*	10 *(47)*
Movies	83 *(397)*	16 *(77)*
Mod Squad or Then Came Bronson	73 *(349)*	26 *(123)*
Mission Impossible	69 *(332)*	30 *(142)*
Bonanza or Gunsmoke	65 *(310)*	34 *(163)*
Ironside or Dragnet	64 *(306)*	35 *(166)*
Sports	56 *(267)*	44 *(209)*
Bill Cosby Show	52 *(250)*	47 *(223)*
Laugh-In or Hee Haw	47 *(223)*	52 *(250)*
Dean Martin or Johnny Cash Show	44 *(211)*	55 *(262)*
Let's Make a Deal	43 *(207)*	56 *(267)*
Cartoons	42 *(204)*	56 *(267)*
Johnny Carson or Joey Bishop	43 *(203)*	56 *(269)*
National Educational Television	39 *(184)*	60 *(288)*
As the World Turns	37 *(177)*	62 *(295)*
Mayberry, R.F.D.	35 *(167)*	64 *(305)*
Dark Shadows	32 *(155)*	66 *(315)*
Black Journal	16 *(76)*	82 *(394)*

Table 66 Television Programs Liked Best *(expressed in percent)*

Question 1B: *Which __one__ of those programs do you like best?*

Television Program		Number Who Watch
Mod Squad or Then Came Bronson	28 *(98)*	*349*
Mission Impossible	17 *(55)*	*332*
News and Weather	16 *(66)*	*427*
As the World Turns	14 *(25)*	*177*
Movies	9 *(35)*	*397*
National Educational Television	9 *(17)*	*184*
Sports	8 *(22)*	*267*
Bill Cosby Show	8 *(19)*	*250*
Ironside or Dragnet	7 *(20)*	*306*
Dark Shadows	7 *(11)*	*155*
Bonanza or Gunsmoke	6 *(17)*	*310*
Laugh In or Hee Haw	6 *(14)*	*223*
Let's Make a Deal	5 *(11)*	*207*
Dean Martin or Johnny Cash Show	5 *(11)*	*211*
Johnny Carson or Joey Bishop	4 *(9)*	*203*
Black Journal	4 *(3)*	*76*
Cartoons	2 *(3)*	*204*
Mayberry RFD	2 *(4)*	*167*

Table 67 Selected Television Programs Usually Watched, by Sex
(expressed in percent)

Selected Television Programs	Sex	
	Male *(148)*	Female *(331)*
News and weather	88 *(130)*	90 *(297)*
Mod Squad	65 *(95)*	77 *(254)*
As the World Turns	15 *(22)*	47 *(155)*
Mission Impossible	70 *(104)*	69 *(228)*

Table 68 Selected Television Programs Usually Watched, by Race
(expressed in percent)

Selected Television Programs	Race	
	White *(123)*	Black *(353)*
News and weather	83 *(102)*	91 *(322)*
Mod Squad	57 *(70)*	79 *(279)*
As the World Turns	20 *(24)*	43 *(152)*
Mission Impossible	62 *(75)*	72 *(256)*

Table 69 Selected Television Programs Usually Watched, by Age *(expressed in percent)*

Selected Television Programs	Age (in years)					
	16-24 *(111)*	25-34 *(148)*	35-44 *(101)*	45-54 *(66)*	55-64 *(31)*	65+ *(20)*
News and weather	82 *(91)*	93 *(131)*	96 *(97)*	96 *(63)*	87 *(27)*	80 *(16)*
Mod Squad	81 *(90)*	78 *(116)*	70 *(71)*	71 *(47)*	58 *(18)*	35 *(7)*
As the World Turns	31 *(35)*	33 *(49)*	44 *(44)*	37 *(24)*	45 *(14)*	55 *(11)*
Mission Impossible	77 *(85)*	71 *(105)*	68 *(69)*	66 *(43)*	71 *(22)*	40 *(8)*

Table 70 Selected Television Programs Usually Watched, by Education *(expressed in percent)*

Selected Television Programs	Amount of Formal Education (last year of school)					
	0 - 4 *(31)*	5 - 6 *(47)*	7 - 9 *(146)*	10 - 11 *(151)*	12 *(82)*	13+ *(17)*
News and weather	94 *(29)*	92 *(43)*	88 *(128)*	87 *(131)*	92 *(76)*	94 *(16)*
Mod Squad	65 *(20)*	49 *(23)*	74 *(109)*	79 *(119)*	77 *(63)*	65 *(11)*
As the World Turns	49 *(15)*	38 *(18)*	41 *(60)*	36 *(55)*	29 *(24)*	19 *(3)*
Mission Impossible	55 *(17)*	62 *(29)*	77 *(103)*	75 *(113)*	71 *(58)*	53 *(9)*

235

Table 71   Selected Television Programs Usually Watched, by Adult
          New Reader Activity Rating *(expressed in percent)*

Selected Television Programs	Adult New Reader Activity Rating			
	Least Active *(13)*	Somewhat Active *(144)*	Active *(257)*	Very Active *(65)*
News and weather	76 *(10)*	84 *(121)*	91 *(234)*	95 *(62)*
Mod Squad	46 *(6)*	67 *(97)*	77 *(198)*	74 *(48)*
As the World Turns	23 *(3)*	41 *(59)*	34 *(88)*	42 *(27)*
Mission Impossible	46 *(6)*	65 *(3)*	73 *(187)*	71 *(46)*

Table 72 Radio Listening *(expressed in percent)*

Question 8: *Do you ever listen to the radio?*

Yes	95 *(457)*
No	5 *(22)*
Total	100 *(479)*

Table 73 Radio Programs Usually or Often Listened To *(expressed in percent)*

Question 8A: *When you listen to the radio, do you usually or often listen to . . .*

Radio Program	Yes	No
News and weather	92 *(422)*	8 *(34)*
Music	91 *(415)*	9 *(42)*
Religious programs	68 *(311)*	32 *(146)*
Talk and interview programs	63 *(286)*	37 *(170)*
Sports	53 *(241)*	47 *(214)*

Base = 457

Table 74 Type of Music which Adult New Reader Enjoys *(expressed in percent)*

Question 9: *Now a question about music. Do you enjoy . . .*

Type of Music	Yes	No
Religious music	78 *(374)*	22 *(104)*
Soul music	74 *(353)*	26 *(124)*
Jazz	69 *(330)*	31 *(147)*
Rock and Roll	68 *(326)*	32 *(153)*
Semi-classical or mood music	55 *(263)*	45 *(216)*
Classical music	45 *(215)*	55 *(264)*
Folk music	42 *(202)*	57 *(274)*
Country music	41 *(195)*	59 *(283)*

Base = 479

Table 75 Use of Communication Media by Adult New Reader
(expressed in percent)

Question 8: *Do you ever listen to the radio?*

Basic Social Characteristics	
Sex	
Male	95 *(141)*
Female	95 *(316)*
Race	
White	94 *(115)*
Black	96 *(339)*
Other	100 *(3)*
Age (in years)	
16 - 24	98 *(109)*
25 - 34	95 *(140)*
35 - 44	97 *(98)*
45 - 54	94 *(62)*
55 - 64	90 *(28)*
65 +	90 *(18)*
Education	
0 - 4	97 *(30)*
5 - 6	91 *(43)*
7 - 9	94 *(137)*
10 - 11	97 *(146)*
12	98 *(80)*
13 +	94 *(16)*
No answer	100 *(5)*
Programs or Classes	
Adult Basic Education	94 *(214)*
Employment Oriented	97 *(188)*
Youth Oriented Employment	100 *(29)*
High School Equivalency	96 *(114)*
Reading Development Programs	96 *(48)*
Other	100 *(35)*

Table 75 Use of Communication Media by Adult New Reader (continued)
(expressed in percent)

Question 8: *Do you ever listen to the radio?*

Basic Social Characteristics	
Employment of Time	
Working Force	
White collar	96 *(26)*
Clerical	97 *(33)*
Craft	100 *(39)*
Blue collar	98 *(39)*
Service	97 *(76)*
Unemployed	97 *(30)*
Retired	86 *(12)*
Keeping house	93 *(86)*
School	93 *(112)*
Family Income	
$ 1 - 2,999	94 *(85)*
3,000 - 5,999	95 *(181)*
6,000 - 9,999	97 *(90)*
10,000 or more	98 *(60)*
No answer	93 *(41)*
Individual Income	
$ 0	84 *(16)*
1 - 2,999	96 *(153)*
3,000 - 5,999	97 *(155)*
6,000 - 9,999	96 *(49)*
10,000 or more	100 *(16)*
No answer	93 *(68)*
Adult New Reader Rating	
Very active	98 *(64)*
Active	96 *(247)*
Somewhat active	93 *(134)*
Least active	92 *(12)*

Newspapers. Questions 4, 5, and 6 relate to the newspaper reading

activity of the adults interviewed. Among the respondents inter-

viewed, only 7 percent do not read newspapers. Of the 93 percent

who do read newspapers, two-thirds read one or two newspapers

regularly, 42 percent read two papers, another 20 percent read

three, and 6 percent read as many as four or five (tables 76 and 77).

The newspapers reported read by respondents include the metropoli-

tan dailies as well as numerous neighborhood papers. Actually,

68 different titles are identified by the readers. These papers

represent divergent interests, radically different contents,

journalistic styles, and editorial policies. They include the

authoritative *New York Times, Daily News,* the most widely read

paper in the United States, the powerful *New York Amsterdam News,*

the highly respected *Wall Street Journal,* the *Los Angeles Times,*

and Baltimore's *News American,* the *Afro-American, The Black Pan-*

ther, Muhammad Speaks, Jewish Daily Forward, Danica, popular *El*

Diario-La Prensa and *East Los Angeles Tribune,* and anti-establish-

ment *Soul* and *Village Voice* (table 78). Table 79 shows the

major newspapers published and read by the majority of adult new

readers in each city, for example, *The Sun* in Baltimore, the *Plain*

Dealer in Cleveland, the *Los Angeles Times,* the *Daily News* in New

York, and the *Philadelphia News.* Several ethnic newspapers at-

tract a significant readership: *Afro-American* in Baltimore, *Call*

and Post in Cleveland, the *Los Angeles Sentinel, New York Amster-*

dam News, and *El Diario-La Prensa* in New York, and *The Philadel-*

phia Tribune.

Figure 1 shows special interest newspapers that are read

by newspaper readers. These papers have no regional limitation

geographically, extending from the *Afro-American* on the East Coast

to *The Black Panther* on the West Coast, with *Muhammad Speaks* in

Chicago. Seven newspapers in languages other than English are re-

ported read, for example, *El Tiempo* in New York, *Amerikanski*

Slovenec in Cleveland, *Pravda* in Philadelphia, *Danica* in Chicago. In addition, the two Catholic papers, *Catholic Review* in Baltimore and *Catholic Universe Bulletin* in Cleveland are mentioned. The newspapers reported by respondents include 19 or more big city dailies, and over 45 local papers with diverse contents and published for special audiences. The list of ethnic newspapers and newsletters identified in the LMRP studies illustrates the range of newspaper audiences and suggests various interests (figure 2). Even this brief survey reveals the many publications aimed at the Black and Mexican American population. These audiences have shown their support of such newspapers which speak to their interests. Equally important and growing in number are the newspapers directed to American Indians, Puerto Ricans, and various nationality groups. The unique and original titles frequently reflect their audience, such as *Pan African Roots*, *El Chicano*, *Americans Before Columbus*, *Svoboda*.

Adult new readers read other than the big city dailies and neighborhood newspapers. About two-thirds of the respondents read a church bulletin or newspaper, one-third read club or organization bulletin, one-third read *Weekly Reader*, and one-third a union paper. A few read the racing forms. *News For You*, a weekly newspaper for the adult new reader which is published on two reading levels, A Edition (the easier one) and B Edition, has been read by 7 percent of the respondents (table 80).[3]

Topics usually read in the newspapers are identified in 17 areas which respondents were asked if they read. A substantial majority, between 50 and 87 percent read 13 separate topical areas. Major areas of interest ranking first in readership include news about world affairs, news about civil rights, advertisements, and television news. Table 81 shows the range of topics and readership. When respondents were asked which of the topics they read would be missed most if the chance to read a newspaper was taken

away, the five most missed topics would be, first, news about
world affairs, then sports, advertisements, the women's section,
and horoscope. The least missed topics, not surprisingly, are
book reviews, death notices, and stocks and bonds (table 82).

Tables 83 to 88 show in some detail who usually or regularly reads five selected columns, that is, topical areas. News
about world affairs is read by more men than women, is of equal
interest to both Black and white respondents, has a higher percentage of readers among respondents who are 35 years of age and over.
Education and income appear to have no direct relation to interest.

More men than women read about sports; race makes little
difference in its popularity; all ages are interested, but readers
in the 45 to 54 age group have special interest, as do readers
with higher incomes. The Women's section of newspapers, as is
expected, interests more women than men. It is read by a higher
percentage of Black women than white, interests somewhat older
age groups, and those with more years of schooling, and with lower
incomes. Advertisements, in general, have no interest to 10 percent of the newspaper readers, are of little interest to 46 percent
and have a great deal of interest to 44 percent (table 89). Advertisements, that is, supermarket ads, other store ads, and want
ads, are read by more women than men, by Black readers more than
white. In general, a high percentage of all groups read advertisements, but slightly more persons who are in the age groups of
25 to 34, 55 to 64, and 65 and over read them than do persons in
the 16 to 24, and 35 to 44 age groups. A higher percentage of
persons with 10 to 12 years of schooling and those with lower
individual incomes read advertisements. Horoscope columns interest women more than men, Black respondents more than white. Between 59 and 64 percent of various age groups, and respondents with
more formal education and with lower incomes read the horoscope
predictions.

The metropolitan dailies print primarily national and international news. It is evident that respondents read them for this information. Local news and neighborhood events and personal and social affairs must be read in small neighborhood newspapers because they are not to be found in the large dailies. Exceptions to this exclusion of local events is apparent in the papers which are brought out in special editions, for example, *East Los Angeles Tribune,* published for the Mexican American population. The neighborhood papers have become more and more important as the editor of *New York* magazine perceptively points out, the neighborhood newspapers "do more than record; they reflect the mood of their neighborhoods, the flow of social change, the concerns of the small citizen."[4] The dailies provide the broad coverage of national and international news and information. Local news and the language requirements of individuals and groups are met by the local papers and through publications of the special interest groups. Such publications add dimension, vitality, and cheerfulness. The news reported meets the daily needs and interest of readers.[5] Another important consideration is the readability level of the newspapers. Research shows the metropolitan dailies to be written at a ninth grade reading level.[6] Obviously the interest factor often surmounts reading difficulties. The satisfaction of personal needs and the local information provided is an important contribution made only by the smaller publications.

Some people read newspapers more often than others. Adult new readers are no exception, 51 percent read a newspaper every day and 33 percent read a paper a few times a week. The remaining percentage of newspaper readers were weekly readers, that is, 9 percent of them read a newspaper about once a week and 4 percent read Sunday editions only. A higher percentage of white readers read newspapers daily, and more Black readers read them a few times a week. Daily readers are in the middle age groups, and particularly among the readers with more formal education, that is, 10 to 13 years of schooling, and those respondents with higher incomes. Men and women in craft and blue-collar occupations and retired read newspapers less (tables 90 to 96).

Newspapers are read or glanced at in many places but most frequently at home. Table 97 shows how varied are the places and differences in percentage of respondents' use ranging from 46 percent who read newspapers both at other people's homes and when traveling, to 20 percent who read newspapers in the library. In contrast, 36 percent read newspapers at school, and 33 percent read at work.

Newspapers are read more often than books or magazines. When respondents were asked, "What do you read most often - newspapers, magazines, or books?" the majority, 56 percent, report reading newspapers most often in comparison with 10 percent who read magazines, and 31 percent who read books (table 99).

Table 76 Newspaper Reading *(expressed in percent)*

Question 4: *Do you ever get a chance to read a newspaper?*

Yes	93 *(444)*
No	7 *(35)*
Total	100 *(479)*

Table 77 Number of Newspapers Read by Adult New Reader *(expressed in percent)*

Number of Newspapers	
0	7 *(35)*
1	24 *(117)*
2	42 *(201)*
3	20 *(95)*
4	5 *(24)*
5	1 *(5)*
No answer	⁑ *(2)*
Total	100 *(479)*

⁑ The percentage is equal to less than 1%.

Table 78 Newspapers Reported Read*(Arranged in descending order)

Question 4 A: *What newspapers do you read?*

Daily News (N.Y.C.)	19 *(92)*
The Sun (Baltimore)	15 *(73)*
The News American (Baltimore)	14 *(69)*
The Plain Dealer (Cleveland)	14 *(69)*
The New York Times	13 *(64)*
The Cleveland Press	12 *(58)*
Afro-American (	12 *(58)*
Philadelphia Daily News	12 *(57)*
The Philadelphia Inquirer	10 *(48)*
Los Angeles Times	9 *(44)*
The Evening Bulletin (Philadelphia)	8 *(39)*
Los Angeles Herald Examiner	8 *(36)*
The Philadelphia Tribune	6 *(28)*
Los Angeles Sentinel	4 *(20)*
El Diario-La Prensa (N.Y.C.)	3 *(14)*
New York Amsterdam News	3 *(14)*
New York Post	3 *(13)*
Call and Post (Cleveland)	3 *(12)*
*Long Island Press**	2 *(11)*
*News Post** (Baltimore)	2 *(11)*
Evening Outlook (Santa Monica)	2 *(8)*
Muhammad Speaks (Chicago)	1 *(7)*
The Black Panther (San Francisco)	1 *(6)*

* Reported read by between 1 and 19 %

* Title not identified

Table 78 Newspapers Reported Read (continued)

Amerikanski Slovenec (Cleveland)

Atlanta Georgia News*

Barn* (Cleveland)

Blue Ribbon* (Los Angeles)

Catholic Review (Baltimore)

Catholic Universe Bulletin (Cleveland)

The Chief (New York)

Christian Science Monitor (Boston)

Cleveland Atlantic*

Daily Times (formerly *Chester Times*)(Chester, Pa.)

Danica (Chicago)

East Cleveland Leader (discontinued)

East Los Angeles Tribune

El Tiempo (New York)

Englewood Breeze*

Enquirer* (Los Angeles)

Forward (Jewish Daily) (New York)

Fronterizio* (Los Angeles)

Germantown Courier (Germantown, Pa.)

Herald American* (Los Angeles)

Il Progresso (New York)

Independent (Long Beach, Calif.)

The Leader (Philadelphia)

Liberation (Monthly) (New York)

National Herald* (Cleveland)

National Observer (Silver Spring, Md.)

New York American Journal*

News of the World (England)

*Title not identified

Table 78 Newspapers Reported Read (continued)

News-Pilot (San Pedro, Calif.)

*Oklahoma Eagle**

Parma Sun Post (Cleveland)

Pravda (Chicago)

Press-Telegram (Long Beach, Calif.)

Soul (Los Angeles)

Southwest Wave (Los Angeles)

Spanish newspaper

Star-News (Pasadena, Calif.)

Student Weekly-New York Times

Svoboda (Jersey City)

*Ten Star** (Baltimore)

The Village Voice (New York)

Wall Street Journal (New York)

Washington Post

West Park Sun (Cleveland)

West Side News (Cleveland)

*Title not identified

Table 79 Newspapers Read in Each City *(expressed in percent)*

Newspapers	
Baltimore (Base = 100)	
The Sun	73 *(73)*
The News American	69 *(69)*
Afro-American	58 *(58)*
News Post*	11 *(11)*
Cleveland (Base = 85)	
The Plain Dealer	81 *(69)*
The Cleveland Press	68 *(58)*
Call and Post	14 *(12)*
Los Angeles (Base = 84)	
Los Angeles Times	52 *(44)*
Los Angeles Herald Examiner	43 *(36)*
Los Angeles Sentinel	24 *(20)*
New York (Base = 103)	
Daily News	89 *(92)*
The New York Times	62 *(64)*
New York Amsterdam News	13 *(14)*
El Diario-La Prensa	13 *(14)*
New York Post	12 *(13)*
Philadelphia (Base = 72)	
Philadelphia Daily News	79 *(57)*
The Philadelphia Inquirer	67 *(48)*
The Evening Bulletin	54 *(39)*
The Philadelphia Tribune	39 *(28)*

* Not identified

Figure 1   Special Interest Newspapers Reported Read*

Black Newspapers

       Afro-American (Washington, D.C.)

       The Black Panther (San Francisco)

       Muhammad Speaks (Chicago)

       New York Amsterdam News

       Soul (Los Angeles)

Spanish Language Newspapers

       El Diario-La Prensa (New York)

       El Tiempo (New York)

European Language Newspapers Other Than Spanish

       Amerikanski Slovenec (Cleveland)

       Danica (Chicago)

       Forward (Jewish Daily) (New York)

       Il Progresso (New York)

       Pravda

Religious Newspapers

       Catholic Review (Baltimore)

       Catholic Universe Bulletin (Cleveland)

*Titles were in response to Question 4

Figure 2   Ethnic Newspapers and Newsletters Identified in LMRP*

Black

B	*The Black Panther*	San Francisco, Calif.
B	*Black Politics*	Berkeley, Calif.
B	*Community Progress*	New Haven, Conn.
B	*The Crow*	New Haven, Conn.
B	*Dig This*	Philadelphia, Pa.
B	*Focus In Black*	New York, N.Y.
B	*Herald-Dispatch*	Los Angeles, Calif.
B	*The Milwaukee Courier*	Milwaukee, Wis.
B	*Mississippi Newsletter*	Tougaloo, Miss.
B	*Muhammad Speaks*	Chicago, Ill.
B	*The New African*	Washington, D.C.
B	*The New Observer*	Washington, D.C.
B	*Nitty Gritty*	Milwaukee, Wis.
B	*The Pacemaker*	Detroit, Mich.
B	*Pan African Roots*	Chicago, Ill.
B	*Struggle!*	Washington, D.C.
B	*Third World*	Washington, D.C.
B	*Voice From Mother Country*	Washington, D.C.
B	*The Washington Informer*	Washington, D.C.

General

G	*Chicory*	Baltimore, Md.
G	*News For You*	Syracuse, N.Y.
G	*Pontiac Flag News*	Pontiac, Ill.
G	*The Prince George's Senior Citizen*	Upper Marlboro, Md.

Hebrew

H   *Forward*   New York, N.Y.

American Indian

I   *Americans Before Columbus*   Albuquerque, N.M.

I   *Fort Apache Scout*   Fort Apache Indian Reser-
                                         vation, Whiteriver, Ariz.

Italian

It   *Il Progresso*   New York, N.Y.

Mexican American

M   *Amigo De La Prensa*   Los Angeles, Calif.

M   *Carta Editorial*   Los Angeles, Calif

M   *Chicano Student Movement*   Los Angeles, Calif.

M   *Chicanismo*   Stanford, Calif.

M   *Compass*   Houston, Tex.

M   *El Chicano*   Colton, Calif.

M   *El Gallo*   Denver, Colo.

M   *El Grito Del Norte*   Milwaukee, Wis.

M   *La Verdad*   San Diego, Calif.

M   *La Voz Del Pueblo*   Berkeley, Calif.

M   *La Voz de los Estudiantes*   Milwaukee, Wis.

Puerto Rican

P   *El Diario-La Prensa*   New York, N.Y.

P   *El Tiempo*   New York, N.Y.

P   *LADO*   Chicago, Ill.

Ukranian

Uk   *Svoboda*   Jersey City, N.J.

Yugoslavian

Y	*Amerikanski Slovenec*	Cleveland, Ohio
Y	*Danica*	Chicago, Ill.

* Key

B	Black
G	General
H	Hebrew
I	American Indian
It	Italian
M	Mexican American
P	Puerto Rican
Uk	Ukranian
Y	Yugoslavian

Table 80 Specialized Reading *(expressed in percent)*

Question 49:   *In your reading, do you ever read . . .*

Types of Newspapers	
A local neighborhood newspaper	62 *(295)*
A church bulletin or newspaper	61 *(294)*
Club or organization bulletin	34 *(162)*
Weekly Reader	33 *(158)*
A union paper	32 *(153)*
Racing forms	9 *(45)*
The newspaper called *News for You*	7 *(35)*

Base ▬ 479

Table 81 Topics Usually Read in Newspaper *(expressed in percent)*

Question 6A: *When you read a newspaper, do you usually read each of these things or not?*

Topic	Yes	No
News about world affairs	87 *(386)*	13 *(57)*
News about civil rights	78 *(344)*	21 *(95)*
Advertisements (supermarket ads, other store ads, want ads)	77 *(341)*	23 *102)*
Television news	74 *(330)*	26 *(113)*
Weather	69 *(307)*	31 *(137)*
News about politics and government	68 *(301)*	32 *(142)*
Movie news	64 *(282)*	36 *(160)*
Your horoscope	59 *(265)*	41 *(176)*
Women's section	56 *(250)*	43 *(190)*
Editorials	54 *(239)*	46 *(203)*
Sports	52 *(231)*	48 *(211)*
Letters to the editor	52 *(228)*	48 *(215)*
Comics	51 *(224)*	49 *(219)*
Advice to the lovelorn	38 *(162)*	62 *(279)*
Death notices	35 *(154)*	65 *(287)*
Book reviews	30 *(140)*	70 *(301)*
Stocks and bonds	13 *(58)*	86 *(381)*

Base = 444

Table 82 Topics Reported Missed Most in Newspaper *(expressed in percent)**

Question 6B: *If you didn't have a chance to read any newspaper for a few weeks, which one of those things you usually read would you miss the most?*

Topic	
News about world affairs	38 *(146)*
Sports	16 *(37)*
Advertisements (supermarket ads, other store ads, want ads)	13 *(43)*
Women's section	12 *(29)*
Your horoscope	11 *(30)*
Comics	8 *(18)*
News about politics and government	8 *(25)*
Television news	7 *(23)*
News about civil rights	6 *(21)*
Advice to the lovelorn	6 *(10)*
Editorials	4 *(10)*
Letters to the editor	4 *(8)*
Weather	3 *(9)*
Movie news	3 *(8)*
Stock and bonds	2 *(1)*
Death notices	1 *(2)*
Book reviews	0 *(0)*

*
Percentages are based on the number of respondents who usually read the section (table   ).

Table 83   Selected Newspaper Columns Usually or Regularly Read by Adult New Reader, by Sex *(expressed in percent)*

Selected Newspaper Columns	Sex	
	Male *(133)*	Female *(311)*
News about world affairs	92 *(122)*	85 *(264)*
Sports	83 *(111)*	39 *(120)*
Women's section	8 *(11)*	77 *(239)*
Advertisements (supermarket ads, other store ads, want ads)	55 *(73)*	86 *(268)*
Your horoscope	36 *(47)*	70 *(218)*

Base = 444

Table 84   Selected Newspaper Columns Usually or Regularly Read by Adul New Reader, by Race *(expressed in percent)*

Selected Newspaper Columns	Race	
	White *(115)*	Black *(329)*
News about world affairs	89 *(102)*	86 *(281)*
Sports	50 *(58)*	53 *(172)*
Women's section	44 *(50)*	61 *(199)*
Advertisements (supermarket ads, other store ads, want ads)	63 *(72)*	82 *(267)*
Your horoscope	49 *(56)*	61 *(209)*

Table 85 Selected Newspaper Columns Usually or Regularly Read by
Adult New Reader, by Age *(expressed in percent)*

Selected Newspaper Columns	Age					
	16-24 *(97)*	25-34 *(144)*	35-44 *(96)*	45-54 *(61)*	55-64 *(29)*	65+ *(15)*
News about world affairs	82 *(79)*	86 *(124)*	90 *(86)*	89 *(54)*	93 *(27)*	93 *(14)*
Sports	54 *(52)*	46 *(66)*	56 *(54)*	62 *(38)*	48 *(14)*	40 *(6)*
Women's section	47 *(45)*	58 *(84)*	53 *(51)*	64 *(39)*	72 *(21)*	60 *(9)*
Advertisements (supermarket ads, other store ads, want ads)	70 *(68)*	84 *(121)*	71 *(68)*	72 *(44)*	93 *(27)*	80 *(12)*
Your horoscope	59 *(57)*	64 *(92)*	54 *(52)*	64 *(39)*	58 *(17)*	47 *(7)*

Table 86 Selected Newspaper Columns Usually or Regularly Read by
Adult New Reader, by Amount of Formal Education *(expressed
in percent)*

Selected Newspaper Columns	Amount of Formal Education					
	0-4 *(25)*	5-6 *(38)*	7-9 *(136)*	10-11 *(144)*	12 *(81)*	13+ *(17)*
News about world affairs	89 *(22)*	87 *(33)*	80 *(109)*	88 *(127)*	95 *(77)*	88 *(77)*
Sports	52 *(13)*	37 *(14)*	49 *(67)*	57 *(82)*	56 *(45)*	53 *(9)*
Women's section	56 *(14)*	34 *(13)*	63 *(75)*	59 *(85)*	60 *(49)*	65 *(11)*
Advertisements (supermarket ads, other store ads, want ads)	76 *(19)*	74 *(28)*	73 *(99)*	80 *(115)*	83 *(67)*	59 *(10)*
Your horoscope	32 *(8)*	47 *(18)*	68 *(82)*	65 *(93)*	65 *(53)*	53 *(9)*

Table 87 Selected Newspaper Columns Usually or Regularly Read by
Adult New Reader, by Family Income *(expressed in percent)*

Selected Newspaper Columns	Family Income			
	$1-2,999 *(80)*	3,000-5,999 *(181)*	6,000-9,999 *(86)*	10,000 and up *(54)*
News about world affairs	81 *(65)*	88 *(159)*	85 *(73)*	100 *(54)*
Sports	50 *(40)*	49 *(89)*	52 *(45)*	58 *(31)*
Women's section	60 *(48)*	49 *(111)*	52 *(45)*	41 *(22)*
Advertisements (supermarket ads, other store ads, want ads)	72 *(58)*	82 *(149)*	79 *(64)*	70 *(38)*
Your horoscope	64 *(54)*	59 *(107)*	52 *(45)*	50 *(27)*

Table 88 Selected Newspaper Columns Usually or Regularly Read by Adult
New Reader, by Individual Income *(expressed in percent)*

Selected Newspaper Columns	Individual Income			
	$0-2,999 *(167)*	3,000-5,999 *(149)*	6,000-9,999 *(45)*	10,000 and up *(16)*
News about world affairs	82 *(137)*	88 *(132)*	89 *(40)*	100 *(16)*
Sports	49 *(83)*	55 *(82)*	60 *(27)*	76 *(12)*
Women's section	63 *(105)*	59 *(88)*	33 *(15)*	19 *(3)*
Advertisements (supermarket ads, other store ads, want ads)	78 *(130)*	82 *(124)*	65 *(29)*	44 *(7)*
Your horoscope	65 *(109)*	64 *(96)*	36 *(16)*	31 *(5)*

Table 89 Interest in Reading Newspaper Advertisements *(expressed in percent)*

Question 5: *In general, how interested are you in reading the advertisements in newspapers -- a great deal, a little, or not at all?*

Amount of Interest	
A great deal	44 *(193)*
A little	46 *(202)*
Not at all	10 *(48)*
No answer	∷ *(1)*
Total respondents who read newspapers	100 *(444)*

Table 90 Frequency of Newspaper Reading *(expressed in percent)*

Question 4B: *Some people read newspapers more often than others. Do you read a newspaper every day, a few times a week, once a week, just on Sunday, or less often than that?*

Frequency of Newspaper Reading	
Every day	51 *(224)*
A few times a week	33 *(146)*
About once a week	9 *(40)*
Sundays only	4 *(19)*
Less often than that	3 *(14)*
No answer	∷ *(1)*
Total respondents who read newspapers	100 *(444)*

Table 91 Frequency of Newspaper Reading, by Sex *(expressed in percent)*

Frequency of Newspaper Reading	Male *(133)*	Female *(311)*
Every day	51 *(69)*	50 *(155)*
A few times a week	31 *(41)*	34 *(105)*
Once a week	11 *(14)*	9 *(26)*
Just on Sunday	5 *(6)*	4 *(13)*
Less often	2 *(3)*	3 *(11)*

Base = 444

Table 92 Frequency of Newspaper Reading, by Race *(expressed in percent)*

Frequency of Newspaper Reading	White *(115)*	Black *(329)*
Every day	62 *(71)*	47 *(155)*
A few times a week	19 *(22)*	38 *(123)*
Once a week	9 *(11)*	9 *(28)*
Just on Sunday	7 *(8)*	3 *(11)*
Less often	3 *(3)*	3 *(11)*

Table 93 Frequency of Newspaper Reading, by Age *(expressed in percent)*

Frequency of Newspaper Reading	Age (in years)					
	16 - 24 *(97)*	25 - 34 *(144)*	35 - 44 *(96)*	45 - 54 *(61)*	55 - 64 *(29)*	65+ *(15)*
Every day	40 *(39)*	50 *(73)*	56 *(54)*	58 *(35)*	52 *(15)*	47 *(7)*
A few times a week	43 *(41)*	31 *(44)*	32 *(30)*	26 *(16)*	35 *(10)*	30 *(5)*
Once a week	11 *(11)*	10 *(14)*	7 *(7)*	8 *(5)*	3 *(1)*	13 *(2)*
Just on Sunday	3 *(3)*	6 *(8)*	4 *(4)*	5 *(3)*	3 *(1)*	0 *(0)*
Less often	3 *(3)*	3 *(4)*	1 *(1)*	3 *(2)*	7 *(2)*	10 *(1)*

Table 94 Frequency of Newspaper Reading, by Education *(expressed in percent)*

Frequency of Newspaper Reading	Amount of Formal Education (last year in school)					
	0 - 4 *(25)*	5 - 6 *(38)*	7 - 9 *(136)*	10 - 11 *(144)*	12 *(81)*	13+ *(17)*
Every day	36 *(9)*	42 *(17)*	46 *(63)*	53 *(76)*	57 *(46)*	70 *(12)*
A few times a week	32 *(8)*	32 *(11)*	38 *(52)*	31 *(45)*	30 *(24)*	30 *(5)*
Once a week	12 *(3)*	16 *(6)*	9 *(12)*	10 *(14)*	6 *(5)*	0 *(0)*
Just on Sunday	12 *(3)*	7 *(3)*	3 *(4)*	4 *(5)*	5 *(4)*	0 *(0)*
Less often	8 *(2)*	3 *(1)*	4 *(5)*	2 *(3)*	2 *(2)*	0 *(0)*

Table 95 Frequency of Newspaper Reading, by Family Income *(expressed in percent)*

Frequency of Newspaper Reading	$1- 2,999 *(80)*	3,000 - 5,999 *(181)*	6,000 - 9,999 *(86)*	10,000 and up *(58)*
Every day	36 *(29)*	51 *(92)*	53 *(45)*	62 *(36)*
A few times a week	40 *(32)*	35 *(63)*	30 *(26)*	23 *(13)*
Once a week	10 *(8)*	8 *(15)*	9 *(8)*	7 *(4)*
Just on Sunday	3 *(2)*	4 *(7)*	8 *(7)*	5 *(3)*
Less often	11 *(9)*	2 *(3)*	0 *(0)*	3 *(2)*

Table 96 Frequency of Newspaper Reading, by Individual Income *(expressed in percent)*

Frequency of Newspaper Reading	$0 - 2,999 *(167)*	3,000 - 5,999 *(149)*	6,000 - 9,999 *(45)*	10,000 and up *(16)*
Every day	40 *(69)*	52 *(78)*	62 *(28)*	56 *(9)*
A few times a week	40 *(66)*	34 *(51)*	20 *(9)*	19 *(3)*
Once a week	10 *(17)*	9 *(12)*	8 *(3)*	19 *(3)*
Just on Sunday	4 *(6)*	3 *(5)*	10 *(4)*	0 *(0)*
Less often	6 *(1)*	2 *(8)*	0 *(0)*	6 *(1)*

Table 97   Places Where Newspapers Are Read *(expressed in percent)*

Question 7:   *In the last six months, have you read or glanced through newspapers at any of these places?*

Place	Yes	No
At home	99 *(438)*	1 *(6)*
At other people's homes	46 *(206)*	53 *(235)*
On the bus, train, plane, streetcar, or at terminals or depots	46 *(206)*	54 *(238)*
At dentist's or doctor's office	45 *(198)*	55 *(245)*
At barber shops or beauty shops	37 *(166)*	63 *(278)*
At school	36 *(162)*	63 *(281)*
At work	32 *(143)*	67 *(299)*
In drugstores, newsstands, or bookstores	26 *(116)*	74 *(328)*
In supermarkets, laundromats, or department stores	26 *(115)*	74 *(329)*
In coffee shops, bars, or restaurants	21 *(93)*	79 *(351)*
In the library	20 *(90)*	79 *(352)*

Base = 444

Table 98 Use of Print Material and Communication Media *(expressed in percent)*

c. Question 4: *Do you ever get a chance to read a newspaper?*

Basic Social Characteristics	Read newspapers during the last 6 months		
	Yes	No	Total
Sex			
Male	90 *(133)*	10 *(15)*	31 *(148)*
Female	94 *(311)*	6 *(20)*	69 *(331)*
Race			
White	94 *(115)*	6 *(8)*	26 *(123)*
Black	92 *(326)*	8 *(27)*	74 *(353)*
Other	100 *(3)*	0 *(0)*	∷ *(3)*
Age (in years)			
16 – 24	87 *(97)*	13 *(14)*	23 *(111)*
25 – 34	97 *(144)*	3 *(4)*	31 *(148)*
35 – 44	95 *(96)*	5 *(5)*	21 *(101)*
45 – 54	92 *(61)*	8 *(5)*	14 *(66)*
55 – 64	94 *(29)*	6 *(2)*	6 *(31)*
65+	75 *(15)*	25 *(5)*	4 *(20)*
Education			
0 – 4	81 *(25)*	19 *(6)*	6 *(31)*
5 – 6	81 *(38)*	19 *(9)*	10 *(47)*
7 – 9	93 *(136)*	7 *(10)*	30 *(146)*
10 – 11	95 *(144)*	5 *(7)*	32 *(151)*
12	99 *(81)*	1 *(1)*	17 *(82)*
13+	100 *(17)*	0 *(0)*	4 *(17)*
No answer	60 *(3)*	40 *(2)*	1 *(5)*
Programs and Classes			
Adult Basic Education	93 *(211)*	7 *(16)*	47 *(227)*
Employment Oriented	97 *(190)*	3 *(6)*	7 *(196)*
Youth Oriented Employment	96 *(28)*	4 *(1)*	2 *(29)*
High School Equivalency	93 *(111)*	7 *(8)*	25 *(119)*
Reading Development	96 *(48)*	. 4 *(2)*	10 *(50)*
Other	97 *(34)*	3 *(1)*	7 *(35)*

∷ The percentage is equal to less than 1%

Table **98** Use of Print Material and Communication Media (continued)
(expressed in percent)

c. Question 4: *Do you ever get a chance to read a newspaper?*

Basic Social Characteristics	Read newspapers during the last 6 months		
	Yes	No	Total
Employment of Time			
Working Force			
White Collar	93 *(25)*	7 *(2)*	6 *(27)*
Clerical	100 *(34)*	0 *(0)*	7 *(34)*
Craft	87 *(34)*	13 *(5)*	8 *(39)*
Blue Collar	85 *(34)*	15 *(6)*	8 *(40)*
Service	97 *(76)*	3 *(2)*	16 *(78)*
Unemployed	94 *(29)*	6 *(2)*	6 *(31)*
Retired	71 *(10)*	29 *(4)*	3 *(14)*
Keeping House	95 *(85)*	5 *(7)*	19 *(92)*
School	95 *(114)*	5 *(6)*	25 *(120)*
Family Income			
$0 - 2,999	89 *(80)*	11 *(10)*	19 *(90)*
3,000 - 5,999	95 *(181)*	5 *(10)*	40 *(191)*
6,000 - 9,999	92 *(86)*	8 *(7)*	19 *(93)*
10,000 or more	95 *(58)*	5 *(3)*	13 *(61)*
No answer	89 *(39)*	11 *(5)*	9 *(44)*
Individual Income			
0	95 *(18)*	5 *(1)*	5 *(19)*
1 - 2,999	93 *(149)*	7 *(11)*	33 *(160)*
3,000 - 5,999	93 *(149)*	7 *(11)*	33 *(160)*
6,000 - 9,999	88 *(45)*	12 *(6)*	11 *(51)*
10,000 or more	100 *(16)*	0 *(0)*	3 *(16)*
No answer	92 *(67)*	8 *(6)*	15 *(73)*
Adult New Reader Rating			
Very Active	100 *(65)*	0 *(0)*	14 *(65)*
Active	98 *(254)*	2 *(4)*	54 *(257)*
Somewhat Active	88 *(126)*	12 *(18)*	30 *(144)*
Least Active	0 *(0)*	100 *(13)*	3 *(13)*

Table 99 Printed Reading Material Preference *(expressed in percent)*

Question 48A: *What do you read most often--newspapers, magazines, or books?*

Reading Material	
Newspapers	56 *(271)*
Magazines	10 *(48)*
Books	31 *(147)*
Don't know	1 *(5)*
No answer	2 *(8)*

Question 48B: *And which do you read least often?*

Reading Material	
Newspapers	17 *(82)*
Magazines	42 *(204)*
Books	34 *(161)*
Don't know	5 *(23)*
No answer	2 *(9)*

Magazines. Questions 10, 11, and 12 asked about magazine reading. To the question, "Do you ever read magazines?" 88 percent responded yes. The interviewers then noted what magazines were reported read by checking one of the 13 categories of types of magazines in which the title could be classified. Because of this classification of the information, magazine reading is recorded by type or group rather than by separate titles with the exception of one magazine, *Reader's Digest* and the two groups of picture magazines, *Life* or *Look* and *Ebony* or *Jet*. It is these five magazines that have the largest readership. Over two-thirds of the respondents read *Life* or *Look,* and 57 percent read *Ebony* or *Jet*. *Reader's Digest* is read by 33 percent of the respondents in contrast to other digests such as *Pageant, Black Digest* which are read by 8 percent. The various types of women's magazines have a fair percentage of readers. The women's magazines concerned with homemaking, that is, *Ladies' Home Journal, McCall's, Good Housekeeping* and *Better Homes and Gardens*, are read by 37 percent of the respondents; love and romance magazines by 20 percent; and women's fashion magazines by 19 percent. The news magazines are read by 21 percent. Other types of magazines, sports, movie, men's, religious, and trade, all have small percentages of readers. For the types of magazines which would be missed most by their readers, *Ebony* or *Jet* have the most devoted readers, 45 percent. Sports magazines would be missed most by 30 percent of their readers. Between 10 and 27 percent of the readers would miss their favorite types of magazines in the various categories shown in tables 100 to 102.

Tables 103 and 104 show the types of magazine stories usually read by the respondents. The lives of real people interest a substantial majority, 84 percent, of the magazine readers. Adventure stories attract 60 percent of readers. About half or less read crime and mystery, travel, love and romance, sports, war, space and science fiction stories. Both men and women read in these areas, but there are differences, except for the interest both show in reading about the lives of real people. More men than women read sports, adventure, war, crime and mystery, and space and science fiction. More women read love and romance.

Magazines like newspapers are read in many places, but most frequently at home by 96 percent of the respondents. Magazines like newspapers are read easily in a variety of places such as the dentist's office, barber shops, on the bus, drugstores, laundromats, and coffee shops. Magazines are read at school, at work, and in the library. Table 106 shows the range of places and percentage of respondents who had read a magazine there in the last six months. Consistently the more active readers as rated by the Reader Activity Index read magazines in a variety of places. Significantly as individuals become more active readers they use the library as a source for magazines. More magazine readers, 26 percent, than newspaper readers, 20 percent, read these materials in the library.

Differences among the magazine readers are shown more clearly in relation to basic social characteristics. More women read magazines than men, more younger respondents 16 to 34 years of age read magazines than those 35 years of age and over. Magazine reading increases as formal education increases. Respondents who are retired and those in blue-collar occupations read magazines less than those in other occupations. A high percentage of respondents, 9 in 10, read magazines in the following groups - the unemployed, those in clerical and service occupations, and in school.

Table 107 shows the relationship between the extent of magazine reading and book reading. Particularly significant is the 64 percent of adult new readers who read both magazines and books as compared to the 45 and 49 percent of the NORC, Adult Samples, 1963 and 1962 respectively.

Table 100 Magazine Reading *(expressed in percent)*

Question 10: *Do you ever read magazines?*

Yes	88 *(420)*
No	12 *(59)*
Total	100 *(479)*

Chart 17 Use of Media for News

Television

News and
weather
program

89% *

Radio

News and
weather
program

92%

Newspaper

News about
world
affairs

87%

News about
civil
rights

78%

News about
politics and
government

68%

Magazine

News (i.e.
*Time, News-
week, U.S.
News and
World Report)*

21%

*The percentages are based on those who use the medium.

269

Table 10: Types of Magazines Read by the Adult New Reader
(expressed in percent)

Question 10A: *What magazines do you read?*

Types of Magazines	
Life or *Look*	67 *(281)*
Ebony or *Jet*	57 *(238)*
Women's (i.e., *Ladies' Home Journal, McCall's, Good Housekeeping, Better Homes and Gardens*)	37 *(157)*
Reader's Digest	33 *(140)*
News (i.e., *Time, Newsweek, U.S. News and World Report*)	21 *(90)*
Love and Romance (i.e., *Modern Romance, True Stories, Tan*)	20 *(84)*
Women's Fashions (i.e., *Glamour, Mademoiselle, Vogue*)	19 *(80)*
Movie or Television (i.e., *Modern Screen, Motion Screen, Photoplay*)	15 *(62)*
Sports (i.e., *Sports Illustrated, Field & Stream*)	14 *(57)*
Men's (i.e., *Playboy, Esquire, Argosy, True*)	11 *(48)*
Religious (i.e., *Sacred Heart Magazine, Catholic Digest, Columbian*)	10 *(41)*
Other digests (i.e. *Pageant, Coronet, Black Digest*)	8 *(34)*
Trade magazines (i.e., *Mechanics Illustrated, Electronics World*)	8 *(32)*
Foreign	2 *(8)*
Art and Music	1 *(5)*
Other	5 *(20)*

Base = 420

Table 102 Magazines Read Which Would Be Missed Most *(expressed in percent)* *

Question 10B: *Which one of these magazines would you miss most if you were unable to get it for several months?*

Magazine		
Ebony or *Jet*	45	*(108)*
Sports (i.e., *Sports Illustrated, Field & Stream*)	30	*(17)*
Women's (i.e., *Ladies' Home Journal, McCall's, Good Housekeeping, Better Homes & Gardens*)	27	*(41)*
Reader's Digest	26	*(36)*
Love & Romance (i.e., *Modern Romance, True Stories, Tan*)	26	*(22)*
News (i.e., *Time, Newsweek, U.S. News & World Report*)	24	*(22)*
Religious (i.e., *Sacred Heart Magazine, Catholic Digest, Columbian*)	24	*(10)*
Life or *Look*	23	*(65)*
Trade magazines (i.e., *Mechanics Illustrated, Electronics World*)	22	*(7)*
Movie or Television (i.e., *Modern Screen, Motion Screen, Photoplay*)	14	*(9)*
Men's (i.e., *Playboy, Esquire, Argosy, True*)	13	*(6)*
Women's Fashions (i.e., *Glamour, Mademoiselle, Vogue*)	10	*(8)*
Other Digests (i.e., *Pageant, Coronet, Black Digest*)	3	*(1)*
Others		
Foreign	25	*(2)*
Art and Music	20	*(1)*
Other	15	*(3)*

* Percentages are based on the number of respondents who have read the magazine (table 101).

Table 103 Types of Stories Read in Magazines *(expressed in percent)*

Question 11: *Do you usually read magazine stories about . . .*

Types of Stories	Yes	No
The lives of real people	84 *(353)*	16 *(67)*
Adventure	60 *(255)*	40 *(164)*
Crime and mystery	51 *(215)*	49 *(204)*
Travel	49 *(209)*	51 *(211)*
Love and romance	49 *(207)*	51 *(211)*
Sports	46 *(193)*	54 *(226)*
War	43 *(181)*	57 *(239)*
Space and science fiction	36 *(149)*	64 *(269)*

Base = 420

Table 104 Types of Magazine Stories Usually Read, by Sex *(expressed in percent)*

Types of Magazine Stories	Sex	
	Male *(123)*	Female *(297)*
Crime and mystery	57 *(70)*	49 *(145)*
Space and science fiction	50 *(62)*	29 *(87)*
Love and romance	25 *(31)*	60 *(176)*
War	61 *(75)*	36 *(106)*
The lives of real people	79 *(97)*	86 *(256)*
Travel	50 *(62)*	50 *(147)*
Sports	78 *(96)*	33 *(97)*
Adventure	69 *(84)*	57 *(171)*

Base = 420

Table 105 Places Where Magazines Are Read *(expressed in percent)*

Question 12: *In the last six months, have you read or glanced through magazines at any of these places?*

Place	Yes	No
At home	96 *(402)*	4 *(16)*
At the dentist's or doctor's office	58 *(244)*	41 *(172)*
At other people's home	56 *(232)*	44 *(186)*
At barber shops or beauty shops	49 *(206)*	51 *(212)*
On the bus, train, plane, streetcar or at the terminals or depots	43 *(179)*	57 *(239)*
At school	38 *(159)*	60 *(256)*
In drugstores, newsstands, or bookstores	32 *(135)*	68 *(283)*
At work	28 *(126)*	71 *(289)*
In the library	26 *(111)*	72 *(302)*
In supermarkets, laundromats, or department stores	25 *(105)*	75 *(312)*
In coffee shops, bars or restaurants	20 *(87)*	79 *(329)*

Base = 420

Table 106 Places Where Adult New Reader Reads Magazines by Adult
New Reader Activity Rating *(expressed in percent)*

Places	Adult New Reader Activity Rating		
	Somewhat Active *(105)*	Active *(249)*	Very Active *(65)*
At home	96 *(101)*	96 *(236)*	98 *(64)*
At other people's home	47 *(49)*	57 *(142)*	63 *(41)*
In the library	18 *(19)*	28 *(70)*	34 *(22)*
At dentist's or doctor's office	40 *(42)*	62 *(155)*	72 *(47)*
At barber shops or beauty shops	44 *(46)*	52 *(130)*	46 *(30)*
On the bus, train, plane, streetcar, or at terminals or depots	22 *(23)*	47 *(117)*	60 *(39)*
At work	21 *(22)*	33 *(82)*	34 *(22)*

Table 107 Distribution of Book and Magazine Reading *(expressed in percent)*

Read Magazines Regularly
(NORC, Adult Sample, 1963)[1]

		Yes	No	
Read Books Within the Year	Yes	45	12	57
	No	20	23	43
		65	35	100 *(648)*

Read Magazines Regularly
(NORC, Adult Sample, 1962)[2]

		Yes	No	
Read Books Within the Year	Yes	49	12	61
	No	21	18	39
		70	30	100 *(2,845)*

Read Magazines Regularly
(LMRP Population Study, 1969)

		Yes	No	
Read Books Within Last Six Months	Yes	64	5	69
	No	24	7	31
		88	12	100 *(479)*

[1] Philip H. Ennis, *Adult Book Reading in the United States,* (Chicago: National Opinion Research Center, University of Chicago, 1965), p. 47.

[2] Ennis, p. 48.

Table 108 Use of Print Material and Communication Media
(expressed in percent)

Question 10: *Do you ever read magazines?*

Basic Social Characteristics	Read Magazines
Sex	
Male	83 *(123)*
Female	90 *(297)*
Race	
White	84 *(103)*
Black	89 *(314)*
Other	100 *(3)*
Age (in years)	
16 - 24	91 *(101)*
25 - 34	91 *(134*
35 - 44	84 *(85)*
45 - 54	88 *(58)*
55 - 64	87 *(27)*
65+	70 *(14)*
Education	
0 - 4	55 *(17)*
5 - 6	77 *(36)*
7 - 9	86 *(125)*
10 - 11	93 *(141)*
12	98 *(80)*
13+	100 *(17)*
No answer	80 *(4)*
Programs and Classes	
Adult Basic Education	88 *(200)*
Employment Oriented	95 *(187)*
Youth Oriented Em- ployment	90 *(26)*
High School Equivalency	90 *(107)*
Reading Development	84 *(42)*
Other	91 *(32)*

Question 10: *Do you ever read magazines?*

Basic Social Characteristics	Read Magazines
Employment of Time	
Working Force	
White-collar	89 (24)
Clerical	94 (32)
Craft	87 (34)
Blue-collar	60 (30)
Service	91 (71)
Unemployed	97 (29)
Retired	57 (8)
Keeping house	86 (79)
School	92 (110)
Family Income	
$ 1 - 2,999	82 (74)
3,000 - 5,999	88 (169)
6,000 - 9,999	87 (81)
10,000 or more	92 (56)
No answer	90 (40)
Individual Income	
$ 0	84 (16)
1 - 2,999	89 (143)
3,000 - 5,999	87 (139)
6,000 - 9,999	82 (42)
10,000 or more	88 (14)
No answer	90 (66)
Adult New Reader Rating	
Very active	100 (65)
Active	97 (249)
Somewhat active	73 (105)
Least active	8 (1)

<u>Comic Book Reading</u>. The readers of comic books constitute 34 percent of the respondents. About one-third express a great deal of liking for the comic books, and two-thirds said that they like them a little. Adults in the 45 to 54 age group read them slightly more than any other age group except the younger groups between 16 and 34 years of age. The greater percentage of readers of comic books is in the group with seven to nine years of schooling and who are participants in library reading development and employment oriented programs, have higher incomes, and are in blue= collar occupations.

Among newspaper readers, 51 percent read comics, but when compared with topics that respondents would miss most only 8 percent reported that they would miss the comics most (tables 109, 110, 111).

Table 109 Comic Book Reading

Question 15: *Do you ever read comic books?*

Yes	34 *(161)*
No	66 *(316)*
No answer	⁑ *(2)*
Total	100 *(479)*

⁑ The percentage is equal to less than 1%

Table 110 Degree of Liking Comic Books *(expressed in percent)*

Question 15A: If Yes: *Would you say you like comic books a great deal, a little, or not at all?*

Degree of Liking	
Great deal	29 *(47)*
A little	67 *(107)*
Not at all	4 *(6)*
No answer	⁑ *(1)*
Total who have read comic books	100 *(161)*

⁑ The percentage is equal to less than 1%

Table 111 Use of Print Material and Communication Media *(expressed in percent)*

d. Question 15: *Do you ever read comic books?*

Basic Social Characteristics	Yes	No	Total
Sex			
Male	36 *(52)*	65 *(94)*	31 *(146)*
Female	33 *(109)*	66 *(222)*	69 *(331)*
Race			
White	33 *(40)*	67 *(81)*	25 *(121)*
Black	34 *(121)*	66 *(232)*	74 *(353)*
Other	0 *(0)*	100 *(3)*	1 *(3)*
Age (in years)			
16 – 24	38 *(42)*	62 *(69)*	23 *(111)*
25 – 34	37 *(54)*	63 *(93)*	31 *(147)*
35 – 44	29 *(29)*	71 *(72)*	21 *(101)*
45 – 54	40 *(26)*	60 *(39)*	14 *(65)*
55 – 64	26 *(8)*	74 *(23)*	6 *(31)*
65+	10 *(2)*	90 *(18)*	4 *(20)*
Education			
0 – 4	16 *(5)*	84 *(26)*	6 *(31)*
5 – 6	28 *(13)*	72 *(33)*	10 *(46)*
7 – 9	41 *(60)*	59 *(86)*	31 *(146)*
10 – 11	31 *(47)*	69 *(104)*	32 *(151)*
12	37 *(30)*	63 *(51)*	17 *(81)*
13+	24 *(4)*	76 *(13)*	4 *(17)*
No answer	40 *(2)*	60 *(3)*	1 *(5)*
Programs and Classes			
Adult Basic Education	35 *(80)*	64 *(145)*	46 *(225)**
Employment Oriented	42 *(82)*	58 *(114)*	7 *(196)*
Youth Oriented Employment	59 *(17)*	41 *(12)*	2 *(29)*
High School Equivalency	39 *(46)*	61 *(73)*	25 *(119)*
Reading Development	70 *(35)*	30 *(15)*	13 *(50)*
Other	26 *(9)*	74 *(26)*	7 *(35)*

* Two of the respondents who attend Adult Basic Education Classes did not answer Question 15

Table 111 Use of Print Material and Communication Media (continued)
(expressed in percent)

d. Question 15: *Do you ever read comic books?*

Basic Social Characteristics	Yes	No	Total
Employment of Time			
Working Force			
White Collar	26 *(7)*	74 *(20)*	6 *(27)*
Clerical	29 *(10)*	71 *(24)*	7 *(34)*
Craft	28 *(11)*	72 *(28)*	8 *(39)*
Blue Collar	43 *(17)*	57 *(23)*	8 *(40)*
Service	36 *(28)*	64 *(49)*	16 *(77)*
Unemployed	39 *(12)*	61 *(19)*	6 *(31)*
Retired	7 *(1)*	93 *(12)*	3 *(13)*
Keeping House	33 *(30)*	57 *(62)*	19 *(92)*
School	39 *(45)*	61 *(75)*	25 *(120)*
Family Income			
$ 1 - 2,999	30 *(27)*	70 *(63)*	19 *(90)*
3,000 - 5,999	37 *(70)*	63 *(119)*	40 *(189)*
6,000 - 9,999	29 *(27)*	71 *(66)*	20 *(93)*
10,000 or more	34 *(21)*	66 *(40)*	13 *(61)*
No answer	36 *(16)*	64 *(28)*	9 *(44)*
Individual Income			
$ 0	26 *(5)*	74 *(14)*	4 *(19)*
1 - 2,999	37 *(60)*	63 *(100)*	34 *(160)*
3,000 - 5,999	31 *(49)*	69 *(110)*	33 *(159)*
6,000 - 9,999	33 *(17)*	67 *(34)*	11 *(51)*
10,000 or more	50 *(8)*	50 *(8)*	3 *(16)*
No answer	31 *(22)*	69 *(50)*	15 *(72)*
Adult New Reader Rating			
Very Active	--	--	--
Active	--	--	--
Somewhat Active	100 *(161)*	--	34 *(161)*
Least Active	--	100 *(316)*	66 *(316)*

Book Reading. Respondents were asked, "During the last six months, have you read any paperback or hard-cover books?" Although 31 percent had not read books, the 69 percent who had are considered in the context of this study to be book readers (table 112). A recent Gallup poll shows an increase of book readers in the U.S. population. In 1971, 26 percent said that they had read a book in the last month in comparison with 21 percent in 1958. The younger persons and those with more formal education were a higher percentage of readers. A majority of the respondents, 56 percent, felt that they liked paperbacks the same as hard-cover books; however a significant number, 20 percent, said that they preferred paperbacks to hard-cover books, and 16 percent preferred hard-cover books (table 113), a further indication, as in many instances, of variety of preferences to be considered. When specific titles read by the respondents are examined it is apparent that a majority of them are published in both formats.

Book readers also were asked, "About how many books have you read in the last six months?" Table 114 shows the distribution in the numerical categories of books read which range from one book read in the last six months by 14 percent of the adult new readers to 21 or more books, read by 7 percent. Two to five books is the average for half the readers, about one-fourth read between six and 20 books. As some research has shown, readers are more apt to underestimate the actual number of books read, consequently it may be that more books were read by LMRP respondents than the data show.

In order to make some comparisons with two earlier studies, the LMRP numerical categories are classified as closely as possible with those cited in the Survey Research Center (SRC) 1968 and Johnstone Adult Education 1962. Allowance must be made for the difference in period of time - for LMRP books read in the last six months - for the other two studies within the last year.

The major difference appears in the two categories of fewer books read - the percentage of LMRP readers in the one to four books category is 57 percent, in contrast to the SRC 36 percent and the Johnstone, 37 percent. Only 16 percent of LMRP respondents are in the five to fourteen category of books read, in contrast to SRC 32 percent and Johnstone 36 percent. An interesting aspect of the readers of 15 to 49 books and the 50 or more books category is that nearly the same percentages are found in all three studies. According to Ennis, book readers who read one to four books are light readers, 5 to 24 books are moderate readers, 25 or more books are heavy readers. According to these standards, over half the book readers in the LMRP study are light readers and one-third are moderate readers. It would seem that the measurement of moderate readers might have too large a numerical range. In the LMRP study the light reader, one to four books, correlates with the reading activity measurement of somewhat active reader who reads one to three books. On the other hand, the LMRP's active reader who reads four to nine books might be designated justifiably as a moderate reader. The LMRP very active reader who reads ten or more books - the maximum is 60 books - might be designated justifiably as a heavy reader (table 115).

A reclassification of number of books read makes possible a comparison between NORC Amalgam 1965 book readers and the LMRP book readers, holding education constant. Table 116 shows that the readers in the LMRP study read as much as the NORC Amalgam readers do. The percentages vary only slightly, with the greatest variance seen in the percentage of readers with less than a high school education who read one book, 12 percent of the NORC Amalgam and 19 percent of the LMRP Population Study. The percentage of readers with more than a high school education who read 21 or more books is 17 percent of the NORC Amalgam and only 8 percent of the LMRP Population Study.

Who are the book readers? Tables 117 to 125 show relation-ships between book reading and basic social characteristics of adult new readers. Slightly more women than men are book readers. Among the women, 20 percent had read within the last six months 11 or more books, which places them in the very active or heavy reader category. Little difference between men and women appears in the number of books read in categories from one to ten. As may be expected because of numerical dominance, more Black readers than white read books. In general, the Black respondents read more books; table 118 shows that a third are in the moderate to heavy categories of book readers. A higher percentage of white readers are in the two to five category of books read.

Fewer respondents in older age groups, 45 years of age and over had read books in the last six months, but those older, more active readers read more than younger respondents did.

Respondents with more education read more books. A signifi-cant difference beginning at the seventh grade of formal educa-tion is evident. It is evident also in the increased number of books read by respondents with more education. The data continue to support that education is a correlate of reading, and in par-ticular, of book reading. The importance of the achievement of variable literacy is reconfirmed because at this stage the reader can use more fully print media.

Occupation or employment of time seems to be a correlate of book reading. School is an obvious stimulus to use of books. A higher percentage of respondents in the white-collar, clerical, and service occupations are book readers. Over 50 percent of the white-collar group reads six or more books. It is noted that among the unemployed group of respondents, one-third read six or more books. Income also seems to make a difference in that those respondents with higher incomes, $10,000 and up, 42 percent, read six or more books. Those respondents with lower incomes do read, but they read fewer books. This analysis leaves many questions unanswered and demonstrates the need for additional analysis of the data.

Book readers were asked, "Thinking back over the last six months, could you name some of the books you have read completely or in part?" Table 126 a-g shows the findings relating to the answers to this question. Of the 330 respondents who had read books, 254 recalled specific book titles, and 54 who were unable to recall specific titles could identify 54 subjects. More than two= fifths identified one to two titles, about a third named three to four, and one-fourth identified five to six titles. Readers reporting one or two titles consistently reported incomplete or fragmentary titles which nevertheless were identifiable. Those reporting the higher number of titles consistently named correct titles and frequently authors, whereas those who did not name specific titles frequently named a magazine title or a subject.

It was possible to classify these specific titles reported into broad categories. Fiction titles, 167, and 110 non-fiction with biography predominate. Other categories include classics, reference and texts, children's, foreign language, health, and child care. Three categories of titles less frequently mentioned are religious, occult, and plays and poetry. The 356 titles thus reported represent a diversity and variety almost equal to the number of individual readers. They illustrate the extreme individuality of reading interests. In spite of this diversity, it is possible to identify general and well defined interests among the respondents. The titles most frequently read, a total of 33, and the authors most frequently mentioned by adult new readers are listed in table f and g respectively. They represent an interesting spectrum of popular and group interests. Of primary interest are the books about the Black experience and history, particularly biographical and autobiographical accounts. They are concerned with the immediate and the current issues and a search for identity. In striking contrast are the other popular titles, chiefly in the current best seller category. These include such titles as *The Valley of the Dolls, The Pimp, Baby and Child Care, Profiles in Courage,* and books about Martin Luther King, Jr. and John F. Kennedy.

The 24 authors who are mentioned most frequently, it would seem, have a consistent and strong appeal. Adult new readers are reading their works. Again may be seen the variability of reading illustrated in contrasting content, styles, and periods represented by such authors as James Baldwin, Ian Fleming, Homer, Langston Hughes, Jack London, Kyle Onstott, Harold Robbins, William Shakespeare, Mickey Spillane, and Richard Wright.

The types of books adult new readers like very much include short stories, novels, biography or autobiography, and historical books. Poetry also is liked very much by 20 percent of the respondents. Of little interest, expressed as not liked at all, are plays, scientific writing, and essays. Black readers appear to have much stronger preferences for the various types, except for scientific writings. Women prefer short stories and novels. Men prefer historical books as well as biographies, which appeal also to women (tables 127 , 128 , 129).

In choosing books they read or want to read, adult new readers usually see or hear about them from many sources which are shown in table 130 . The chief source for a majority of the respondents is friends. A second major source is school. Over a third hear about books from family, and slightly less than a third name the library and bookstore. Other sources such as newsstand and drugstore, radio or television, and church, are noted by respondents. The book club, as a source, is not used.

Although the sources from which adult new readers get the books they read are the same, a change in rank is noted. Friends remain the chief source of books for 38 percent of respondents. The library, school, and bookstore become sources from which books are obtained. Members of the family and newsstands or bookstands are also sources (table 131).

One measure of reading interest and activity is the ownership of books. Adult new readers were asked, "Do you have any books of your own?" A substantial majority, 84 percent, do have their own books. The subject areas are diverse and reflect the reading interests and informational needs that have been reported by respondents in several instances. Reference and religious books are owned by eight in ten of the respondents, five in ten own health and nutrition and Black history or stories about Black people.

Light reading is represented among a third or more of respondents who own books in several categories - adventure, crime and mystery, science fiction, sports, love and romance, and war. Women own more books about homemaking in subject areas of child care, health and nutrition, how to manage or budget money, and home decorating or furnishing. More men own books on crime and mystery, sports, adventure, war, building or making things, Although these subjects reflect interests and responsibilities because of sex, it is noted that men and women have similar interests and own books in the various subject areas (tables 132, 133, 134).

The purposes and reasons for reading indicate both practical and pleasure areas of reading. About half the respondents read for both pleasure and relaxation and for information. Nearly a third report that they read more for information, and 18 percent read more for pleasure and relaxation. Nearly everyone reads for reasons relating to education and learning, which is to be expected in the context of the sample of respondents. A large percentage also read to help with school work and learning. A majority read for employment reasons (tables 136 to 146).

Respondents were asked several questions about the use of books in relation to daily tasks and in the context of work or job, home life, club or group activites, and classes. Tables 137 to 146 show with what things books had helped, or in relation to which things special reading had been done. Books had been used to help "with anything" by 90 percent of the respondents. The particular uses in which they were of help are in concrete practical areas. Books were a help in school work or school studies to 63 percent of the respondents, and 58 percent found them helpful in improving and learning English, and in reading. Books were useful in the areas of homemaking and raising children for 47 percent of the respondents, and in job placement or job improvement and building and repairing things for 17 percent.

Tables 139 to 142 show the types of subject areas in which special reading was done by the respondents of whom 15 percent used reading materials to help prepare or improve work or job. Other types of reading were primarily for help in areas of health and vocational and technical jobs requiring manuals. In connection with family and home life responsibilities and interests, 30 percent of the respondents had done special reading. The usual homemaking subjects are noted with additional subjects of sex and hygiene. Two final areas in which special reading or help from reading materials were reported are in connection with club work and classes, 37 percent and 51 percent respectively. In both instances, the use would be stimulated by the activity and would be of a voluntary nature rather than required.

Table 112 Adult New Reader's Book Reading in Last Six Months
(expressed in percent)

Question 16: *During the last six months, have you read any paperback or hard-cover books?*

Yes	69 *(330)*
No	31 *(149)*
Total	100 *(479)*

Table 113 Preferences for Paperback Over Hard-cover *(expressed in percent)*

Question 22: *Comparing paperbacks to hard-cover books, would you say that you like paperbacks more, less or about the same as hard-cover books?*

Extent of Liking	
Same	56 *(267)*
More	20 *(96)*
Less	16 *(77)*
Don't know	8 *(39)*
Total	100 *(479)*

Table 114 Number of Books Read in the Last Six Months *(expressed in percent)*

Question 16A: *About how many books have you read in the last six months?*

One	14 *(45)*
2 - 5	50 *(165)*
6 - 10	16 *(52)*
11 - 20	10 *(35)*
21 or more	7 *(22)*
No answer	3 *(11)*
Total	100 *(330)*

Base = 330

Table 115 Number of Books Read *(expressed in percent)*

Number of Books Read	Survey Research Center (SRC) 1948*	Johnstone Adult Education (books read in last year) 1962**	LMRP (books read in last six month 1969
1 - 4	36	37	57
5 - 14	32	36	16
15 - 49	18	16	15
50 or more	14	11	12
Total	100 (1,151)	100 (2,845)	100 (319) ∷

(20 percent of the users account for 70 percent of the book use)

* Bernard Berelson, *THE LIBRARY'S PUBLIC,* (New York: Columbia University, 1949), p. 7.

** Philip H. Ennis, *ADULT BOOK READING IN THE UNITED STATES,* (Chicago: National Opinion Research Center, University of Chicago, 1965), p. 43

∷ Eleven respondents who answered Question 16 did not answer Question 16A.

Table 116 Number of Books Read in Last Six (6) Months, Among Readers Only, by Education *(expressed in percent)*

Number of Books Read	Education					
	Less than high school		High school or better		Total	
	NORC*	LMRP	NORC	LMRP	NORC	LMRP
One book	12	19	9	10	10	14
Two to five books	55	50	41	53	45	52
Six to ten books	14	17	20	16	18	16
Eleven to twenty books	9	8	13	13	12	11
Twenty-one or more books	10	6	17	8	15	7
Total	100 (209)	100 (134)	100 (503)	100 (181)	100 (712)	100 (315)∷

* NORC Almagam, 1965. Philip H. Ennis, *ADULT BOOK READING IN THE UNITED STATES*. (Chicago: National Opinion Research Center, University of Chicago, 1965), p. 42.

∷ Four respondents who answered Question 16A did not respond to the question on education, Question 34A.

Table 117 Book Reading by Adult New Reader, by Sex *(expressed in percent)*

Books Read	Sex	
	Male *(148)*	Female *(331)*
Yes	65 *(96)*	71 *(234)*
No	35 *(52)*	29 *(97)*

Number of Books Read, by Sex	Male *(96)*	Female *(234)*
1	13 *(12)*	14 *(33)*
2 - 5	49 *(47)*	50 *(118)*
6 - 10	17 *(16)*	15 *(36)*
11 - 20	7 *(7)*	12 *(28)*
21 or more	7 *(7)*	7 *(15)*
No answer	7 *(7)*	2 *(4)*

Table 118 Book Reading by Adult New Reader, by Race *(expressed in percent)*

Question 16: *During the last six months, have you read any paperback or hard-cover books?*

A: *About how many books have you read in the last six months?*

Books Read	Race	
	White *(123)*	Black *(353)*
Yes	63 *(77)*	70 *(250)*
No	37 *(46)*	30 *(103)*

Number of Books Read, by Race	White *(77)*	Black *(250)*
1	12 *(9)*	14 *(35)*
2 - 5	57 *(44)*	48 *(121)*
6 - 10	12 *(9)*	17 *(43)*
11 - 20	9 *(7)*	11 *(27)*
21 or more	5 *(4)*	7 *(17)*
No answer	5 *(4)*	3 *(7)*

Table 119 Book Reading by Adult New Reader, by Age *(expressed in percent)*

Question 16: *During the last six months, have you read any paperback or hard-cover books?*

A: *About how many books have you read in the last six months?*

Books Read	Age					
	16-24 *(111)*	25-34 *(148)*	35-44 *(101)*	45-54 *(66)*	55-64 *(31)*	65+ *(20)*
Yes	77 *(85)*	70 *(104)*	75 *(76)*	58 *(38)*	55 *(17)*	45 *(9)*
No	23 *(26)*	30 *(44)*	25 *(25)*	42 *(28)*	45 *(14)*	55 *(11)*

Number of Books Read, by Age	16-24 *(85)*	25-34 *(104)*	35-44 *(76)*	45-54 *(38)*	55-64 *(17)*	65+ *(9)*
1	12 *(10)*	11 *(11)*	12 *(9)*	26 *(10)*	12 *(2)*	34 *(3)*
2 - 5	51 *(43)*	53 *(55)*	52 *(40)*	47 *(18)*	41 *(7)*	28 *(2)*
6 - 10	15 *(13)*	15 *(16)*	16 *(12)*	16 *(6)*	23 *(4)*	11 *(1)*
11 - 20	12 *(10)*	10 *(10)*	12 *(9)*	5 *(2)*	6 *(1)*	22 *(2)*
21 or more	8 *(7)*	8 *(8)*	4 *(3)*	3 *(1)*	12 *(2)*	11 *(1)*
No answer	2 *(2)*	3 *(4)*	4 *(3)*	3 *(1)*	6 *(1)*	0 *(0)*

Table 120 Book Reading by Adult New Reader, by Amount of Formal
Education (expressed in percent)

Question 16: During the last six months, have you read any paperback
or hard-cover books?
A: About how many books have you read in the last six months?

Books Read	Education					
	0-4 (31)	5-6 (47)	7-9 (146)	10-11 (151)	12 (82)	13+ (17)
es	55 (17)	47 (22)	68 (100)	69 (105)	80 (66)	100 (17)
o	45 (14)	53 (25)	32 (46)	31 (46)	20 (16)	0 (0)

Number of Books Read, by Formal Education	0-4 (17)	5-6 (22)	7-9 (100)	10-11 (105)	12 (66)	13+ (17)
	24 (4)	26 (6)	16 (16)	10 (10)	10 (7)	12 (2)
- 5	29 (5)	50 (11)	51 (51)	55 (59)	47 (31)	35 (6)
- 10	18 (3)	9 (2)	18 (18)	17 (18)	12 (8)	18 (3)
1 - 20	5 (1)	5 (1)	8 (8)	9 (9)	20 (13)	12 (2)
1 or more	12 (2)	5 (1)	5 (5)	5 (5)	9 (6)	18 (3)
o answer	12 (2)	5 (1)	2 (2)	4 (4)	2 (1)	5 (1)

Table 121 Book Reading by Adult New Reader, by Employment *(expressed in percent)*

Question 16: *During the last six months, have you read any paperback or hard-cover books?*

A: *About how many books have you read in the last six months*

Books Read	Employment				
	White Collar *(27)*	Clerical *(34)*	Craft *(39)*	Blue Collar *(40)*	Service *(78)*
Yes	70 *(19)*	77 *(26)*	54 *(21)*	60 *(24)*	70 *(55)*
No	30 *(8)*	23 *(8)*	46 *(18)*	40 *(16)*	30 *(23)*

Number of Books Read, by Employment	White Collar *(19)*	Clerical *(26)*	Craft *(21)*	Blue Collar *(24)*	Service *(55)*
1	16 *(3)*	12 *(3)*	0 *(0)*	17 *(4)*	15 *(8)*
2 - 5	32 *(6)*	58 *(15)*	55 *(11)*	46 *(11)*	67 *(34)*
6 - 10	16 *(3)*	23 *(6)*	5 *(1)*	21 *(5)*	7 *(4)*
11 - 20	26 *(5)*	7 *(2)*	15 *(3)*	8 *(2)*	7 *(4)*
21 or more	5 *(1)*	0 *(0)*	20 *(4)*	4 *(1)*	7 *(4)*
No answer	5 *(1)*	0 *(0)*	5 *(1)*	4 *(1)*	2 *(1)*

Table 122 Book Reading by Adult New Reader, by Employment of Time
(expressed in percent)

Question 16: During the last six months, have you read any paperback
or hard-cover books?
A: About how many books have you read in the last six months?

Books Read	Employment of Time			
	Unemployed (31)	Retired (14)	Keeping House (92)	School (120)
Yes	68 (21)	43 (6)	64 (59)	80 (96)
No	32 (10)	57 (8)	36 (33)	20 (24)

Number of Books Read	Unemployed (21)	Retired (6)	Keeping House (59)	School (96)
1	14 (3)	17 (1)	17 (10)	12 (12)
2 - 5	48 (10)	17 (1)	46 (27)	51 (49)
6 - 10	23 (5)	17 (1)	17 (10)	18 (27)
11 - 20	9 (2)	17 (1)	13 (8)	9 (8)
21 or more	0 (0)	17 (1)	5 (3)	7 (7)
No answer	5 (1)	17 (1)	2 (1)	3 (3)

Table 123 Book Reading by Adult New Reader, by Family Income *(expressed in percent)*

Question 16: *During the last six months, have you read any paperback or hard-cover books?*
A: *About how many books have you read in the last six months*

Books Read	Family Income			
	$1-2,999 *(90)*	3,000-5,999 *(191)*	6,000-9,999 *(93)*	10,000 and up *(61)*
Yes	70 *(63)*	71 *(136)*	58 *(54)*	80 *(48)*
No	30 *(27)*	29 *(55)*	42 *(39)*	20 *(12)*

Number of Books Read, by Family Income	$1-2,999 *(63)*	3,000-5,999 *(136)*	6,000-9,999 *(54)*	10,000 and up *(48)*
1	21 *(13)*	12 *(16)*	14 *(8)*	10 *(3)*
2 - 5	44 *(28)*	52 *(71)*	54 *(28)*	44 *(21)*
6 - 10	18 *(11)*	15 *(20)*	14 *(8)*	17 *(8)*
11 - 20	11 *(7)*	8 *(11)*	7 *(4)*	19 *(9)*
21 or more	3 *(2)*	9 *(12)*	7 *(4)*	6 *(3)*
No answer	3 *(2)*	4 *(5)*	4 *(2)*	4 *(2)*

Table 124 Book Reading by Adult New Reader, by Individual Income
(expressed in percent)

Question 16: During the last six months, have you read any paperback
or hard-cover books?
A: About how many books have you read in the last six months?

Books Read	Individual Income			
	$0-2,999 (179)	3,000-5,999 (161)	6,000-9,999 (51)	10,000 and up (16)
Yes	70 (126)	68 (109)	70 (36)	63 (10)
No	30 (53)	32 (51)	30 (15)	37 (6)

Number of Books Read by Individual Income	$0-2,999 (126)	3,000-5,999 (109)	6,000-9,999 (36)	10,000 and up (10)
1	17 (21)	11 (12)	17 (6)	0 (0)
2 - 5	45 (57)	55 (60)	47 (17)	40 (4)
6 - 10	18 (23)	14 (15)	19 (7)	30 (3)
11 - 20	11 (14)	8 (8)	6 (2)	30 (3)
21 or more	6 (7)	9 (10)	3 (1)	0 (0)
No answer	3 (4)	3 (3)	8 (3)	0 (0)

Table 125 Use of Print Material and Communication Media *(expressed in percent)*

a. Question 16: *During the last six months, have you read any paperback or hardcover books?*

Basic Social Characteristics	Yes	No	Total
Sex			
Male	65 *(96)*	35 *(52)*	31 *(148)*
Female	71 *(234)*	29 *(97)*	69 *(331)*
Race			
White	63 *(77)*	37 *(46)*	26 *(123)*
Black	70 *(250)*	29 *(103)*	76 *(353)*
Other	100 *(3)*	0 *(0)*	⁑ *(3)*
Age (in years)			
16 - 24	77 *(85)*	23 *(26)*	23 *(111)*
25 - 34	70 *(104)*	30 *(44)*	31 *(148)*
35 - 44	75 *(76)*	25 *(25)*	21 *(101)*
45 - 54	58 *(38)*	42 *(28)*	14 *(66)*
55 - 64	55 *(17)*	45 *(14)*	6 *(31)*
65+	45 *(9)*	55 *(11)*	4 *(20)*
No answer	50 *(1)*	50 *(1)*	⁑ *(2)*
Education			
0 - 4	55 *(17)*	45 *(14)*	6 *(31)*
5 - 6	47 *(22)*	53 *(25)*	10 *(47)*
7 - 9	68 *(100)*	32 *(46)*	30 *(146)*
10 - 11	69 *(105)*	31 *(46)*	32 *(151)*
12	80 *(66)*	20 *(16)*	17 *(82)*
13+	100 *(17)*	0 *(0)*	4 *(17)*
No answer	60 *(3)*	40 *(2)*	1 *(5)*
Programs and Classes			
Adult Basic Education	70 *(160)*	30 *(69)*	58 *(227)*
Employment Oriented	77 *(152)*	23 *(44)*	49 *(196)*
Youth Oriented Employment	83 *(24)*	17 *(5)*	8 *(29)*
High School Equivalency	79 *(93)*	21 *(26)*	30 *(119)*
Reading Development	24 *(12)*	76 *(38)*	13 *(50)*
Other	71 *(25)*	29 *(10)*	9 *(35)*

⁑ The percentage is equal to less than 1%

Table 125 Use of Print Material and Communication Media (continued)
(expressed in percent)

a. Question 16: *During the last six months, have you read any paperback or hardcover books?*

Basic Social Characteristics	Yes	No	Total
Employment of Time			
Working Force			
White-Collar	70 *(19)*	30 *(8)*	6 *(27)*
Clerical	77 *(26)*	23 *(8)*	7 *(34)*
Craft	54 *(21)*	46 *(18)*	8 *(39)*
Blue-Collar	60 *(24)*	40 *(16)*	8 *(40)*
Service	70 *(55)*	30 *(23)*	16 *(78)*
Unemployed	68 *(21)*	32 *(10)*	6 *(31)*
Retired	43 *(6)*	57 *(8)*	3 *(14)*
Keeping House	64 *(59)*	36 *(33)*	19 *(92)*
School	80 *(96)*	20 *(24)*	25 *(120)*
Family Income			
$ 1 - 2,999	70 *(63)*	30 *(27)*	19 *(90)*
3,000 - 5,999	71 *(136)*	29 *(55)*	40 *(191)*
6,000 - 9,999	58 *(54)*	42 *(39)*	19 *(93)*
10,000 or more	80 *(48)*	20 *(13)*	3 *(61)*
No answer	66 *(29)*	34 *(15)*	9 *(44)*
Individual Income			
$ 0	53 *(10)*	47 *(9)*	4 *(19)*
1 - 2,999	73 *(116)*	27 *(44)*	33 *(160)*
3,000 - 5,999	69 *(109)*	31 *(51)*	33 *(160)*
6,000 - 9,999	70 *(36)*	30 *(15)*	11 *(51)*
10,000 or more	63 *(10)*	37 *(6)*	3 *(16)*
No answer	67 *(49)*	33 *(24)*	15 *(73)*
Adult New Reader Rating			
Very Active	100 *(65)*	0 *(0)*	14 *(65)*
Active	85 *(218)*	15 *(39)*	54 *(257)*
Somewhat Active	32 *(46)*	68 *(98)*	30 *(144)*
Least Active	7 *(1)* *	93 *(12)*	3 *(13)*

* The one inactive reader who claims to have read a book must have failed to respond to Question 16A

Table 126 Books Read by Adult New Reader

Question 17: *Thinking back over the last six months, could you name some of the books you have read completely or in part?*

a. Adult New Readers' Responses to Naming Specific Books Read within Last Six Months *(expressed in percent)*

Responses	94 *(311)*
No response	6 *(19)*
Total	100 *(330)*

Base = 330

b. Readers Reporting Specific Books Read Completely or in Part within Last Six Months

Specific book titles	254
Subjects	54
Magazine titles	3
No answer	19
Total	330

c. Readers Reporting Specific Books Read Completely or in Part
    within Last Six Months *(expressed in percent)*

Number of
Reported Titles

1 - 2	44 *(111)*
3 - 4	30 *(77)*
5 - 6	26 *(66)*
Total	100 *(254)*

Base = 254

d. Specific Titles Read by Adult New Reader, by Category

Category

Popular fiction	167
General non-fiction	56
Biography and autobiography	55
Classics	15
Reference and school texts	11
Childrens	11
Foreign language	11
Health and child care	9
Religious	8
Occult	7
Plays and poetry	6

Base = 254

e. Titles Dealing with Minority Cultures, by Category

Category

Spanish Culture	3
Black Culture	
Fiction	21
Biography and autobiography	32
General non-fiction	30
Plays and poetry	6

The Autobiography of Malcolm X by Malcolm X and Alex Haley

Soul On Ice by Eldridge Cleaver

The Holy Bible

Valley of the Dolls by Jacqueline Susann

Black Like Me by John H. Griffin

Martin Luther King, Jr. (books by and about)

Manchild in the Promised Land by Claude Brown

Peyton Place by Grace Metalious

The Pimp: The Story of My Life by Iceberg Slim [Robert Beck]

Rosemary's Baby by Ira Levin

Nigger: An Autobiography by Dick Gregory

To Sir, With Love by Edward R. Braithwaite

Airport by Arthur Hailey

Black Boy by Richard Wright

Baby and Child Care by Benjamin Spock

The Pearl by John Steinbeck

Pictorial History of the American Negro by Langston Hughes and
    Milton Meltzer

Gone With the Wind by Margaret Mitchell

Soul Brothers and Sister Lou by Kristin Hunter

Little Women by Louisa M. Alcott

Black Rage by William H. Grier and Price M. Cobbs

John F. Kennedy (books about)

The Arrangement by Elia Kazan

The Slave by Isaac B. Singer

Go Up For Glory by Bill Russell and William McSweeny

Invisible Man by Ralph Ellison

To Kill a Mockingbird by Harper Lee

Profiles in Courage by John F. Kennedy

Of Mice and Men by John Steinbeck

The Adventurers by Harold Robbins

The Learning Tree by Gordon Parks

From the Back of the Bus by Dick Gregory

The Love Machine by Jacqueline Susann

g. Authors Most Frequently Mentioned by Adult New Readers

Baldwin, James	*Another Country.* Dell
	Blues for Mr. Charlie. Dell
	Giovanni's Room. Dell
	Go Tell It on the Mountain. Dell
Bennett, Lerone B., Jr.	*Before the Mayflower: A History of the Negro in America 1619-1966.* Penguin
	Confrontation: Black and White. Penguin
	What Manner of Man: A Biography of Martin Luther King. Simon & Schuster
Cleaver, Eldridge	**Soul On Ice.* Dell
	Post-Prison Writings and Speeches. Random
Fleming, Ian	*Doctor No.* Signet
	From Russia with Love. Signet
	Goldfinger. Signet
	On Her Majesty's Secret Service. Signet
	You Only Live Twice. Signet
Gregory, Dick	**Dick Gregory from the Back of the Bus.* Dutton
	*Nigger: An Autobiography. Pocket Books
Hailey, Arthur	**Airport.* Bantam
	Hotel. Bantam
Hemmingway, Ernest	*For Whom the Bell Tolls.* Scribner
	The Sun Also Rises. Scribner
Homer	*Iliad.*
	Odyssey.
Hughes, Langston and (Meltzer, Milton)	*Best of Simple.* Hill and Wang
	Black Magic: A Pictorial History of the American Negro. Prentice-Hall
Jones, James	*From Here to Eternity.* Signet
	Go to the Widow-Maker. Dell

* Titles most frequently mentioned

London, Jack

Call of the Wild.

Great Short Works of Jack London.
Harper & Row

Malcolm X and Haley,
Alex

Autobiography of Malcolm X. Grove

Malcolm X Speaks. Grove

Metalious, Grace

Peyton Place. Pocket Books

Return to Peyton Place. Dell

Onstott, Kyle and
Horner, Lance

Mandingo. Fawcett World

Master of Falconhurst. Fawcett World

Black Sun. Fawcett World

Falconhurst Fancy. Fawcett World

Parks, Gordon

A Choice of Weapons. Noble & Noble

The Learning Tree. Fawcett World

Robbins, Harold

The Adventurers. Pocket Books

The Carpetbaggers. Pocket Books

Seventy-Nine Park Avenue. Pocket Books

Where Love Has Gone. Pocket Books

Shakespeare, William

Hamlet.

Macbeth.

Othello.

Romeo and Juliet.

The Taming of the Shrew.

mentioned only "Shakespeare"

Spillane, Mickey

Kiss Me, Deadly. Signet

My Gun Is Quick. Signet

"Mickey Spillane" mysteries

Steinbeck, John

The Grapes of Wrath. Bantam

Of Mice and Men. Bantam

The Pearl. Bantam

The Wayward Bus. Bantam

Susann, Jacqueline	*The Love Machine.* Bantam
	The Valley of the Dolls. Bantam
Wallace, Irving	*The Man.* Fawcett World
	The Plot. Pocket Books
Wright, Richard	*Black Boy.* Harper & Row
	Long Dream. Ace
	Native Son. Harper & Row
	The Outsider. Harper & Row
Yerby, Frank	*Goat Song.* Dial
	Pride's Castle. Pocket Books

Table 127 Extent of Interest in Types of Books *(expressed in percent)*

Question 45: *Now I want to know how you feel about particular kinds of books. For example, poetry. Do you like to read poetry books very much, a little, or not at all?*

Types of Books	Very Much	A Little	Not at All	No Answer
Poetry	23 (112)	38 (183)	38 (179)	1 (5)
Plays	19 (91)	35 (168)	45 (216)	1 (4)
Short Stories	53 (253)	32 (151)	14 (69)	1 (6)
Scientific writing	19 (91)	30 (143)	50 (239)	1 (6)
Essays	18 (88)	32 (151)	48 (232)	2 (8)
Novels	46 (222)	30 (145)	23 (108)	1 (4)
Biography or autobiography	57 (271)	35 (146)	12 (58)	1 (4)
Historical books	44 (209)	35 (168)	20 (97)	1 (5)

Table 128 Types of Books Liked Very Much by Adult New Reader, by Sex (Based on Question 45) *(expressed in percent)*

Types of Books	Sex	
	Male *(148)*	Female *(331)*
Poetry	16 *(23)*	27 *(89)*
Plays	15 *(21)*	21 *(70)*
Short stories	43 *(63)*	57 *(190)*
Scientific writings	27 *(39)*	16 *(52)*
Essays	12 *(17)*	21 *(71)*
Novels	37 *(54)*	51 *(168)*
Biography or auto-biography (that is, the lives of people)	52 *(77)*	58 *(194)*
Historical books	50 *(75)*	40 *(134)*

Table 129 Types of Books Liked Very Much by Adult New Reader, by Race
(Based on Question 45) *(expressed in percent)*

Types of Books	Race	
	White *(123)*	Black *(353)*
Poetry	19 *(23)*	25 *(89)*
Plays	15 *(18)*	21 *(73)*
Short stories	45 *(55)*	55 *(196)*
Scientific writings	27 *(33)*	16 *(57)*
Essays	11 *(14)*	21 *(74)*
Novels	39 *(47)*	49 *(174)*
Biography or auto-biography (that is, the lives of people)	45 *(55)*	61 *(214)*
Historical books	45 *(56)*	43 *(151)*

Table 130 Places Where Adult New Reader Chooses Books *(expressed in percent)*

Question 18A: *In choosing the books you've read or want to read, where do you usually see or hear about them?*

Friends	58 *(190)*
School	41 *(136)*
Member(s) of the family	36 *(118)*
Library	31 *(101)*
Bookstore	31 *(101)*
Newsstand or bookstand	26 *(86)*
Newspapers or magazines	20 *(65)*
Drugstore, grocery store, supermarket, 5 & 10 cent store	19 *(64)*
Radio or television	17 *(56)*
Church	8 *(28)*
Other	4 *(14)*
Book club	1 *(5)*
At work	1 *(4)*

Base = 330

Table 131 Places Where Adult New Reader Gets Books *(expressed in percent*

Question 18B: *Thinking back over the last six months, where did you get the books you read?*

Friends	38 *(123)*
Library	36 *(117)*
School	30 *(100)*
Bookstore	29 *(92)*
Member(s) of family	21 *(69)*
Newsstand or bookstand	19 *(64)*
Drugstore, grocery store supermarket, 5 & 10 cent store	16 *(51)*
Church	3 *(10)*
Newspapers or magazines	3 *(10)*
Radio or television	1 *(5)*
Other	5 *(16)*
Book club	1 *(5)*
At work	1 *(3)*

Base = 330

Table 132 Ownership of Books *(expressed in percent)*

Question 20: *Do you have any books of your own?*

Yes	84 *(402)*
No	16 *(77)*
Total	100 *(479)*

Table 133 Subject Areas of Book Ownership *(expressed in percent)*

Question 20A: If yes: *Are any of these books about....*

Subject Area	Yes	No
Reference book, like a dictionary or encyclopedia	89 *(356)*	11 *(43)*
Religious books, like the Bible	88 *(352)*	11 *(45)*
Cooking*	73 *(204)*	23 *(68)*
Health and nutrition	51 *(204)*	47 *(191)*
Black history or stories about black people	50 *(200)*	49 *(196)*
Sewing, knitting or crocheting*	49 *(138)*	45 *(127)*
Child care	41 *(166)*	57 *(228)*
Home decorating or furnishing	40 *(161)*	58 *(233)*
Adventure	40 *(158)*	59 *(238)*
Ways to better self (like how to get a better job)	38 *(151)*	60 *(244)*
Crime and mystery	35 *(137)*	64 *(259)*
Building or making things	34 *(136)*	64 *(259)*
Science fiction	34 *(134)*	64 *(259)*
Sports	32 *(129)*	67 *(267)*
Love and romance	32 *(128)*	66 *(266)*
War	29 *(118)*	69 *(276)*
How to manage or budget money	24 *(96)*	75 *(300)*

Base = 402

* Only asked if respondent was female. (Base = 282, the total number of women who owned books)

Table 134 Subject Areas of Book Ownership, by Sex *(expressed in percent)*

Subject Areas	Sex	
	Male *(148)*	Female *(331)*
Childcare	19 *(23)*	51 *(143)*
Health and nutrition	34 *(41)*	58 *(163)*
Love and romance	20 *(24)*	37 *(104)*
Crime and mystery	38 *(45)*	33 *(92)*
Science fiction	30 *(37)*	34 *(97)*
Black history or stories about black people	46 *(55)*	52 *(145)*
Sports	47 *(56)*	26 *(73)*
Adventure	43 *(52)*	38 *(106)*
War	35 *(42)*	27 *(76)*
How to manage or budget money	18 *(21)*	26 *(75)*
Ways to better self (like to get a better job)	36 *(43)*	38 *(108)*
Building or making things	47 *(56)*	28 *(80)*
Home decorating or furnishing	25 *(30)*	46 *(131)*
Reference book, like a dictionary or encyclopedia	88 *(105)*	89 *(251)*
Religious book, like the Bible	80 *(96)*	91 *(256)*
Sewing, knitting or crocheting	--	49 *(138)*
Cooking	--	72 *(204)*

Table 135 Purpose in Reading *(expressed in percent)*

Question 46: *When you read, do you read more for pleasure and relaxation, or more for information?*

Response		
Pleasure and relaxation	18	*(88)*
Information	31	*(147)*
Both	49	*(234)*
Do not know	2	*(10)*
Total	100	*(479)*

317

Table 136 Reasons for Reading *(expressed in percent)*

Question 21: *Here are some reasons people have for reading. Are any of these true for you?*

Reasons for Reading	
To help educate yourself	95 *(453)*
For enjoyment	88 *(420)*
To help with school work	83 *(397)*
To learn to do something	83 *(396)*
For employment	59 *(281)*

Table 137 Use of Books for Help "with anything" *(expressed in percent)*

Question 19: *Have you ever used books to help you with anything?*

Yes	90 *(433)*
No	10 *(46)*
Total	100 *(479)*

Table 138 Use of Books *(expressed in percent)*

Question 19A: If yes: *What things did they help you with?*

Particular Use	
School work, or school studies (tests in school, school subjects--science, geography, history, etc.)	63 *(278)*
Improving or learning English, reading ability and vocabulary	58 *(257)*
Homemaking, nutrition, meal planning (sewing, interior decorating, planning economical meals)	28 *(125)*
Raising children, family relations (better mother and/or wife)	19 *(88)*
Job placement or job improvement in present job or in another line of work	17 *(76)*
Building, making or repairing things (carpentry, automobiles, machinery, welding, etc.)	10 *(43)*
Other	5 *(20)*
Human relations	2 *(8)*
Medical information	1 *(7)*
Religion	1 *(5)*

Base = 433

Table 139 Reading in Relation to Work or Job *(expressed in percent)*

Question 24B: *Have you done any special reading to prepare for your present work, or to improve yourself on this job?*

Yes	15 *(74)*
No	30 *(142)*
No answer	55 *(263)*
Total	100 *(479)*

Table 140 Type of Reading Done in Relation to Work or Job *(expressed in percent)*

Question 24C: If Yes to B: *What reading have you done?*

Category	
Health: nurses training/aide, medicines, first aid, medical terminology.	27 *(20)*
Technical books: welding, wires, metal, oil burners, air conditioning, refrigeration, tools and machine, blueprint, electronic.	22 *(16)*
Manuals: training, science of job, vocational materials (unspecified).	15 *(11)*
Child care: growth and development of children. Homemaking: cooking, food.	12 *(9)*
Educational: lesson planning, teaching methods, counseling.	9 *(7)*
Basic or general education: reading, math, grammar.	9 *(7)*
Clerical/sales: secretary, clerical work, filing.	3 *(2)*
Other (list was kept by interviewers)	2 *(1)*
No answer	2 *(1)*

Base = 74

Table 141 Other Special Reading in Relation to Work *(expressed in percent)*

Question 24D: *In connection with your work, is there any (other) special reading you have to do?*

Yes	6 *(29)*
No	38 *(182)*
No answer	56 *(268)*
Total	100 *(479)*

Table 142 Type of Special Reading Done in Relation to Work
(expressed in percent)

Question 24E: If Yes to D: *What special reading do you have to do?*

Health: nurses training/aide; medicines; first aid; medical terminology.	21 *(6)*
Child care: growth and development of children, homemaking, cooking, foods.	17 *(5)*
Manuals: training, science of job, vocational materials (uspecified).	17 *(5)*
Educational: lesson planning; teaching methods, counseling.	9 *(3)*
Clerical/sales: secretary, clerical work, filing.	6 *(2)*
Basic or general education reading, math, grammar.	6 *(2)*
Technical books: welding, wires, metal, oil burners, air conditioning, refrigeration, tools and machine, blueprint, electronic.	3 *(1)*
Other (list was kept by interviewers)	9 *(3)*
Don't know, vague, irrelevant answers	6 *(2)*

Base = 29

Table 143 Reading for Home Life *(expressed in percent)*

Question 26   *In connection with your family and home life, is there any special reading you have done?*

Response	
Yes	30 *(142)*
No	70 *(336)*
No answer	⠆ *(1)*
Total	100 *(479)*

⠆ The percentage is equal to less than 1%

Table 144 Subject of Reading for Home Life *(expressed in percent)*

Question 26A   *If* Yes: *What kind of things about your home life or relationships with family and children did you want to read about?*

Subject	
Child care	48 *(68)*
Health	41 *(58)*
Homemaking, cooking	40 *(57)*
Family relationships	35 *(50)*
Sex, hygiene	27 *(38)*
Ethnic background (Black culture, Spanish, etc.)	25 *(36)*
Budgeting	23 *(32)*
Bible	13 *(19)*
Other	5 *(7)*

Base = 142

Table 145 Reading Done in Connection with Club *(expressed in percent)*

Question 27C: *In connection with your club or group activities, have you used any special information or help from reading materials?*

Yes	37 *(72)*
No	62 *(118)*
No answer	1 *(2)*
Total of the respondents who are members of a club	100 *(192)*

Table 146 Reading Influenced by Classes *(expressed in percent)*

Question 29: *Because of the things you learned in your class(es), did you go on to read any other things?*

Yes	51 *(203)*
No	49 *(190)*
No answer	° *(1)*
Total	100 *(394)*

Base = 394

° The percentage is equal to less than 1%

325

READERS' OPINIONS ABOUT 24 SELECTED BOOKS

A major objective in the survey of adult new readers was to gain information about the readers' opinions of a few selected books. These opinions, it was thought, would reflect to some degree the readers' interests in subjects and types of reading materials. Adult new readers who were interviewed in the survey responded to four questions about specific titles. The titles were grouped in four sets of six carefully selected books. The respondent was asked if he thought a specific title would be helpful or not, if he had read it or not, and if he had read it, whether he liked it very much, a little, or not at all.

The 24 titles included in the four questions were selected from a basic list established on the bases of information gained from the initial exploration, "Survey of Reading Materials Evaluated by Specialists in Selected Public Libraries," the popular titles reported by Fader in *Hooked on Books,* and the LMRP staff's knowledge about books and readers. Reader access to a majority of these titles was verified by an analysis of bibliographies published by 28 public libraries and agencies, for example, *Suggested Books for Beginning Adult Readers,* Reading Center's Project, Cleveland Public Library, 1967; *Bibliography of Materials for the Adult Basic Education Student,* U.S. Office of Education, Adult Education Programs, and the National University Extension Association.

The titles were selected on the basis of the following characteristics: subject appeal, accessibility, reading grade level, interest level, cultural significance, age group appeal, title self-explanatory (figure 3).

Books Thought to Be Helpful

The first question on selected titles brought together the practical books. Between 60 and 72 percent of the readers indicated that they had found, or would find helpful, the following books: *Health in the Later Years, Get Your Money's Worth, Write Your Own*

Figure 3 , Characteristics of
24 Selected Books Used in LMRP
Population Study Questionnaire

	Subject Appeal*	Accessibility*	Reading Grade Level (Gunning)	Interest Level-High	Interest Level-Low	Cultural Significance	Age Group Appeal	Title Self-Explanatory
LETTERS FROM VIETNAM	X**	X	NA**	X				X
PEREZ AND MARTINA	X	X	NA		X	X	Child	
THE HOLY BIBLE	X	X	NA	X				X
Reader's Digest books	X	X	6.5	X				X
HOT ROD	X	X	8.1	X			Young Adult	X
James Bond stories	X	X	4.4	X				X
Perry Mason mysteries	X	X	4.8	X				X
ABC'S OF HAND TOOLS	X	X	10.9					X
BLACK LIKE ME	X	X	7.7	X		X		X
DIANE'S NEW LOVE	X	X	7.0		X		Young Adult	X
SELECTED POEMS	X	X	NA	X		X		X
LOVE AND SEX IN PLAIN LANGUAGE		X	10.0	X			Young Adult	X
PROFILES IN COURAGE	X	X	14.7	X				X
THE AUTOBIOGRAPHY OF MALCOLM X	X	X	8.3	X		X		X

Characteristics of 24 Selected Books Used in LMRP Population Study Questionnaire (cont.)

Book	Subject Appeal	Accessibility*	Reading Grade Level (Gunning)	Interest Level-High	Interest Level-Low	Cultural Significance	Age Group Appeal	Title Self-Explanatory
PEOPLE AND PLACES	X	X	17.0	X				X
LIFE WITH THE LUCKETTS		X	4.4		X	X		
CALL THEM HEROES	X	X	6.4	X		X		X
UP FROM APPALACHIA		X	7.0			X	Young Adult	X
WRITE YOUR OWN LETTERS	X	X	NA					X
HEALTH IN THE LATER YEARS	X	X	17.0	X			Senior Citizen	X
SHANE	X	X	6.8					X
GETTING AND HOLDING A JOB	X	X	9.6	X				X
BABY AND CHILD CARE	X	X	9.8	X				X
GET YOUR MONEY'S WORTH	X	X	5.0	X				X

*Assumed to be accessible in library collections based on bibliographies published by libraries and agencies, (Appendix : Sources of Adult New Reader Material)

**X = Category Applies or NA = Not Applicable

Letters, Getting and Holding a Job, and *Baby and Child Care.* The
two most frequently read were *Baby and Child Care* and *Getting and
Holding a Job,* respectively by 26 and 10 percent of the respondents.
ABC'S of Hand Tools was the title found helpful by the least number
of respondents. Perhaps this reflects the bias of women who were
predominant in the survey of readers (table 147).

Books of Interest to Adult New Readers

The most frequently read books are the *Holy Bible* and the
Reader's Digest books, read respectively by 85 and 65 percent of
the respondents. Other most read titles are *The Autobiography of
Malcolm X* (25 percent), *Black Like Me* (23 percent), *Profiles in
Courage* (19 percent), James Bond stories (21 percent), and Perry
Mason mysteries (23 percent). The remaining eleven titles are
read by less than ten percent of the respondents.

Over 50 percent of the respondents, who have read the specific
book or author, express an interest in reading the following books:
Reader's Digest books (77 percent), *People and Places* (67 percent),
Black Like Me (67 percent), *Profiles in Courage* (73 percent), and
Perry Mason mysteries (55 percent).

Titles of particular interest to respondents who had *not* but
would like to read the books are: *Profiles in Courage* (54 percent),
People and Places (52 percent), *Black Like Me* (50 percent), *The
Autobiography of Malcolm X* (44 percent), and *Letters from Vietnam*
(42 percent).

Whenever a specific book has been read, the reader's reaction
usually has been favorable. Among the 24, 19 titles are liked very
much by over 50 percent of the respondents (table 151). The other
five titles which were less appealing are *Perez and Martina, Hot Rod,
Love and Sex in Plain Language, Life with the Lucketts,* and *Shane.*
In the application of the MAC Checklist, these titles are not found to
be as appropriate for the adult new reader because of varying factors.

Perez and Martina is a picture book designed for children; *Hot Rod* and *Love and Sex in Plain Language* have limited audience - the teenage reader. *Life with the Lucketts* contains values and attitudes which are offensive to some readers.

Table 147 Books Which the Adult New Reader Thinks Would Be Helpful
(expressed in percent)

Question 23 A. *Now I have the names of a few books. As I read each one, please tell me if you think it would be helpful, or not helpful to you.*

B. *Have you had a chance to read (NAME OF BOOK)?*

(a) *Write Your Own Letters: Simple Letters for Adults* by Jeannette B. Rosenfeld and Angelica W. Cass

	Helpful	Not helpful	Don't know	
Have read	8	✕	✕	8
Have not read	56	25	10	91

No answer 1
100 *(479)*

(b) *ABC'S OF HAND TOOLS* by General Motors, Public Relations Staff

	Helpful	Not helpful	Don't know	
Have read	6	0	✕	6
Have not read	38	43	12	93

No answer 1
100 *(479)*

(c) *HEALTH IN THE LATER YEARS* by Robert E. Rosenberg

	Helpful	Not helpful	Don't know	
Have read	6	✕	✕	6
Have not read	66	19	8	93

No answer 1
100 *(479)*

✕ The percentage is equal to less than 1%

331

(d)   *GET YOUR MONEY'S WORTH* by Aurelia Toyer

	Helpful	Not helpful	Don't know	
Have read	6	1	0	7
Have not read	65	18	9	92

No answer   1
100 *(479)*

(e)   *BABY AND CHILD CARE* by Benjamin Spock

	Helpful	Not helpful	Don't know	
Have read	23	3	⋇	26
Have not read	37	31	4	72

No answer   2
100 *(479)*

(f)   *GETTING AND HOLDING A JOB* by Bernard Schneider

	Helpful	Not helpful	Don't know	
Have read	10	⋇	0	10
Have not read	57	24	8	89

No answer   1
100 *(479)*

⋇ The percentage is equal to less than 1%

Table 148 Books in Which the Adult New Reader Expresses Interest
(expressed in percent)

Question 38 A. *Now I am going to read you the names of some more books. For each book, please tell me if you think you would like to read it or not.*

B. *Have you had a chance to read (NAME OF BOOK)?*

(a)   *CALL THEM HEROES* by New York City Board of Education

	Want to read	Would not want to read	
Have read	2	0	2
Have not read	39	57	96
		No answer	2
			100 *(479)*

(b)   *LOVE AND SEX IN PLAIN LANGUAGE* by Eric Johnson

	Want to read	Would not want to read	
Have read	5	∷	5
Have not read	37	56	93
		No answer	2
			100 *(479)*

(c)   Reader's Digest books

	Want to read	Would not want to read	
Have read	64	1	65
Have not read	13	19	32
		No answer	3
			100 *(479)*

∷ The percentage is equal to less than 1 %

(d) *LETTERS FROM VIETNAM* edited by Bill Adler

	Want to read	Would not want to read	
Have read	5	ӿ	5
Have not read	42	52	94
		No answer	1
			100 *(479)*

(e) *PEOPLE AND PLACES* by Margaret Mead

	Want to read	Would not want to read	
Have read	7	ӿ	7
Have not read	52	39	91
		No answer	2
			100 *(479)*

(f) *THE HOLY BIBLE*

	Want to read	Would not want to read	
Have read	83	2	85
Have not read	5	7	12
		No answer	3
			100 *(479)*

ӿ The percentage is equal to less than 1 %

Table 149 Books in Which the Adult New Reader Expresses Interest
(expressed in percent)

Question 44 A. *Now I have the names of a few more books. For each book, please tell me if you think you would like to read it or not.*

B. *Have you had a chance to read (NAME OF BOOK)?*

(a) *UP FROM APPALACHIA* by Charles Raymond

	Want to read	Would not want to read	
Have read	2	፠	2
Have not read	23	73	96
		No answer	2
			100 *(479)*

(b) *THE AUTOBIOGRAPHY OF MALCOLM X* with the assistance of Alex Haley

	Want to read	Would not want to read	
Have read	23	፠	23
Have not read	44	32	76
		No answer	1
			100 *(479)*

(c) *PEREZ AND MARTINA, A PORTORICAN FOLK TALE* by Pura Belpré

	Want to read	Would not want to read	
Have read	1	፠	1
Have not read	20	78	98
		No answer	1
			100 *(479)*

፠ The percentage is equal to less than 1%

(d)   *BLACK LIKE ME* by John Griffin

	Want to read	Would not want to read	
Have read	23	ⅹ	23
Have not read	50	26	76

No answer   1
100 *(479)*

(e)   *SELECTED POEMS* by Langston Hughes

	Want to read	Would not want to read	
Have read	8	0	8
Have not read	37	54	91

No answer   1
100 *(479)*

(f)   *PROFILES IN COURAGE* by John F. Kennedy

	Want to read	Would not want to read	
Have read	19	ⅹ	19
Have not read	54	26	80

No answer   1
100 *(479)*

ⅹ The percentage is equal to less than 1%

Table 150 Books in Which the Adult New Reader Expresses Interest
(expressed in percent)

Question 47 A. *Here is the last list of book names. Again, for each book, will you tell me if you think you would like to read it or not.*

B. *Have you had a chance to read (NAME OF BOOK)??*

(a) *DIANE'S NEW LOVE* by Betty Cavanna

	Want to read	Would not want to read	
Have read	∷	∷	∷
Have not read	24	75	99
		No answer	1
			100 *(479)*

(b) James Bond stories by Ian Fleming

	Want to read	Would not want to read	
Have read	20	1	21
Have not read	29	48	77
		No answer	2
			100 *(479)*

(c) *HOT ROD* by Henry Felsen

	Want to read	Would not want to read	
Have read	2	∷	2
Have not read	12	85	97
		No answer	2
			100 *(479)*

∷ The percentage is equal to less than 1%

Table 150 Books in Which the Adult New Reader Expresses Interest (Question 47A) (continued)

(d) *SHANE* by Jack Scheafer

	Want to read	Would not want to read	
Have read	10	✕	10
Have not read	25	63	88
		No answer	2
			100 *(479)*

(e) Perry Mason mysteries by Erle Stanley Gardner

	Want to r read	Would not want to read	
Have read	22	1	23
Have not read	33	43	76
		No answer	1
			100 *(479)*

(f) *LIFE WITH THE LUCKETTS* by Phyllis Morris

	Want to read	Would not want to read	
Have read	1	0	1
Have not read	16	82	98
		No answer	1
			100 *(479)*

✕ The percentage is equal to less than 1%

Table 151 Titles "liked very much" by Adult New Reader, Based on Questions 23C, 38C, 44C, and 47C *(expressed in percent)*

Diane's New Love	100 *(3)**
Baby and Child Care	86 *(128)*
Profiles in Courage	85 *(94)*
The Holy Bible	84 *(419)*
Black Like Me	83 *(110)*
Selected Poems	82 *(40)*
The Autobiography of Malcolm X	81 *(108)*
Getting and Holding a Job	81 *(52)*
Perry Mason mysteries	78 *(104)*
Reader's Digest books	76 *(311)*
ABC'S of Hand Tools	76 *(28)*
Health in the Later Years	75 *(32)*
Write Your Own Letters	71 *(49)*
James Bond stories	66 *(102)*
Call Them Heroes	62 *(8)*
Up from Appalachia	60 *(10)*
Get Your Money's Worth	58 *(31)*
Letters from Vietnam	54 *(24)*
People and Places	53 *(34)*

* The number in parentheses is the number of respondents who have read the book.

Table 152 Readers' Opinions about 24 Selected Books *(expressed in percent)*

Questions 23C, 38C, 44C, 47C If Yes to B: *How did you like (NAME OF BOOK) -- very much, a little, or not at all?*

	Very much	Little	Not at all
LETTERS FROM VIETNAM	54 *(13)*	42 *(10)*	4 *(1)*
PEREZ AND MARTINA	43 *(3)*	43 *(3)*	14 *(1)*
THE HOLY BIBLE	84 *(353)*	15 *(59)*	∷ *(2)*
Reader's Digest books	76 *(234)*	23 *(72)*	1 *(4)*
HOT ROD	50 *(5)*	50 *(5)*	0 *(0)*
James Bond stories	66 *(67)*	28 *(29)*	6 *(6)*
Perry Mason mysteries	78 *(81)*	19 *(20)*	3 *(3)*
ABC'S OF HAND TOOLS	76 *(22)*	21 *(6)*	3 *(1)*
BLACK LIKE ME	83 *(91)*	17 *(19)*	0 *(0)*
DIANE'S NEW LOVE	100 *(3)*	0 *(0)*	0 *(0)*
SELECTED POEMS	82 *(33)*	18 *(7)*	0 *(0)*
LOVE AND SEX IN PLAIN LANGUAGE	48 *(12)*	44 *(11)*	8 *(2)*
PROFILES IN COURAGE	85 *(80)*	14 *(13)*	1 *(1)*
THE AUTOBIOGRAPHY OF MALCOLM X	81 *(88)*	18 *(19)*	1 *(1)*
PEOPLE AND PLACES	53 *(18)*	44 *(15)*	3 *(1)*
LIFE WITH THE LUCKETTS	50 *(3)*	50 *(3)*	0 *(0)*
CALL THEM HEROES	62 *(5)*	38 *(3)*	0 *(0)*
UP FROM APPALACHIA	60 *(6)*	40 *(4)*	0 *(0)*
WRITE YOUR OWN LETTERS	71 *(29)*	27 *(11)*	2 *(1)*
HEALTH IN THE LATER YEARS	75 *(24)*	25 *(8)*	0 *(0)*
SHANE	72 *(36)*	24 *(12)*	4 *(2)*
GETTING AND HOLDING A JOB	81 *(42)*	19 *(10)*	0 *(0)*
BABY AND CHILD CARE	86 *(110)*	13 *(17)*	1 *(1)*
GET YOUR MONEY'S WORTH	58 *(18)*	32 *(10)*	7 *(2)*

∷ The percentage is equal to less than 1%

Notes

1. Louis Harris, "But Do We Like What We Watch," *Life,* 71 (Sept. 10, 1971): 42.

2. Ibid.

3. *News For You* (Syracuse, N.Y.: Laubach Literacy, Inc.).

4. *New York,* 4 (May 24, 1971): 3.

5. Jack Deacy, "What the Big Dailies Don't Tell You About What's Going On In the City," *New York,* 4 (May 24, 1971): 44.

6. Taher A. Rasik, "A Study of American Newspaper Readability," *Journal of Communication,* 19 (Dec. 1969): 317-324.

7. *Publishers' Weekly,* 199 (March 1, 1971): 28.

9.

READING BEHAVIOR AND PATTERNS

Reading Developmental Patterns

A particular concern in the survey of readers has been to learn about the developmental reading patterns of the adult new reader, his perception of his own reading behavior, and his comparison of his reading behavior with that of others, such as parents and friends. Several questions were asked that related to his attitude toward reading and the amount or extent of his reading at different periods in his life. The data are analyzed in relation to how he felt about reading and how much he read during four designated periods of his life: as a child through the age of 12; between the ages of 12 and 19; now; and during most of his adult years, between the ages of 20 and now. The analysis of data is summarized in tables 153 and 171 . A special analysis of data further summarizes this interesting information and compares it with similar data collected by Ennis who has assisted in the special analysis.

Table 153 Experienced Periods in Life of Little Reading *(expressed in percent)*

Question 31: *Have there been any periods in your life when you read very little or not at all?*

Yes	70 *(333)*
No	30 *(145)*
No answer	⁑ *(1)*
Total	100 *(479)*

⁑ The percentage is equal to less than 1%

Table 154 Period in Life When Read Very Little *(expressed in percent)*

Question 31A: If Yes: *When was this? Do you remember at what age?*

Period in Life	
Under 12	16 *(52)*
12 - 16	24 *(80)*
17 - 20	25 *(85)*
21 - 29	18 *(59)*
30 - 44	8 *(25)*
45 - 64	3 *(11)*
65 and over	0 *(0)*
No answer	6 *(21)*

Base = 333

Table 155 Period in Life When Read the Most *(expressed in percent)*

Question 32: *At what times in your life have you read the most?*

Period in Life	
Under 12	4 *(17)*
12 - 16	19 *(91)*
17 - 20	19 *(94)*
21 - 29	25 *(119)*
30 - 44	20 *(96)*
45 - 64	8 *(37)*
65 and over	1 *(6)*
No answer	4 *(19)*
Total	100 *(479)*

Table 156 Attitude Toward Reading at Different Periods in Life
(expressed in percent)

Question 36: *Some people have felt different about reading at different times in their life.*

Period in Life	Like A Lot	Like A Little	Not Very Interested
A: *When you were a child--through the age of 12--how did you feel about reading?*	38 (182)	30 (144)	32 (151)
B: *Between the ages of 12 and 19, how did you feel about reading?*	41 (198)	39 (187)	20 (94)
C: *How about now?*	69 (329)	25 (121)	6 (27)
D: If applicable, (R is over 20): *During most of your adult years--between the ages of 20 and now, how did you feel about reading?* *	62 (261)	31 (131)	6 (23)

* 60 respondents were under 20.

Table 157 Attitude Toward Reading: Like a Lot, by Sex *(expressed in percent)*

Period in Life (in years)	Sex	
	Male *(148)*	Female *(331)*
Under 12	26 *(38)*	44 *(144)*
12 - 19	34 *(50)*	45 *(148)*
Now	69 *(102)*	69 *(227)*
20 and over	54 *(72)**	64 *(189)***

* 25 males were 20 years of age or under.

** 35 females were 20 years of age or under.

Table 158 Attitude Toward Reading: Like a Lot, by Age *(expressed in percent)*

Period in Life	Age					
	16-24 *(111)*	25-34 *(148)*	35-44 *(101)*	45-54 *(66)*	55-64 *(31)*	65+ *(20)*
Under 12	33 *(37)*	37 *(55)*	44 *(44)*	44 *(29)*	32 *(10)*	30 *(6)*
12 - 19	53 *(59)*	35 *(52)*	44 *(45)*	39 *(26)*	32 *(10)*	25 *(5)*
Now	64 *(71)*	73 *(108)*	73 *(73)*	68 *(45)*	65 *(20)*	55 *(11)*
20 and over	51 *(26)**	70 *(104)*	61 *(62)*	56 *(37)*	71 *(22)*	45 *(9)*

* 60 respondents in the 16-24 age group are over 20.

Table 159 Attitude Toward Reading: Not Very Interested, by Sex
(expressed in percent)

Period in Life (in years)	Sex	
	Male (148)	Female (331)
Under 12	45 (67)	25 (84)
12 - 19	26 (38)	17 (56)
Now	7 (10)	5 (17)
20 and over	10 (12)*	4 (11)**

* 25 males were 20 years of age or under.

** 35 females were 20 years of age or under.

Table 160 Attitude Toward Reading: Not Very Interested, by Age
(expressed in percent)

Period in Life (in years)	Age (in years)					
	16-24 (111)	25-34 (148)	35-44 (101)	45-54 (66)	55-64 (31)	65+ (20)
Under 12	33 (37)	32 (48)	27 (27)	29 (19)	36 (11)	40 (8)
12 - 19	6 (7)	24 (35)	16 (16)	21 (14)	32 (10)	55 (11)
Now	6 (6)	5 (7)	6 (6)	3 (2)	3 (1)	25 (5)
20 and over	0 (0)	5 (7)	7 (7)	8 (5)	3 (1)	15 (3)

Table 161 Attitude Toward Reading: As a Child (less than 12 years of age), by Book Reading *(expressed by percent)*

	Read Books		
	Yes	No	
Like a lot	28	10	38
Like a little	40	21	61
	68	31	99 *(477)*
		No answer	1 *(2)*
			100 *(479)*

Table 162 Attitude Toward Reading: As a Teenager (12-19 years of age), by Book Reading *(expressed in percent)*

	Read Books		
	Yes	No	
Like a lot	32	9	41
Like a little	37	22	59
	69	31	100 *(479)*

Table 164 Amount of Reading at Different Periods in Life *(expressed in percent)*

Question 37: *Now we are interested in how much you have read at different times in your life.*

Period in Life	A Good Deal	Some	Hardly
A: *When you were a child --through the age of 12--how much did you read?*	30 *(144)*	41 *(196)*	28 *(138)*
B: *Between the ages of 12 and 19, how much did you read?*	36 *(174)*	44 *(211)*	19 *(90)*
C: *What about now?*	58 *(280)*	33 *(159)*	8 *(36)*
D: *If applicable (R is over 20): During your adult years--between the ages of 20 and now, how much did you read?**	54 *(226)*	38 *(157)*	7 *(30)*

* 60 respondents were under 20.

Table 163 Attitude Toward Reading: Now, by Book Reading *(expressed in percent)*

	Read Books Yes	No	
Like a lot	53	15	68
Like a little	15	16	31
	68	31	99 *(477)*
		No answer	1 *(2)*
			100 *(479)*

Table 165 Amount of Reading: A Good Deal, by Sex *(expressed in percent)*

	Sex	
Period in Life (in years)	Male *(148)*	Female *(331)*
Under 12	19 *(28)*	35 *(116)*
12 - 19	30 *(44)*	39 *(130)*
Now	57 *(85)*	59 *(195)*
20 and over	49 *(60)**	56 *(166)***

* 25 males were 20 years of age or under.

** 35 females were 20 years of age or under.

Table 166 Amount of Reading: A Good Deal, by Age *(expressed in percent)*

Period in Life	Age (in years)					
	16-24 *(111)*	25-34 *(148)*	35-44 *(101)*	45-54 *(66)*	55-64 *(31)*	65+ *(20)*
Under 12	30 *(33)*	28 *(41)*	32 *(32)*	35 *(23)*	29 *(9)*	25 *(5)*
12 - 19	48 *(53)*	32 *(47)*	36 *(36)*	35 *(23)*	29 *(9)*	25 *(5)*
Now	58 *(65)*	61 *(91)*	64 *(65)*	50 *(33)*	48 *(15)*	50 *(10)*
20 and over	49**(25)*	61 *(90)*	54 *(55)*	45 *(30)*	58 *(18)*	35 *(7)*

* 60 respondents were under 20

Table 167 Amount of Reading: Hardly Any, by Sex *(expressed in percent)*

Period in Life	Male (148)	Female (331)
Under 12	38 (57)	24 (79)
12 - 19	37 (37)	53 (53)
Now	9 (13)	7 (23)
20 and over	12 (15)*	5 (15) **

* 25 males were 20 years of age or under.

** 35 females were 20 years of age or under.

Table 168 Amount of Reading: Hardly Any, by Age *(expressed in percent)*

Period in Life (in years)	Age in Years					
	16-24 (111)*	25-34 (148)	35-44 (101)	45-54 (66)	55-64 (31)	65+ (20)
Under 12	27 (30)	30 (44)	26 (26)	29 (19)	29 (9)	35 (7)
12 - 19	7 (8)	20 (29)	20 (20)	23 (15)	29 (9)	45 (9)
Now	8 (9)	6 (9)	5 (5)	9 (6)	13 (4)	15 (3)
20 and over	8 (4)	5 (8)	6 (6)	9 (6)	6 (2)	20 (4)

* All bases are weighted

Note: 60 respondents are under 20

351

Table 169 Amount of Reading: As a Child (less than 12 years of age), by Book Reading *(expressed in percent)*

	Read Books		
	Yes	No	
A good deal	23	7	30
Some	45	24	69
	68	31	99 *(476)*
		No answer	1 *(3)*
			100 *(479)*

Table 170 Amount of Reading: As a Teenager (12-19 years of age), by Book Reading *(expressed in percent)*

	Read Books		
	Yes	No	
A good deal	29	7	36
Some	40	23	63
	69	30	99 *(475)*
		No answer	1 *(4)*
			100 *(479)*

Table 171 Amount of Reading: Now, by Book Reading *(expressed in percent)*

Read Books

	Yes	No	
A good deal	47	11	58
Some	21	20	41
	68	31	99 *(475)*

No answer 1 *(4)*

100 *(479)*

Reading developmental patterns in the special analysis which follows are derived from the data based on answers to the question, "Now we are interested in *how much* you have read at different times in your life. A. When you were a child - through the age of 12 - how much did you read? Would you say a good deal, you read some, or you hardly read at all?" and "B. Between the ages of 12 and 19, how much did you read? Would you say you read a good deal, you read some, or you hardly read at all?" These two questions confront each other for reading up to age 12 and reading up to age 18. The LMRP results are compared with Ennis' earlier study which compares the extent of reading at comparable ages for a group of college graduates. Yes equals a good deal and No equals some and hardly at all.

Reading to Age 12

	Yes	No	
Reading to Age 19 Yes	19 *(93)*	17 *(51)*	36 *(144)*
No	11 *(81)*	53 *(254)*	64 *(335)*
	30 *(174)*	70 *(305)*	100 *(479)*

Elementary School[1]

	Yes	No	
High School Yes	23	24	47
No	2	51	53
	25	75	100 *(872)*

Note that both LMRP group and the college educated group had a similar level of reading up to age 12 -- 25 percent for the college group and 30 percent for LMRP new readers. Then by the end of high school there is seen the losses of readers among the LMRP group.

The next pair of tables shows LMRP group and their reading patterns as they change from age 19 to the present compared to the college group (19 years to the time in college). Note especially the fact that the college group is picking up readers -- 24 percent starters and 2 percent deserters compared to 17 percent starters and 11 percent deserters for the LMRP group.

Reading to Age 19

		Yes	No	
		Yes	No	
Reading Now	Yes	29	39	68
	No	8	24	32
		37	63	100 (479)

High School^2

		Yes	No	
College	Yes	43	31	74
	No	4	22	26
		47	53	100 (872)

The current level of LMRP group is almost that of the college group when they were in college, but again there is a greater slippage, losing readers faster than they are gaining them, but not as greatly divergent compared to the earlier age. This must reflect the impact of the programs in which they have been participating.

The next table combines for LMRP group the reading before
age 12 and age 19 -- reading at either time makes the person
an early reader -- and compares it to current reading. This table is
contrasted with one from a national study of people with less
than a high school education.

Early Reading
(To Age 19)

		Yes	No	
	Yes	37	32	69
Current				
	No	10	21	31
		47	53	100 *(479)*

Less than
High School
Early Reading [3]

		Yes	No	
	Yes	19	11	30
Current Reading				
	No	28	42	70
		47	53	100 *(686)*

The parallels are interesting. The two samples have identical
early rates of reading (47 percent). LMRP readers however have
reversed the ratios of deserters (31 percent) to late starters (69
percent) compared to the population as a whole (70 to 80 percent).
Also the ratios of regular readers to non-readers are reversed. The
combination results in a rate of current reading double the national
sample. LMRP sample held almost 80 per cent of its early readers
while the national sample held only about 40 percent of its early

readers. Then among the early non-readers the LMRP sample converted about 60 per cent into current readers while the national sample only got about 20 per cent of early non-readers into current readers. How much of this has to do with the sample of selected persons who are readers and who might be more motivated to read, and how much it was dependent on the impact of the programs is impossible to tell. The implications of these data are not clear without further analysis.

Adult New Reader's Perception of His Reading

The analysis of the data concerned directly with the adult new reader's perception of his reading is summarized in charts 18 to 22, and tables 172 to 184. It is noted that over half of the respondents considered that they had reading problems and over two-thirds felt that they had overcome these problems. The majority felt that they were fair readers. Nearly two-thirds felt that they read more than their parents. Over a third read more than their friends and another third read less. A significant percentage, 61 percent, read aloud to other people and particularly to children, and some read to a husband or wife, friends, parents, and other relatives. The respondents are able to evaluate and compare their reading with those close to them.

Chart 18 Reading Problems of Adult New Readers

Question 33: *Have you had any kind of reading problems that you have had to overcome?*

TOTAL SAMPLE

| YES: 55% | NO: 45% | (N=479) |

BY SEX

Male | YES: 56% | NO: 44% | (N=148)

Female | YES: 54% | NO: 46% | (N=331)

BY RACE

Black | YES: 56% | NO: 44% | (N=353)

White | YES: 53% | NO: 47% | (N=122)

BY AGE

16-24 | YES: 54% | NO: 46% | (N=111)

25-34 | YES: 55% | NO: 45% | (N=148)

35-44 | YES: 50% | NO: 50% | (N=101)

45-54 | YES: 60% | NO: 40% | (N=65)

55-64 | YES: 58% | NO: 42% | (N=31)

BY FORMAL EDUCATION

Grade

0-4 | YES: 78% | NO: 22% | (N=31)

5-6 | YES: 74% | NO: 26% | (N=46)

7-9 | YES: 61% | NO: 39% | (N=145)

10-11 | YES: 51% | NO: 49% | (N=151)

12 | YES 38% | NO: 62% | (N=82)

Chart 19 Adult New Readers Who Have Overcome Reading Problems
(expressed in percent)

Question 33A: If Yes: *Did you overcome these problems?*

TOTAL SAMPLE

| YES: 68% | NO: 32% | (N=261) |

BY SEX

Male

| YES: 62% | NO: 38% | (N=82) |

Female

| YES: 69% | NO: 31% | (N=179) |

BY RACE

Black

| YES: 71% | NO: 29% | (N=196) |

White

| YES: 57% | NO: 43% | (N=64) |

BY AGE

16-24

| YES: 71% | NO: 29% | (N=59) |

25-34

| YES: 64% | NO: 36% | (N=80) |

35-44

| YES: 70% | NO: 30% | (N=59) |

45-54

| YES: 77% | NO: 33% | (N=39) |

55-64

| YES: 56% | NO: 44% | (N=18) |

BY FORMAL EDUCATION

Grade
0-4

| YES: 63% | NO: 37% | (N=29) |

5-6

| YES: 61% | NO: 39% | (N=32) |

7-9

| YES: 63% | NO: 37% | (N=89) |

10-11

| YES: 75% | NO: 25% | (N=75) |

12

| YES: 71% | NO: 29% | (N=31) |

Question 50:   *Would you say that you read a great deal, some, a
               little, or hardly anything?*

Evaluation of Amount of Reading	
A great deal	42 (202)
Some	35 (169)
A little	17 (82)
Hardly any	5 (25)
No answer	∺ (1)
Total	100 (479)

∺ The percentage is equal to less than 1%

Chart 20 Self-Evaluation of Reading Skills

Question 51:   *Would you say you are a good reader, a fair
               reader, or a poor reader?*

Good	30% (145)
Fair	54% (261)
Poor	14% (65)
Don't know	2% (7)

Chart 21 Self-Evaluation of Reading Skills, by Use of Media
          (expressed in percent)

Self-
Evaluation   Television
    Good   YES: 92%

    Fair   YES: 91%

    Poor   YES: 83%

                                Radio
    Good   YES: 96%

    Fair   YES: 97%

    Poor   YES: 88%

                              Newspapers
    Good   YES: 97%

    Fair   YES: 95%

    Poor   YES: 75%

                               Magazines
    Good   YES: 94%

    Fair   YES: 90%

    Poor   YES: 66%

                                Books
    Good   YES: 79%

    Fair   YES: 70%

    Poor   YES: 37%

                              Own Books
    Good   YES: 89%

    Fair   YES: 84%

    Poor   YES: 69%

Table 173 Evaluation of Reading Skills (Self-Perception), by Adult New Reader Activity Rating (expressed in percent)

Evaluation of Reading Skills	Adult New Reader Activity Rating			
	Least Active	Somewhat Active	Active	Very Active
Good	15 (2)	19 (27)	33 (84)	49 (32)
Fair	23 (3)	54 (78)	58 (150)	46 (30)
Poor	62 (8)	26 (37)	7 (18)	3 (2)
Don't know	0 (0)	1 (2)	2 (4)	2 (1)
No answer	0 (0)	0 (0)	⁑ (1)	0 (0)
Total	100 (13)	100 (144)	100 (257)	100 (65)

⁑ The percentage is equal to less than 1%

Table 174 Other Than School Reading When a Child (expressed in percent)

Question 52: When you were a child, did you read any books besides those in school?

Yes	56 (266)
No	44 (210)
No answer	⁑ (3)
Total	100 (479)

⁑ The percentage is equal to less than 1%

Table 175 Active Reading of Friends When a Child *(expressed in percent)*

Question 53: *When you were a child, did you have any close friends who read a lot?*

Yes	48	*(231)*
No	29	*(137)*
Don't know	23	*(111)*
Total	100	*(479)*

Chart 22 Frequency of Being Read to When a Child

Question 54: *Do you recall your parents or other relatives reading to you at home when you were a child?*

0	10	20	30	40	50	60	70	80

Yes ▓▓▓▓▓▓▓▓▓▓▓▓▓▓▓▓▓▓▓▓▓▓▓▓▓▓ 62% *(297)*

No ▓▓▓▓▓▓▓▓▓▓▓▓ 38% *(182)*

Question 54A: *Would you say they read to you very often, fairly often, or only occasionally?*

Very often ▓▓▓▓▓▓▓▓ 31% *(92)*

Fairly often ▓▓▓▓▓▓▓▓ 33% *(96)*

Occasionally ▓▓▓▓▓▓▓▓ 36% *(107)*

Table 176 Reading Other Than in School When a Teenager *(expressed in percent)*

Question 55: *When you were a teenager, did you read any books besides those for school?*

Yes	64 *(304)*
No	35 *(170)*
No answer	1 *(5)*
Total	100 *(479)*

Table 177 Presently Have Active Readers As Friends *(expressed in percent)*

Question 56: *Do you now have any close friends who read a lot?*

Yes	61 *(292)*
No	24 *(116)*
Don't know	15 *(71)*
Total	100 *(479)*

Table 178 Reading Activity Compared with Friends *(expressed in percent)*

Question 57: *At the present time, would you say that you read more, less, or about the same as most of your friends do?*

More	36 *(171)*
Less	28 *(132)*
Same	31 *(148)*
No answer	5 *(28)*
Total	100 *(479)*

Table 179 Reading Activity Compared with Parents *(expressed in percent)*

Question 58: *Would you say that you now read more, less, or about the same as your parents did?*

More	60 *(287)*
Less	16 *(79)*
Same	12 *(57)*
Don't know	18 *(54)*
No answer	⁑ *(2)*
Total	100 *(479)*

⁑ The percentage is equal to less than 1%

Table 180 Reading Activity Compared with People with Whom Reader Lives *(expressed in percent)*

Question 59: *Would you say that you now read more, less, or about the same as the people who live with you?*

More	38 *(183)*
Less	29 *(139)*
Same	24 *(103)*
Live alone	7 *(33)*
Don't know	4 *(21)*
Total	100 *(479)*

At the end of the LMRP rather long interview with many
questions, respondents were asked "Is there anything else you
would like to tell me about your reading." and their comments
are classified. Table 184 shows values in reading as perceived by
readers, readers' attitudes toward reading, and problems perceived.

Table 181 Respondents Who Read Aloud to Other People *(expressed in percent)*

Question 60: *Do you ever read aloud to other people?*

Yes	61 *(290)*
No	39 *(188)*
No answer	* *(1)*
Total	100 *(479)*

* The percentage is equal to less than 1%

Table 182 To Whom Respondent Reads Aloud *(expressed in percent)*

Question 60A: If Yes: *Who do you read to?*

Person Read To	
Children	71 *(206)*
Husband or wife	16 *(46)*
Friends	13 *(37)*
Parents	6 *(16)*
Other relatives	17 *(43)*
Others	21 *(63)*

Base = 290

Table 183 Readers Choosing to Comment Further About Their Reading
(expressed in percent)

Question 61: *Is there anything else you would like to tell me about your reading?*

Comments	50	*(241)*
"No, everything answered"	13	*(61)*
Total Response	63	*(302)*
No response	37	*(177)*
Total	100	*(479)*

Table 184 Readers Choosing to Comment Further About Their Reading
(expressed in percent)

Question 61:   *Is there anything else you would like to tell me about your reading?*

Comments	
Values in reading as perceived by readers	
Pleasure & relaxation	11 *(26)*
Gain information	6 *(15)*
Understanding & comprehension	5 *(12)*
Help in daily life	4 *(11)*
Ability to communicate improved	3 *(8)*
Vocabulary enlarged	2 *(5)*
Reader's attitude toward reading	
Like very much	6 *(14)*
Like	19 *(46)*
Like some	1 *(2)*
Dislike	3 *(6)*
Reading problems as perceived by readers	
Too slow	9 *(22)*
Little time	5 *(13)*
Started too late	2 *(4)*
Little education	3 *(6)*
English as a second language	10 *(24)*

Base = 247

Question 61: *Is there anything else you would like to tell me about your reading?*

Comments	
Vocabulary problems	8 *(18)*
Pronunciation	3 *(7)*
Spelling	1 *(3)*
Sense of improvement	15 *(34)*
Desire for improvement	13 *(30)*
Miscellaneous	20 *(47)*
Needs and interests as perceived by readers	
Black history	1 *(2)*
Bible	1 *(3)*
Magazines	1 *(3)*
Newspapers	2 *(4)*
Good reading material	3 *(6)*
Foreign language material	1 *(2)*
Reading habit	4 *(9)*
Miscellaneous	7 *(17)*

Base = 247

What reading means to the adult interviewed is expressed
best in their own words. The difficulties, the benefits, the pleasures
are illustrated in several selected comments that the respondents
chose to make.

It's coming along. If the books at school were more interesting,
I'd like it better. They start you off with a book for foreign
people and if they had a better story to it instead of Spot
went to catch a rabbit and then keep repeating the same stuff,
it would be better.

I just read newspapers. I very seldom read any books.

I just started reading this Harpers magazine and I am finding
it to be quite interesting. I read other books centered
around the functioning of the Credit Union frequently.

I read every night to my daughter age 5, and she belongs to
two book clubs. (Got idea from the Parent's Magazines)

I'm going to read more about history and news events. I'd like
to know about what's going on in the world. Some people might
lie about it. I'd like to check up on it. In the work I do,
I like to know how other countries do it and if it's better and
their techniques are better, I could use their ideas to do my
job better.

I like to read books that have a lot of pictures and are
about people. I've heard of such as our movie starts. I still
have to use a dictionary a lot.

Now that they have this Negro history thing, this is something
new to me -- because of this I like to read much more and enjoy
it more.

I wanted to go back to our reading class but we didn't have
people to come to keep the class going, maybe they will start it
again next year.

I try very much to read but there is so little time except for my music and teaching.

I'm not a good reader. I didn't have much of an education. My wife helps me. I'm a poor reader but I manage.

I don't like to read a lot, it makes me nervous, and I stumble over words. I have a problem pronouncing words. Sometimes when I read I go to sleep. If I do find an interesting book it's hard to get away from. It usually takes me a long time to read a book. That's all.

I would like to read faster than I do now. I am a very slow reader.

When I read to myself -- I read a lot faster than my eyes can adjust to. When I was in school they had a machine that projects -- read faster than the machine projected -- this was embarrassing when they say raise hand -- I would pretend to have finished along with the rest of the class.

Some things I can't make out. When I get to these words and can't make them out I just lay the paper or magazine down.

I still have trouble understanding what some of those long words really mean in the paper without my dictionary.

Adult New Reader: 16 to 24 Years of Age

The youngest age group of adult new readers between 16 and
24 years of age is of special concern to adult education agencies.
A large proportion of this age group is considered to be dropouts
not only from high school but also from society. They constitute
a new minority which may prove unassimilable as Cervantes points
out in his study on causes and cures of the problem.[4] Through no
fault of their own, they are all too often educationally deficient
and without employment.[5,6,7]

The LMRP findings contain data which have particular significance because of limited knowledge of reading materials for this
minority group. Educators working in various communication media
require objective information for planning and implementing programs.[8] The following brief analysis of selected data describes
a few social characteristics of this group of adult new readers,
their use of communication media, and reading behavior which has
relevance in planning reading programs for young adults.

Sex and Race. The adult new readers in the 16 to 24 age group who
were interviewed in the LMRP survey of readers constitute 23 percent (N=111) of the total sample of 479 respondents. In this
youngest age group 41 percent are males and 59 percent are females.
In comparison with the total sample there are fewer women. No
differences appear in the proportion of white to Black respondents
in the total sample of respondents and in this youngest group. In
both races, however, the percentage of males increases slightly,
with a comparable decrement in the female sample (tables 6a, 6b, and
185).

Amount of Formal Education. The 16 to 24 age group has had more
education than the older age groups. Of this group, 30 percent
have completed between seven and nine years of formal schooling,

372

38 percent have completed 10 to 11 years of schooling, and 29 percent have completed 12 years. Only 20 percent of the respondents in the 25 to 34 age group have completed 12 years of schooling, and only eight percent in the 35 to 44 age group have completed 12 years of schooling. The median years of formal education is 11.02, which is a full grade higher than the average of 10.2 years for the total sample (tables 7a and 186).

Table 185 Distribution of Males and Females Among White and Black
Respondents 16 to 24 Years of Age *(expressed in percent)*

	Male	Female	Total
White	15 (17)	11 (12)	26 (29)
Black	26 (29)	48 (53)	74 (81)
Total	41 (46)	59 (65)	100 (111)

Table 186 Education of the Adult New Reader: 16 to 24 Years of Age
(expressed in percent)

Amount of Formal Education: Last Year Completed in School	
0 - 4	0 *(0)*
5 - 6	☼ *(1)*
7 - 9	30 *(33)*
10 - 11	38 *(42)*
12	29 *(32)*
13 or more	3 *(3)*
Total	100 *(111)*

Median = 11.02

☼ The percentage is equal to less than 1%

Table 187 Reading Activity Rating of Adult New Reader: 16 to 24 Years of Age *(expressed in percent)*

Final Combined Score	Rating	Percent of Respondents
0	Least Active	4 *(4)*
1 - 4	Somewhat Active	25 *(28)*
5 - 7	Active	58 *(65)*
8 - 10	Very Active	13 *(14)*
	Total	100 *(111)*

Participation in Adult Education Classes or Programs. Among the
respondents in the 16 to 24 age group, 86 percent report going to
adult education classes and programs within the last year. This
percentage is higher than the participation among the respondents
who are over 45 years of age. The youngest age group participates
most frequently in adult basic education, Manpower Development and
Training, and high school equivalency programs. This youngest
group also has a higher percentage of respondents who participate
in employment oriented programs in contrast to the non-participa-
tion of the respondents who are over 45 years of age, with the
exception that the older group participates in Manpower Development and Training (Chart 14).

Use of Free Time. Going to the movies is a popular free time
activity for all age groups, but as is to be expected, it is the
most popular activity for this youngest age group as well as those
from 25 to 34 years of age. Dances are a major free time activity
for the youngest group as are going to a bar, cocktail lounge or
tavern, and going to the pool hall or bowling alley. The neighborhood centers and Y activities are of lesser interest. Although
fewer report going to church, synagogue, mosque, over half attend.
In contrast, three-fourths of the respondents over 25 years of age
attend church, synagogue, mosque. Nearly everyone goes to the
park or a zoo (table 25).

Use of Television. News and weather are watched by 82 percent of
the younger age group, as compared to 90 percent plus for older
ones. Mod Squad and Mission Impossible had the highest percentage
of regular viewers among this age group, 81 percent and 77 percent-
respectively. As the World Turns is watched less by the younger
age group (31 percent) than the older age groups (table 69).

Use of Radio. Youth compose the largest radio listening audience, with 98 percent of the 16 to 24 age group listening to radio, as compared with 95 percent of the general sample.

Use of Newspapers. Although newspaper readership is 93 percent among the total number of respondents, the readership among the 16 to 24 age group is somewhat less, 87 percent. The frequency of reading newspapers similarly is less among the youngest age group with 40 percent reading newspapers every day. In comparison, a majority of the respondents 25 years of age and over read newspapers every day. On the other hand, a majority of the youngest readers do read newspapers at least once or a few times a week (table 93). The selected newspaper features - news about world affairs, sports, women's section, advertisements, and horoscope - usually or regularly read by the youngest group of readers parallels features read by all respondents. Within these five interest areas the 16 to 24 age group reads most regularly news about world affairs and advertisements, 82 percent and 70 percent respectively (table 85).

Use of Magazines. Persons in the 16 to 24 age group read slightly more magazines than the general sample, 91 percent, compared to 88 percent for the study sample(table 108).

Use of Comic Books. Readership of comic books among the youngest age group does not differ significantly from the 45 to 54 age group. Fewer persons report reading comic books who were in the 35 to 44 age group and 55 and over(table 111).

Use of Books. Among the 16 to 24 age group, 77 percent indicate that they had read a book within the last six months. In contrast, of the 65 years or over age group, 45 percent indicated that they had read a book in the last six months (table 119).

The number of books read during this six month period does not differ significantly by age until the 45 to 54 age group, when the number of books read declines. Among the youngest group, 12 percent said they had read one book in the last six months, 51 percent had read from two to five books, 15 percent had read from six to ten books, and 11 percent had read from 11 to 20. Fewer younger people, 8 percent, had read 21 or more books (table 119).

Type of Book Liked Very Much. Persons in the 16 to 24 age group tend to like novels and essays somewhat more than the other age groups, and to like history and plays somewhat less than the others.

Use of the Public Library. Of the youngest age group, 89 percent use the public library, which is slightly more than the older age groups (85 percent).

Reading Development. Of the 16 to 24 age group, 54 percent indicated that they had reading problems that they had to overcome. This does not differ significantly from the other age groups until the age of 65 is reached (Chart 18). Of this group, among those who did report having reading problems, 71 percent report that they have overcome them (Chart 19). Reading tends to increase with age until age 30 and then declines. The most reading occurs during the 21 to 29 age period, with the 17 to 20 and the 30 to 44 age periods being the second most frequent periods in which respondents read the most. The sample indicates that 24 percent read very little during the 12 to 16 age period; 26 percent report that they had read little during the 17 to 20 age period; and 18 percent, during the 21 to 29 age period. Those who read least when under 12 years of age comprise 16 percent. After age 29, the percentages decline greatly and range from 0 to 8 percent.

377

Of the 16 to 24 age group, 64 percent indicated that they liked reading a lot, which was slightly lower than the percentages for the older age groups except for those over 65. The percentages for the age group 25 to 44 was 73 percent. However, a higher percentage of the youngest age group indicated that they liked to read very much when they were younger, aged 12 to 19 (53 percent), than the older age groups which averaged about 37 percent during this 12 to 19 age period . The percentage of persons in the youngest age group, 16 to 24 years, who said they now are not very interested in reading (6 percent) is about the same as that of the older age groups. However, only 6 percent of this youngest group report that they were little interested in reading at ages 12 to 19, while the comparable percentages for the older age groups are much higher: 24 percent for ages 25 to 34, 16 percent for ages 35 to 44, 21 percent for 45 to 54, and 32 percent for 55 to 64 years of age .

Participatnts in the study were asked whether they read a great deal, some, or hardly at all (little). The 16 to 24 age group did not differ from older age groups in terms of moderate reading ("some"reading). Of this youngest age group, 36 percent said they read some, which is about the same percentage as the older groups. Fewer persons in the youngest age group said they read a great deal compared to the older groups, although the difference is slight. In addition, slightly more persons in this group said they read "a little" than did the older age groups. One-fourth (25 percent) of this young group said they read a little, while 39 percent reported reading a good deal (table 166). About the same percentage of persons in the 16 to 24 age group indicated they read hardly at all (8 percent) as did the other groups which ranged from 5 to 15 percent. However, only 7 percent of this youngest group indicated that they had read hardly at all when they were between 12 and 19 years of age. The older age groups reported that this was the case for over 20 percent of them (table 168).

The following profiles of individual younger adult new readers help to personalize the preceding more statistical analysis. These readers are: Lorenzo Coppola, a somewhat active reader; Maria Gomez, an active reader; Susan Mathews, an active reader; Stephen Kalis, an active reader; Polly Burke, an active reader; and Tina Sperry, a very active reader.

Somewhat active: reading score - 4. A 23-year-old barber, Lorenzo Coppola is rated as a somewhat active reader. He was educated in Italy and the United States, where he completed the eighth grade. He left school at 16 due to an automobile accident. He would like to be a plumber.

In his spare time, Mr. Coppola visits his friends and relatives, plays cards, takes drives, and reads magazines and books. Although he has read no books in the past six months, he has read *Life* and *Field and Stream*. He belongs to a labor union but holds no office. He has been to the library, although not during the past six months. He goes to dances, the park or zoo, to movies, and to the pool hall. He watches television: news and weather, *Let's Make a Deal, Bonanza* or *Gunsmoke, the Dean Martin Show* or *Johnny Cash Show,* the movies, *Mod Squad* or *Then Came Bronson,* sports, cartoons, *Mayberry RFD, Laugh-In* or *Hee-Haw,* and *As the World Turns.* His favorite is *Mod Squad* or *Then Came Bronson.* His radio listening includes music - rock, semi-classical, mood - and sports. Mr. Coppola also reads two daily metropolitan newspapers in addition to an Italian language newspaper.

The only kind of book Mr. Coppola owns is reference books, and the only book listed in the questionnaire that he would care to read is *Love and Sex in Plain Language.* During his teenage years of 12 to 16 he liked to read the most. He has read only as a necessity throughout most of his life. He rates himself as a fair reader who hardly reads. This is reflected in his statement that the present time is the period in which he has read the least.

Active: reading score - 5. Maria Gomez is an 18-year-old cafeteria worker who would like to become a key punch operator. She has lived in her present city for less than a year. She attended grammar school through the eighth grade in Puerto Rico and left school because of poor grades. Her primary language is Spanish and she says she speaks only a little English. She does not attend any adult classes.

Maria spends her free time listening to records and the radio, playing cards or games, taking drives or walks, going to exhibits or concerts, reading magazines or books, playing pool, and going to movies, to a neighborhood center, and to dances. Watching television is also a pastime. She usually watches the news, *Let's Make a Deal*, *Bonanza* or *Gunsmoke*, the movies, *Mod Squad*, sports, cartoons, *Mayberry RFD*, *Laugh-In* or *Hee Haw*, *As the World Turns*, the Bill Cosby show, *Dark Shadows*, and National Educational Television programs.

Maria is an active reader. She reads a daily metropolitan newspaper and a Spanish newspaper a few times a week. She would miss the women's section the most. She also reads her church news bulletin. She reads women's and fashion magazines and enjoys stories about love and romance, war, lives of people, travel, and adventure. She reads comic books. Of the many books she has read in the last six months, she can only remember one, *Doña Barbaro*. Books have helped Maria to improve her English and she likes to read all types. She sees and gets her books from the library and from school. She uses the library frequently. Besides borrowing books, she has visited the library to read magazines and newspapers, listen to records, ask for information, and to study.

Of the books named by the interviewer, she would like to read *Call Them Heroes, Love and Sex in Plain Language,* the Reader's Digest books, *Letters from Vietnam, People and Places, Perez and Martina, Write Your Own Letters, Get Your Money's Worth, Baby and Child Care,* and *Getting and Holding a Job.*

Maria considers herself a poor reader who reads little and has not overcome her reading problems. She has always liked to read, and when she was a child her parents read to her occasionally. She presently reads more than her parents did, but less than the people with whom she lives. She reads aloud to students in school. She now reads more than when she was younger.

[Maria tried to answer the questionnaire, but did not always understand the questions. Much of the interview was interpreted by an assistant - *Interviewer's comment*]

Active: reading score - 7. Susan Mathews is 19 years of age, of African origin, and working for her high school diploma in a high school equivalency program. She left school before graduating because she was pregnant. She is a full-time worker in a garment factory, but would like to become a practical nurse.

By the Reading Activity Index she is rated as an active reader. She reads the local newspapers once a week. She reads most of the sections, features, and columns regularly. Her favorite part is the comics section. She reads *Life* or *Look, Reader's Digest, Jet, Vogue,* and *Tan.* She would miss the *Reader's Digest* most if she could not get it for a few months. Mrs. Mathews has read 16 books in the last six months. Among them were *The Learning Tree, The Boston Strangler,* a story about Martin Luther King, and one about Abraham Lincoln.

Books have helped her in school, at home, on the job, and in her everyday life. Since starting classes, she has a better understanding of people and can communicate better with them.

She uses the library to take her child there, to borrow books, ask for information, hear a lecture, read a book or magazine, take a tour of the library, and to study there. The library is a major source of her books, and she also gets them at newsstands, book stores, drugstores, and in school.

From the list of books in the questionnaire, Mrs. Mathews has read the Reader's Digest books, the Bible, *Selected Poems* by Langston Hughes, *Baby and Child Care,* and *Getting and Holding a Job.* She is interested in reading *Up From Appalachia, Autobiography of Malcolm X, Black Like Me, Profiles in Courage,* the Perry Mason mysteries, the James Bond stories, *Diane's New Love, Call Them Heroes,* and *Love and Sex in Plain Language.*

Mrs. Mathews reads for information and pleasure. She owns books on child care, Black history, adventure, sports, money management, relition, and sewing. She enjoys short stories, novels, and biographies.

In her free time, she likes to take walks or drives and to bowl. She goes to dances, the movies, the YWCA, and to church. She watches television regularly: the news and weather, *Let's Make a Deal, Bonanza,* the movies, *Mod Squad* cartoons, *Mayberry RFD, Laugh-In,* the Bill Cosby show, *Ironside,* and her favorite, *Mission Impossible.* She listens to all kinds of radio programs; her favorite types of music are soul, jazz, mood, and religious.

As she grows older, Mrs. Mathews has become more interested in reading. She is reading more now than ever before. She reads aloud to her child, as her parents did for her. She rates herself as a fair reader who reads some.

Active: reading score - 5. Stephen Kalis is 18 years of age. He has lived in this city for one year. He completed the eighth grade in Greece and left at the age of 15 because of poor grades. Stephen's first language is Greek.

He is employed currently as a carpenter's apprentice. He is enrolled in an adult basic education program and also one sponsored by private industry. Stephen is learning to read, write, and speak English. In addition, he is studying mathematics, American history, and carpentry. He says, "When I came here I couldn't say anything, and now it sure makes me feel different. It makes me feel good."

Stephen watches television regularly. He views National Educational Television, news, situation comedies, crime and mystery programs, soap operas, sports events, variety shows, talk shows, and cartoons. He enjoys television movies the most. His radio listening includes music, news, and religious programs.

He likes to visit, listen to records, take walks and drives, read, go to movies, bowl, go to the park, and to dances. He belongs to a union and attends church. He has been to the library to borrow a book.

As an active reader, Stephen reads newspapers, magazines, and books. He has read four books in the last six months: *Stories of Famous Men,* the Reader's Digest books, *The Men and Stars* and another book whose title he cannot recall. He reads *Life* and a motorcycle magazine, *Cycle.* His favorite is *Life.* He enjoys all types of magazine stories except romance. He reads the newspaper a few times a week, primarily for world news. He also reads the local newspaper, his church and union newsletters, and the *Weekly Reader.* He owns books on health and nutrition, crime and mystery, sports, adventure, war, building things, and reference. Stephen reads primarily for pleasure. His reading has helped him in school, in work as a carpenter in reading blueprints, and in his daily life. He enjoys reading all kinds of literature except poetry and plays. His sources of books are his friends, family, and school.

Stephen shows an interest in reading *Call Them Heroes, Letters From Vietnam, People and Places,* the Bible, *Up From Appalachia, Profiles in Courage,* and the Perry Mason mysteries. He would find all of the books helpful except *Baby and Child Care.*

He has liked to read always. He rates himself as a fair reader who reads a little. His parents did not read to him when he was a child. He now reads aloud to his own child, as well as for his schooling.

Polly uses the library frequently to study in, to borrow books, read, see a movie or an exhibit, listen to records, and ask for information.

When she was a child, Polly liked to read a lot, but she has lost interest in reading as a teenager. Her parents read to her very often when she was a child. She now reads to her parents. She rates herself as a good reader who reads some.

Active: reading score - 5. Polly Burke, 17 years of age, is still attending high school. Of African ancestry, she is is in the eleventh grade, and is participating in a Neighborhood Youth Corps and a Work Study Program. She also works part-time as a waitress in a restaurant. She would like to be a telephone operator or file clerk.

Polly reads books, comic books, magazines, and newspapers. She cannot remember the number of books she has read in the last six months. She reads newspapers at least once a week, reading the national, international and local news, the women's page, television news, and advertisements. She says that the advertisements are the most important part of the newspaper to her. Polly reads several types of magazines: women's, fashion, movie and television, men's, *Reader's Digest, Ebony, Jet, Life* or *Look,* and trade maga-

zines. In these magazines she enjoys the crime and mystery, human
interest, and adventure stores.

She owns books on all kinds of topics: child care, love and
romance, Black history, budgeting money, home decoration, cooking,
and reference. She reads for pleasure and for information. She
enjoys short stories the most.

Polly has read *Baby and Child Care* and *Getting and Holding a
Job* which she found helpful. She has read *Love and Sex in Plain
Language* and the Reader's Digest books. She would be interested
in reading *Call Them Heroes, Letters from Vietnam, People and Places,
Up from Appalachia, Black Like Me, Profiles in Courage, Diane's New
Love,* and *Life with the Lucketts.*

Polly enjoys watching on television the news, game shows,
movies, crime and mystery programs, and situation comedies. Her
radio listening includes music and news. She likes to go to dances,
taverns or bars, and bowling alleys or pool halls. She visits
friends and relatives in her free time and listens to records, plays
cards and other games, takes drives, and reads.

Very active: reading score - 8. Mrs. Tina Sperry is a high
school graduate attending Manpower Development and Training and an
electronic computing program for key punch operator sponsored by
private indistry. She is studying English, mathematics, and basic
office skills, which have led her to read other things. She says
that her classes "make me want to work harder."

In the last six months she has read five books: *House on
Green Apple Hill, Macbeth,* a life of Martin Luther King, Jr., a
story about John F. Kennedy, and another book she could not remem-
ber. From the list in the interview she has read the Reader's
Digest books, the Bible, *The Autobiography of Malcolm X, Black Like
Me, Selected Poems* by Langston Hughes, *Profiles in Courage,* the
James Bond stories, *Shane,* and the Perry Mason mysteries. She would

like to read *People and Places* and *Letters from Vietnam*. Books
have helped Mrs. Sperry in obtaining a better job. She owns books
on the following subjects: health and nutrition, Black history,
adventure, self-improvement, reference, and religion. Her major
sources for books are her friends and family, and the bookstore.
She enjoys poetry, plays, short stories, novels, biographies, and
histories. She reads the newspapers every day in addition to
church, club, and union newsletters. Mrs. Sperry usually reads
all of the columns listed in the questionnaire except the comics.
Her favorite feature is the horoscope. Her magazine reading includes *Life*, the *Reader's Digest*, and news, fashion, women's and
movie magazines. *Vogue* is her favorite magazine. She enjoys the
crime, human interest, travel, sports, and adventure stories in
these magazines.

In her free time, Mrs. Sperry visits friends and relatives,
takes drives and walks, takes judo lessons, and reads. She also
enjoys watching television and listening to the radio. She watches
a great deal of television and her favorite program is *Ironside*.
Her radio listening includes news, music, and religious and talk
shows. Mrs. Sperry belongs to a modeling group for which she has
read special materials.

She is rated as a very active reader. She perceives herself
as a good reader who reads a great deal. As a child she did not
like to read, but did read books other than for school. At the
present, 21 years of age, she likes to read a lot and has friends
who like to read. When she was a child her parents read aloud to
her fairly frequently, and now Mrs. Sperry reads aloud to her child.
Reading has given Mrs. Sperry enjoyment and has helped her in job
placement.

Notes

1.   Philip H. Ennis, *Adult Book Reading in the United States*
(National Opinion Research Center, Report No. 105)   (Chicago:
University of Chicago, 1965): p. 38.

2.   Ibid.

3.   Ibid., p. 35.

4.   Lucius F. Cervantes, *The Dropout; Causes and Cures* (Ann Arbor:
The University of Michigan Press, 1965).

5.   Daniel Schreiber, editor, *Profile of the School Dropout* (New
York: Random House, Inc., 1967).

6.   Harlem Youth Opportunities Unlimited, Inc., *Youth in the Ghetto*
(New York: Harlem Youth Opportunities Unlimited, Inc., 1964).

7.   David Gottlieb and Anne L. Heinsohn, editors, *America's Other
Youth; Growing Up Poor* (Englewood Cliffs, N.J.:   Prentice-Hall,
Inc., 1971).

8.   Richard Cortright, July 1971:   personal communication.

10

Findings and Implications

The study of adult new readers has identified special segments
in the population, their social characteristics, and reading behavior
and interests. Findings are based on interviews with 479 persons drawn
from a random sample of adults in adult basic education, job training
and library reading programs in the ghetto areas of Baltimore, Cleveland
Los Angeles, New York, and Philadelphia. Only a few of the findings
are summarized here.

Among the reader respondents, less than one-third are men, while
69 percent are women. Interviewers identified three-fourths as
Black, while one-fourth were reported as white. Nearly all speak
English, and one-fourth also speak a second language. More than
half the readers are under the age of 35, and three-quarters are
under the age of 45. The median age is 33.2 years. The average
period of residence in the present locality is 24 years yet one-third
have lived all their lives in the city. In terms of formal education,
that is the last year completed in school, adult new readers have
attended an average of 10.2 years. Nearly two-thirds have completed
between seven and eleven years of school. Nearly a fifth have less
than a sixth grade schooling and an equal number have completed high
school. A majority of readers, 58 percent, have participated in
adult basic education programs, 30 percent in high school equivalency, 19 percent in Work Incentive Programs, 16 percent in Manpower
Development and Training, and 13 percent have participated in public
library reading development programs.

More than half of the readers are in the labor force, one-fourth
in school, and nearly a fifth keep house. Of those employed, 18 perce
are in blue collar and 18 percent in craft occupations, 16 percent in
clerical, and 12 percent in white collar occupations. Over one-third,
36 percent, are in service occupations. Although the family incomes
range from zero to $10,000 and over, nearly 20 percent have incomes

less than $3,000, and 40 percent between $3,000 and $6,000. The median income for individuals is approximately $3,500, and for families, $5,000.

Although heterogeneous groups of readers exist, certain homogeneous groups are identified clearly. The Black population dominates the sample primarily because of residence in the ghetto area of cities which were surveyed. The Puerto Rican American and Chicano or Mexican American are represented. Over one-fourth of the respondents are identified as part of the white population. The person who has English as a second language also is identified.

The use of the various communication media is common to all groups. Everyone watches television; 95 percent listen to radio; 93 percent read newspapers and half of these newspaper readers read them every day. Among the 88 percent who read magazines, *Life* or *Look*, *Ebony* or *Jet*, women's magazines and *Reader's Digest* are particularly popular. The favorite types of magazine stories are about lives of real people, adventure, crime and mystery, travel, and love and romance. Fewer persons, 69 percent, read books. The majority of respondents report reading two to five books in the last six months, ranging from popular fiction to the occult, and poetry.

In the context of the study, the diversity and variety of reading interests and various uses of materials are extensive. The number and variety of interests and needs almost equal the number of individual readers. Reading patterns span a range of life interests, responsibilities, and roles as adults. Nevertheless, within this great diversity, certain preferences, common interests and titles have been identified in each phase of the research by readers, teachers, and librarians. Three titles that were reported again and again are *The Autobiography of Malcolm X, Soul on Ice* by Cleaver, and the *Bible*. Among the 33 most frequently read books reported by readers, half are concerned with Black literature and biography.

The Reading Activity Index measurement of the adult new reader's use of print materials shows that a third of the respondents are least active readers, about a third are somewhat active readers, a fourth are active readers, and slightly over 10 percent are very active

389

readers. Agreement is shown between the actual estimation of the reader's perception of his own reading and the measurement of his reading activity by the Reading Activity Index. Readers also are able to perceive their reading problems and evaluate changes in their reading skills and interests. The individual's ability to evaluate his reading has significant implications in that such information can be useful to librarians and teachers in advisory and counseling activities.

Appeals to readers, sometimes classified as reasons for reading, tend to center around informational or instrumental values. The practical materials relating to homemaking, child care, job training and advancement, and school work are helpful when they provide aid and solutions for everyday problems such as writing letters, credit buying, cooking, getting a driver's license, filing tax forms, reading maps, magazines, and newspapers. Personal and social development are important areas of interst. The biographies of the lives and problems of persons, unknown or famous, as well as sensitive portrayals of characters in fiction with whom readers can identify have special appeal. Popular best sellers are another special interest Survival, civil rights, the counter culture are topics of deep concern.

The reader perceives other benefits from reading, such as, a better job, self-confidence, ability to communicate better with others, pleasure and relaxation. Readers view learning as something that gives them confidence and more personal and social security.

The interest in local, national, and international news is a common thread in priority uses of the media -- television, radio, and print. The implications are rather clear that libraries should build on this interest. Libraries can fulfill a significant function by providing and promoting print resources that give objective coverage and in depth studies of current events and issues not found in the brief reports from the electronic media. Materials and services should be correlated and promoted along with the television and radio news coverage of the moment. Equally valuable would be a continuing analysi of current news to determine significant subjects of long range interest in order to build collections in depth.

Adult new readers in general recall titles that may be classified as fictional and biographical accounts with ethnic appeals. Apparently readers recall what is most meaningful and enjoyable to them. Although a significant amount of reading is required and stimulated by school studies, the titles recalled seem not to be related directly to school. The range and volume of reading materials which libraries might provide are great.

Librarians and teachers will interpret these data in numerous ways that are relevant to building library collection. Subject interests and clues to kinds and types of reading materials are immediately evident. The individuality of interests and needs is a major factor in use of reading materials. The reading patterns span a range of life interest and responsibilities in relation to roles of adults, life styles, and life cycle.

It is evident not only that reading materials must meet a diversity of interests, needs, and abilities, but also, they must be in every possible format, and cover numerous subjects. Special authentic materials pertinent to the interests, life styles, and problems of potential readers have immediate appeal.

Information about job opportunities, career and vocational guidance, and counseling materials as well as curriculum related selections are areas for collection building. Materials related to new occupations and preparation for advancement are important in light of the findings on aspirations of adult new readers.

The newspaper and magazine reading reflect the same diversity and similarities as book reading. Access to local neighborhood newspapers and publications is of primary importance as a source of information and interest to citizens of a community.

The identification with others and the satisfactions gained from experience recorded by others who have made it and who express ethnic pride have strong appeals. Implications for building library collections are obvious in subject areas of biographies, ethnic history, and culture.

The need for materials in Spanish is confirmed. The evidence of a variety of backgrounds and first languages would seem to indicate the importance of identifying and providing materials not only in the first language of literacy but also subject and cultural material of special group interest in English.

At various points in the LMRP analysis the data reinforce the finding that the critical stage in reading development is the variable literacy stage, that is, formal education at seventh grade level. It is at this stage the library service in reading materials and reading guidance would seem to be crucial. At this point the range and volume of reading resources can be most useful to the adult new reader.

Education is an important correlate of reading. The increased years of formal schooling and higher reading achievement level are correlates of greater reading activity. Magazine reading and book reading continue to increase in relation to more education.

Several conclusions and problems in relation to methodological aspects of the survey of readers are evident.

The respondents, with few exceptions, spoke freely and openly. They were cooperative and friendly. The response within this special segment of the population appears to be similar to the Ennis sample of persons who made up a voluntary and more highly selective sample.

Respondents were able to identify patterns of reading during their life, perceive and evaluate their own abilities, compare their reading with others close to them, and report reasons for reading in relation to daily activities.

Although the assessments of frequency of reading, extent of reading, and comparative evaluations are very general, they appear to be accurate and acceptable.

Respondents were able to recall specific titles of books, names of newspapers and magazines. They could supply titles read within the last six months. They appear to remember what is important to them. Recall of reading in chronological order was not attempted.

When asked about specific titles to get an idea if books were read, or, if not, would they be interested in them, the answers were accurate and honest. It is noteworthy that most of the titles had not been read. Those titles mentioned most often as having appeal were corroborated by interests and titles reported by respondents in answers to other questions.

It has been possible to construct a biographical review of major characteristics of each individual and his reading interests, habits, and pattern of reading, including his own perception of himself. The statistical aggregate analysis is individualized and humanized by the profiles developed about each reader through rearrangement of questions in the interview to form logical life patterns and by use of the computer.

Although the personal interview is structured and precise, personal comments and open-end questions yielded interesting information. Some specificity is illustrated in newspapers and books read.

If more freedom of opportunity for follow-up questions had been observed it might well have resulted in discovering attitudes and findings not revealed.

The major question about the survey of readers relates to problems and obstacles encountered in selecting the survey sample. Although the sample does contain a percentage of persons above the sample education limitation and proportional representation is observed, the lack of control group for comparisons is a serious matter.

Four major recommendations based on this study of adult new readers are -

1. This analysis leaves many questions unanswered and demonstrates the need for additional analysis of the data.

2. The various aspects of adult new readers' social characteristics and communication habits and patterns of use of the communication media should be explored in depth. Particular segments
only touched on through the questionnaire interviews might be developed.
Further study is needed on the group who reads little or not at all.

3. A major question arises about the differences and similarities to be found in the large population of white adults who are poor,
functionally illiterate, and developing basic education skills and their
use of reading resources.

4. A recommendation perhaps inherent in the study but nevertheless supported by the data about adult new readers is the necessity
for careful evaluation of reading materials in light of all that can
be learned about the user and potential users of the materials and
the context in which it will be used.

PART 3: NATIONAL ADULT PROGRAMS STUDY

    11. THE STUDY

    12. THE PROGRAMS

    13. THE READING MATERIALS

11.

THE STUDY

Introduction

The National Adult Programs Study is the phase of the Library Materials Research Project concerned with gathering data about the nature and use of reading materials within the context of 11 national adult basic education programs and job training programs. The participants or students in these programs are adult new readers as defined in the research project. The National Adult Programs Study examines the general characteristics of the local programs, their main purposes, services, and goals. The research also gathers data on the characteristics of program participants, their age, sex, ethnic background, and education.

This study focuses on the identification of reading materials which are not instructional, are not strictly instructional, or which extend beyond the boundaries of being strictly instructional. It is assumed that some of these programs may not be using reading materials at all, but because such programs do exist, they should generate and stimulate the creation or use of reading materials. The objectives of the study have been to identify the various types of reading materials used and needed, the specific titles used, and reading materials locally produced by teachers and students which have been stimulated by the programs.

Research Design

The initial step of this study was the identification of current national programs. In the study, national programs are defined as those which now operate in at least five of the nine regions into which the U.S. Office of Education divides the country. A program is defined as an administrative and functional structure engaged in providing services to the adult new reader.

The literature, documents, articles and other publications

describing 28 national programs were collected and reviewed. Descriptions of the programs were prepared which included information on the following facets of the programs: administration and funding, historical developments and changes, eligibility requirements for participants and a profile of enrolled participants, methods of instruction, reading materials used, and the number and locations of programs throughout the nation.

On the basis of this information, 11 national programs were chosen that fulfilled the definition of a national program in service to the adult new reader and also had the continuity and permanence assured by being in operation for at least two years. The programs selected were: (1) Adult Basic Education (ABE), (2) Concentrated Employment Program (CEP), (3) Job Corps, (4) Laubach Literacy, Inc., (5) Manpower Development and Training Centers (MDTA), (6) Neighborhood Youth Corps (NYC), (7) New Careers, (8) Opportunities Industrialization Centers, Inc., (9) Upward Bound (UPB), (10) Vocational Education, Special Needs Program, and (11) Work Incentive Program (WIN). Background information about these programs has been presented previously in this report.

Geographic locations were selected with the intent of achieving maximum area representation. It was felt that maximizing area representation would ensure the collection of the widest possible range of data on the use of reading materials in the 11 national programs.

For selection of the geographic sample, the U.S. Department of Health, Education, and Welfare's division of the nation into nine regions.was used. The three largest metropolitan areas in each of the nine regions were identified, as were the locations of each of the 11 types of programs operating in the selected cities. From this group, a stratified sample was drawn. Programs were classified by the 11 types of programs and by the nine regions. A sample of two of each of the 11 types of programs was drawn from each region using a table of random numbers. This

398

process yielded a total of 198 programs. Some could not be located, possibly because they had moved or been discontinued. The final sample included 178 programs (appendix 4 , Stratified Sample of Programs and Their Locations in the National Adult Program Study).

The instruments used to collect the data on the programs were two mail questionnaires (appendix 5 , LMRP National Programs Study: Questionnaire for Administrators; and appendix 6 , LMRP National Programs Study: Questionnaire for Teachers). The questionnaire for administrators acquired information which provided a general description of the local program - its purposes, its main services, and the characteristics of program participants. The questionnaire for teachers focused on the variety, type and extent of usage of reading materials, and also what types of reading materials are needed currently and in the future for various clientele groups.

Three questionnaires were sent to each program in the sample, one for the program administrator and two for teachers. The administrator was asked to give the teacher questionnaires to two teachers on the program staff who were closest to the reading materials.

The questionnaires were designed in the fall of 1969, and approved by the Bureau of Research, U.S. Office of Education in December 1969. A pretest of the questionnaires was conducted using programs in Milwaukee, Wisconsin. The questionnaires were then revised and sent to the sample in January 1970. The total sample consisted of 178 programs. Questionnaires were sent to 178 administrators and to 356 teachers. The number of administrator questionnaires returned was 97, or 54 percent. Teachers returned 124 questionnaires, or 37 percent (table 188). Table 189 shows the programs represented by the administrators and teachers' responses to the questionnaires.

Table 188 Response to National Adult Program Study Questionnaires
(expressed in percent)

Number of programs in sample	100 *(178)*
Number of Questionnaires for Administrators sent	100 *(178)*
Number of Questionnaires for Administrators returned	54 *(97)*
Number of Questionnaires for Teachers sent (two to each program)	100 *(356)*
Number of Questionnaires for Teachers returned	35 *(126)*
Number of complete responses (all three questionnaires returned)	30 *(54)*
Number of programs from which the administrator and one teacher questionnaire were returned	42 *(74)*
Number of programs which returned Questionnaire for Administrators only	37 *(65)*

Table 189 Response to National Adult Program Study Questionnaires, by Program *(expressed in percent)*

Program	Response			
	Questionnaire for Administrators	Questionnaire for Teachers "A"	Questionnaire for Teachers "B"	Total Sample for each Question-naire
Adult Basic Education	61 *(11)*	33 *(6)*	50 *(9)*	*18*
Concentrated Employment Program	53 *(9)*	35 *(6)*	41 *(7)*	*17*
Job Corps	80 *(12)*	73 *(11)*	67 *(11)*	*15*
Laubach Literacy Program	60 *(9)*	53 *(8)*	33 *(5)*	*15*
Manpower Development and Training Skills Center	64 *(9)*	57 *(8)*	64 *(9)*	*14*
Neighborhood Youth Corps	61 *(11)*	44 *(8)*	44 *(8)*	*18*
New Careers	41 *(7)*	18 *(3)*	24 *(4)*	*17*
Opportunities Industriali-zation Centers	53 *(8)*	27 *(4)*	33 *(5)*	*15*
Upward Bound Project	24 *(4)*	6 *(1)*	0 *(0)*	*17*
Vocational Education for the Disadvantaged	50 *(7)*	21 *(3)*	21 *(3)*	*14*
Work Incentive Program	56 *(10)*	22 *(4)*	22 *(4)*	*18*
Total	55 *(97)*	35 *(62)*	36 *(64)*	*178*

12

THE PROGRAMS

The study of the national programs collected information about the major characteristics of the programs - their purposes, services, methods, and materials. The questionnaires for administrators and teachers gathered information in these two areas and about four characteristics of the program participants - their age, sex, race or nationality, and educational level.

Characteristics of Program Participants

Age of Participants

Although a wide range of age groups are represented in the programs, the participants tend to be young. Over 50 percent are in the 16 to 24 age group, and one-third of the programs draw more than 75 percent of their participants from this age group. Only 14 percent of the programs have a majority of participants over the age of 25.

With the exception of this large number of programs in which the younger group of students is predominant, the remaining programs have a wide range of age groups that do not exhibit any particular concentration. Between one-fourth and one-third of the programs draw between one-fourth and one-third of their participants from each of the major age groups - 16 to 24, 25 to 34, and 35 to 44. If a program is not predominantly young, it tends to be a mixed group with each of the major age groups well represented. As the age of participants increases, the proportion of participants of that age decreases; thus the 25 to 34 age group is second largest, and the 35 to 44 age group is third largest (chart 23).

Sex

The program administrators reported a somewhat higher rate of participation by women than by men. The mean percentages for the programs studied were 46 percent men and 54 percent women.

Race and Ethnic Characteristics

The largest racial group represented in the programs is Black, with a median of 66 percent. A majority of programs contain over 50 percent Black enrollment and more than one-third of the programs have over 75 percent Black enrollment. The second largest racial group is white, not including persons of Spanish origin, with a median of 18 percent.

The ethnic groups represented in the programs include American Indians, persons of Spanish origin - Mexican Americans or Chicanos, Puerto Ricans, Cubans - and others. These groups are represented in less than 50 percent of the programs, and have medians of zero. Among these groups, the Mexican American group is largest. However, as the chart indicates, this is still a very small group, with only 8 percent of the programs drawing 25 percent or more of their enrollment from the Mexican American group (chart 14).

Educational Levels

The educational levels of the program participants and the distribution of these levels varies widely among the programs. Thirty-one percent of the programs have a majority of participants who are at the high school level, that is, have completed grade 8, 9, 10, or 11. Another 24 percent of the programs have a majority of participants who have completed less than the eighth grade. Eleven percent of the programs have a majority of participants who have completed no more than the fourth grade. A few programs, 7 percent, have a majority of participants who have completed the twelfth grade.

A large majority of the programs have a wide range of educational levels represented among their participants. Most programs draw one-fourth or less of their participants from each of the four basic educational levels - grades 0 to 4, 5 to 8, 8th completed, and 9 to 11. Thus, the most salient characteristic revealed by

these data is the very wide range of educational levels represented in the individual programs (chart 25).

The main characteristics of the program participants may be
summarized briefly. The majority of participants in the national
adult programs studied are Black, young, and possess a formal
education ranging from grade one to twelve. The most salient
characteristic is the diversity of the students enrolled in the
programs. Most program participants tend to be young - between
16 and 24 years of age - but persons of all ages participate in
the programs. The median percentage of white program participants
is 18 percent, and over half the participants are Black. Other
minority groups represented include American Indians, Mexican
Americans or Chicanos, and Puerto Ricans. Somewhat more women
than men participate in the programs. This diversity of the
students' backgrounds and educational levels presents a challenge
to the teacher, who must provide materials appropriate to the
diverse needs of the students.

Chart 23 Age Representation in National Programs

Percent of Age Groups
Represented in Programs,
by Quartiles*

Percent of Programs

		0	10	20	30	40	50	60	70	80

0%
- 16-24   3
- 25-34   32%
- 35-44   33%
- 45-54   35%
- 55+   52%

1-24%
- 16-24   28%
- 25-34   17%
- 35-44   40%
- 45-54   57%
- 55+   47%

25-49%
- 16-24   28%
- 25-34   35%
- 35-44   24%
- 45-54   7%
- 55+   0%

50-74%
- 16-24   7%
- 25-34   12%
- 35-44   2%
- 45-54   0%
- 55+   0%

75-100%
- 16-24   33%
- 25-34   2%
- 35-44   0%
- 45-54   0%
- 55+   0%

* For example: The second quartile of the chart (25-49%) indicates
that 28% of the programs draw between 25% and 49% of their students from the 16-24 age group, that 35% of the programs draw
between 25% and 49% of their students from the 24-35 group.

Chart 24 Race and Ethnic Groups Represented in the National Adult Programs

Percent of Each Group
in Programs, by Quartiles

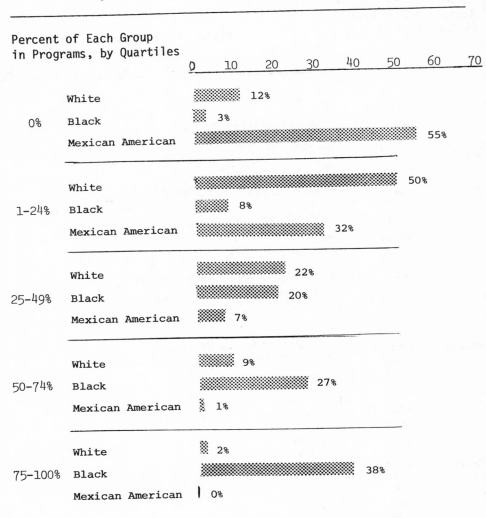

| | | 0 | 10 | 20 | 30 | 40 | 50 | 60 | 70 |

0%
White 12%
Black 3%
Mexican American 55%

1-24%
White 50%
Black 8%
Mexican American 32%

25-49%
White 22%
Black 20%
Mexican American 7%

50-74%
White 9%
Black 27%
Mexican American 1%

75-100%
White 2%
Black 38%
Mexican American 0%

Chart 25 Educational Levels Represented in National Programs

Percent of Each Grade Level
in Programs, by Quartiles

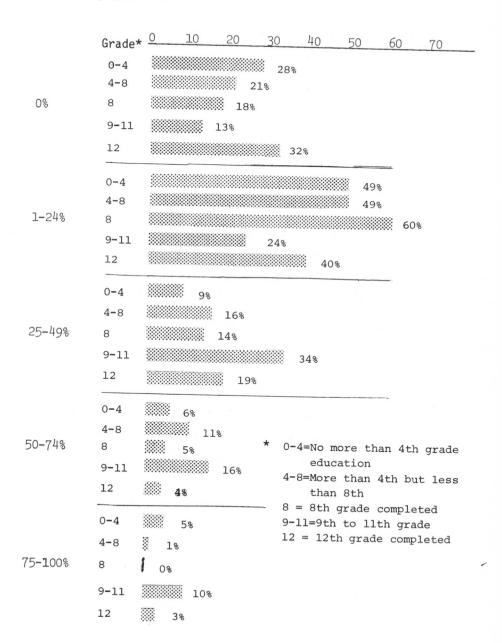

	Grade*	Percent
	0-4	28%
	4-8	21%
0%	8	18%
	9-11	13%
	12	32%
	0-4	49%
	4-8	49%
1-24%	8	60%
	9-11	24%
	12	40%
	0-4	9%
	4-8	16%
25-49%	8	14%
	9-11	34%
	12	19%
	0-4	6%
	4-8	11%
50-74%	8	5%
	9-11	16%
	12	4%
	0-4	5%
	4-8	1%
75-100%	8	0%
	9-11	10%
	12	3%

* 0-4=No more than 4th grade
      education
  4-8=More than 4th but less
      than 8th
  8 = 8th grade completed
  9-11=9th to 11th grade
  12 = 12th grade completed

Characteristics of National Adult Programs

The study of the 11 national adult programs obtained information in two areas relating to the characteristics of the programs and the use of reading materials in these programs. Data about the programs include the length of time the programs have functioned, the program purposes, and the main services offered by these types of educational programs - adult basic education, job training, and high school equivalency. Data about the characteristics of reading materials include the types of reading materials used, the use of materials in various instructional methods, and the sources of these materials.

Length of Time National Programs Have Served Participants

In 1969, when this study was made, most of the programs were relatively new. The median length of time programs had been serving participants directly was 4.2 years. Eighty-eight percent of the programs had been functioning for less than seven years, and 36 percent of them for less than four years. The greatest expansion of the programs occurred in 1965-66, when 42 percent began to provide services (table 190).

Primary Purposes of the National Programs

Each program administrator was asked to state the primary purpose of his program. These statements of purpose supplement the statements derived from the literature describing the programs and those stated in the legislative authorizations for the programs. Administrators tend to mention the main services their programs provide. Two-thirds of the administrators specify their program's major purpose as providing adult basic education, skill training, literacy skills, or other specific services. About one-third of the administrators, however, report a broader scope of objectives that they are trying to achieve. This more general conceptualization of program purpose includes such goals as aiding "human renewal," conducting a "socialization process," "building self-reliance and independence," "promoting social adjustment," and "providing equal opportunity for the disadvantaged."

The fact that two-thirds of the program administrators define only basic services as their purpose does not necessarily mean that they lack awareness of the broader goals mentioned by the other third. The former may assume that these broader purposes are implicit because most of the programs were created specifically to serve the needs of unemployed and disadvantaged persons. It seems reasonable to assume that programs which are conceived with broad rather than narrow definitions of purpose will use a wider variety of reading materials, while those programs conceived in narrower terms will tend to use reading materials limited to instruction in basic skills.

Main Services Provided by National Programs

The programs studied provide a variety of services in the major areas of instruction and counseling. The instructional services include: adult basic education, which is provided by 75 percent of the programs; high school equivalency, by 67 percent; and specific job training, by 56 percent. Nearly half, 47 percent, report instruction in English as a second language, and only 16 percent include the traditional high school curricula. Counseling is a major service offered by 85 percent, and job placement service is provided by 65 percent of the programs. Work experience or work orientation services are provided by 68 percent of the programs (table 191).

The chief areas of emphasis in the adult basic education programs are communication skills, computational skills, social living skills, and specific subject areas. Sixty-eight percent of the programs provide instruction in the communication skills of reading, writing, and speech; and 59 percent offer instruction in mathematics and arithmetic. Thirty-one percent of the programs offer instruction in the social living skills which include health, personality development, counseling, consumer education, driver education, and legal education. Instruction in specific subject areas is less prevalent. Sixteen percent of the programs offer social studies and civics, 13 percent offer humanities, and 8 percent offer instruction in science (table 192).

Among the 68 percent of the programs providing job training, five major occupational areas are emphasized. Skilled crafts and trades constitute the largest number of courses. These include a wide range of training in various skills and trades, particularly automobile mechanics and welding, and such crafts as carpentry, plumbing, television and appliance repair, and heavy equipment operation.

Instruction in the field of clerical, secretarial and office work constitutes the second area of emphasis. Specifically, this area includes instruction in clerical and bookkeeping skills, typing, and keypunching.

Instruction in subjects related to health constitutes a third important area of emphasis. Training in the various health areas covers a wide range of specific occupations at various levels of skill and knowledge. These occupations include practical nurse, laboratory technician, medical technologist, nurse's aide, hospital orderly, and other hospital staff supportive positions.

Training for service workers constitutes a fourth important field of instruction. This category of training is for positions as cooks, waitresses, food checkers, and also preparation for work as hairdressers, bakers, maintenance engineers, and sales clerks.

Finally, training in the area of community and public service is a significant occupational category. The most frequently offered training in this area is preparation for becoming teacher aides. Training was also frequently reported in a variety of social service and human relations skills. Occupations in this area include training of workers in social service, human relations, community development, and various other welfare and urban programs.

This summary far from exhausts the range of occupational instruction reported by administrators of the national adult programs. Over a hundred other occupations are mentioned. The diversity and variety in the training and types of preparatory work suggest the complexity and potential of reading materials that might be used in such programs.

Table 190 Length of Time Programs Served Participants *(expressed in percent)*

Question 3: *How long has your program been directly serving participants?**

1-3 years (1967-69)	36
4-6 years (1964-66)	52
7-9 years (1961-63)	7
10 years or more (1960 or before)	5
Total	100

Median = 4.2 years   Base = 94

* LMRP National Programs Study, Questionnaire for Administrators

Table 191 Main Services Provided by National Programs (expressed in percent)

Question 2: *In order to achieve your purpose, what main services do you provide?**

Service	
Adult basic education	75 (73)
High School Equivalency	67 (65)
English as a second language	47 (46)
Traditional high school curriculum	16 (15)
General work experience or work orientation	68 (66)
Specific job training	56 (54)
Work evaluation and assessment	53 (51)
Counseling services	85 (82)
Job placement	65 (63)
Other	26 (25)

* Questionnaire for Administrators

412

Table 192 Areas of Emphasis in Adult Basic Education Programs*
(expressed in percent)

Communication Skills	68 *(65)*
Reading, writing, speech and conversation	
Computational Skills	59 *(56)*
Mathematics and arithmetic	
Social Living Skills	31 *(29)*
Health, personality development, counseling, consumer education, driver education, legal education	
Social Studies and Civics	16 *(15)*
Science	8 *(8)*
Humanities	13 *(12)*
History, minority history, art, literature, religion	
General Education Degree and Civil Service Examination Preparation	10 *(9)*

* Questionnaire for Administrators, Question 2.

13.

THE READING MATERIALS
Their Nature and Use
Sources and Types of Materials

Reading materials are used by 97 percent of the national adult programs reporting in this study. These materials are obtained primarily by purchasing them with funds from program budgets. Donations of materials by corporations, the programs' staff, and school districts constitute a second major source of program collections. The third major source of reading materials is borrowed materials, primarily from local public libraries (table 193).

The study examined the extent to which teachers use reading materials in their classrooms which are not strictly instructional. The median percentage of use of materials of this type is 27 percent. Over 25 percent of the teachers report that more than 50 percent of the reading materials they use are not strictly instructional, and 12 percent of the teachers use over 80 percent not strictly instructional reading materials in their classes. At the other extreme, about one-third of the teachers use less than 20 percent not strictly instructional materials, and another third use from 20 to 40 percent. Table 194 indicates in more detail materials used which are not strictly instructional.

More than eight types of reading materials not strictly instructional are used in the adult classes of the national programs studied. Paperback books are the most widely used type of material, and are used by 79 percent of the teachers. Magazines are used by 62 percent, newspapers and pamphlets by 50 percent, and hardcover books by 41 percent. Other types of materials used by teachers include newspapers devised for the adult new reader, newsletters, comic books, maps, atlases, and almanacs (table 195).

Specific Reading Materials Used by Teachers in National Adult
Programs

In an attempt to find out what books are read widely by students in the programs, teachers were asked to list the titles and
authors of six books most frequently read by their students. The
question was not answered by 35 percent of the teachers who returned the questionnaires. Because 97 percent of the teachers
said that they do use reading materials in their programs, obviously the failure to list specific titles does not imply that the
teachers do not use reading materials. There are several possible
explanations for this non-response rate. The question may have
been overly ambitious in expecting teachers to take the time and
effort necessary to answer the question. Or it may be that teachers have either too much or too little information to answer the
question. It may have been impossible to select six books either
because the variety of reading materials used may be too great,
or teachers may lack knowledge about their students' reading habits, or lack feedback from students' reactions to materials they
have read.

A partial explanation for this non-response rate is the fact
that teachers interpreted the question in two different ways. Some
saw the question as referring only to reading outside the classroom
or recreational reading, while others felt it referred to instructional materials used in the classrooms, such as dictionaries and
basic English and mathematics textbooks. Many teachers who did not
answer the question stated that they could not do so because they
did not know what was read by their students outside the classroom.
One teacher said, "It is impossible to tell from the 1500 titles
in our library." Another who teaches in a Job Corps program reports that they have an honor system for borrowing books, which
makes it impossible to tell who has checked out what books. Pre-
sumably, many of the teachers who did not list specific titles might

415

have done so if they had interpreted the question to include materials used in the classroom, as did most.

Some teachers, instead of listing specific titles, mentioned the genre of materials read or the names of the series used in their programs. They report that the students read westerns, romances, and stories, and that they use Reader's Digest, Science Research Associates, and some other series material.

An analysis of the specific titles reported by the 65 percent of the teachers answering the question reveals a great variety of material. Altogether, 317 different titles are mentioned by 81 teachers. Of this total, 219 are mentioned once, 19 are mentioned twice, and only nine are mentioned more than twice. Within this last group of nine books which are mentioned from three to eight times, seven deal with Black oriented subject matter. They are: *Soul on Ice* by Eldridge Cleaver, *The Autobiography of Malcolm X*, *Stories of Twenty-three Famous Negro Americans* by John King and Marcet King, *Call Them Heroes* by the New York City Board of Education, *The Fire Next Time* by James Baldwin, *Lilies of the Field* by W.E. Barrett, and *Manchild in the Promised Land* by Claude Brown. The other two books are basic reading texts, *Be a Better Reader* by N.B. Smith and *Step Up Your Reading Power* by Jim Olsen, which is actually a series of five books. The 19 titles named twice also deal chiefly with either basic language skills or ethnic oriented literature.

Although the 319 titles named by teachers show much diversity, they can be grouped into 12 interest areas. Five general areas are literature, history and government, science, biography, and religion. Other significant areas of reading interests include ethnic literature, problems of race relations, and cultural development. The ethnic literature deals mainly with Black oriented subject matter, and to a limited extent with material oriented toward persons of Spanish origin (table 196).

How the Reading Materials Are Used

Teachers were asked how they use the reading materials in the programs. The most common uses of the reading materials are for independent reading (77 percent) and suggested reading (74 percent). Some teachers have students present oral reports on the readings. Teachers in the Laubach Literacy program use the Laubach instruction method, in which each student has a tutor, and all instruction is conducted on a one-to-one basis.

Over half of the teachers use reading materials in directed reading (open book lesson) and in programmed instruction for individualized reading. Only 30 percent report the use of reading materials as required reading. In addition, teachers report other uses. A frequent practice reported by several teachers is the use of reading materials selected by the students as a basis for group or class discussion (table 197).

Topics Emphasized and Needed in Reading Materials

Teachers were asked to indicate by ranking what topics are currently being emphasized in the programs, and what topics they think should receive more emphasis. Among the topics currently being emphasized in the reading materials, basic information (English, science, mathematics) receives the most emphasis. Job information ranks second, followed by stories, reference books, consumer education, and community participation. Family life (sex education and child care, etc.) ranks sixth in current emphasis, and literature about specific ethnic and nationality groups ranks seventh. Topics least emphasized in the reading materials are health, homemaking, art, music, religion, and poetry.

Teachers also indicated by ranking the topics they think deserve more emphasis in the reading materials. The ranking of these topics differs significantly from the ranking of the various ones currently being emphasized. Consumer education and job information share the top position in terms of needed emphasis in reading materials. In terms of current emphasis, however, consumer education ranks fifth. Job information ranks high on both indices, on the other hand, indicating that even though it is currently the second most emphasized topic, teachers think that even more emphasis is needed. Literature about ethnic and nationality groups ranks third in terms of needed emphasis, but is ranked eighth in terms of current emphasis. Basic information, ranked first in current emphasis, ranks sixth in terms of needed emphasis. Stories and reference books also ranked significantly higher in terms of current emphasis than in terms of needed emphasis. The remaining topics did not differ greatly in their rankings on the two indices. Generally, teachers feel that increased emphasis is needed in reading materials about consumer education, job information, and ethnic literature; while current emphasis stresses the more traditional areas of basic information, stories, and reference books. The exception is job information which receives current emphasis. Yet it is a topic that teachers feel needs even more emphasis in reading materials (table 198).

Table 193 Sources of National Programs Reading Materials *(expressed in percent)*

Sources	Percent of Programs*
Purchased material	91
Donated material	37
Borrowed material	21
Rented material	2
Other sources	11

Base = 90 programs

* Percentages add up to more than 100% because most administrators listed multiple sources of materials. Although primary and secondary sources were asked for in the questionnaire, the respondents did not make this distinction. (appendix , Questionnaire for Administrators, Question 8a)

Table 194 Materials That Are Not Strictly Instructional *(expressed in percent)*

Question 1*: *Considering the reading materials used in your classes, what percent of these materials are not strictly instructional materials?*

Percent of Materials Not Strictly Instructional	Teachers' Responses
0 - 19	34
20 - 39	34
40 - 59	9
60 - 79	11
80 - 100	12

Base = 105   Median = 27%

* LMRP National Programs Study, Questionnaire for Teachers

420

Table 195 Types of Reading Material Used *(expressed in percent)*

Question 2*: *What types of reading materials are these?*

Type	Percent of Teachers
Paperback books	79
Magazines	62
Newspapers (daily)	50
Pamphlets	50
Hard-cover books	41
Instruction sheets	35
Newspapers (devised for the adult new reader)	31
Newsletters	15
Other	19

* LMRP National Programs Study, Questionnaire for Teachers

Table 196 Subject Classifications of Reading Material Cited by Teachers*

Subject Area	Frequency
Language skills	73
Literature	52
Ethnic orientation	40
Occupations	29
High school equivalency material	20
History and government	18
Science	18
Family life	14
Biography	10
Religion	5
Problems of race relations	3
Cultural development	2

* Titles are classified under all applicable categories. See question
  #8, LMRP National Programs Study, Questionnaire for Teachers,
  appendix   .

Table 197 Utilization of Reading Materials *(expressed in percent)*

Question 4*: *How are these reading materials used?*

Independent reading	77 *(97)*
Suggested reading	74 *(93)*
Directed reading (open book lesson)	55 *(69)*
Programmed instruction (individualized)	51 *(64)*
Required reading	30 *(38)*
Others (discussion)	14 *(17)*

Base = 126

* LMRP National Programs Study, Questionnaire for Teachers

Table 198 Topics Emphasized and Needed in the Reading Materials

Question 3: *What subjects or topics are emphasized in the reading materials?* *

Question 5A: *What subjects or topics are needed in the reading materials?* *

Please rank them on a scale of one to seven in order of emphasis. Number 1 = most emphasis.

Subject or Topic	Ranking of: Topics Emphasized	Topics Needed
Basic information (English, geography, math, history, etc.)	1	6
Job information	2	1*
Reference books (dictionary, encyclopedia, etc.)	3	8
Family life (sex education, marriage, child care, etc.)	4	5
Consumer education	5	1*
Stories (e.g., romance, war, mystery, fiction, etc.)	6	12
Community participation	7	4
Literature about specific ethnic or nationality groups	8	3
Health	9	7
Housing	10	9
Homemaking (cooking, sewing, etc.)	11	10
Law	12	11
Poetry	13	14
Religion	14	15
Art and music	15	13

* LMRP National Programs Study, Questionnaire for Teachers
* Consumer education and Job information tied for first place in the ranking by teachers of topics needing more emphasis in reading materials.

Needed Reading Materials Reported by Administrators

Program administrators were asked, "Do you think that there
is a need for reading materials in your program?," and if so, "What
types of reading materials are needed?" Virtually all administrators (98 percent) think that there is a need for reading materials,
and 36 percent specified the types of reading materials they think
are needed. Administrators identify two general categories of
needs: those which relate to the reading skill level and degree of
difficulty, and those which relate to the substantive content of
the materials.

The most frequently reported need is for reading materials
in a particular subject area, written on a simple, elementary level.
Although administrators express the need for reading materials
written at all levels of difficulty from grade 1 through 12, the
primary need is for materials ranging from first to eighth grade
level. Some administrators indicate that the need is for reading
materials written below the fourth grade level with controlled
vocabularies of 100, 200, 500, 1,000, and 1,500 words.

The statement of need for materials written at an elementary
level is strongly related to the subject areas in adult basic
education and job training programs. Administrators stress the
lack of elementary reading level materials for use in instruction
in vocational and occupational training, and a lack of vocationally
related materials for use in instruction in basic education skills -
language and arithmetic. Basic reading materials are needed for
training in specific vocations such as automobile mechanics and
office work. Elementary materials are needed in related vocational
areas of work experience and job preparedness as well as in relation to "everyday life situations" encountered by adults, such as
consumer buying, health, birth control, prenatal care, drug addic-
tion, cooking, and other specific subject areas which also reflect
the need for materials of more relevance to adults. Very few

administrators mention a need for materials in more traditional subject areas such as English, civics, and geography.

Another subject area of need in addition to the vocational and practical, is that of materials for specific ethnic and minority groups. In particular, administrators cited the need for information on the culture and history of Blacks and American Indians. Others point out a need for materials about disadvantaged persons living in an urban society and the problems they face. They mention the need of materials about minority group social and psychological situations, "character building" stories about members of minority groups, biographies about non-white Americans, and books that encourage ethnic pride. Finally, several administrators express a need for materials of interest to adults to be read for enjoyment and pleasure only, but written with a controlled vocabulary.

Needed Reading Materials Reported by Teachers

Teachers were asked to indicate whether they think there is a need for reading materials which presently do not exist. According to 72 percent of the teachers, new, additional materials are needed. Only 15 percent of the teachers feel there is no need for additional materials. More than three-quarters of the teachers express an opinion as to what should be included in the needed materials. Most of the needs mentioned correspond closely to the needs administrators express. However, teachers were able to be more specific in discussing these needs, as well as identifying some areas not named by administrators.

The most frequently expressed desire of the teachers, also shared by administrators, is for elementary level materials that are of interest and relevance to adults. Although teachers report the need for reading materials for all grade levels, they express a particular need for materials at the basic grade levels of one to five. Most teachers report that little material written at this level is of interest to adults. Existing materials at this basic level simply are not believable to adults who are neither unintelligent nor lacking in adult life experiences even though they have limited vocabularies and reading skills.

Related to the need for relevance and believability is the criticism of the "moralizing" and "lessons" contained in existing materials which usually have been written with children in mind. The values and experiences expressed in the "lessons" do not reflect the values, life styles, and life experiences of disadvantaged adults who are students in the programs. Consequently, these materials fail to motivate program participants. Teachers stress that believable, interesting, and relevant materials at this level are needed to create interest and motivation among the students.

Teachers strongly recommend that in place of existing materials which so often contain moralizing lessons, materials that emphasize the worth of the individual and his contribution to society be created. Some teachers suggest that materials be written which would help people develop positive attitudes and values, and convince them that their efforts in the program will pay off. One teacher suggests that some adult education success stories might accomplish this purpose.

Teachers made specific suggestions on substantive topics to be emphasized in new reading materials. They confirmed the preferences stated previously for material dealing with consumer education and job training. More material is needed on how to find and hold a job, and descriptions of occupations for men and women. Again, they emphasize the need for more materials on health, child care, birth control, and homemaking skills. Other teachers report a need for newspapers for adult new readers and "realistic" biographies of Black people.

In the area of instructional materials, suggestions were made for English grammar texts that are geared to adult interests, and collections of short reading selections with questions on reading comprehension and vocabulary. Further suggestions include requests for programmed instruction materials in workbook form and phonics materials. Many teachers report materials are needed on at least three different levels of difficulty to serve adequately the wide range of educational levels represented in the adult classes.

Representative comments made by the teachers reveal strong opinions and illustrate the major areas of inadequacies and needs.

Many materials seem aimed at a younger age level and seem somewhat insulting, equating a limited vocabulary with a lack of experience. Information is often dated or moralistic.

Adult oriented in format, tone and subject. Adult material too often tries to teach "lessons" - to moralize - this especially true of biography and some fiction. Adults we teach have a more sophisticated view of life and can draw on their own moral conclusions. I would like biographies that are realistic.

There is a terrible need for reading materials on a beginning (to grade 5) level with a content that appeals - or even means *anything* to young adult readers, especially those for specific ethnic or nationality groups - other than the suburban WASP.

Adult interest content written at a level which can be handled by people with limited ability and of interest to Black and Puerto Rican adults.

Our prime need is reading material on Hispanic history as it relates to the Mexican American. We also need stories in which they can make some sort of identification with the characters.

Need material at a reading level suited to student but geared to adult interests and experiences. 2. More reading material needed in Family and Community Life Values 3. More reading material appealing to the Negro male student (not Afro-American culture). 4. Health reading materials.

There is very little material in any field for the adult beginning reader that is not insulting to his intelligence.

Any materials designed specifically for adults - honest information, no trite or unimportant and trivial data so often found in our present materials.

More adult real life reading material. Lower level reading material appealing to mature grown ups to teach basic skills. Materials to evaluate current, every day experiences.

English grammar texts containing exercises geared to adults' interests rather than those of high school students.

High interest level for illiteracy groups. Consideration should be given to the culturally deprived adult and younger school dropout with emphasis on the worth of the individual.

Reading Materials Written by Program Staff

About 40 percent of the teachers indicate that their programs do use materials specifically written by the teachers or other members of the staff. A wide range of forms and types of materials are reported. The majority of materials written by teachers are basically instructional materials prepared for use in grammar, spelling, and composition exercises. Some teachers report that they have written programmed instruction workbooks for use in grammar exercises, and phonics materials for spelling instruction. Staff members have written simple short stories and dialogues for use in teaching English as a second language. Generally, most materials appear to have been written for use in grammar instruction.

Many teachers have written materials that are other than strictly instructional in nature and which are suited more to the students' "felt needs" and individual interests. Some teachers have written short stories of interest to their students which use the vocabulary they are studying. Several teachers report writing simplified newspaper articles on current events. Consumer education and job information are popular topics of staff-written articles, again reflecting the importance which these topics have for students in these programs. Teachers also have written material relating to the vocations the students are studying. Descriptions of jobs, application procedures, and work rules - all written on a beginning basic level - are common examples of materials written by staff. Examples of other types of materials written by the teachers include a handbook on finding and furnishing an apartment, a simplified driver education handbook, and a handbook on community services and resources. Homemaking skills, health and nutrition facts, recipes, voter registration information, and citizenship material are also topics on which material has been prepared by staff members.

Materials Written by Students

In a majority of programs (59 percent) students themselves have written reading materials. Although students write materials as part of class assignments, writing frequently has broader purposes than individual classwork. More often than not, the material also is for the benefit of the other students in the program. The most common type of material written is autobiographical. It usually concerns the student's personal history, experiences, and his interests, ambitions, and goals. This type of material often is written in the form of a job application. Autobiographical material is used as "get acquainted" papers to be read to the class. Another form of the biographical sketch written by students is the "Who Am I?" type of personal statement.

The second most common type of material written by students is the news article. These articles are published in the program's newspaper or newsletter which usually is put out by the students themselves. Short stories and poetry also are frequently written by students. Most short stories concern personal life experiences and also are published in the program's newspaper. Other types of materials produced by students include book reviews, letters, job descriptions, and essays. In these essays students often express their opinions on current events. Several teachers report that students have written simple one-act plays about Black history and job situations. One play focused on the problems of newly arrived immigrants to the United States.

Relationship Between Reading Materials and Student Success

Teachers were asked to comment on the relationship of reading materials to the success or failure of the student. Teachers who expressed an opinion on this (80 percent) emphasized one factor repeatedly: the relationship between reading materials and student success depends directly on how relevant and interesting the

materials are to the student. Materials that lead to students'
success are defined as those which create interest, and interesting materials foster motivation in students. With such interest
and motivation, teachers indicate, learning is much more likely to
occur. To summarize, the teachers observe that the relationship
is one of interesting reading material which creates motivation
and in turn leads to student success. Quotations from the teachers'
comments illustrate this relationship:

> Those who read more, no matter what "quality" of material
> selected, are more successful. This is related to motivation.

> Those students who read beyond the required assignments
> appear to increase their rate and comprehension faster
> than those who do not read outside of class.

> If reading materials are not meaningful to the student,
> then the student is bored and most probably will not
> attend class.

> Reading materials are most important to the success or
> failure of our students in that we must give them something
> of interest *to them* that they are able to read.

> To the extent that we use materials interesting to the
> student we hold and maintain his interest, and help him
> to success.

> Trainees who have found interesting material at an accept-
> able level have invariably increased their reading speed
> and comprehension.

If an *interest* in reading and an appreciation of the
pleasure from it can be aroused, success is bound to
be greater.

Teachers stress the difficulties they encounter when the
majority of adult education materials lack interest and relevance
for the students. They point out that it is easier to teach and
the program is more successful when appropriate materials are
available. As one teacher said, "Without proper reading materials
the instructor's task is all the more difficult. With them, a
well balanced program can be developed, one that will be dynamic
and of interest to both pupils and teachers alike."

Teachers report that they often rely on "pulp" magazines of
the "true romance" variety and on popular novels often selected by
the students. They are of the opinion that students who "read more
material" regardless of its "quality" improve their reading skills
and are more successful in the program than students who read less
material. They say that if students have interesting and relevant
material available, they invariably increase their reading speed
and comprehension. The important factor is the reinforcement of
the reading habit and skills derived from the knowledge, enjoyment,
and the information in the substantive content of the material
rather than the rewards derived from reading successfully at a particular level.

Students tend to do well when they have material which interests them, but may "fail completely" when it does not gain their
interest. One teacher reports:

While the material in Katz' *Eyewitness: the Negro in American History* is sometimes on a reading level considerably
above the test-indicated abilities of some of the students
who read it, they struggle through and get it because they
are fascinated. On the other hand, books such as *Learning*

Your Language are on an easier level, but the content is so childish and/or remote from the lives of the students that they have difficulty *wanting* to understand it.

I have found very little in the way of adequate reading materials for adults. I have used mostly magazines and newspapers. There is definitely a need for better reading materials. Most reading materials in use today have a low interest level for adults. We are attempting to fit the reading material to the interests of the students as in an individual reading program. One main difficulty is that in the teaching of remedial reading, relevancy is difficult to obtain without the materials becoming too difficult. Therefore, we are using magazines and books that are not known for their literary quality, but rather for their content, i.e. romance stories, etc. Since there is no specific set of books used here, as in a classroom library, books read by these girls are picked at random. The basic type of book read is of the cheap sex novel variety, and the titles are irrelevant. A few of the girls read mystery magazines, such as the monthly Alfred Hitchcock magazine containing short stories. All other reading materials, as listed in #3 are read by the girls under the guidance and direction of a tutor.

Students in this group *all* devour True-Confessions-type books. We work from this point toward "stories." There is a need to identify ethnically, and stories of aspiration are popular. The second way in which we work is to communicate regularly on paper, and...reading out "letters" helps by creating the need to read.

It appears that in order to circumvent the problem of inappropriate or lack of materials, teachers turn to alternative sources. They themselves write materials on topics of interest to the students, such as consumer education and job information; they use confessional magazines and popular paperbacks considered to be without literary value; they use materials written and selected by students. Several teachers report the use of series publications which are both successful in achieving program goals and of interest to the students - Reader's Digest Series, Science Research Associates, and Laubach Literacy materials.

A few teachers, less than 10 out of 106 who responded to this question, are of the opinion that reading materials have no effect on student success. Most of them give no explanation for their opinions. One teacher feels the student's individual motivation is the primary determinant of success in the program. Another says that the reading material can encourage or discourage a student but that it cannot determine the student's success or failure in the program. A few teachers report that the reading materials are irrelevant to the program's goals. One teacher feels that the reading materials were irrelevant to success for the General Education Degree examination for which the students were preparing.

Conclusions and Implications

Participants in the National Programs Study when compared to the sample of readers in the Population Study, are somewhat younger, more are men even though women still predominate. The dominant group is Black, but more Mexican Americans are represented.

Certain major characteristics concerning the use of reading materials in the classes or programs have been identified. The median use of non-instructional materials is 27 percent and the most common format of reading material is the paperback book. Teachers report using a great variety of materials. Variety remains the salient aspect. Among the more than 300 specific titles no widely used favorites are reported with the exception of a few titles such as *Soul on Ice, The Autobiography of Malcolm X,* and the Reader's Digest series.

The most significant persistent theme present throughout the study is the almost identical criticisms of the materials reported by teachers. Materials are not suitable for adults, they either offend the intelligence and experience of the adult or are written for children. The latter may be at a simple elementary level, but they fail to relate to adult interests, particularly adults who are from a disadvantaged background or who are members of a minority group. Values are of moral nature intended for children. Much of the available material does not motivate or interest adults sufficiently to achieve learning.

The major conclusion is the lack of adequate appropriate reading materials despite the existence of series and adult education materials, particularly at the beginning levels of reading. The implications for publishers, librarians, and editors are clear: the need to create new materials and to identify existing materials which frequently are hidden within important and unknown works. Biographies, short stories, poetry, current issues from the political and social science publications are important sources. Pertinent parts of such publications might be republished in other formats. Content and format then would have adult appeal. Materials written by students and teachers should be encouraged and opportunities for publication made. Materials are needed for use in instruction in vocational and occupational training and in basic education skills - language and arithmetic - and in specific subject areas.

Materials of interest to adults, to be read for enjoyment and pleasure, on the culture and history of a minority group, but with a controlled vocabulary, are needed.

Libraries have the professional skill and resources that should make it possible to: coordinate services with adult education agencies, provide advisory services both for students and teachers, search for material that fits class and individual needs, and support reading guidance services which assist the student to find materials for continuing reading and becoming an independent reader.

It is recommended that an extension of this study be carried out to investigate the use of and need for reading materials in the context of adult basic education and library reading development programs' objectives, with a more complete sample than the LMRP achieved, and through field studies possibly by means of in-depth interviews, observation, and case studies.

PART 4 MATERIALS ANALYSIS STUDY

14.

THE STUDY

Introduction

The Materials Analysis Study is the central part of the LMRP investigation. It permeates the entire study and provides the overarching design throughout the project. More narrowly defined, in this part of the report it is the phase of the research which focuses directly on the LMRP objective, to develop meaningful criteria for the evaluation of a range of materials - materials both currently available and those yet to be published which the adult new reader could use successfully to gain enjoyment and personal satisfaction. An annotated bibliography of titles selected on the basis of the findings in the LMRP studies and tested with the criteria is the other major product. This bibliography, *Materials for the Adult New Reader*, is designed primarily for professional use. As in the supportive studies, the Materials Analysis Study is concerned with library reading materials in relation to the context for use of the material.

Various factors complicate the problem of definition of library materials. The concept of what constitutes library materials encompasses almost every medium of communication. Multimedia centers contain all types of materials. Multimedia library services are providing materials through many professional and quasi= professional agencies. The limitation of the scope of the LMRP study to print materials was necessary because the extent and variety of materials in all media would be impossible to survey. The vast range and variety of published materials from existing and ever emerging areas of publishing, presented a staggering problem of establishing a representative, appropriate, and manageable collection for purposes of analysis. Lack of knowledge about materials satisfactory and useful to the adult new reader further complicates this identification.

Public libraries provide direct service to adults in various educational activities which they conduct or organize in cooperation with other educational agencies. Such programs and services create opportunities for those who have acquired reading skills and want to continue learning, to gain new knowledge and insights through the use of library reading materials.

One important factor for consideration is the use of materials in formal education. Reading materials in a classroom situation are classified as instructional and supplementary. Instructional materials are prepared for purposes of teaching reading skills and developing reading abilities. They are primarily for formal instruction under the guidance of a teacher. These materials, often programmed, have developmental sequences and frequently use audiovisual as well as print materials. Materials which are not of the instructional type frequently are described as supplementary. They reinforce and supplement more formal curriculum material. They are used for independent and follow-up reading. They help to complete the adult's search for knowledge and facts, furnish enrichment and enjoyment, and broaden his reading choices. They include a wide range of reading content to satisfy the diverse interests, needs, and abilities of the adult reader. The diverse purposes for which materials may be used include not only improvement of skills and instrumental use of information, but also understanding and use of a vast range of ideas, beliefs, and insights recorded by others. Such materials help to bridge the gap between minimal literacy and independent, mature reading. It is this type of material that this study is concerned with. Instructional materials are included only when they are of a supplementary nature. Foreign language materials are excluded because of other programs such as Proyecto Leer,[1] which are concerned exclusively with these materials. All these factors inevitably required that arbitrary limitations be imposed to create a manageable study collection.

Reading materials, for purposes of this study, are those print materials that serve broad reading purposes, that place emphasis on substantive content rather than the development of reading skills, that have been prepared specifically for the adult new reader and are adaptable to his level of use and interests. They provide a volume of reading range. They include materials evaluated and selected in relation to the context of use in daily life situations of home, job, club, street, school, and adult education programs. Context of use involves three basic aspects: the individual user's personal interests and daily needs, the occasions for use with library-created reading situations, and the occasions for use stimulated by agency programs and adult learning situations. The more formal class situations involve some study aspects which will use print materials or stimulate and generate their use in independent reading.

The Adult New Reader

Habitual readers tend to forget that to read is one of the great victories of life. Adult new readers realize better than anyone else how great the achievement is. Malcolm X in his autobiography describes the situation common to millions of adults with reading problems, "...every book I picked up had a few sentences which didn't contain from one to nearly all the words that might as well have been in Chinese."[2] He takes action by copying page after page of the dictionary, writing day after day, reading, and reviewing the meanings. He testifies, "I suppose it was inevitable that as my word-base broadened, I could for the first time pick up a book and read and now begin to understand what the book was saying. Anyone who has read a great deal can imagine the new world that opened."[3] "I knew right there in prison that reading had changed forever the course of my life."[4] Men and women interviewed in the Library Materials Research Project agree.

Respondents often commented that for them reading improvement opened up new worlds.

It is assumed in this study that an individual in today's society must be at an eighth grade level of reading achievement to be considered functionally literate. The adult reader goes beyond this to achieve complete literacy when he is able to read critically, to evaluate what he reads, to integrate facts and ideas, and to use concepts gained to help understand further reading. The adult then becomes a discriminating, independent reader.

Many comtemporary writers of distinction and the men and women interviewed in the LMRP survey of readers substantiate the values of reading and its influence in their lives. James Baldwin writes in *Go Tell It on the Mountain*,

> He left Fifth Avenue and walked west towards the movie houses. Here on 42nd Street it was less elegant but no less strange. He loved this street, not for the people or the shops, but for the stone lions that guarded the great main building of the Public Library, a building filled with books and unimaginably vast, and which he never yet dared to enter. He might, he knew, for he was a member of the branch in Harlem and was entitled to take books from any library in the city. But he had never gone in because the building was so big that it must be full of corridors and marble steps, in the maze of which he would be lost and never find the book he wanted. And then everyone, all the white people inside, would know he was not used to great buildings, or to many books, and they would look at him with pity. He would enter on another day, when he had read all the books uptown, an achievement that would, he felt, lend him the poise to enter any building in the world.[5]

Readers' feelings and opinions are demonstrated in a few selected statements made in response to the open-ended question in the LMRP Population Study, "Is there anything else you would like to tell me about your reading?"

I like to read to myself. I like to go to the library to look at books. I read what I like; maybe some people say, "Read this, it's a good book." I don't pay attention. I like to pick my own books. I like technical books.

It builds my vocabulary and it helps my imagination. It helps me in spelling.

From Plato I learn people to be honest and to love freedom and for nice education to read. From Kennedy I read every peoples should have courage and what to do for defense of this country and to love this country, America. From biography of Dwight Eisenhower I learn American troops won with courage from Germany in Normandy. My brains get grown up bigger. Too much for one day.

I like it. I think reading has helped me out. I have hopes of completing high school and going to college.

Reading has helped me a great deal. Well, to understand myself and others. Helped me to relax more. Better outlook for employment and most of all, better my love life.

Only thing I can say, that if you form a habit of reading, you can learn more about life and it also helps to relax your mind.

I have found out that the more I read, the more I
learn about different things. Since I started reading about two years ago, I became more interested in
reading. I can talk about many more subjects now and
also I can give information to other people. I can
answer in class about current events and world affairs.

Adults interviewed also were aware of specific benefits gained
from improvement in reading skills. A few selected comments point
out problems that reading helped to solve.

It helped me to sharpen my vocabulary.

Well, reading I find very useful in everyday walk of
life. It enabled me to help my kids with their
homework.

It is very useful and it is very depressing not
to know how to read. It also provides comfort
when I am alone.

I am just learning to read better in English as well
as in Spanish.

I now can read good enough to read street signs on
the corner.

In talking to people, it's easier. It's helped on
jobs. It's changed me completely around.

The place of reading in the lives of six adults, three women
and three men, interviewed for the Population Study, illustrate
various reading behavior patterns and interests. They represent
the four areas of reading activity: least active, somewhat
active, active, and very active, as measured on the Reading Activity

Index established in the Population Study. As previously reported, over half of the adult new readers are active readers, a third are somewhat active, 14 percent are very active, while three percent are classified as least active. Each reader described in the biography is anonymous in the study, and has been assigned a pseudonym.

A least active reader. Sadie Johnson is a 54 year old housewife who has lived in this city for 26 years. Her total family income is less than $1,500. She identifies Africa as the origin of her ancestors. She attended grammar school through the sixth grade in a small town in Mississippi. Her reason for leaving school was to support herself. At the present, she is studying English, reading, writing, and spelling in a public library reading development program. Her classes have changed her life. She has improved her personal relations. She understands and communicates better with other people.

Mrs. Johnson is rated as a least active reader because she has read no books in the past six months and does not read magazines, newspapers, or comic books. She owns no books. When she does read she enjoys plays the most. She also reads for information, to help in her school work, and to improve her English, reading ability, and vocabulary.

She has been to the library in the past six months to borrow books and attend lectures. In her free time, she takes drives or walks, goes to the neighborhood center, and attends church. Mrs. Johnson watches television news and weather, *Bonanza* or *Gunsmoke*, *Mod Squad, Mayberry RFD*, the Bill Cosby show, *Ironside,* and cartoons. Her favorite program is *Ironside*. Her radio listening includes music - country, rock-and-roll, soul, mood, religious, and classical; news; sports; religious programs; and talk shows.

Mrs. Johnson perceives herself as a poor reader who hardly reads. She says that she has no reading problems. In her childhood and teenage years, she liked to read, but her attitude in adult years has changed. She now likes to read only a little.

A somewhat active reader. Maria Fields is 28 years of age and a housewife. She attended five years of grammar school in rural Italy and left school at age 11 to support herself. Her first language is Italian.

She has not read any books in the last six months. Of the books listed, she would like to read *Diane's New Love*. She reads the newspapers at least once a week, either an Italian paper or an English metropolitan daily. She enjoys the news of the world, weather, the comics, advertisements, political news, and television news. She also reads *U.S. News and World Report*. She likes to read the stories about war and the lives of persons. Mrs. Fields reads to improve her English, for enjoyment, and for information. She owns no books, but uses the library to borrow books, to read magazines and newspapers, and takes her children there.

In her free time, she goes to dances, to the park or zoo, to the movies, and to church. She usually watches the following television programs: news and weather, *Let's Make a Deal*, Johnny Carson or Joey Bishop, *Bonanza* or *Gunsmoke*, *Black Journal*, the *Dean Martin* or *Johnny Cash Show*, movies, cartoons, *Mayberry RFD*, *Laugh-in* or *Hee-Haw*, the *Bill Cosby Show*, *Ironside*, and educational television. Her favorite program is *Johnny Carson* or *Joey Bishop*. She listens to the radio: news, sports, and music - country, western, rock-and-roll, soul, and semi-classical.

Mrs. Fields perceives herself as a poor reader who reads little. She always has liked to read, but as a child and teenager she did not read other than for school. At present she reads more than her parents did and the people with whom she lives. She read most between the ages of 17 and 20.

Melvin Roberts, a 32 year old blue-collar worker earning $6,000 a year, also is rated in the study as a somewhat active reader. Although he has not read a book during the past six months and does not read magazines, he reads two metropolitan newspapers daily. He also reads church, club, and union newsletters, and occasionally comic books. The newspaper articles he enjoys most are those on world affairs. He usually reads newspaper articles or features, weather, comics, sports, editorials, stocks and bonds, advertisements, news about civil rights and politics, obituaries, and television news.

Mr. Roberts owns books on war and religion as well as reference books. He enjoys reading, especially historical books. He reads to educate himself. He is studying English, reading, and spelling in adult basic education classes. Of the titles on the interview list, he would like to read *Call Them Heroes, Letters from Vietnam, People and Places, Up from Appalachia, Selected Poems* by Langston Hughes, *Profiles in Courage, Hot Rod, Shane,* and the Perry Mason mysteries. He has read the Reader's Digest books, the Bible, and the James Bond books. He would not find *Write Your Own Letters* helpful.

In his spare time, Mr. Roberts takes drives or walks, goes to dances, visits "a park or a zoo", the movies, a pool hall, and attends church. He is a sports enthusiast and belongs to a labor union. On the radio he listens to music - country, jazz, mood, religious, and folk; to news, sports, and talk shows. His television watching includes news and weather which he would miss most, *Bonanza* or *Gunsmoke,* the *Dean Martin* or *Johnny Cash Show,* the movies, *Mod Squad* or *Then Came Bronson,* sports, cartoons, *Laugh-in,* the *Bill Cosby Show, Ironside,* and *Mission Impossible.*

Throughout his life, Mr. Roberts has read little. As a child in a small Pennsylvania town, he read only school books although his parents occasionally read to him. As a teenager, he did not read books except school textbooks. At age 17 he left school after completing the eighth grade because he had to support himself. He reads now more than at any other time in his life, and he has friends who read a lot. Mr. Roberts perceives himself as a fair reader who read a little.

An active reader. Mrs. Dolly Weber is rated an active reader. She is 47 years of age and of African origin. She has completed eight years of school. At age 14 she left school to help her parents on their farm. She now works full-time as a housekeeper in a nursing home. She currently is participating in an adult basic education and a high school equivalency program where she is studying basic mathematics, language skills, and American history.

In her free time Mrs. Weber watches television. She usually watches the news and weather, *Gunsmoke,* the *Dean Martin Show,* movies, *Mod Squad, Mayberry RFD, Hee-Haw, As the World Turns, Ironside,* and *Mission Impossible.* She would miss *As the World Turns* most if she could not watch television. She also enjoys reading, visiting, and taking drives and walks. She likes to go to movies, to "the park or zoo," and to taverns. She belongs to a church and is active in her labor union and neighborhood organization. She listens to radio: religious programs, news, and music.

Mrs. Weber reads the *Reader's Digest, Ebony,* and *Time.* She reads the *Reader's Digest* regularly because she can get it where she works. She enjoys the human interest stories in these magazines. Mrs. Weber reads the newspaper a few times a week, and also her church, union and club newsletters. She likes to read the news - world, political, civil rights; letters to the editor and editorials; the women's section; advertisements; and the horoscope which she would miss most if she could not get the newspaper. She has read one book in the past six months. It was a mystery, *The Late Claire.* She owns books on health and nutrition, child care, and cooking. She reads for pleasure and relaxation as well as for information. She enjoys short stories and historical books. She gets information about books from the librarian at the nursing home where she works. Her major source of books is the library where she has borrowed a book and asked for information in the past six months.

Mrs. Weber has read *Life with the Lucketts* which she liked only "a little," and Reader's Digest books, and the Bible. She indicated an interest in the Perry Mason mysteries, *Letters from Vietnam, People and Places, Black Like Me,* Malcolm X, and *Profiles in Courage.*

Mrs. Weber liked to read when she was a child and also as a teenager. Her parents read to her occasionally. She read books other than for school. Her interest decreased in her young adult years when she was not at all interested in reading. She has returned to enjoying reading at the present time.

She feels she has not overcome her reading problem of pronunciation. Books have helped her in school, daily life, and in homemaking. She says, "I wish I had more time for reading. I wish I could understand what I read better."

By the Reading Activity Index, Matt Polanski also is rated an active reader. When 15 years of age, he left school because he had to support himself and his family. His second language is Polish. He is employed as an upholsterer for custom-built furniture. Now 39, Mr. Polanski is enrolled in adult basic education classes, and also an investment class in stocks and bonds.

As an active reader, he reads the daily newspapers in addition to the *Wall Street Journal* and *Barron's National Business & Financial Weekly.* He also reads his neighborhood paper, church, union and club news bulletins. He reads the news columns, stocks and bond quotations, editorials and letters to the editor, and book reviews. *Life* and the sports magazines are among those he usually

451

reads. War, human interest, and travel stores interest him the
most. In the past six months, Mr. Polanski has read two books,
one on how to invest money, and the other, *The Shooter's Bible*.
He has found that books have helped him in his school work, his
language skills, and in building things. He owns books on ways
to better himself in addition to religious and reference books.
His sources of books are friends, the library, the book store,
drugstore, and school. His main reason for reading is for information, to build things, and to help in his studies.

In the last six months, Mr. Polanski has been to the public
library to borrow books and to study. In his free time he reads,
listens to records - light music - and the radio, watches television - news, movies, the *Dean Martin Show*- plays cards, games,
and bingo, and visits friends and relatives. He belongs to two
clubs, a Polish organization and a sports or hobby club. He also
belongs to the YMCA. Pastimes which he also enjoys are movies,
walks in the park, and going dancing.

Only recently has Mr. Polanski begun to like reading. As a
child and a teenager, he did not read books other than for school,
although he had friends who were active readers. When he was a
child his parents often read to him. He feels that he has overcome
his reading problem. He rates himself a poor reader who reads a
little. "It's like this: before I fix anything, I go to the library and read up on it. I've been trying to improve my reading
in general. I read to help me with whatever interests me at the
time." In contrast, he is rated as an active reader by the Reading Activity Index.

A very active reader. Rich Sanders is 18 years of age. He
has lived in this city since he was four. His first language is
English and he also speaks French. Currently, Rich is in school
in an adult basic education program. He would like to get into
computer training. After completing eleventh grade, he left school

452

to support himself.

Rich always has liked to read. In the past six months he has read 25 books, among them are *Master of Falconhurst, Slave, We Charge Genocide, A Hundred Years of Lynching, A Handbook of Revolutionary Warfare,* and *Autobiography of Malcolm X.* From the list in the LMRP questionnaire, Rich has read *Profiles in Courage* and the Bible. He also indicated interest in reading *Letters from Vietnam, Get Your Money's Worth,* and *Getting and Holding a Job.* Rich reads *Time, Life, Sports Illustrated,* and *National Geographic* magazines regularly. He especially enjoys the human interest, travel, and sports articles. Among the magazines which he reads, he would miss *Sports Illustrated* most. He usually reads two of the daily newspapers every day, and a local neighborhood paper. He reads the news, sports, editorials, and book review sections faithfully. He is most partial to the sports news.

His free time is spent reading, visiting, listening to records and the radio, watching television, playing cards, going bowling, to dances, to the YMCA, and to bars. His radio listening includes music and sports shows. On television Rich likes the adventure programs, news, sports, and the *Johnny Carson Show.* Sports play an important part in his leisure time activites, as seen in his reading habits.

Rich is rated a very active reader. He considers himself a good reader who reads a great deal. There has never been a time in his life that he did not read a great deal. However, he has no friends who are active readers. His parents read to him frequently when he was a child. He feels that he reads less than his parents did.

Background for the Analysis of Reading Materials

The experiences of the librarians and specialists on the staffs of the cooperating public libraries and other libraries providing materials service in the area of the LMRP were a base of departure for the study of reading materials. Although these librarians felt the inadequacy of knowledge and experience, as the MacDonald study showed, they had experimented and developed reading lists for inexperienced readers. MacDonald's study documented 13 major programs.[6] In the initial stage of the Materials Analysis Study, the LMRP staff drew upon the knowledge gained in these special programs.

Cleveland's Reading Centers Project, although not continued, generated a valuable bibliography and film based on the special book collection used in the program. New Haven's Library Neighborhood Center demonstration explored new ways of bringing books and other media to individuals for their life enrichment. Enoch Pratt Free Library in Baltimore set up an experimental, flexible library program as part of the Community Action area program. This reading program drew upon all types of materials - paperbacks, newspapers, children's books, and pamphlets. An important factor was the librarians' responsiveness to immediate needs when subjects and title interests were identified. Brooklyn Public Library's Reading Improvement Program indicated that a wide range of materials is necessary, and identified titles which were successful. Keller reported successful use of such materials as simplified classics, the Thorndike-Barnhart beginning dictionary, and remedial readers such as the Mott Basic Language Series, Reader's Digest Skill Builders, the Turner-Livingston Series, and Science Research Associates' publications. Of interest to readers at the fourth grade reading level were such titles as: *The Good Earth* by Pearl Buck, *What Makes Sammy Run?* by Bud Schulberg, *Ethan Frome* by Edith Wharton, and *Animal Farm* by George Orwell.[7]

The Free Library of Philadelphia in the Reader Development Program initiated in 1967, made available to individuals and organizations materials which could be used by adults and young adults who read on or below the eighth grade level. The annotated, graded reading lists of paperback books, workbooks, pamphlets, and periodicals are an important guide and source for comparison. Los Angeles Public Library Federal Bookmobile Project reports contained valuable insights and choices of materials. The Kalamazoo Public Library program, although discontinued, published a rather comprehensive bibliography similar to the Office of Education adult basic education list of materials. Special materials on a beginning level were developed for this program.

These examples suffice to show the use of knowledge and experience available at the time. Data from research studies reviewed previously in this report, the librarians' experiences, bibliographic products of library experimental programs, all provided a foundation for the Materials Analysis Study.

Procedures

The problem of establishing evaluative criteria for the selection and creation of reading materials is most complex because of the diversity and variety both among potential readers and in the materials, themselves. Although this problem is present when serving any adult segment of the population, it takes on particular significance when directed to the evaluation of materials for adults on whom the LMRP focuses.

The development of the criteria has been based on an analysis of the characteristics of existing reading materials. It has relied heavily on the findings of the supportive studies which surveyed readers, studied materials within the context of adult use, and analyzed the indigenous literature for the identification of reader groups, subject interest, opinions and attitudes of readers,

and types and content of materials. These studies provide the
bases for new insights and confirmation in regard to categories
and content in the criteria, as well as new suggestions for the
bibliography of reading materials for adult new readers. Each
major phase of the Materials Analysis Study has been influenced
by these other studies, as well as by the data gathered within
the Materials Analysis Study itself. The latter in turn supplied
important data for the other studies which particularly were useful in the construction of the data-gathering instruments. Changes
and new directions have been possible because of the project's
policy of continuing revision.

The procedures involved in the Materials Analysis Study have
been -

1. the identification and organization of a collection of
materials for study purposes;

2. a survey of librarians' opinions about a selected list
of books;

3. personal interviews about materials and problem areas
with adult educators and librarians;

4. examination of special reading development and general
collections in public libraries;

5. the formulation of the instrument of evaluation;

6. the testing of the instrument through application to
materials, and librarians' and graduate library school students' reactions and critical suggestions;

7. the final analysis of the reading collection through the
application of the criteria established through the investigation;

8. the selection and description of the reading materials
for adult new readers.

Notes

1. Proyecto LEER (to READ) is a joint project of the Bro-Dart Foundation and the Books for the People Fund, Inc. The Project identifies books and other instructional materials in Spanish for children, young adults, and adults which are appropriate for public and school libraries; reviews materials; and publishes selected annotated lists, *Proyecto LEER Bulletin,* for library procurement.

2. Malcolm X with Alex Haley, *The Autobiography of Malcolm X* (New York: Grove Press, 1964), p. 171.

3. Ibid., pp. 172-73.

4. Ibid., p. 179.

5. James Baldwin, *To Tell It on the Mountain* (New York: Dell Publishing Co., 1952), p. 37.

6. Bernice MacDonald, *Literacy Activities in Public Libraries* (Chicago: American Library Association, 1966).

7. Richard L. Keller, "How the Brooklyn Public Library Helps the Functionally Illiterate," ALA: *Adult Services Division Newsletter* (Fall 1967), pp. 5-13.

15.

READING MATERIALS

Adult New Reader (ANR) Collection

The building of the Adult New Reader (ANR) Collection for study and analysis was a first concern. Consequently, in phase one of the Materials Analysis Study, the initial collection of materials which were to be evaluated was selected. The information about the materials came from many sources - librarians, adult new readers, teachers, reading specialists, publishers, both trade and indigenous, and the LMRP Staff. The search for materials in special categories and the analysis of these materials continued during the entire period of the Materials Analysis Study.

The specific sources from which the ANR Collection was compiled include -

1. bibliographies published by public libraries, adult basic education programs, and reading specialists for use with readers and students (appendix   , Sources of Adult New Reader Materials);

2. a representative paperback collection selected from the Fader list;[1]

3. recent titles selected from current publications, *Black World* (formerly *Negro Digest*), *ERIC News*, *Library Journal*, *Newsweek*, *Publishers' Weekly*, *Time*, *Wilson Library Bulletin* during the period of January 1968 to December 1971;

4. titles reviewed in ethnic publications such as *El Chicano*, *Americans Before Columbus*, and *The Black Panther*;

5. specific titles recommended by librarians and teachers through survey questionnaires and field visit interviews;

6. examination of collections for reading development programs;

7. bibliographies in special subject areas published during

458

the period of the research;

8. metropolitan and university book shops with special
ethnic materials, for example Drum & Spear Bookstore (Washington, D.C.);

9. materials developed by writers and indigenous groups in
the inner-city environment and by ethnic publishers;

10. findings and suggestions from information gained from
interviews with readers in the Population Study and responses from teachers and administrators who answered the mail
questionnaire in the National Adult Programs Study, and the
analysis of the materials in the Indigenous Literature Study.

The search for materials resulted in the ANR study collection
which contains three types of materials: (1) books, hardcover and
paperback; (2) materials in other than book formats: booklets,
broadsides, forms, leaflets, magazines, maps, newsletters, newspapers, pamphlets, and posters; and (3) indigenous literature, as
defined in Part 5 of this report. The collection totals approximately 1,900 items. Of this number, 1,000 are books, 800 are in
other formats, and 100 are classified as indigenous literature.

The collection is supported by the extensive bibliography,
the Bibliographic Record, which draws together data on approximately 4,200 titles that were identified during the study. The
Bibliographic Record contains standard bibliographic information,
brief notes from the published library bibliographies, annotations
by reading specialists, special comments from teachers and librarians, notes based on analysis by LMRP staff, and reading grade
levels noted by adult basic educators and librarians. The Record
contains additional titles not acquired for the study collection.
These titles are differentiated in the Record by a color coding
system. (appendix   Example of Bibliographic Record)

More important than the organization and control of the data
made possible by this Record was the continual use of the data for

four major purposes -

1. reference and information;

2. a basis for the selection of titles for the questionnaire
which surveyed librarians' opinions of materials;

3. a basis for the formulation of interview questions asked
in the field trips;

4. a contributing source for decisions in selection of titles
for the final bibliography.

A further important result is its usefulness to researchers,
graduate students in library science and adult education, and
writers of material for adult new readers.

Survey of Librarians' Opinions About Specific Titles

Librarians' opinions about materials for the adult new reader
were obtained at the beginning of the Materials Analysis Study
through a mail questionnaire sent to 11 of the public libraries
cooperating with the research project. These opinions were used
in the analysis of the titles and in the development of the list
of selected titles included in the Population Study to learn the
readers' opinions.

The librarians who are adult service specialists ranked two
groups of titles which had been identified in LMRP as being listed
most frequently on the bibliographies used as sources for the ANR
collection. On a three point scale the librarians evaluated
99 specific titles. They judged the usefulness of the material
in relation to relevancy of the subject, format appeal, and suitable cultural background. The first group of 77 titles appeared
on bibliographies 7 to 17 times. The second group of 22 titles
appeared 1 to 6 times, and were chosen to obtain more information
about their value in the areas of title appeal and subject interest (appendix 89, Survey of Librarians Opinions About Specific Titles.

Librarians in at least seven or more of the participating libraries were familiar with 24 of the 77 titles in the first group. These titles are of a practical nature and half are Reader's Digest publications (figure 4).

The librarians evaluated all 99 titles as satisfactory, unsatisfactory, or of uncertain usefulness in relation to three categories: subject is relevant, format appeals, and cultural background suitable. The 40 titles listed in figure 5 were judged by librarians in two-thirds of the nine libraries to be satisfactory in one or more of the three categories.

Only five titles were judged to be satisfactory in all three categories by librarians in eight of the nine libraries. Those titles were *The Autobiography of Malcolm X*, Holt's *Basic Dictionary of American English*, *Invisible Man* by Ralph Ellison, *Martin Luther King* by Edward T. Clayton, and *Selected Poems* by Langston Hughes. *The Autobiography of Malcolm X* and Ellison's *Invisible Man* are not included on the library bibliographies first analyzed in this study. These titles, nevertheless, apparently were being used.

The interest in Black history and biography is supported further by librarians' suggestions of additional titles not on the questionnaire but popular with adult readers. Three titles recommended by more than one library are *Great Negroes, Past and Present* by Russell L. Adams, *Before the Mayflower* by Lerone Bennett, Jr., and *Manchild in the Promised Land* by Claude Brown.

Most of the librarians were not able to name any titles as unsatisfactory or as "disasters". One librarian found unsatisfactory Stanwix House Publications, the Morgan Bay Mysteries published by Harr Wagner, and books by Angelica Cass. Another attributed the lack of "disaster" experiences to cautious book selection and to lack of awareness of specific rejections by readers when they took place. This perceptive observation may

Figure 4 Titles with Which Seven or More Libraries Are Familiar

Brice, Edward W. *Arithmetic*

Cass, Angelica W. *Your Family and Your Job*

Crabtree, Arthur P. *You and the Law*

Crothers, George D. *American History*

Goss, Jocelyn P. *The Thomases Live Here*

Holt, Rinehart & Winston. *Basic Dictionary of American English*

McCarthy, Agnes and Reddick, Lawrence. *Worth Fighting For*

Morris, Phyllis. *Life With the Lucketts*

New York City Board of Education. *Call Them Heroes*

Reader's Digest. *First at the Finish*

Reader's Digest. *Guides to High Adventure*

Reader's Digest. *"I Fell 18,000 Feet"*

Reader's Digest. *Men Who Dare the Sea*

Reader's Digest. *Mystery of the Mountains*

Reader's Digest. *A Race to Remember*

Reader's Digest. *Santa Fe Traders*

Reader's Digest. *Second Chance*

Reader's Digest. *"Send for Red!"*

Reader's Digest. *Valley of 10,000 Smokes*

Reader's Digest. *What's on the Moon?*

Reader's Digest. *Workers in the Sky*

Rosenfeld, Jeanette B. and Cass, Angelica W. *Write Your Own Letters*

Starks, Johnetta. *Measure, Cut and Sew*

Toyer, Aurelia. *Get Your Money's Worth*

Figure 5

Librarians' Opinions About Specific Titles

	Subject Relevant	Format Appeals	Cultural Background Suitable
Alesi, G.E. and Pantell, D.F. *Family Life in the U.S.A.*	X		
Archer, E. *Let's Face It: A Guide to Good Grooming*	X	X	X
Beck, J.H. *Understanding the Automobile*	X	X	
Brice, E.W. *Arithmetic*	X	X	X
Cass, A.W. *Your Family and Your Job*	X		
Clayton, E.T. *Martin Luther King: the Peaceful Warrior*	X	X	X
Crabtree, A.P. *You and the Law*	X		
Crothers, G.D. *American History*	X		
Ellison, R. *Invisible Man*	X		
Epstein, S. and B. *George Washington Carver: Negro Scientist*	X		X
Felsen, H.G. *Hot Rod*	X	X	
Hughes, L. *Selected Poems*	X	X	X
Goss, J.P. *The Thomases Live Here*	X		
Holt, Rinehart & Winston *Basic Dictionary of American English*	X	X	
Keller, H. *The Story of My Life*	X		
Kennedy, J.F. *Profiles in Courage*	X	X	X
Lasher, W.K. *How You Can Get a Better Job*	X		
Laubach, F.C. and Hord, P.J. *A Door Opens*	X		
Laubach, F.C. *Going Forward*	X		
Laubach Literacy, Inc. *News for You, edition A*	X		
Malcolm X, with Haley, Alex *The Autobiography of Malcolm X*	X	X	X
McCarthy, A. and Reddick, L. *Worth Fighting For*	X	X	X
Morris, P.D. *Life With the Lucketts*	X	X	X

Figure 5 (continued) Librarians' Opinions About Specific Titles	Subject Relevant	Format Appeals	Cultural Background Suitable
New York (City) Board of Education *Call Them Heroes*	X		X
O'Connor, G. *Helping Your Children*	X		
Reader's Digest *First at the Finish*	X	X	X
Reader's Digest *Guides to High Adventure*	X	X	X
Reader's Digest *"I Fell 18,000 Feet"*	X	X	X
Reader's Digest *Men Who Dare the Sea*	X	X	
Reader's Digest *Mystery of the Mountains*	X	X	X
Reader's Digest *A Race to Remember*	X	X	X
Reader's Digest *Santa Fe Traders*	X	X	X
Reader's Digest *Second Chance*	X	X	X
Reader's Digest *"Send for Red!"*	X	X	X
Reader's Digest *Valley of 10,000 Smokes*	X	X	X
Reader's Digest *What's On the Moon?*	X	X	X
Reader's Digest *Workers in the Sky*	X	X	X
Rosenfeld, J.B. and Cass, A.W. *Write Your Own Letters*	X	X	X
Starks, J. *Measure, Cut, and Sew*	X	X	X
Toyer, A. *Get Your Money's Worth*	X	X	X

very well explain the lack of knowledge, generally, about unsatisfactory titles.

It may be concluded that unfortunately a number of titles
which are out-of-date and irrelevant in content and format are
perpetuated on reading lists. These older publications, in pre-
senting the cultures and values of minorities, tend to use stereotypes, misconceptions, and biases. Titles such as Fitch's *One God*,
The Browns and Their Neighbors, and *Good Manners in the United
States* by Simonson and Roe, although appearing on the reading
lists, evidently were not being used by librarians. In contrast,
the title *Write Your Own Letters,* which appeared most frequently
on 17 of the bibliographies used as sources for the ANR Collection, is reported to be satisfactory by seven out of nine libraries; only two libraries had no experience with it. Further confirmation of the value of such a title or subject is the fact that
a majority of readers interviewed in the Population Study expressed
interest in this same title.

The *Home and Family Life Series* appeared on 11 of the bibliographies, yet the librarians reported in seven out of the nine
libraries no experience with these titles. Those librarians who
had used this series judged it to be satisfactory for subject,
although half of them judged the format and cultural background
as not satisfactory.

The Reader's Digest *Science Reader* series and McGraw-Hill's
What Job for Me? series are listed frequently on the bibliographies
but were unknown in half of the libraries. However, those librarians who had experience with them judged them to be satisfactory.

More attention needs to be given to screening and revising
the bibliographies. It appears that librarians whose leadership
in this area of service is recognized, prepare reading lists for
adult new readers. These lists, which are accepted by other librarians for selection and guidance, are used beyond their period

of usefulness. Such standard lists require revision not only to replace out-of-date materials, but also to add new and popular trade publications along with local materials.

Selected Data from LMRP Field Trips

The information gained in this survey and through first analysis of materials in the initial study collection was augmented by significant data collected on field trips to the cooperating public libraries and agencies. These data, collected through personal interviews, observations, examination and discussion of materials, became an integral part of the Materials Analysis Study (appendix 2 , LMRP Field Trips).

The major accomplishments achieved in these visits and conferances with librarians, reading specialists, and adult educators included -

1. information and opinions from librarians about types of materials, reader interests, specific titles, and problems encountered in materials service for adult new readers;

2. the examination of public library collections being used with individual adult new readers and in adult education classes;

3. extension of knowledge about the readers as well as materials based on the firsthand experience of the practicing librarian and teacher;

4. collection of materials produced locally and materials not easily acquired;

5. testing the instruments - criteria and questionnaires - being developed for the analysis of materials and collection of data about readers and their reading.

Discussions with librarians and examination of materials during the field trips made possible certain conclusions based on varying points of view about reading materials, the readers, and problems in reading guidance and materials service.

Children's Books for Adult New Readers. The advisability of
whether or not to use children's books with adult new readers is
a problem yet to be solved. Children's books are included in
most reading lists for adults with limited reading abilities.
The ALA/ASD Committee on Reading Improvement for Adults selected
a few children's books, "which will not offend the adult reader
in subject matter, textual presentation, or illustrations. The
Committee recommends that children's books be eliminated from use
as rapidly as possible and that each title used be tested very
carefully and reactions noted."[2] The consensus of librarians and
consultants interviewed about the use of children's books seems
to be that titles which contain adult concepts may be used successfully. Biographies and science books written at an elementary
reading level are particularly useful, as are introductory materials on such subjects as government, voting, cooking, and automobile repairs.

When asked, "How do you feel about the use of children's books
with the adult new reader?" librarians' responses indicate specific purposes for which they would use them. The responses have
been edited for this report.

Generally, only with mothers who want to read to their
children.

They are used particularly in the sciences. It depends
on the book and the patron's need.

Yes, to some extent. Biographies [written for children]
are particularly popular. Often the librarian suggests
the use of children's books for topics unfamiliar to
the reader.

Adults don't seem to mind - a matter of assessing their level.

Not used extensively. Use those with adult concepts, for example, biographies of Jackie Kennedy and Eleanor Roosevelt. Adults prefer to struggle with adult books - stretch the mind.

Use some children's books. Worried about turning someone off by giving someone "Run, Spot, Run," but feel that if you really like people, don't have to worry about talking down.

Not much used - don't like to.

The findings of LMRP research are in agreement with the librarian who stated succinctly, "Should keep in mind that these [ANR] are mature people with mature problems and should have relevant material on their reading level." The problem of the use of children's books by adult new readers was not investigated further in this research project because librarians indicated their limited usefulness; teachers emphasized the importance of using only adult material; and readers, themselves, did not report reading children's books.

Of the 254 book titles named by readers interviewed in the Population Study, only 11 children's titles were named. It is likely that even these, for example, "The Three Bears" and books by Dr. Seuss, were read by adult new readers who were reading to a child. In the National Programs Study, teachers did not report using children's books. Both librarians and teachers emphasize the importance of using adult materials which may be adapted or are appropriate for adults improving their reading.

Materials for Persons of Spanish Origin. Librarians working with persons of Spanish origin, chiefly Puerto Rican, Cuban, and Chicano populations, emphasize that the women, like women with similar responsibilities, have an interest in materials about homemaking skills, home management, and child training. Much information on cooking, sewing, and child care is a primary need because they are learning to live in a new environment and culture. The ethnic emphasis is not always the determining factor in choice of reading materials. For recreational reading women, especially young women, enjoy romance and love stories.

Sociological and Anthropological Studies. Some sociological and anthropological studies of minority groups in the population, although considered to have scholarly reliability and repute, are rejected by some readers who are members of the group studied. For example, some Puerto Rican and Chicano adult readers find offensive and undesirable the way of life and values reported by Oscar Lewis in *La Vida*[3] and *The Children of Sanchez*.[4] The findings and interpretations by several sociologists and anthropologists in studies about the Black population have generated a literature of controversy. Many Black scholars and readers disagree with the interpretations and judgments which have been made chiefly by white scholars oriented toward the dominant culture. Examples of continuing controversy are the Moynihan report and interpretations of it by others.[5,6] Alternative concepts and interpretations are presented by Valentine and others.[7,8] As perceptive and informed an observer as Stan Steiner, author of *La Raza; the Mexican Americans*[9] and *The New Indians*,[10] has been criticized by Chicanos and Indians because, although he writes authoritatively, he is not a member of the minority groups.

Values in the Materials. The most significant aspect of any material may well be the values supported in the material. Whether the material is acceptable or not, is biased or not, is considered by the reader to be dangerous or not, depends to a great extent on the adult reader's own evaluation of the values found in the material.

Coordination of Library Materials Service with Other Agencies.
The coordination of library materials services with other educational and community service organizations presents problems.
Librarians identified several obstacles. One commented that
"there is an attempt on the part of the library to coordinate
service with other agencies, but it is difficult, primarily because adult education instructors rank supplementary services
low in their priorities. They, too, must contend with insufficient time. The [adult education] agency's definition of enrichment reading differs from the library's - to the former it means
arithmetic, spelling, grammar." Another librarian stresses that
a two-way approach is necessary and that the librarian must have
information about civic agencies at his fingertips.

Location of ANR Collections. Where to locate the collection of
ANR materials for convenient use by the adult new reader is an
unsolved problem in some libraries. The LMRP staff observed that
special collections often are scattered in a hit-and-miss arrangement. Some are kept with large-print books. Sometimes the
materials are displayed as small collections in an accessible
spot. Librarians commented:

> Very seldom does the adult new reader use the collection.

> Tutors and sometimes family members get the books for the
> poor reader. The exceptions seem to be some of the high-
> ly motivated foreign born who want to learn English.

> Son, daughter, teacher, are the contact - not very often
> the adult new reader himself.

> People do come on their own. Some adult basic educa-
> tion classes either meet in or make periodic visits to

the library, and material also circulates.

Librarians' Criticisms of Materials. Criticisms of materials not
liked were characterized by librarians as: "series programmed
reading texts for children," "too old," "too brief," "no real
information, although a technical book," "too childish," "cartoons offend," "poor grammar," "too cluttered with captions,"
"too small," and "how-to-do-it books not popular with tenants."

Librarians reported a miscellany of materials liked by
readers: books in Spanish, Scriptographic booklets by J.C. Fer-
guson Publishing Company, *You and Your Job* series, Reader's
Digest books, Urban Education Studies, The Golden Legacy series,
Grolier Large Type Dictionary, Berlitz *English*, Cortina Method
Language Books, *News for You,* romances for young girls, Black
history, poetry, and biography.

Notes

1. Daniel N. Fader and Elton B. McNeil, *Hooked On Books: Program and Proof* (New York: Berkley Publishing Co., 1966).

2. ALA/ASD Committee on Reading Improvement for Adults, "Books for Adults Beginning to Read," *Wilson Library Bulletin,* 41, no.1 (September 1966), p.4.

3. Oscar Lewis, *La Vida* (New York: Random House, 1966).

4. Oscar Lewis, *The Children of Sanchez* (New York: Random House, 1961).

5. Daniel P. Moynihan, editor, *On Understanding Poverty: Perspectives from the Social Sciences* (New York: Basic Books, Inc., 1969).

6. Lee Rainwater and William L. Yancey, *The Moynihan Report and the Politics of Controversy...Including the full text of The Negro Family: the Case for National Action* by Daniel Patrick Moynihan (Cambridge, Mass.: The M.I.T. Press, Massachusetts Institute of Technology, 1967).

7. Charles A. Valentine, *Culture and Poverty, Critique and Counter-Proposals* (Chicago: University of Chicago, 1968).

8. Eleanor B. Leacock, editor, *Culture of Poverty: A Critique* (New York: Simon & Schuster, 1971).

9. Stan Steiner, *La Raza: the Mexican Americans* (New York: Harper & Row, 1970).

10. Stan Steiner, *The New Indians* (New York: Harper & Row, 1968).

16.

DEVELOPMENT OF CRITERIA FOR ANALYSIS OF MATERIALS
Background, Assumptions, and Procedures

As the LMRP research yielded new data and results concerning readings and materials, the Materials Analysis Study focused on the formulation of a precise instrument that could be used as a guide to specific categories in evaluation. The instrument developed under the continuing revision policy over the four year research period has resulted in the *MAC Checklist - Materials Analysis Criteria: Standards for Measurement* (figure 8).[1]

Preliminary to the development and formulation of criteria for evaluation of materials, certain underlying assumptions were made. In the context of this study, traditional criteria commonly used by librarians for the evaluation and selection of reading materials are considered inadequate. Traditional criteria emphasize authority, intent of author, quality, literary value, permanence, moral tendency, standard formal language, and disregard readability measurements.[2] Materials' relevance to adult new readers' life styles, personal and social motivations, values, interests, and needs is essential to satisfactory use of the material. Detailed analysis and precise description of materials for adult new readers will aid in objective selection and informed reading guidance.

The approach in establishing criteria in the MAC Checklist may be summarized as twofold: an analysis of characteristics of the adult new reader through insights gained from sociological and educational studies in research, the growing body of experience in the field, and LMRP research findings; and an analysis of reading materials from the several aspects outlined in the MAC Checklist. The procedures in developing criteria in the MAC Checklist are multiple -

1. the application of the continuing revision concept as an integral approach to the development of this evaluative

instrument as it has been applied in other parts of the investigation;

2. an analysis of the characteristics of the adult population who might be adult new readers through the findings of the sociological and educational studies concerned with life style, interests, and roles of adults, the experience of specialists, teachers, and librarians working directly with adult illiterates, new literates, and adults becoming independent, mature readers;

3. analysis of research on the characteristics of reading materials in the areas of legibility and readability;

4. the analysis of the reading materials in the ANR Collection to identify major characteristics, that is, source, format, adult roles, subjects, values, structure and development, language, illustrations and special features, reading level, and reading appeal;

5. an analysis of findings and conclusions from LMRP supportive studies: survey of adult new readers, the study of context of use in adult education programs, and analysis of creative writings by individuals sharing the backgrounds and environments of adult new readers;

6. evaluation and testing of criteria by librarians and reading consultants;

7. the analysis and testing of the materials by LMRP staff through application of the criteria;

8. continuing revision of the MAC Checklist in relation to the formulation of the organization and structure of the content, the layout and format, and the directional statements.

As the research evolved in the major phases, the LMRP investigation identified significant factors which determined the direction taken toward the final formulation of criteria. The

474

dominance of Black respondents interviewed in the Population Study
pointed to a greater emphasis on the study of materials concerned
with Black culture and literature. The more precise identification of reading interests and needs based on reading reported by
adult new reader respondents resulted in broadening the scope of
the collection to include more best sellers, ethnic literature,
and classics. The importance of identifying adult roles, attitudes, and values as treated in the reading matter or content
became central to analysis. It was assumed that elemental value
units are recognized by all groups of people, but that differences
arise from the rank ordering of value preferences.

Any precise determination of common attitudes toward established values and goals on the part of adult new readers has been
impossible to arrive at because of the great diversity in the
potential readers' ethnic, cultural, socioeconomic, and environmental backgrounds. The various culture of poverty theories are
limited and interpreted from conflicting points of view. The
influence of situational factors are dominant considerations.
Attitudes and values long established within the dominant culture
are being questioned by increasing numbers of persons.

MAC Checklist and Problems in Development

In the development of the MAC Checklist under the continuing
revision concept, 21 versions of the criteria were formulated and
tested. Substantial changes in the six principal versions were
made on the basis of new findings in the four major studies. These
versions which are the 6th, 10th, 11th, 13th, 17th, and 21st,
represent the key points in the formulation of the MAC Checklist.

The first tentative criteria consisted of the more traditional categories used by librarians in evaluating materials. These
main categories are: bibliographic information, appearance and
format, content, and presentation. As the MAC Checklist was

revised and expanded throughout the study it became more complex. However, basic categories which were used in the first version of the criteria were kept throughout: bibliographic information, appearance and format, content, and appeal. The emphasis given to these categories varied throughout the development of the MAC Checklist, but as the criteria were developed it became apparent that an additional section for measuring readability was necessary.

The essential and primary part of the total evaluation of material is the analysis of content. In the development of the MAC Checklist it is in this area that the greatest problems were encountered. Decisions on questions resulting from the formulation of these categories necessarily preceded all others. From whose point of view should content analysis be approached - the author, the reader, or the evaluator? Is it necessary to develop separate sets of criteria for fiction and nonfiction? What measures of readability should be considered? Is it possible to structure content analysis around roles and values? These questions finally were resolved through application of the various versions of the Criteria to the titles in the ANR Collection and in the light of staff discussions based on the knowledge gained in testing the criteria.

In the early stages of development of criteria it seemed that different sets of criteria were needed to evaluate adequately fiction and nonfiction. An attempt was made to formulate particular criteria for the materials defined as fiction or imaginative literature under categories such as universal situations and universal problems and style of writing. The impracticality of defining such general categories and applying separate sets of criteria to fiction and nonfiction became apparent. The necessity for a set of criteria that would measure all types of materials was established as the major objective. The *MAC Checklist - Materials Analysis Criteria: Standards for Measurement* (figure 8) achieves this goal.

In developing and testing the MAC Checklist, over 600 titles
from the ANR Collection were evaluated by the LMRP staff. In
addition, the MAC Checklist was applied to a separate collection
of indigenous literature. This analysis of these materials contributed to the important categories of roles, subjects, values
and attitudes, and language and style of writing.

When the 10th revision of the checklist had been formulated -
midpoint in the study - the general validity of the categories was
confirmed and some changes suggested on the basis of a special
conference between a panel of librarians and reading specialists
and the LMRP staff (appendix 10 MAC Checklist, 10th Revision).
Although this revision is complicated and overly detailed, it
foreshadows the final Criteria. For the first time, the title,
Standards of Measurement, was used and reflected the direction in
which the Criteria was developing. This checklist is divided into
two parts - Descriptive Information and Content Analysis. The
distinguishing feature of the 10th revision is the descriptive
paragraphs which precede and qualify each major category. The
next version of the Criteria was streamlined considerably by re-
placing the lengthy introductions with short descriptive directions.
At this point the three readability formulas, the Flesch Reading
Ease, Gunning Fog Index, and Smog Grading were incorporated (appendix 11 MAC Checklist, 11th Revision).

Ongoing revisions of the MAC Checklist concentrated on the
refinement of various aspects of the criteria: content analysis,
evaluative methods, precise directions, format, and organization.
Changes were made in the content analysis section by defining life
roles and revising the subject and value categories in relation
to life roles. Procedures for evaluative ratings and a new format
were developed. At this point the final form and pattern of the
MAC Checklist was established. At this time special consideration

was given to opinions and criticisms of practicing librarians who, individually and in staff discussions, evaluated the criteria. Further revisions refined directions and determined layout of the Checklist. Important additions were the worksheets for use in computing readability scores. The final major addition was the Quantitative Evaluation Scale developed to supplement the more qualitative evaluation of the other sections in the Criteria.

Bibliographic Evaluation. The first section of the MAC Checklist draws together the bibliographic aspects and provides for a critical evaluation. These aspects include: author, title, illustrator, publisher, series, edition, language of the text, date, price, physical format, and type of literature. On the basis of continuous testing, it was decided that it is necessary to provide this minimum bibliographic data about the materials for the purposes of identification and classification of the material and to assess the source and origin, that is, author and publisher.

In the early stages of the development of the MAC Checklist these bibliographic aspects merely were identified and accepted as factual and traditional points to record. As it became evident that many authors and publishers were unknown or had primarily local significance, it was apparent that they must be considered and evaluated. The assessment of the authority of the author, the competence of the illustrator, and the reliability of the publisher are the core of the bibliographic evaluation. These factors are always to be considered and at times may be the determining factor in the final evaluation. Series, editions, and dates, as in any evaluation, are essential considerations in judging the material's usefulness.

The location of the publisher and the costs are of critical importance in acquisition and budgetary considerations. For these reasons it was decided to include the address of the publisher and the price of the material as an aid in the selection and acquisition process. Although several of the MAC Checklist revisions omit this information because prices and addresses are subject to many changes, the importance of such data has been established in testing of the criteria and upon the urgent recommendations of various advisors who recognized the need for this information. It became evident also that many successful and potentially useful materials are not listed in the standard bibliographic publishing aids. A great deal of the material with which this study is concerned is published by new or obscure presses. Also, an estimate of price is useful even though subject to change.

Finally, the Bibliographic Evaluation includes an identification of the physical format and type of literature. The categories itemized are familiar and traditional, but include such classifications as booklets, broadsides, readers, and workbooks which are types of formats less frequently found in library collections.

Content Analysis. Essential to the total evaluation of materials for the adult new reader is the content analysis aspect. The general categories considered in the first versions of the MAC Checklist were derived from the first analysis of materials in the ANR Collection as well as studies directly related to definitions of values and analysis of life style of the four major groups in the population - American Indians, Blacks, whites, and Chicanos and Puerto Ricans. A comparison of the major categories incorporated into the preliminary revisions with the categories in the final revision shows the the extent of the refinement. The detail of the preliminary revisions gradually became more manageable and precise. At the same time, the five general categories first identified remain throughout in some classification but become more clear-cut and definable and less confusing.

The extent of changes made may be seen by reviewing a few of the five early classifications: reading interest which included consumer, vocational and civic education, housing, personal development, health, human relations; reading experience which included universal situation and problems, inspirational, fantasy, escape, empathy; points on cultural disadvantages such as political and social assumptions, problem solution through action, view of the minority group; style and vocabulary; and constructive cultural elements. Such terms were not definable and did not lend themselves to objective evaluation. However, the ideas remain and can be traced through the periods of the MAC Checklist development.

As the insights and data gained from the application of various tentative Criteria versions to analysis of the materials and the preliminary data were tabulated from the Population Study and National Adult Programs Study, it was decided to incorporate the concept of adult roles and to correlate this classification with subjects and value classifications. It had become apparent that a judgment about points of view found in the material content could be described adequately only through analyzing values and attitudes. It was decided that a most significant consideration in the analysis of the content might well be the precise and accurate identification of the values and attitudes promoted or rejected. Attitudes and values are equally difficult to identify and to evaluate. It is a hazardous area of criticism. Although in some materials the feelings and attitudes portrayed are very obvious, frequently they are implicit, obscure, and unobserved. The well informed, sensitive, experienced evaluator who is aware of various values and attitudes among individuals and groups, will categorize as objectively as possible the treatment and presentation in the material. Then and only then can judgment be made regarding relevancy and appeal to potential readers or the material be described so that the reader has information on which to base his choice.

The existence of a vast range of subjects and topics required the categorization of subjects into general classifications. A pattern of control is accomplished by the parallel grouping of subjects in relation to the personal roles of adults. The subject interests are classified in eight general categories corresponding to the role classification. These general areas include: personal development, learning, family role, group role, work role, citizenship, education, and leisure role. The impossibility of classifying all knowledge and possible subjects into a few selected areas is self-evident. The subject list on the MAC Checklist represents a refinement and selection based on findings from various phases of the research. The first subject interests list was developed by a subject analysis of the study collection and by matching topics with life-task orientation. The life-task orientation which is based on Havighurst's developmental tasks, served as a starting point. These tasks which are based mainly on middle-class goals in the decades of the 1930's and 1940's were broadened to define the interests and needs of a segment of the population primarily made up of urban ghetto residents with various ethnic backgrounds, different life styles, and educational deprivations.

Several subjects were identified as having current, special interests. For example, survival in various aspects - environmental, political, economic, personal, and social - is a topic of importance. Major concerns were identified in the areas of health, law, and dissent. Civil rights, consumer problems, housing, legal aid are a major concern to minority groups of young adults, the Black community, Chicanos, and American Indians. Topics of special interest which were identified in the analysis of indigenous literature include: survival, legal rights, revolution, personal identity, and the Black experience. Interest in practical information for daily living, popular fiction and classics, the occult, and news was indicated by readers interviewed in the Population Study. The great interest of persons of all ages in ethnic culture and literature was confirmed both by readers and teachers. Figure 6 shows the variety of subjects which are important for inclusion in reading collections for adult new readers. The list includes more specific topics of interest to adult new readers than can be itemized in the Criteria.

The general category of Structure and Development, the fourth part of the Content Analysis section of the MAC Checklist, provides a way to analyze the materials in relation to intellectual challenge and style. Intellectual challenge is defined as treatment or manner of presentation in terms of plot, characters, setting, style, and richness of ideas. These aspects are based on the indicators of maturity established by the Gray and Rogers rating scale developed in their appraisal of reading maturity.[3] The MAC Checklist in no way parallels their complex levels of evaluation. It presents a simplified, general outline which is applicable to fiction and nonfiction. Although a background in literary criticism and writing can provide the basis for critical insight in depth, the

Figure 6   Subjects of Interest to Adult New Readers

Personal Development

Alcoholism	Love
Drugs	Personal Identity
Friendship	Self-Preservation
Hate	Sexuality
Health	Social Poise
	Survival

Literature

Autobiography

Biography

Plays - Drama

Novel

    classic   popular

    humor   romance

    mystery science
                    fiction

Poetry

The Occult

Learning

Anthropology

Arts

Basic English

Ecology

Environment

History

Language

Mathematics

Nature

Amerindian Culture & History

Chicano Culture & History

Black Culture & History

Religion, Mythology

Science - Space

Technology

Education

Adult Basic

Advanced

High School Equivalency

Self-Education

Vocational & Technical

Citizenship

African Nationalism

Civil Liberties

Consumer Buying

Community Development

Counter-Culture

Current Events

Daily Tasks - driving, etc.

Dissent

Draft

Housing

Income Tax	Third World
Legal Aid	Urban Affairs
Politics	Welfare

Family Role

Child Care	Family Relationships
Divorce	Marriage
Family Conflicts	Parenthood
Daily Tasks - buying food, etc.	

Figure 6   Subjects of Interest to Adult New Readers, continued

Work Role

Auto Mechanics	Drafting	Nursing
Barbering	Earning money	Nutrition
Beautician	Electronics	Plumbing
Brickmasonry	Employment	Seamanship
Business Machines	Health	Secretarial
Careers	Housekeeping	Service
Carpentry	Labor Relations	Telephone Company
Cooking		Welding

Group Role

Membership in a Group

Peer

Ethnic

Political

Religious

Neighborhood

Responsibility to Others

Survival

Leisure Role

Arts & Crafts

Letter Writing

Music

Reading

Sports

Travel

Africa

Mexico

Puerto Rico

evaluation of the five characteristics is possible within the framework of the Criteria. Such evaluation is an important part of the analysis of content and essential to the overall evaluation.

Measurement of Readability. The measurement of readability takes into account factors not measured by readability formulas but considered in the context of this study to be equally important. This third section of the MAC Checklist includes factors for evaluation which affect comprehension and enjoyment, as well as ease and speed of reading. The factors to be evaluated in a general way include physical, visual, and literary aspects of print materials, that is, typography, special features, learning aids, language, and measurement of readability by the Gunning Fog Index Formula. Study and tests have confirmed that these various factors are related directly to readability. It is essential to consider them in relation to the readability score and content. Aspects of type, spatial arrangements, printing surfaces, illustrations, and other special features are analyzed and rated. In addition, the clarity and appropriatemess of learning aids and language are judged. [4,5]

The evaluation of language is of special importance in evaluating materials. Language may clarify or confuse, be appropriate or inappropriate, authentic or false. Single words, terms, and phrases which reflect life styles, values, and attitudes are acceptable although unfamiliar. Consciously or unconsciously, explicitly or implicitly, biases and prejudices are revealed. Nevertheless, the aesthetic, social, and personal meanings can be evaluated without a technical grasp of the field of linguistics and communication.

The MAC Checklist defines five types of language based on dictionary definitions. The broader problem in making judgments about the use of language relates to recognition of terms in the context of the evaluator's biases and potential reader reaction.

It is necessary to recognize terms "so charged with emotive potential that their use, with or without conscious pejorative intent,
to describe certain ethnic, social or religious groups generally
provoke an adverse reaction on the part of these groups."[6] Many
words carry overtones of racial and ethnic superiority that offend.
An objective evaluation and description of language in the context
of the content analysis is required.

Currently there is a great debate among reading specialists
and educators about the usefulness of grade level prediction by
readability formula. What can one learn from a readability formula? A readability formula indicates the relative difficulty or
grade level of reading material. Readability formulas measure
style. Actually, they measure only one aspect of style - difficulty - based on sentence length and vocabulary. No formula
developed to date measures content. No formula measures how good
or how poor a writer's style is. Formulas do not take into consideration at all organization, word order, format, or imagery.
Nor does any formula take into account the differing purposes,
maturity, or intelligence of readers. When working with readability
formulas it is important to remember that a piece of writing is
not necessarily good because of a good readability score.[7]

The question of whether or not to use readability formulas
was raised early in the development of criteria. The search for a
practical and reliable mathod of ascertaining the readability
level of materials for adult new readers involved much research
and experimentation. Formulas first under consideration were:
Dale-Chall, Flesch Reading Ease, Farr-Jenkins-Patterson Reading
Ease, Thorndike, and the Cloze Readability Procedure. It was
decided that measurement by formula is necessary to the criteria.
The determination of reading levels is helpful in assessing the
reading ease of material. The evaluator gains a more accurate
picture of reading level in relation to content and is able to

make comparisons with levels established by librarians, publishers, or teachers. The Dale-Chall, Farr-Jenkins-Patterson, and Thorndike formulas were rejected for purposes of this study, because of difficulty of calculation and inappropriateness for adult materials. Although the possible use of the Cloze Readability Procedure was explored, it was considered to be too complex and no further consideration was given to it.[8]

After research and consultation with reading experts, it was decided that two or three formulas were the maximum that could be used. Three formulas were incorporated into the 11th revision of the MAC Checklist. These formulas were: Flesch Reading Ease, Gunning Fog Index, and the Smog Grading formula (appendix 11 , MAC Checklist, 11th Revision).[9,10,11] Approximately 300 titles were analyzed with these three formulas. In evaluating titles, the LMRP staff members kept a record of the time required to compute each of the three formulas. A comparison of the amount of time spent on computing each score showed that the Gunning and Smog formulas required the least time, approximately 15 and 10 minutes respectively, whereas the Flesch Reading Ease formula required 20 or more minutes for each computation. Also, scores were compared for consistency of grade level prediction. It was found that the Smog scores varied from the Flesch and Gunning. As a result it was decided to omit the Smog formula from the MAC Checklist.

In the 12th revision of the MAC Checklist, the Flesch and Gunning formulas were used. Detailed instructions, explanations, examples, and work sheets for calculating the readability ratings were developed and tested. These two formulas were applied to titles from the ANR Collection to test the work sheet directions and accompanying work sheets. The Fry Reading Graph for Estimating Readability was incorporated into the 15th revision of the MAC Checklist.[12] The three formulas - Flesch, Fry, and Gunning - were applied to approximately 500 titles analyzed with the MAC Checklist during the period of major analysis of the ANR Collection, May, 1970 through August, 1971. In finalizing the criteria it was decided to eliminate the Flesch and Fry formulas and retain the Gunning Fog Index. Robert Gunning's Fog Index is mathematically an easy formula to compute and is an accurate measure of the difficulty of adult materials.

Quantitative Evaluation. The quantitative evaluation has been developed to serve as a supplement to qualitative measurements obtained in the analysis. The numerical ratings are based on judgments established for various categories in the preceding analysis. A rating scale ranging from one to nine is used to evaluate each of the four groups of questions relating to Bibliographic Evaluation, Content Analysis, Measurement of Readability, and Appeal to Readers. These rating scores serve as an index for computation of the quantitative evaluation score. A simple, straightforward mathematical procedure is used that requires merely following directions and no special mathematical explanation.

Figure 7   Materials Analysis Criteria No. 1

Library Materials in Service to the Adult New Reader
Tentative Criteria for Evaluation of Reading Materials
for the Adult New Reader

A. Bibliographic Information:

- author
- title
- edition
- series
- pages
- publisher (include address)
- price
- date

B. Appearance and Format:*

- size (width, height, thickness)
- shape (number of inches)
- cover (hard-cover, soft-cover, paperback)
- binding (color, quality of material, sturdy but pliable)
- paper (opaque, good quality, without glare)
- type size (be specific: 18 pt., 14 pt., 10 pt., etc.)
- type clarity (intensity: dark, medium, or light)
- leading (between letters, between lines, between words)
- margins (generous to the point of making the page look uncluttered and uncrowded)
- illustrations (suitable color, black & white, appropriate to subject)
- charts and maps (easily understood, purposeful, appropriate to subject)

C. Content:

- title appeal (suggests content-appeal, invites potential reader)

- subject (specific subject, relevant to everyday needs, vocationally oriented, enrichment within reader's need or readiness)
- scope (accuracy of facts, authenticity, relevance quotient, introductory, general, or specific treatment)
- organization (length of book, skills and concepts presented in logical order, glossary, index, table of contents, suggestions for further reading, directions about the use of the book, anthology, bibliography, biography, episodic, essay, fictional situation)
- idea diversity (original, important, trivial, stimulating)
- treatment (factual, imaginative, type or genre of literature)

D. Author:
- purpose
- intent
- accomplishment
- tone and attitude
- background for the subject
- relation of illustrations to author's purpose

E. Presentation:
- vocabulary load (related to various patterns of everyday speech, diversity and difficulty, word length)
- sentence structure (length, complex or simple, relation to vocabulary)
- paragraphs
- style (technical, pedantic, factual, vivid, dramatic, realistic, exciting, artistic)
- reading difficulty (readability scores: publisher, librarian, reviewer, reading specialist, other, LMRP)

F. Publisher:
- purpose
- intent

- reliability
- cost related to product
- comparative costs

G. Usefulness and Value:
- ethical and spiritual development
- job training
- job advancement
- self-improvement
- family living
- social relationships
- general education
- civic competence
- interpersonal relationships
- leisure-time
- health
- retirement
- cultural understanding

H. User:
- library
- other agencies
- ethnic group
- program use
- occupational
- income-level groups
- students
- age groups

* An attempt will be made to design rating scores for each category.
May 1968.

Figure 5   MAC Checklist

MAC CHECKLIST -

MATERIALS ANALYSIS CRITERIA: STANDARDS FOR MEASUREMENT

CONTENTS

For use with the handbook

The Adult New Reader and His Reading

INTRODUCTION

MAC Checklist - How to Judge Reading Materials

What is MAC Checklist?

- A guide for judging key points in various types of reading materials ranging from books to broadsides
- Itemizes in convenient checklist form the aspects of reading material which are to be judged critically

Who will use MAC?

- Librarians, Library Community Coordinators, ABE Teachers, Reading Specialists, Library School Professors and Students, Editors

Why use MAC?

- To analyze and to judge bibliographic data, content, readability, and appeal to readers

What MAC does

- Serves as a guide for annotations which record specific aspects of the reading material
- Supplies qualitative and quantitative evaluation for use in selection of reading materials and reading guidance with readers

How to use MAC

- Read the material to be analyzed
- Follow directions on MAC Checklist

MAC Checklist - Materials Analysis Criteria: Standards for Measurement

> A checklist of criteria to use in analyzing reading materials
> — books, pamphlets, magazines, newspapers, leaflets — which will
> provide the adult new reader with information and ideas, give personal
> satisfaction and pleasure, while aiding in the development of his
> reading skills.

I BIBLIOGRAPHIC EVALUATION

I-A Bibliographic Data

> Circle the appropriate category for each item: Very Good = VG,
> Good = G, Poor = P, Unable to judge = U. Formal bibliographic
> citation should be entered on MAC Summary Record and Annotation

I-A 1 Author(s) _____   Authority   VG G P U

I-A 2 Title _____   ☐ explains ☐ misleads

I-A 3 Competence of Illustrator   VG G P U   ☐ not applicable

I-A 4 Reliability of Publisher   VG G P U

I-A 5 Quality of Series   VG G P U

I-A 6 Quality of Edition Original VG G P U   Revised   VG G P U
                        Abridged   VG G P U   Rewritten VG G P U
                        Enlarged   VG G P U   Partially VG G P U
                                                Revised

I-A 7 Language of Text (other than English) _____
I-A 8 Price_____   I-A 9 Date_____

> Indicate format by checking (X) in space indicated. More than one
> may apply.

I-B Physical Format

Book: hard-cover	__	Leaflet	__	Poster	__
Book: paperback	__	Magazine	__	Reader	__
Booklet	__	Maps	__	Textbook	__
Broadside	__	Newsletter	__	Workbook	__
Collection	__	Newspaper	__	Other____	
Form	__	Pamphlet	__		

I-C Type of Literature

Autobiography	__	Humor	__	Scientific account	__
Biography	__	Novel	__	Short story	__
Essay of Information	__	Personal essay	__	Tract ____	
Folklore	__	Play	__	(specify)	
Historical account	__	Poetry	__	Travel account	__
How-to-do-it	__	Reference	__	Other ____	

494

II CONTENT ANALYSIS

Content analysis includes four major aspects which are vital in the evaluation of reading materials for the adult new reader. These aspects are: personal roles, subjects, attitudes and values, and structure and development. A critical analysis is necessary for an objective evaluation and description of the material

II-A Personal Roles

> Indicate whether the roles as defined are identifiable in the material by checking (X) the category which applies: Dominant = D, Secondary = S, Not Applicable = NA. More than one may apply.

II-A 1 *The Role of the Person in his own Development:* Growth and self-development which enables one to meet individual and social expectations at various periods during life. Subject areas relevant to the personal development role are: individual identity, religious and spiritual beliefs, social relationships, personal health, understanding the arts, literature, nature, and science.   D __ S __ NA __

II-A 2 *The Role in the Family:* Role as a member of family with parents, brothers, and sisters, grandparents, and extended family. Subject areas relevant to the family role include: marriage, parenthood, child care, family relationships, and home management.   D __ S __ NA __

II-A 3 *The Role of the Person in the Group:* Role as a member of society in relation to others. Subject areas relevant to group role include: friendship patterns, responsibility for others, acceptance or rejection of group norms, and identification with ethnic groups and the community.   D __ S __ NA __

II-A 4 *The Role of the Person as a Participant in Political and Social Life:* Influence on the development of established law, government, politics, social welfare, and counter-social structures. Subject areas relevant to this role include: law, government, counter positions, citizenship, civil liberties, current events, and community development.   D __ S __ NA __

II-A 5 *The Role of the Person as a Participant in Education:* Education and learning in acquiring knowledge and skills for everyday living and personal enjoyment. Subject areas relevant to this role include the various fields and types of knowledge -- arts, science, technology.   D __ S __ NA __

II-A 6 *The Role of the Person in Work:* The choice, preparation, and work in an occupation which brings satisfaction and income. Subjects relevant to the work role include: careers, employment, and labor and industrial relations.   D __ S __ NA __

II-A 7 *The Role of the Person in his Leisure:* Participation in activities which provide pleasure and enjoyment during one's free time. Subjects relevant to these activities include: arts, crafts, learning, reading, and sports.   D __ S __ NA __

II-A 8 *Other*   D __ S __ NA __

II-C Attitudes and Values

Attitudes and values for the purposes of this checklist mean an author's feeling or position with regard to any norm, object, situation, ideal, or principle treated *in the material analyzed.*

Indicate the author's point of view toward the attitudes and values treated in the material by checking the appropriate column:
+ = promotes or supports the attitude or value
- = criticizes or rejects the attitude or value
o = presents attitude or value in a neutral manner
U = Unable to judge
Analyze the content for attitudes and values dealt with either explicitly or implicitly in the material. If no attitude and value analysis is appropriate go to Section III.

II-C 1 Personal Development	+	-	o	U		II-C 5 Political/Social Role	+	-	o	U
Cooperation						Evolutionary Change				
Creativity						Law and Order				
Freedom						Legal Justice				
Hate						Citizen Participation				
Leadership						Patriotism				
Love						Revolutionary Change				
Material Things						Status Quo				
Personal Identity						Traditionalism				
Physical Appearance						Other _____				
Physical Fitness										
Sexuality						II-C 6 Work				
Success						Earning a Living				
Survival						Economic Security				
Other _____						Job Satisfaction				
						Service Orientation				
II-C 2 Learning						Other _____				
Enjoyment										
Gain Facts						II-C 7 Orientation to Time				
Gain Skills						To the Present				
Gain Appreciation						To the Past				
Self Advancement						To the Future				
Other _____						Other _____				
II-C 3 Family Role						II-C 8 Spiritual/Aesthetic				
Authority of Father						Creative Arts				
Authority of Mother						Formal Religion				
Extended Family						Literature				
Family Solidarity						Music				
Other _____						Nature				
						Personal Religion				
II-C 4 Group Role						Other _____				
Advancement										
Alienation						II-C 9 Science & Technology				
Conformity						Environment				
Group Identity						Nature				
Survival						Other _____				
Other _____										
						II-C 10 Other				
						_____				
						_____				
						_____				

II-B Subjects

Check (X) Subjects present in material being analyzed. Check (X) in appropriate column the term which describes treatment of specific subjects: Authentic = A, Inaccurate = I, Unable to judge = U.

II-B 1 Personal Development   A I U
Alcoholism
Drugs
Friendship
Hate
Love
Personal Identity
Self Preservation
Sexuality
Social Poise
Survival
Other _____

II-B 1a Learning
Arts
History
Language
Nature
Religion
Science
Technology
Other _____

II-B 2 Family Role
Child Care
Divorce
Family Conflicts
Family Relationships
Home Management
Marriage
Parenthood
Other _____

II-B 3 Group Role
Membership in a Group
  -Ethnic
  -Neighborhood
  -Peer
  -Political
  -Religious
Responsibility to
  others
Survival
Other _____

II-B 4 Work Role
Careers
Employment
Labor Relations
Unemployment
Other _____

II-B 5 Citizenship   A I U
Civil Liberties
Community Development
Current Events
Housing
Law
Legal Aid
Politics
Urban Affairs
Welfare
Other

II-B 6 Education
Adult Basic
  Arithmetic
  Reading
  Writing
  Consumer Affairs

High School
Equivalency
  Business
  English
  History
  Mathematics
  Science

Vocational &
Technical
  Business
  Crafts
  Job Training

Advanced

Self Education

Other _____

II-B 7 Leisure Role
Arts and Crafts
Reading
Sports
Travel
Other _____

II-B 8 Other
_____
_____
_____
_____

497

III THE MEASUREMENT OF READABILITY

The measurement of readability considers factors which affect comprehension and enjoyment, as well as ease and speed of reading. The factors to be analyzed include physical, visual, and literary aspects of printed material: typography, special features, learning aids, language, and measurement of readability by the Gunning Fog index formula[1].

III-A Typography

> Legibility means the perception of letters and words. Judge the legibility of typographic elements in the materials: type, spatial arrangements, and printing surfaces as having High Legibility = H, Moderate Legibility = M, Low Legibility = L, Illegibility = I.

III-A 1 Type

III-A 1a Style of type   ☐ H ☐ M ☐ L ☐ I

Style of type is appropriate to content   ☐ yes   ☐ no

III-A 1b Size of type   ☐ H ☐ M ☐ L ☐ I

Size of type is appropriate to content   ☐ yes   ☐ no

III-A 1c Judge type legibility   ☐ acceptable   ☐ not acceptable

III-A 2 Spatial Arrangements

III-A 2a Outer Margins ☐ adequate ☐ inadequate ☐ obscure print

Inner Margins ☐ adequate ☐ inadequate ☐ obscure print

III-A 2b Judge legibility of overall spatial arrangement considering margins, page layout, spacing between heading and text, spacing between lines of text.

☐ H ☐ M ☐ L ☐ I   ☐ acceptable   ☐ not acceptable

III-A 3 Printing Surfaces

III-A 3a Texture ☐ dull ☐ glossy ☐ acceptable ☐ not acceptable

III-A 3b Print on reverse side shows through

☐ yes ☐ no   ☐ acceptable   ☐ not acceptable

III-A 3c Quality of paper ☐ acceptable ☐ not acceptable

III-A 3d Color of type on printing surface

	H	M	L	I
Black on White				
White on Black				
Black on Color				
Color on Color				

Judge color or type and printing surface   ☐ acceptable   ☐ not acceptable

III-A 3e Judge overall legibility of printing surfaces ☐ H ☐ M ☐ L ☐ I

II-D Structure and Development

II-D 1 Intellectual Challenge, i.e., Treatment or Manner of Presentation

> Check (X) in appropriate column to indicate characteristics of plot, characters, setting, style, and richness of ideas: Factual, Stereotyped, Average, Above Average, Original, Universal, Not Applicable. In some material these traditional stylistic elements will not be significant. More than one may apply.

	Factual	Stereo-typed	Average	Above Average	Original	Universal	Not Applicable
Plot							
Characters							
Setting							
Style							
Richness of Ideas							

II-D 1a

> Indicate by checking (X), whether in your judgment, plot, characters, setting, style, and richness of ideas are simple, average, complex, or not applicable. More than one may apply.

	Simple	Average	Complex	NA
Plot				
Characters				
Setting				
Style				
Richness of Ideas				

II-D b

> Judge the importance and relationship of each stylistic characteristic. Indicate by checking (X), whether plot, characters, setting, style, and richness of ideas are primary, secondary, integral, or not applicable. More than one may apply.

	Primary	Secondary	Integral	NA
Plot				
Characters				
Setting				
Style				
Richness of Ideas				

II-D 2 Analysis of Style

> Check (X) in space provided, characteristics of style present in the material being analyzed. More than one may apply.

Dramatic ___   Imaginative ___   Scholarly ___
Factual ___   Journalistic ___   Scientific ___
Fantasy ___   Poetic ___   Technical ___
Humor ___   Popular ___   Other _____

III-B 3 Diagrams

Diagrams in content ☐ yes ☐ no   Needed but missing ☐

Technique _____ ☐ not known
       (write in)

Supportive of text ☐ yes ☐ no

Logical placement ☐ yes ☐ no

	VG	G	P	NA
Accuracy of Content				
Artistic Quality				
Black & White				
Color				
Reproduction				
Technical Quality				

III-B 4 Tables, Charts, Graphs

	Tables	Charts	Graphs
Included in content	☐ yes ☐ no	☐ yes ☐ no	☐ yes ☐ no
Needed but missing	☐	☐	☐
Supportive of text	☐ yes ☐ no	☐ yes ☐ no	☐ yes ☐ no
Logical placement	☐ yes ☐ no	☐ yes ☐ no	☐ yes ☐ no

	VG G P NA	VG G P NA	VG G P NA
Accuracy			
Black & White			
Character Alignment			
Color			
Explanatory Statement			
Reproduction			
Spacing			

III-B Special Features - Maps, Illustrations, Diagrams, Tables & Charts

> Evaluate the special features in the material being analyzed.
> Answer where applicable, yes/no, and rate specific qualities:
> Very Good = VG, Good = G, Poor = P, Not Applicable = NA.

III-B 1 Maps

Maps included in content ☐ yes ☐ no   Needed but missing ☐

If "yes" answer the following:

Supportive of text ☐ yes ☐ no

Adequate number ☐ yes ☐ no

Logical placement ☐ yes ☐ no

	VG	G	P	NA
Accuracy of Content				
Clarity of Legends				
Clarity of Symbols				
Color Identification				
Consistency of Scales				
Precision of Scales				
Reproduction				
Technical Accuracy				

III-B 2 Illustrations

Cover Illustration ☐ yes ☐ no   Needed but missing ☐

☐ explains   ☐ misleads   ☐ appeals

Illustrations in content ☐ yes ☐ no   Needed but missing ☐

Technique _____   ☐ not known
          (write in)

Supportive of text ☐ yes ☐ no

Logical placement ☐ yes ☐ no

	VG	G	P	NA
Accuracy of Content				
Artistic Quality				
Black & White				
Color				
Reproduction				
Technical Quality				

III-E Readability Formula - Gunning Fog Index

> Robert Gunning in *The Technique of Clear Writing* states, "The aim of readability research has been to single out those factors of writing style that can be measured, and to take the added, important step of finding out to what degree each affects reading difficulty." He bases his readability formula, the Fog Index, on two language factors, *sentence length* and *hard words*.
>
> Terminology: *Hard Words* - words composed of three or more syllables
> *Fog Index* - reading grade level required for understanding the material

Procedure

1 Select three 100 word samples, one near the beginning, but not opening paragraph, one near middle, and one near the end.

2 Count number of sentences in each 100 word sample. Determine the average sentence length by dividing the number of words by the number of complete sentences.

3 Count the number of words of three syllables or over to get the number of hard words. Do not count proper nouns, easy compound words like "bookkeeper", or verb forms in which the third syllable is merely the ending.

4 Add together the number of polysyllabic words and average sentence length, then multiply by .4 which yields the reading grade level.

5 Repeat computation for each sample of 100 words.

6 Compute average of the three samples.

Example

		I	II	I	II
				Evaluator's work space	
1	Number of sentences in 100 word sample[1]	6			
2	Average Sentence Length 100 ÷ 6 (put answer in column II)		16.6		
3	Number of hard words (put answer in column II)		+2		+
4	Add figures in column II =		18.6		
5	Multiply this sum by .4		x.4		
6	Reading Grade Level is Seventh Grade, fourth month for first 100 word sample		7.4		
7	Compute the score for 2nd 100 word sample		6.6		
8	Compute the score for 3rd 100 word sample		22.8		
9	Compute the average of the three reading grade scores		3) 36.8		3)
	Fog Index =		12.2		

---
[1] Malcolm X and Alex Haley, *Autobiography of Malcolm X* (New York, N.Y.: Grove Press, 1966) p. 39, paragraph 1.

III-C Learning Aids

Check (X), if applicable, in the appropriate column to indicate when the learning aids in the material being analyzed are clear, unclear, useful, not useful. More than one may apply.

	Clear	Unclear	Useful	Not Useful	Needed but Missing
Answers					
Appendix(es)					
Bibliography(ies)					
Chapter summaries					
Exercises to test skills					
Explanatory phrases in text					
Footnotes					
Follow up projects					
Glossary					
Index to illustrations					
Index to text					
Introduction					
Question guides					
Reading guides					
Self-pacing techniques					
Table of contents					
Vocabulary definitions					
Other _____					

III-D Language

Check (X), if applicable, in the appropriate column to indicate whether the language is appropriate or inappropriate, and whether it clarifies or confuses reading ease and understanding. More than one may apply.

	Appropriate	Inappropriate	Clarifies	Confuses	Unable to Judge
Argot: peculiar to particular group					
Colloquial: conversational style					
Dialect: regional speech pattern					
Formal: standard, traditionally correct					
Slang: informal, nonstandard, including so called "unacceptable"					
Technical: terms peculiar to the subject					
Other _____					

V QUANTITATIVE EVALUATION

The following numerical rating scale and accompanying questions serve
as a supplement to the preceding measurements in the MAC Checklist
Sections I through IV. The numerical rating of each question is to
be an overall integrated evaluation of the section to which it refers.
In assigning each rating it is necessary to take into account all of
the factors considered in that section.

Rate each question using the following scale from one to nine, or 0 if not
applicable. Do not total scores until all 4 groups of questions are rated.

1	definitely inferior	6	somewhat good
2	very poor	7	good
3	poor	8	very good
4	somewhat poor	9	definitely superior
5	fair	0	not applicable

Rating
Questions Related to Each Section of the MAC Checklist   Score

I Bibliographic Evaluation

I-A What is your overall assessment of the reliability and
authority of the material (bibliographic data) ?   _____

I-B What is your overall judgment of the material's physical
format?   _____

I-C How would you evaluate the material as representative of
this type of literature?   _____

GROUP I TOTAL = _____

II Content Analysis

II-A How would you judge the overall development of the dominant
personal roles in the material, taking into consideration
completeness, credibility, and portrayal?   _____

II-B How would you rate the treatment of the subjects covered in
the material with respect to authenticity, accuracy, and
verisimilitude?   _____

II-C Are the attitudes and values treated in the material portrayed in a convincing and believable manner?   _____

II-D How would you evaluate the overall development of the material
with respect to complexity and appeal to the adult new
reader's interest?   _____

II-D How would you judge the overall development of the characters? _____

II-D How would you evaluate the treatment of the setting in the
material?   _____

II-D How would you rate the style of the material with respect to
its clarity, appropriateness to the subject, and integration
of its stylistic elements?   _____

II-D How meaningful or penetrating is the richness of ideas expressed in the material?   _____

GROUP II TOTAL = _____

IV APPEAL TO READERS

IV-A Potential Reader(s)

> On the basis of your findings evaluate the appeal of the book to the potential reader in each of the following categories as: Major = M, Secondary = S, or Unable to Judge = U. Check (X) the appropriate column listed below. More than one may apply.

Sex

    M S U

  Men

  Women

Age

  15-18 years

  19-24

  25-34

  35-44

  45-54

  55-64

  65 and over

  Any age

Special Background Appeal

  Rural

  Urban

  Suburban

Ethnic Emphasis

    M S U

  American Indian

  Black American

  White American

  Cuban

  Mexican American

  Puerto Rican American

  African

  Asian

  European

  South American

  Other

IV-B Reader Appeal

> Check (X) appropriate qualities in the material which may attract the potential reader.

Informational	__	Aesthetic	__	Adventure	__
Interpretive	__	Intellectual	__	Pleasure	__
Problem solving	__	Spiritual	__	Relaxation	__
Personal security	__	Social security	__	Other	_____

Using the rating scores entered in the 4 Groups of questions, compute the following to arrive at a description of the title being evaluated.

	Question Groups				
	I	II	III	IV	
a. Enter the total rating scores for each Group	___	___	___	___	(line a)
b. Go to next line (these figures to use with line d)	3	8	5	2	(line b)
c. Enter the number of questions rated 0 (not applicable) for each Group	___	___	___	___	(line c)
d. Subtract line c from line b (line b — line c)	___	___	___	___	(line d)
e. Go to next line	x9	x4.5	x9	x9	(line e)
f. Multiply line d by line e (line d x line e)	___	___	___	___	(line f)
g. Divide line a by line f $\dfrac{\text{line a}}{\text{line f}}$	___	___	___	___	(line g)
h. Add the four decimal numbers in line g	___				(line h)
i. Divide the number in line h by 5 $\dfrac{\text{line h}}{5}$	___			= Average Decimal Score	(line i)

j. Use the following "MAC Evaluation Scale" to convert line i (Average Decimal Score) into a description

MAC Evaluation Scale

Score	Description	Score	Description
0 - .11	definitely inferior	.56 - .67	somewhat good
.12 - .22	very poor	.68 - .78	good
.23 - .33	poor	.79 - .89	very good
.34 - .44	somewhat poor	.90 - 1.00	definitely superiod
.45 - .55	fair		

Enter the appropriate description _____

Questions Related to Each Section of the MAC Checklist (continued)

III The Measurement of Readability

III-A How do you judge the <u>typography</u> for overall legibility and appearance?

_____

III-B What is your judgment of the <u>special features</u> (maps, illustrations, diagrams, tables, charts, and graphs) with respect to appropriateness, clarity, and appearance?

_____

III-C How would you assess the overall clarity and usefulness of the <u>learning aids</u> employed in the material?

_____

III-D What is your assessment of the <u>language</u> used in the material taking into consideration its clarity and appropriateness?

_____

III-E How would you judge the <u>readability level</u> of the material for the adult new reader?

_____

GROUP III TOTAL = _____

IV Appeal to Readers

IV-A How would you evaluate the material for its appeal to the <u>potential group</u>?

_____

IV-B What is your judgment of the material's appeal to the <u>potential reader</u>?

_____

GROUP IV TOTAL = _____

Add the rating scores for each group of questions and record them in the four spaces provided below. Count the number of questions which were rated 0 (not applicable) and record each of these four numbers in the space below each group total. Using these two sets of numbers completed the Quantitative Evaluation by performing the computations on the next page.

	I	II	III	IV
Group Totals	___	___	___	___
Number of Questions Rated 0	___	___	___	___

Enter the four Group Totals in the spaces on line a of the next page. Then enter the number of questions rated 0 (not applicable) for each group on line c of the next page.

507

Complete the evaluation of the material by summarizing
the data and insights gained from the detailed analysis
in the MAC Checklist. Describe the material and identify
potential readers according to what has been learned in
the analysis. It is important to use all knowledge and
judgments gained from the MAC Checklist. On the basis of
this data, appraise the material in a critical annotation
and compare it with other titles on the same subject.

The MAC Summary Record and Annotation is designed for
reference purposes. For convenience it may be detached
and filed separately.

The MAC Summary Record and Annotation provides a a comprehensive, precise evaluation for librarians and readers to
use in selection and reading guidance.

This page may be used for special notes

VI MAC SUMMARY RECORD AND ANNOTATION

Evaluator's Summary of the Material Analyzed

Potential Reader(s) _____

Ethnic Emphasis _____

Primary Subject _____

Readability Score _____

Quantitative Evaluation _____ _____
                                 Score   Description

Author _____

Title _____

Publisher _____

        Address _____

Edition _____ Date _____ Pages _____ Price _____

Utilize your MAC Checklist analysis to summarize the essential points about the material as determined in your evaluation for each category in the following areas.

I. Bibliographic Evaluation (Bibliographic Data, Physical Format, Type of Literature)

II. Content Analysis (Roles, Subjects, Attitudes & Values, Structure & Development)

III. Measurement of Readability (Typography, Special Features, Learning Aids)

IV. Appeal to Readers

Annotation

Describe in a brief critical note essential facts about the material,
based on the Materials Analysis Criteria, including what it is about,
what is said, how well it is said, the point of view, strengths and
weaknesses, and for whom you would recommend it. Compare and contrast
with other materials.

_____
Evaluator's Name

_____
Department

_____   _____
Date of Evaluation   Library

Notes

1. The Materials Analysis Criteria will be referred to as *MAC Checklist* although during its development variations of this final title for the Criteria were used.

2. Helen E. Haines, *Living with Books; the Art of Book Selection* 2nd ed. (New York: Columbia University Press, 1965): 122-155.

3. William S. Gray and Bernice Rogers, *Maturity in Reading; Its Nature and Appraisal* (Chicago: University of Chicago Press, 1956): 98-103.

4. Miles A. Tinker, *Legibility of Print* (Ames, Iowa: Iowa State University Press, 1963).

5. George R. Klare, *The Measurement of Readability* (Ames, Iowa: Iowa State University Press, 1963).

6. "U.N. Group Urges Dropping of Words with a Racist Tinge," *The New York Times,* December 14, 1968

7. Klare, *The Measurement of Readability.*

8. John R. Bormuth, "The Cloze Readability Procedure," *Elementary English Journal,* 65 (April 1968): 429-437.

9. Rudolph F. Flesch, "A New Readability Yardstick," *Journal of Applied Psychology,* 32 (June 1948): 221-233.

10. Robert Gunning, *The Technique of Clear Writing* (New York: McGraw-Hill, 1952).

11. G. Harry McLaughlin, "Smog Grading, a New Readability Formula," *Journal of Reading,* 12 (May 1969): 639-646.

12. Edward Fry, "A Readability Formula That Saves Time," *Journal of Reading,* 11 (April 1968): 513-516, 575-577.

17.

FINDINGS AND IMPLICATIONS

The major finding of the Materials Analysis study is the in-
strument created for the analysis of reading materials, the *MAC
Checklist - Materials Analysis Criteria: Standards for Measurement.*
The MAC Checklist is divided into six parts: I Bibliographic
Evaluation, II Content Analysis, III The Measurement of Readability,
IV Appeal to Readers, V Quantitative Evaluation, VI MAC Summary
Record and Annotation. It is to be used in analyzing reading
materials of various types which will provide the adult new reader
with information and ideas and give personal satisfaction and
pleasure while aiding in the development of his reading skills.
It is a guide for judging key points in reading materials. It
itemizes in convenient checklist form the aspects of reading materials which must be judged critically.

It is proposed that the analysis of the material by means of
this MAC Checklist will serve as a guide to the evaluation of materials for possible use with adult new readers, or for that matter,
for adults not necessarily identified as adult new readers. It
must be emphasized that many differences exist among various groups
of new or less experienced readers, and that establishing the usefulness and appeal of materials for a particular group of readers
will depend on how well the evaluator can relate his analysis to
the individuals in the group. Even greater caution must be taken
in classifying adults as illiterate or new readers. It appears,
more often than not, that adults *will not* read or choose not to
read rather than that they *cannot* read.

Certain basic principles derived from the Materials Analysis
Study are considered essential to the kind of selection and evaluation of reading materials required for building library collections of interest and satisfaction to adult new readers, for use
in adult education and reading development programs, and for

provision of reading guidance service to individuals and groups. Criteria essential to the evaluation of materials in the content of such service, whether in school, college, or public library, necessitates adaptations and changes in the use of standard library criteria in such areas as authority and format. Significant new approaches developed for the MAC Checklist in the area of content analysis require the identification of personal roles of adults portrayed in the material, the values and attitudes presented, and subjects as related to the roles of adults. These same categories must be evaluated along with readability measurements. In addition, an overall judgment is made by a quantitative evaluation. The findings of the LMRP investigation support the following conclusions and implications.

The diversity and variety of reading interests and various uses of reading materials is extensive. The number and variety of interests and needs almost equals the number of individual readers. Reading patterns span a range of life interests, responsibilities, and roles as adults. Certain preferences, common interests, specific titles, and types of format are identifiable. Recurring subject interests and titles were identified in each phase of the research. Topics of deep concern are survival, civil rights, the counter-culture, job training, and practical skills. Essays of social and personal development, biography, and poetry have special appeal. Materials with authentic ethnic cultural background are of chief interest. These materials should be honest and authentic without derogatory, biased terms and interpretations. Materials should be evaluated and described precisely in regard to the attitudes and values found in the materials. Materials should be selected that have particular concepts, values, and attitudes found within ethnic cultures and local communities.

Diversity in physical format of materials as well as content is of particular importance. Different types of format frequently signify a type of content not found in the usual book and newspaper sources. The full range of various types of formats brings a dynamic quality to a reading collection. This type of material which is often ephemeral brings to collections current events and new information and ideas. Paperbacks and pamphlets are the popular formats which have cover appeal, ease of handling, and economy. They continue to increase the range of choice among authors and subjects and make more accessible the old and the new. Booklets and leaflets are a convenient format for workbooks and programmed series. Many leaflets and forms are free or inexpensive and available from business, government, and social agencies. They provide a range of information on daily problems such as social security, drugs, tax reports, legal procedures, and credit buying. Broadsides and posters are unique for content and format. Newspapers and newsletters are indigenous products from the community. They communicate information about local persons, events, and concerns not found in the metropolitan dailies.

A review of the reading levels established for the titles analyzed in the ANR Collection shows an interesting pattern of grade levels. The application of readability formulas to titles in the ANR Collection identified materials in five grade levels ranging from first grade to twelfth grade level and over. The analysis of reading levels for 276 selected titles which met the MAC Checklist criteria shows the range of materials in each of five grade level categories - grades 1-3, 4-5, 6-8, 9-11, 12 and over. Because both the Gunning Fog Index and the Fry Graph for Estimating Readability, unlike the Flesch Reading Ease formula, predict a numerical grade level the results of these two formulas can be compared (table 199).

Table 199 Comparison of Application of Gunning and Fry Formulas

Grades	Gunning Fog Index	Fry Graph
1 - 3	6	21
4 - 5	29	31
6 - 8	77	91
9 - 11	52	36
12 and over	24	∷
Total	186	179

∷ Fry Graph measures levels up to grade 12

These figures indicate the lack of acceptable materials at the beginning grade levels. It is concluded that insufficient materials of interest and appeal to adults at the beginning level exist, and materials need to be written. This conclusion is also supported by the findings of the National Adult Programs Study discussed in Part 3 of this report.

Experience and skill gained by extensive use of the MAC Checklist facilitates and permits efficient and thorough evaluation. Close scrutiny of various aspects of the materials as outlined in the MAC Checklist are essential to critical reading and objective appraisal of the material. Although not all categories in the MAC Checklist are applicable to every item evaluated, each category should be considered.

The traditional dependence upon well known and approved publishers and authors is no longer possible. Unknown and new authors appear. Publishers spring up locally. New publications from local, underground, and special interest groups are numerous. Ephemeral, transitory materials all add to the complexity of judging reliability. No longer is it possible to classify easily publishers as reliable and accepted. A careful search for identification of sources and reliance on evaluators' judgments, or again, on the information gained from the publication, is necessary.

Although the instrument of evaluation developed in this research is designed to evaluate materials for a specific group, namely, adult new readers as identified in the LMRP study, the application of the MAC Checklist to a wide range of materials has proved that this instrument can be used in the evaluation of materials for general adult readers.

Certain conclusions about the methodology used in the Materials Analysis Study may be made. The productive methodology was the continuous use of pertinent research findings identified during the research as well as preliminary to it. The close contact maintained through field trips with librarians and community coordinators who were serving directly adult new readers resulted in useful information, advice, and criticism. Although continuous revision involved incorporation of new data and constant changes with testing and retesting, in retrospect it is evident that it was a feasible approach for development of the criteria. It is recognized that continuous revision is a slow process which requires patience and time.

The completion of the Materials Analysis Study leads to the conclusion that the significant aspect of evaluation is the depth and precision of the analysis. When the MAC Checklist is used properly, it draws together and provides a record of detailed information, critical judgment, and descriptive summary about the material and serves as a selection and reading guidance aid. It is recommended that the MAC Checklist be used for the evaluation of materials in any type of library, particularly school, college, and public library. Admittedly, it takes time to read and analyze materials in the detail demanded by the MAC Checklist. The usefulness of the materials analysis criteria for a library's program of reading materials service depends upon the philosophy of service and competence of the staff.

It is recommended that the MAC Checklist be used by librarians, teachers of adults, editors, and professional reviewers. An additional important use of the MAC Checklist is for educational purposes as a teaching instrument in graduate library schools and library staff development programs.

The Materials Analysis Study raises many questions and suggests areas in which further studies would be desirable. The problem of whether to use children's materials with adults learning to read and improving reading skills is a complex issue that surfaced during the Materials Analysis Study in discussions with librarians.

This problem needs to be explored in depth through an experimental study.

The findings of the LMRP investigation support hypotheses that can serve as a basis for three major studies about reading materials for adult new readers. It is recommended that these studies be carried out as a logical continuation of the Library Materials Research Project to insure further use of the research findings.

It is recommended that a readability formula be developed specifically to assess the reading level of materials for adults. Such a formula should take into consideration adult vocabulary, concepts, and life experiences. Ideally, such a formula would not use the traditional numerical grade levels as a measurement. The importance of the development of such a formula is reinforced by opinions of the reading specialists, adult educators, and librarians consulted during the Materials Analysis Study.

It is recommended that the Guided Reading vs. Independent Reading Study, a part of the original LMRP research design, be carried to completion. This study proposes to test reading materials identified and evaluated in the four studies of the Library Materials Research Project in a controlled field situation. The proposed research provides an experimental design to collect facts not gathered in other parts of the LMRP. An experimental and a control group from a metropolitan public library area would provide the setting and the sample for this investigation. It is suggested that two hypotheses be subjected for study: that materials in a special collection selected by criteria established in the preceding studies of the LMRP will be more satisfying and more frequently used by the participants in the reading groups than materials in the collection which do not meet the criteria; and that participants with reading guidance service will engage in more reading and have more success finding material to meet their needs and interests than participants in the independent reading group.

It is recommended that multiple criteria for a selection of reading materials be programmed for computer storage and retrieval in a pilot project to test human versus machine evaluation in a simulated book selection and reading guidance environment. The selected bibliography of reading materials for adult new readers that evolves from the LMRP analysis of materials would serve as an initial data base.

The final results of the Materials Analysis Study are the *MAC Checklist - Materials Analysis Study: Standards of Measurement* and a bibliography of selected titles for adult new readers. It is hoped that the analysis of materials by means of the MAC Checklist will serve as a guide to evaluation of that material for possible use with adult new readers. Because of the differences among various groups of new readers and the individual reading differences of each person, the establishing of usefulness and appeal of the materials for a particular group of readers will depend on how well the evaluator can relate the analysis to the individuals in that group. Finally, the decision and choice of reading material will be made by the reader. The librarian or adult educator will need to determine whether the attitudes and values expressed in material are meaningful and of interest to the individuals in a particular community. His ability to do this will rest on his knowledge and understanding of the community and will be verified or gainsaid by the reader himself.

PART 5   INDIGENOUS LITERATURE STUDY

18.

THE STUDY

The Indigenous Literature Study further extends the Materials Analysis Study and focuses in this phase of the LMRP investigation on a special literature that has its sources in the creative products of individuals and groups and in local publishing efforts.[1] The general purpose of the study has been similar to that of the larger Materials Analysis Study, that is, to identify and analyze these materials for their similarities to and differences from other materials in the ANR Collection and in relation to the evaluative criteria developed in this research. As the Indigenous Literature Study progressed, it was possible to define more precisely the meaning and character of this area of reading materials and to determine specific objectives and methodology for the special studies concerning this literature. These special studies carried out as doctoral dissertations have gathered data about two aspects of these materials in relation to their use by adult new readers. One study is directed to the relative satisfaction which the adult new reader expresses in the values and themes of the indigenous literature of his own cultural group.[2] The other study is concerned with the relative competence in reading which the adult new reader demonstrates in using the indigenous literature of his own cultural group as contrasted with the literature of another cultural group.[3,4]

The study of indigenous literature had been included in the research design because it was evident that reading materials to meet the interests and needs of particular groups in the population are being created and developed outside traditional publishing channels. Readers in adult basic education and library programs are expressing their ideas and feelings in writings that are read by others in their reference group. Teachers create material to personalize studies and to fit a task. These materials increasingly are being identified by educators and librarians, by authors and publishers. Some have been printed for private distribution. Some have been published as trade publications. It is comparatively easy because of technological developments in printing and reproduction equipment and with small capital investments to publish individual and group works. The findings and insights gained in the analysis of the indigenous literature have been incorporated into the criteria and bibliography resulting from the entire study as well as being reported here.

Finding materials was the first concern in initiating the Indigenous Literature Study. The material generally has been identified and procured through other than the usual trade channels. The majority of items in the collection were identified: by examination of the stock found in bookstores in Chicago, Newark, Baltimore, and Washington, D.C.; from titles reported as read by respondents interviewed in the Population Study; and through reviews, announcements, and special bibliographies. The Indigenous Literature Study (ILS) Collection that has been analyzed includes approximately 186 items. When classified by format there are approximately 31 books, 62 pamphlets, 66 newspapers, 17 broadsides, and 10 little magazines and newsletters. The sources from which the collection was acquired vary because of the lack of bibliographic control.

The diversity in content and format among the items in the collection seems to indicate that a representation of this type of literature has been analyzed. The examination of the literature through application of the MAC Checklist contributed to the refinement of the Checklist itself because new categories and omissions or modifications of other categories was possible on the basis of this testing procedure.

Indigenous literature in the context of the LMRP investigation is defined on the basis of an examination of the ILS Collection assembled for analysis. The term, indigenous literature, refers to a

work or body of literature that has all or most of the characteristics defined under seven categories: author, content, language,
treatment, publication, distribution, and audience.

Author. The author has his origins in a particular ethnic,
minority, or regional group, or is closely allied to it
experientially; that is to say, the author does not deal
with the group from the point of view of an alien, nor as
a social scientist. The contribution of the author is
that he speaks from the point of view of a member of the
group and not of the ethnologist.

Content. The major content or theme of the work has its
origins in the group and is reflective of the individual
and group experience, regardless of the mode of treatment
or depth of analysis.

Language. The language is usually representative of the
group idiom, street language, slang, or jargon. The work
may use words or phrases in a language other than English,
or it may be entirely in a language other than English.

Treatment. The treatment of the material varies. It
may take the form of creative literature - novel, drama, visual
essays, poetry, biography and autobiography; social and critical analysis of the group; and ideological tracts and
treatises - political, economic, racial, and social.

Publication. The work is published locally rather than
by trade publishers. It may serve as a source for later
trade publication.

Distribution. The work is distributed locally or region-
ally. It may reach national distribution through the established trade distribution network or through other agents.

Audience. The primary audience for the work is the group
from which the author originates and to which he speaks.

This statement of criteria serves to define the phrase indigenous literature in terms appropriate to the materials. It focuses attention upon those characteristics of the materials which make them relevant to the cultural, socioeconomic, and value orientations of the adult new reader. It separates this body of materials from the usual trade publications that may interest adult new readers.

Perhaps the most relevant general statement that can be made about indigenous literature is the tautology that it is *indigenous*. It is a product of a particular ethnic or minority culture or group. The author originates in the group. The content of the literature is focused on the group. Publication is by members of the group. The work is directed toward the group. The members of the group form its primary audience. It is a literature that bears organic relationship to its culture. It is not, in a sense, literature that is superimposed by the majority culture upon the members of the minority group.

The detailed analysis of the materials in the ILS Collection identified the characteristics of these materials in the categories established by the MAC Checklist which was used for the analysis. These characteristics are discussed in relation to the structural framework established by the MAC Checklist.

Bibliographic evaluation shows the close connection between source of the materials and the environmental influences. The authority of the author and the reliability of the publisher are for the most part assumed to be very good because they speak for the group, are usually not commercial, and are unknown.

The materials in the ILS Collection are in the form in which they first were published. Although for some collections of poetry prior publication had been in one of the journals such as *Black*

World (*Negro Digest*) or *Phylon*. The language of publication is
English for the materials about Black culture. The Chicano materials are in English, English and Spanish, or Spanish. The format
of publication is usually paperback book, newspaper, or pamphlet.
Poetry is the type of indigenous literature most frequently published. Other types of literature are not represented to a comparable extent. The use of the poetic form appears to provide the
personal quality which permits the communication of a shared experience between author and reader. Frequently the vocabulary
and allusions used by the poet are part of the common idioms of
the group.

The analysis of the indigenous literature in terms of categories in the content analysis section of the MAC Checklist reveals
certain patterns and interests. Of the seven personal roles defined in the Checklist, three roles appear most frequently -
the role of the person in his own development, the role of the
person in the group, and the role of the person as a participant
in political and social life. The roles concerning the family or
work were rarely present in the material, and then appeared as
secondary.

The subject categories identified follow the same general
pattern as shown in the dominant roles. Within each of the three
categories - personal development, group role, and citizenship -
some subjects frequently identified in the materials are: personal development - friendship, hate, love, personal identity, self=
preservation, survival, alcoholism, drugs; group role - membership
in an ethnic group, survival, membership in a political group,
membership in a religious group; citizenship - civil liberties,
politics, urban affairs, community development.

The stylistic quality of the material varies, and some of the
material being published has no intrinsic literary merit. The
expression of the experiences of the individual who communicates

those experiences to others is more important than artistry of expression. Much of the material is of average or above average quality, with some individual poems or collections being outstanding. A variety of styles and modes of expression are used. There are works of lyricism, didactic poems, free verse. The language is that of the streets and ghettos, the academic community, and the urban slum.

The physical format of indigenous literature includes a large proportion of titles reproduced by offset printing from typewritten copy. A few unique publications are mimeographed. Illustrations are few. Standard language generally is used. When argot and slang are used, they convey a sense of forthrightness, an undiluted sense of life.

Perhaps the most important characteristic of the literature, one from which others derive, is that it is a product of a particular ethnic or minority group, and achieves its uniqueness in terms of the shared life and thought experiences of the members of this group. The literature in a sense is involuted in that its origins and primary audience are in the group. The content is largely reportorial, dealing with the relationships between the indivudual, the group of which he is a member, and the majority culture. The literature explores and comments upon these relationships, often with an underlying theme of social criticism. Due to this organic relationship with the group, the authority of the author and publisher is high, and this lends credence to the views expressed in the literature.

Another aspect of this literature is the role it serves in unifying the members of the group. The literature functions to establish a sense of self-identity for members of the group; and also establishes a sense of group separateness and identity. This is fostered by the large amount of material that is published in the form of poetry, for poetic expression requires a shared heritage and sympathy for it to communicate fully. By having a language and allusion unique to the members of the group, one which is not fully shared by the majority culture, the literature reflects and contributes to a feeling of self-integrity.

A special study related to the LMRP investigation focuses on the reading comprehension of adult new readers of two ethnic groups, Blacks and Mexican Americans, in relation to reading materials that center around their cultural backgrounds. The basic conclusion of this investigation is that there is evidence that publications centering around culture themes of ethnic groups may well improve the adult new reader's ability to apply and use what he reads, and consequently the publishing of such materials is likely to fill a serious gap. "Application" and "use" are conceived of in terms of the reader's use of the material to solve his problem.[5]

19.

BLACK INDIGENOUS LITERATURE

A special collection of Black literature was acquired from
Black ghetto bookstores in Washington, D.C. and other Black ghetto
areas. These materials were evaluated by application of the MAC
Checklist (figure 9). In turn, the evaluations were analyzed
to determine the effectiveness and applicability of the MAC Checklist to the Black indigenous literature. This evaluation provided
another way to test the accuracy and usefulness of the Criteria.

This particular analysis deals with one specific type of
indigenous material - that originating in the Black community.
The questions to be answered include: What constitutes indigenous
material? Can indigenous material be readily evaluated using the
MAC Checklist? How does indigenous literature stand up under this
evaluation? Is indigenous material appropriate for adult education
programs? From the answers to these questions, other areas of
consideration concerning indigenous literature can be broached.

It seems that the first question of what constitutes indigenous material has been adequately satisfied by the identification
in the context of this study of indigenous literature, as previously defined.

To look at the MAC Checklist evaluations of the material acquired from the Drum and Spear Bookstore in the Black ghetto in
Washington, D.C. and from other Black ghettos is to confirm an
affirmative answer to the question of using the Criteria to evaluate indigenous literature. Most of the evaluation was done with
ease and indicates no more problems than with the regular trade literature. If any of the items present difficulty, it is the magazine
or periodical material. These involve more time in evaluating
simply because the contents and types of literature are diverse,
dissimilar, unrelated, and miscellaneous. But even they can be
used within the confines of the MAC Checklist as the evaluations

532

show. It is only a matter of adjustment and adaptation.

It may prove worthwhile here to make a closer examination of the individual sections of the Checklist and see how each section stands in relation to the indigenous material.

Bibliographic Evaluation. The information under bibliographic data rates on a par with the regular trade literature. The biggest difference is the smaller scale of operations of the indigenous publishers and the greater anonymity of the authors. They are less well known than writers being published by trade publishing houses, although this is not necessarily the case, witness the example of Gwendolyn Brooks, the well known poet who is being published by the large publishing house of Harper and Row and by the Black indigenous Broadside Press. Amiri Baraka (Leroi Jones) is doing the same with indigenous publishers in Newark, New Jersey.

More often than not, the physical format of indigenous material is in a softcover form: paperback books, broadsides and leaflets, pamphlets and booklets, newsletters and magazines, and newspapers. There is a very good reason for this. The primary concern of the authors and publishers is to get as much information as possible to their constituents. Something that is easily handled and used is best for this purpose. It should be noted that there is not always a sharp delineation between magazine and newspaper in the indigenous material; at times one rather merges into the other.

There is a preponderance of two types of literature, essays of information and poetry. The former can be accounted for by the sense of urgency that pervades the Black community. Because of the Black man's plight, he must be informed about what is causing his condition and told ways of remedying his situation. Political theorizing and information of propagandistic type lend themselves to the essay form. Concerning the frequency of poetry as a type of literature, the blues must be taken into account. The blues form and its imagery are meaningful. Blacks essentially sing when they talk. Their songs are inevitably blues because their lives are filled with the stuff of which blues are made. Poetry is the closest way of capturing the feeling of Black language, hence the abundant production of poetry.

Content Analysis. Undoubtedly content is the most important aspect of the indigenous literature. Practically all the subdivisions of the Content Analysis section of the MAC Checklist are applicable to the literature. All the personal roles are covered by the literature and some of the individual pieces of literature include all the roles, with Personal, Group, and Political/Social roles being predominant.

The subject matter is inclusive of all seven categories and their subdivisions. Family, Education, and Leisure are treated less than other subjects; foremost is Personal Development.

The attitudes and values espoused by the writers are ones that lean towards self-sufficiency and independent action. The writers' attitudes are usually anti-establishment and pro-Black liberation. This is not to say that traditional viewpoints are lacking, but the traditional values can be expressed easily through the regular trade publishers.

In the area of structure and development, the indigenous literature rates well with the regular trade material. Much of it is factual, the political writing, simple to average in complexity, with richness of ideas being primary. The other portion of the literature, poetry, is original, average to complex in style, with the style being primary. Style ranges from factual to humorous to imaginative to journalistic to poetic to popular to scholarly.

Measurement of Readability. On the whole, the measurement of readability of indigenous material rates well using the MAC Checklist.

Typography is usually good or very good. Special features is the category where the literature fares best. Illustrations abound as a special feature, and they more than do justice to the texts they supplement. If there are photography, they are evocative of the mood the author wanted, and if there are drawings or sketches, they are skillfully done to stimulate the desired reaction. Other kinds of special features are conspicuously absent.

Indigenous materials are weak in learning aids in the traditional sense, but because of their very nature, there is an inherent overall learning aid that the material conveys to its readers. It is designed for the disadvantaged minority and is written appropriately for them as a learning vehicle.

The language is almost always formal in the prose works, that is to say, it is correct English, though not formal in the sense of being stilted. As often as not, slang is liberally interspersed throughout to add a flavor of authenticity and simplicity to the work. Poetry on the other hand, is less formal in any accepted sense of the word. It incorporates more argot and slang than the prose does. It aims at sounding as Black people sound. Here, the Black idiom is truly able to come out.

Measurement of readability by the formulas tends to predict reading levels higher than the true level. The long sentences and proper nouns account for the higher ratings. The one fiction piece analyzed, *The Uncertain Sound*,[6] is an exception in that its scores were indicative of its real reading level.

Appeal to Readers. The audience to which the indigenous material is directed seems to be the younger generation - younger than 40 years of age. This may not be the desired effect since it is imperative that all elements of the Black community be reached in order to achieve effectiveness. However, the attitudes and values displayed in the material tend to point up this observation.

Quantitative Evaluation. The scores recorded for this section are invariably high for indigenous literature. The lowest rating computed is somewhat good. Nearly all of the rest of the material is rated as good, very good, and definitely superior.

It is evident that the MAC Checklist both evaluates the indigenous literature adequately and that the Checklist is verified by successful use with the literature.

It is not far from the concept of written indigenous literature to that of living oral indigenous literature which is produced by local Black drama groups and the line poetry reading sessions given by the young Black poets. There is Black drama activity from Seattle to Kansas City, from Cleveland to Washington, D.C. The local Black theatre movement owes its inspiration, if not its inception, to Amiri Baraka and the Black Arts movement in Harlem in the 1960's. Adult educators can add new dimensions and opportunities for adult students by directing them to drama and poetry activities going on in local areas, as well as by conducting such activities in the adult education programs.

It would appear that the avenues open to the librarian or the adult education coordinator are unlimited. There is much that can and should be done to stimulate the interest and motivation to learn on the part of the adult new reader.

It is the desire of the Library Materials Research Project to stress the importance of indigenous literature in the education and reading improvement of adult new readers. The evaluations obtained from analyzing the individual pieces of indigenous literature corroborate this belief.

It is recommended on the basis of the various analyses and studies of indigenous literature that libraries and adult education institutions particularly in large urban areas make special efforts to acquire indigenous reading materials from bookstores and other channels. Stores which stock Black literature are springing up in

all the metropolitan areas and are the best sources. A basic
principle in building appropriate, interesting collections, not
only for the Black population, but also for all ethnic groups is
to search for special sources, frequently obscure and unknown.

Figure 9 Black Indigenous Literature: a Few Examples

Books

Bryant, L.A. *Know Thyself.*
Floyd, Tom. *Integration Is a Bitch!*
Gaskin, Ruth L. *A Good Heart and a Light Hand.*
Johnson, Alicia L. *Realities vs. Spirits.*

Pamphlets

Knight, Etheridge. *Poems from Prison.*
Randall, Dudley. *Cities Burning.*
Robinson, Odee. *The Black Dreamer.*

Magazines

ALAFIA, A Magazine of the Black Arts, New York, N.Y.
Black News, Brooklyn, N.Y.

Broadsides

Chiri, Ruwa. *Sixteen South Street*
Glover, Jon. *Black Frustrations, Two Black Poems*

Photographic Essay

Lewis, Roy and Perkins, Eugene. *West Wall.*

Informational Essay

Boutelle, Paul and others. *Murder in Memphis, Martin Luther
King and the Future of the Black Liberation Struggle.*

Notes

1. Helen H. Lyman, "Proposal for Research...Library Materials in Service to the Adult New Reader: (Madison: The University of Wisconsin-Madison Library School, 1968), p.30.

2. Laurence L. Sherrill, "The Affective Responses of Ethnic Minority Readers to Indigenous Ghetto Literature: A Measurement" (Ph.D. dissertation, University of Wisconsin-Madison, 1972).

3. Yekutiel Deligdisch, "The Reading Comprehension of Adult New Readers in Relation to Their Ethnic Backgrounds" (Ph.D. dissertation, University of Wisconsin-Madison, 1971).

4. Several graduate students at the Library School, University of Wisconsin-Madison assisted in the various analyses related to the indigenous literature. I am indebted to Emil Levinson for analysis of the general collection and to Beacher J.E. Wiggins for special analysis of Black indigenous literature.

5. Deligdisch, "Reading Comprehension".

6. Herman Cromwell Gilbert, *The Uncertain Sound* (Chicago: Path Press, Inc., 1969).

PART 6   PRINCIPAL FINDINGS AND RECOMMENDATIONS

20

INTERPRETATIONS AND FINDINGS

This report on the research project, Library Materials in Service to the Adult New Reader, is addressed primarily to those persons who are in positions to make practical use of the findings, that is, librarians in public library materials service programs and teachers in adult basic education programs, administrators in public library and adult education agencies, library school educators, students of library science, and reading specialists. The findings also will be useful to persons either teaching or doing research in the field of adult education and to editors and publishers publishing materials in various areas of interest which are considered in this study.

The two major aspects investigated in this research are the characteristics and reading behavior of the adult new reader and the reading materials for this group of readers. During the five-year period from July 1967 to May 1972 data have been collected and analyzed through four major studies designed to survey a sample of readers in five cities, investigate the nature and use of reading materials in the context of adult basic education, job training, and library reading programs, and analyze reading materials from regular trade publications and within the indigenous literature.

No previous research investigates the problem of adult literacy in relation to library reading materials. The study has been possible because of the existence of public library and adult education programs in this area of service and their cooperation with the research. The findings and experience of previous researchers have been drawn upon in the design and in the analysis of the research. The LMRP investigation takes its place among the more general studies relating to adult reading interests and library use which were carried out during the period from the 1920's to the present. The findings about this special segment of readers defined in this research as adult new readers present original data and explore a relatively unknown area. The LMRP statistical analyses and comparisons contribute more current data and add to the knowledge of what is known from other studies about adult reading. The findings of the study are directed toward the solution of the problem which is the appraising of reading content and levels in materials accurately and matching the print materials to the readers' abilities, skills, and interests.

The major finding of the LMRP research is the criteria in the form of a checklist for a qualitative and quantitative analysis of print materials. The results of the study about the adult new reader, his characteristics and attitudes provides a descriptive analysis and specific information about the adult new readers' social characteristics and activities, reading behavior and reading activity. Within the research project, extensive use has been made of data analyzed in the process of carrying out various phases of the study for the development of instruments of analyses and in revisions indicated for the criteria. The continuous revision proved to be a feasible approach for the development of the criteria.

Similar use has been made of data gained in the National Adult Programs and Materials Analysis Study. Because of what has been learned about the reader and his use of materials in the context of daily living and continuing education, the criteria for analysis of reading materials has precise categories identified in the various phases of the LMRP investigation.

Reading materials and adult new reader are defined for the LMRP investigation. Reading materials in this context are those print materials that serve broad reading purposes, that place emphasis primarily in the substantive content rather than the development of reading skills, and that either have been prepared specifically for the adult new reader or are useful to his level of interests and reading achievement. For the purposes of this research the adult new reader is identified as 16 years of age and over, his native language is English or he is learning English as a second language, his formal education has not extended beyond grade 11. An individual in today's society must be at an eighth grade level of reading achievement to be functionally literate. Bridging the gap between literacy skill and independent discriminating reading is the ultimate aim of this study.

In general the findings and conclusions of the study have several immediate and future uses. The data generate hypotheses for future research. The data provide a foundation for decision making and provision of service to adults in public library programs. The aggregate statistical findings can be useful in planning literacy and adult basic education materials service. An important consequent of the study in the near future will be the production of a bibliography of evaluated reading materials for the adult new reader. A second product, not originally envisioned, is an analysis of the characteristics of the adult new reader and of the criteria and its use which will be presented in the form of a handbook.

The major limitations of the data relate to the limitations within the survey sample of adult new readers as defined in the context of this study. Generalizations about the Black population of adult new readers are justifiable, it would seem, because the data are based on a greater percentage of the sample. In several instances where comparisons are possible, general population statistics corroborate the LMRP sample statistics. The many variables in the reading situation result in complexity which makes it most difficult to isolate one or more variables for study. Environmental problems for the adult new reader population add to this complex situation. Weaknesses in the LMRP investigation have been created because of the problems and the limitations in the survey sample for the Population Study and the mail questionnaire method used in the National Adult Programs Study. The major problems encountered have been in drawing the reader sample and defining literacy levels.

Some of the strengths in the LMRP investigation have been in the validity of the questionnaire instrument and in the skill of the personnel who carried out the interviews in the Population Study. The continuing

543

testing and revision of the criteria for evaluation have served to strengthen the result in the final criteria for analysis of materials. The various procedures for collecting data combined to achieve balance between sources of data acquired in the academic environment and in the field. The contribution of the advisory committee and the consultants added valuable insights and guidance.

The importance of the interrelationships among the four major phases of the LMRP investigation became more and more significant as findings and results from one study could be related to another. Data about readers or materials in its initial form and analyzed only partially were of immediate value for background information on social characteristics and for current reading interests and opinions of readers. The Materials Analysis Study gained momentum and new direction with emphases on Black readers' interests and needs and special ethnic materials when the interview data had been scanned. Specific titles and types of materials newly identified were analyzed. New insights contributed useful information for evaluation of the content of materials. It has been possible to make revisions based on what was learned about subject interests, attitudes, and values of the special groups identified, that is, Black, Chicano, Puerto Rican, Indian. Reading materials have been identified and evaluated in relation to new knowledge and insights gained.

A particular value of the findings set forth in this report is that they provide resources in data and instruments for research use and for the educating and training of graduate students in library studies and library personnel in staff development programs. Specifically these resources include: the report itself; the research design; the research instruments for collection of data and analysis, that is, the questionnaires and the Reading Activity Index; the criteria for analysis of materials; and any future hypotheses based on these findings.

The MAC Checklist provides an instrument of evaluation which has been tested in various situations. It has been found to be useful in evaluation of reading materials in particular for the adult new reader as defined in the context of this project and also for adult readers in general. It provides a structured approach. Through it a descriptive analysis of the reading materials may be achieved along with the evaluation of the specific factors as well as an overall evaluation. The process of analysis is incorporated within the procedure required in using the checklist. The form provides an organization facilitating the use of the criteria and outlining what to consider in the analysis. It is necessary only to check specific categories. It saves time and effort. The disciplined approach makes unnecessary lengthy writing of annotations and guards against having no record or note. It serves as a guide and a reminder of points to consider. It makes possible an objective appraisal of bibliographic and readability factors and a quantitative rating. This focus on specific aspects of the material is new, not so much in practice, as in the attempt to place the analysis in an efficient structural form. Many of the points included are evaluated automatically by experienced librarians.

The use of the criteria requires looking at material in its entirety -- sources, subjects, ideas, roles portrayed, values and attitudes presented, language, structure and development, readability level, legibility, and an overall quantitative rating. Such an analysis when combined with insights and understanding of values and attitudes in the life styles of individual users and the community can be used in selection and reading guidance. The criteria analysis is an additional aid for building a collection of reading materials with breadth and depth which insures the right of the reader to wide choices and represents the diversity of values and opinions found in the community. The analysis further makes it easier and more possible to bring the materials to the attention of potential readers.

The data gained in various phases of the study support the
interpretation that a primary concern in evaluating reading materials
for adult new readers is the analysis of content in relation to subject
interests, values and attitudes, structure and development, measurement
of readability in aspects ranging from legibility and learning devices
to readability levels. The evaluation of materials for instrumental,
pleasure, and enjoyment uses which relate to role of adults as portrayed
in the material gains importance in interpreting principles of selection.

The criteria can be used successfully by experienced and inexperienced
librarians. The majority of persons, librarians and graduate students in
library science,who used the MAC Checklist in evaluating a wide range of
materials found it satisfactory and a valuable measure of the work. It
is concluded on the basis of numerous tests that the criteria is valid,
useable, and an instrument with great potential.

Points that are questioned frequently by interested librarians
and specialists are stated and answered by two skeptics who comment
on the MAC Checklist.

I think we had a profitable morning last Wednesday discussing
your "Materials Analysis Criteria," as I hope you do too. As I
told you my first reaction, before you talked with us, was that it
was too involved and complex. Now, especially after hearing from
you how it has been used, I believe that you have developed a tool
which will be valuable in a variety of ways. First, it will give us
an objective way to evaluate the kind of book which libraries have
traditionally turned down as "trivial" or "poorly written," but which
is in great demand especially in inner city branches. It provides
a framework which forces us to consider in detail varous aspects
of a book or other publication. It also makes us consider the
attitudes and values in the material - which may not be the traditi
ones. The length of the checklist, which troubled some of us, does
not seem so burdensome when it is recognized as an aid for selectin

materials for special groups, or for evaluating special problem
books. Even though it probably would not be used _routinely_ by
experienced librarians, I think it would be very useful as a staff
training device.[1]

I was dubious about this kind of structural approach to a book,
especially a work of art. I found, however, that instead of
demeaning and de-mystifying the work, this analysis actually
indicated that it was all the more remarkable. It is indeed
helpful to know what to look for and to be able to pinpoint a
book's focus, or foci, as on page 7. It made me realize in this
case that a standard solid novel, while not a masterpiece was
also a valuable social document.[2]

It is a controversial instrument primarily because of the time and
effort exacted and the background knowledge in other fields such as
sociology, literacy, psychology, adult education, and reading which is
demanded. It is to be expected the MAC Checklist is used most effectively
and advantageously depending upon the evaluator's depth of knowledge and
understanding about life styles, values, materials, and needs of various
smaller segments of the population. It is recognized that knowledge
of characteristics of readers, reading studies, and reading materials
is important. The findings of the LMRP investigation present much that
is needed as background to its use. An additional aid will be the handbook
on the use of the criteria with essays about each segment of the population which is being prepared to use in conjunction with the MAC Checklist.

Because of the differences among various groups of adult new
readers and the individual reading differences of each person, the establishing of usefulness and appeal of the materials for a particular group of
readers will depend on how well the evaluation can relate the analysis to
the individuals in the group. Finally, the decision and choice of reading

material will be made by the reader. The librarian or adult education teacher will need to analyze the materials so that the user is able to choose wisely on the basis of information available and his own interests and needs. The ability of the librarian or adult educator to determine whether the attitudes and values expressed in material are meaningful and of interest to particular groups or individuals rests on his knowledge of the community and the material. The reader himself will verify or disprove his judgment.

Indigenous literature from all ethnic groups adds vitality and significance to a library materials collection for adult new readers. Although not easily identified or acquired, these materials will add appeal and increase use of the collection. The authors and publishers are frequently obscure and unknown, consequently, it is necessary to explore and search for special sources of these materials. It is concluded that the traditional dependence upon well known and approved authors and publishers is not sufficient guide for acquiring materials either indigenous or trade publications. Now authors and publishing firms and presses from local, underground, and special interest groups increasingly are sources for new relevant materials. It is evident that librarians and teachers may be an active source for finding new authors and works. Locally produced materials can gain and have gained national recognition and distribution. It is concluded on the basis of analysis of the indigenous literature through application of the MAC Checklist that publications centered around cultural themes of ethnic groups may help to improve reading skills and have strong appeal to readers. One result of this study is the definition formulated to describe what is meant by indigenous literature. It is a literature that is the product of a particular ethnic or minority culture or group.

What has been learned about the adult new reader? The data provide descriptive information about the adult new reader in relation to general and specific characteristics, the nature and use of materials in the context of use in daily life and continuing education activities,

548

reading interests and needs, reading behavior and patterns. This descriptive information is presented in approximately 250 tables, charts, and figures, in which quantitative data are analyzed and frequently compared with other data. Further detailed analyses have been presented throughout this report and are not to be repeated in this brief summary. Also, a composite of different measures of reading use of print materials, newspapers, magazines, comic books is combined into the Reading Activity Index. The following outline showing the composition of the sample draws together highlights about respondents interviewed in the survey of readers.

Composition of the Sample
N = 479 [*]

Respondent Characteristics	Percent
Sex of Respondent	
Men	31
Women	69
Race of Respondent	
Black	74
White	26
Other	::
Language(s) Spoken	
English	75
English and Spanish	15
English and Other	9
Median Age in Years	33.7 years
Median Years in Present Locality	24 years
Median Amount of Formal Education	10.2 years
Median Age When Left School	16.9 years
Main Reason for Leaving School	
Graduated	15
Lack of Money	40
Didn't go to High School	28

[*] except where noted otherwise

:: The percentage is equal to less than 1%

Participation in Adult Classes or Programs (N = 394)

Adult Basic Education	58
High School Equivalency Program	30
Work Incentive Program	19
Manpower Development and Training	16
Public Library Program	13
Other	35

Employment of Time

Working Force	53
Not in Working Force	
Retired	3
Keeping House	19
In School	25

Occupation in Current Employment (N = 218)

White Collar	12
Clerical	16
Craft	18
Blue Collar	18
Service	36

Median Family Income	$5,009
Median Individual Income	$3,449
Member of Club or Group, or Society or Union	40
Officer of Organization (N = 192)	36
Gone to Public Library	87

	Percent
Communication Media	
Watch Television	99
Majority Interest in News and Weather	89
Movies	83
Mod Squad	73
Mission Impossible	69
Listen to Radio	95
Listen to News and Weather (N = 457)	92
Listen to Music (N = 457)	91
Newspaper Readers	93
Read Every Day (N = 444)	50
Read a Few Times a Week (N = 444)	34
Read About Once a Week (N = 444)	9
Sundays Only (N = 444)	4
Less Often Than That (N = 444)	3
A Great Deal of Interest in Newspapers (N = 444)	44
A Little Interest in Newspapers (N = 444)	46
No Interest (N = 444)	10
Major Interest in News About World Affairs (N = 444)	87
Major Interest About Civil Rights (N = 444)	78
A Great Deal of Interest in Advertisements (N = 444)	44
Magazine Readers	88
Read *Life* or *Look*	67
Read *Ebony* or *Jet*	57
Book Readers	69
Comic Book Readers	34
Owner of Books	84
Reading Activity Index	
Least Active Readers	3
Somewhat Active Readers	30
Active Readers	53
Very Active Readers	14

	Percent
Purposes and Reasons for Reading	
Read for Pleasure and Relaxation	18
Read for Information	31
Read for Both	49
Read for Education	95
Read for Enjoyment	88
Read for School Work	83
Read to Learn to Do Something	83
Read for Employment	59
Reading Has Helped	90
Reading Helped in Preparing for Present Job	15
Reading in Connection with Home Life	30
Reading in Connection with Club or Group Activity (N = 192)	37
Reading Influenced by Classes (N = 394)	51
Had Reading Problems	55
Overcame Problem (N = 261)	68
Evaluation of Amount of Reading	
A Great Deal	42
Some	35
A Little	17
Hardly Any	5
Self-Evaluation of Reading Skills	
Good	30
Fair	54
Poor	14

	Percent
Read to When a Child	62
Other Than School Reading When a Child	56
Reading Other Than School Reading When a Teenager	64
Active Reading of Friends When a Child	48
Presently Have Active Readers as Friends	61
Reading Compared with Friends	
More	36
Less	28
Same	31
Reading Compared with Parents	
More	60
Less	16
Same	12
Reading Compared with People with Whom Reader Lives	
More	38
Less	29
Same	24
Read Aloud to Other People	61

In reporting materials read most frequently the majority mentioned newspapers. Magazines are mentioned least. Books are mentioned by three in ten of the respondents. The most frequently mentioned type of books read are popular fiction and biographies and autobiographies. Short stories, novels, biographies and historical books are the types of literature respondents prefer; and a fifth of the respondents like plays and poetry very much. Among books owned by respondents books on practical subjects are first, for example, reference (dictionary, encyclopedia), health and nutrition, child care, home decorating. The fictional type of books are mentioned less frequently. Over half of the respondents have no preference of paperbacks to hardcover books, one-fifth preferred paperbacks.

The miscellany of materials liked by readers is corroborated in various parts of the LMRP investigation by librarians and teachers and readers' own statements reflect similar interests. These various areas are representative only but indicate how sensitive and informed the library staff must be to select materials. For example, important areas and titles include: books in Spanish, You and Your Job Series, Reader's Digest books, romances for young girls, Black history, poetry, biography.

Certainly adult new readers need to have information that is accurate and up to date on subjects suggested by many teachers and librarians. These subjects include: abortion laws, divorce laws, lending laws, mental health, social security rights, health, sex, marriage, family, consumer buying, space technology, race relations, counter-culture, urban life. They need to have access to sample forms, regulations, notices, mail order catalogues, driver's manuals, voting ballots, banking forms. They need to find creative literature - poetry, drama, classics, best sellers, ethnic and national history and culture.

Teachers as well as librarians emphasize the need for materials on basic education, consumer education and job information. Also

high on teachers' lists of needed materials are literature about
ethnic and nationality groups, stories, and reference books. Libraries
should be able to provide such material and stimulate publication of
needed materials. Although specific subject areas are emphasized, a
range of subject interests is noted. Again it is concluded that a library
collection of some range and depth to which adult new readers have easy
access is most important.   The extensive amount of counseling seems
to indicate the need for information in this area both for teachers and
students. Job information, career information, and technical material
about career and work should have interested clientele in view of the
occupational aspirations reported by respondents interviewed and
indicated by students in employment oriented and job training programs.

Materials are needed at all reading levels but most of all at
the beginning, one to fourth grade level, and with interest and relevance
to adults. Authentic, unmoralizing stories with adult appeal are desired

Evidence of the reliability and authenticity of the creative
literature and interpretive studies depended upon for concepts, understanding and research findings have been confirmed within the LMRP
investigation. It is significant that several works influential in
the development of the LMRP research plan are found to be of great
importance in the reading of the adult new reader, for example,
The Autobiography of Malcolm X, *Manchild in Promised Land*, *Nigger*,
Black Boy, *From These Ashes*.

The nature and use of reading materials as reported by librarians
and teachers indicate the need for supplemental materials. It appears
the programmed learning series with audio visual materials, the workbooks,
the skills in reading require and stimulate the use of materials not
strictly instructional. The changing concepts in teaching with emphasis
on the learner and learning rather than the teacher and teaching involves
the more extensive use of supplemental materials. The context of
continuing education for adults creates opportunities for coordinated
public library services in materials for students, teachers, and program
personnel.

It seems clear that an opportunity exists for public, school, even college libraries to become primary sources for borrowed materials for independent and suggested reading by adult students in continuing education programs. Teachers need materials for study and continuing professional education.

The single most significant factor in serving the person and groups who are developing reading skills and gaining maturity in reading may be the respect and understanding between the library user or potential user, the individual or community, and the library personnel. Learning the interests and needs of the adult new reader, understanding his life style and values will give the librarian insight into serving the individual or the group. The main indicator of success or failure will be the use that the adult new reader makes of the reading materials.

Adult new readers have a variety of interests. Regardless of the number of years of schooling, adults are continuing education at various levels. For example, the age group 25 to 44 years of age, continue education in high school equivalency programs for the purpose of acquiring the high school diploma and accreditation it represents.

Education is a correlate to reading activity, a fact which has been identified by earlier studies. The circular nature in the dependent relationships between the current education system and print oriented library service and reading distort this finding. The cycle can be broken at any stage. The cycle can be entered at any stage. At the fifth and sixth grade level the crucial factor in further development is access to appropriate materials. It appears that informed relevant guidance by the librarian and teacher at this stage is most important for the adult new reader's continuation of his reading and reading development.

The partial literacy level of 40 percent of active readers confirms that many readers not only are capable of making use of print materials but do make use of them. An increase in reading activity with increase

in formal education achieves a point where as a mature reader the adult
can make productive use of a wide range and variety of materials. The
more active a reader is, the more varied is his use of print materials
and other resources. The relationship between book reading and variable
literacy is clear.

The diversity in subjects, titles, and formats mentioned by newspaper
magazine, and book readers reflect the individuality of reading. The use
of newspapers, books, and magazines as stimulated by daily activities
and voluntary study and reading suggest the multitude of possibilities
public libraries may choose to follow. The expanded use of these print
resources and the potentialities which the information about the reader
and reading materials in this report suggest will be seen by the concerned
imaginative librarian and teacher. The implications are clearly in the
direction of strong collections of reading materials in every possible
format, on subjects of practical interest and ethnic appeal, with support
for values and attitudes related to the life style and experiences of
ther reader, as well as opening up new experiences about the world and
other persons. This latter type of materials which can answer questions
about the universe and current events and satisfies natural curiosity
and interest has significance for library service not explored sufficientl

News events, local, national, international, constently of primary
interest to a majority of adult new readers using television, radio,
newspapers and magazines as communications sources for what is
happening. A significant function libraries can fulfill in this area
of interest would be to collect, organize, and promote the use of
materials related to news of the moment. An extension of such service
would be to analyze the significance of the current news in terms of
long range interest and to build collections in depth. Equally important
is an extensive collection of neighborhood newspapers, language and ethnic
newspapers for local news.

The single fact about the adult new reader which is essential to
recognize is his adulthood. Whether 16 or 65 years of age he is adult,
has adult responsibilities, and a life time of experiences equal to the

years of his life. To those experiences and years may be added the
experiences and years of other lives. The records of the lives and
thoughts and aspirations as told by novelists and writers, by reporters
and script writers. Is it any wonder that adult new readers prefer to
read about lives of other persons: biographies and autobiographies, news
of the world, and fiction. In the search for identity these records
are sources. The degree of validity, the authenticity, and the meaning-
fulness of the materials which they find may depend solely on the access
to library collections of sufficient breadth and depth and the professional
librarianship they encounter in the library staff.

Maslow has said that the search for identity is the search for
values. It is a characteristic search of the twentieth century. The
theoretical construct set forth in Maslow's hierarchy of needs presents
a philosophical foundation on which to base library policy and principles.

Maslow's concept that "basic needs or values are related to each
other in a hierarchical and developmental way, in order of strength and
of priority"[3] has important implications for library provision of service
in reading materials for the segment of the population identified as
adult new readers in the LMRP investigation.

The various stages of social and personal development at which an
individual or social group may be have important implications in relation
to planning and guidance services if librarians and teachers identify
and relate the stage of need to the library resources that may meet that
need.

The process of growth is the process of becoming a person in Maslow's
concept the ultimate goal being self-realization a point of autonomy,
creativity, and productivity for the individual. Before this stage can
be accomplished the basic needs both physiological and psychological must
be gratified. Healthy development is a matter of gratification in steps:
basic needs, security and safety; belonging as in family, community or
point of interdependence and love; gain respect, esteem, approval, and
self respect and dignity; self-actualization or self-realization, that is,

freedom for fullest development of talents and capacities. At the risk
of oversimplification, this concept has direct relationship to librarianship.[4] The library service program based on this conceptual development
of individuals is relevant to life values and subject interest of adult
new readers. The search for identity and survival has been identified
in all phases of the LMRP investigation as of major importance. The
resources represented in the reading materials with which LMRP is
concerned are products of human experience and knowledge of ourselves
and our environment. They can serve as strong forces in the growth
of readers as well as assist in development of reading skills.

The rising expectations of individuals and groups have created a
revolution of expectations. Misconceptions and myths about persons
who are different are being disproved and questioned. The rigidity
of institutions and slowness to anticipate and to respond to change
create stresses and tensions that seem irreconcilable and insolvable.
When the problems are not solved and the expectations realized destruction
and frustration result.

The expectations can be realized. The institutions can change.
The public library is an education institution capable of flexibility
and change. The library staff sensitive to the expectations of the men
and women in their library community and with a wide and varied knowledge
of resources,print materials and other communication media can anticipate
respond, act to advance the realization of the expectations.

21

RECOMMENDATIONS

The findings and conclusions of the LMRP investigation support several recommendations and serve as a basis for further studies in addition to those directly related to library materials service. Several studies are recommended as logical continuations of the Library Materials Research Project to insure further use of the research findings.

The research data from the survey of readers has not been analyzed as fully as was intended. A statistical analysis to establish correlations and influential factors related to reading behavior and reading interests is desirable.

It is recommended that the selective annotated bibliography of materials for the adult new reader which is in the process of completion be published as planned for use by the profession and to serve as an initial data bank in a computer storage pilot project.

It is recommended that the MAC Checklist be used by librarians, teachers of adults, editors, and professional reviewers. Also an important use of the MAC Checklist is for educational purposes as a teaching instrument in graduate library schools, library staff development programs, adult reading, and adult education courses.

The complex issue of whether to use children's materials with adults learning to read and improving reading skills is an issue that should be explored in depth through an experimental study.

It is recommended that the Guided Reading vs. Independent Reading Study, a part of the original LMRP research design, be carried to completion. This study proposes to test reading materials identified and evaluated in the four studies of the Library Materials Rsearch Project in a controlled field situation. The proposed research provides an experimental design to collect facts not gathered in other parts of the LMRP. An experimental and a control group from a metropolitan public library area would provide the setting and the sample for this investigation. It is suggested that two hypotheses be subjected for study: that materials

in a special collection selected by criteria established in the preceding
studies of the LMRP will be more satisfying and more frequently used by
the participants in the reading groups than materials in the collection
which do not meet the criteria; and that participants with reading
guidance service will engage in more reading and have more success
finding materials to meet their needs and interests than participants
in the independent reading group.

It is recommended that multiple criteria for a selection of reading
materials be programmed for computer storage and retrieval in a pilot
project to test human versus machine evaluation in a simulated book
selection and reading guidance environment. The selected bibliography
of reading materials for adult new readers that evolves from the LMRP
analysis of materials would serve as an initial data base.

It is recommended that a readability formula be developed specifically
to assess the reading level of materials for adults; an experimental
study be conducted to test reading materials indentified and evaluated
as appropriate for adult new readers.

It is recommended that an extension of the National Adult Programs
Study be carried out to investigate in depth and with more complete
sample than LMRP achieved, the uses and need for reading materials in
context of adult basic education programs.

It is suggested that the public library should present opportunities
for older adults to develop basic education skills and enjoy the use
of library reading materials in a variety of formats. It is concluded
that this group constitutes a potential library clientele of significant
dimensions and with major literacy problems. It also appears that this
oldest group is more comfortable in the less structured educational
atmosphere which the library can offer.

In the LMRP survey of readers, it is shown that the oldest group
of adults 45 years of age and over participate far more in adult basic
education programs than the youngest adults, but they also participate
in employment oriented programs and are attracted to library reading

development programs. It has been shown that this aging population uses public libraries and has less education. Previously in this report, it has been noted that in the United States the larger proportion of illiterates is concentrated in the oldest group who are 65 years old and over. They constitute about 45 percent of all illiterates. Of these older persons who have problems of illiteracy 38.4 percent are men, and 52.0 percent are women. The data support further recommendation for a special study be carried out to determine needs and interests of the older population and what type of materials are needed.

The lack of appropriate reading materials, particularly at the elementary level of reading skills, suitable to adult experience and intelligence results in serious handicap for adult new readers and for adult programs achievement of learning goals. Adults require material from first to sixth grade level with content related to adult experiences and the ethnic, racial backgrounds and life styles of potential readers.

The need to create new materials and to identify existing materials to meet current interests is uppermost. The implications for librarians, editors, and publishers are clear. Materials are needed for use in instruction in vocational and occupational learning and in basic education skills and selected subject areas such as biographies, short stories, poetry, current issues. Equally important are materials of interest to adults to be read for enjoyment and pleasure, to learn about ethnic culture and history.

Basic books for home use and ownership, as well as library lending are indicated as particular areas of publishing in which publishers will request manuscripts and do direct marketing, for example, dictionaries, encyclopedias, cookbooks, sewing manuals, consumer information, practical aids in vocational and service occupations, homemaking, Bibles, biographies and histories, anthropology, and series.

Independently owned and directed publishers in ethnic fields by ethnic staffs would seem to be one answer to the creation of acceptable and consequently more useful books. The small press publishers produce poetry, plays, novels, history, tracts, and biographies originating with individuals within the culture of the group. These presses should be encouraged and supported.

It appears that market and audience exist for ethnic background and cultural material in traditional human interest areas, when and only when they are written by persons in the ethnic group. Such materials must be truly accurate, authentic, and of aesthetic quality. No stereotypes, myths, misconceptions, racism, nationality or class bias will be tolerated.

Although this research supports the conclusion that insufficient materials of interest to adults at a beginning level and with authentic ethnic content exist the extent of demand and use has not been ascertained. It is recommended that the publishing industry identify the markets and authors, and manufacture and distribute the materials which must be written.

In summary it is recommended that public, school, and college libraries develop professional skills and resources to coordinate materials services for adult education agencies, provide advisory service to students and teachers, search for materials that fit class and individual needs, and support reading guidance services for students. To enable librarians and teachers to achieve these goals it is recommended that universities develop education programs and curriculum to educate and train future professional staff who may work in this exacting and rewarding area of service to adults.

Notes

1. Emily W. Reed, December 22, 1970: personal communication

2. R.W. Porst, April, 1972: graduate student in library science.
comment after analyzing John Updike's *Rabbit Redaux*.

3. Abraham H. Maslow, *Toward A Psychology Of Being* Second Edition
(Princeton, N.J.: D. VAn Nostrand Co., 1962, 1968): p. 153.

4. Ibid.: pp. 199-200.

RECOMMENDED READINGS

rown, Ina C. *Understanding Other Cultures*. Englewood Cliffs, N.J.: Prentice-Hall, 1963.

ahill, Susan and Cooper, Michele F., editors. *The Urban Reader*. Englewood Cliffs, N.J.: Prentice-Hall, 1971.

lark, Kenneth B. *Dark Ghetto: Dilemmas of Social Power* (Harper Torchbooks). New York: Harper & Row, 1965, 1967.

ader, Daniel. *The Naked Children*. New York: Macmillan, 1971.

etzels, J.W., "The Problem of Interests: A Reconsideration." *Reading: Seventy-Five Years of Progress*. Proceedings of the Annual Conference on Reading held at the University of Chicago, 1966. Compiled and edited by H. Alan Robinson. University of Chicago Press, December 1966. Vol. 18, ch. 9.

ottlieb, David and Heinsohn, Anne Lienhard. *America's Other Youth: Growing Up Poor*. Englewood Cliffs, N.J.: Prentice-Hall, 1971.

ay, William S. and Rogers, Bernice. *Maturity in Reading*. Chicago: University of Chicago Press, 1956.

iffith, William S. and Hayes, Ann P., editors. *Adult Basic Education: The State of the Art*. Chicago: University of Chicago, Department of Education and U.S. Government Printing Office, May, 1970.

nnerz, Ulf. *Soulside: Inquiries into Ghetto Culture and Community*. New York: Columbia University Press, 1969.

dian Voices: The First Convocation of American Indian Scholars. San Francisco: The Indian Historian Press, 1970.

elan, Lola M., editor. *Low-Income Life Styles*. U.S. Department of Health, Education, and Welfare. Welfare Division, Division of Research Publication no. 14, Washington, D.C., U.S. Government Printing Office, 1968.

are, George R. *The Measurement of Readability*. Ames, Iowa: Iowa State University Press, 1963.

ning, Frank W. and Many, Wesley A., editors. *Basic Education for the Disadvantaged Adult: Theory and Practice*. Boston: Houghton Mifflin Company, 1966.

ubach, Frank C. and Laubach, Robert S. *Toward World Literacy: The Each One Teach One Way*. Syracuse, N.Y.: Syracuse University Press, 1960.

cock, Eleanor Burke, editor. *The Culture of Poverty: A Critique*. New York: Simon & Schuster, 1971.

bow, Elliot. *Tally's Corner: A Study of Negro Streetcorner Men*. Boston: Little, Brown and Co., 1967.

RECOMMENDED READINGS (continued)

Lyman, Helen Huguenor, editor. *Library Trends*. Issue on Library Programs and Services to the Disadvantaged. Urbana, Ill.: University of Illinois Graduate School of Library Science, v. 20, no. 2 (October, 1971).

McCord, William, et al. *Life Styles in the Black Ghetto*. New York: W. W. Norton & Co., 1969.

Maslow, Abraham. *Motivation and Personality*. Harper, 1954.

Maslow, Abraham. *Toward a Psychology of Being*. Second edition. (An Insight Book) Princeton, N.J.: D. Van Nostrand, 1962, 1968.

Moore, Truman. *The Slaves We Rent*. New York: Random House, 1965.

Rogers, Carl R. *A Therapist's View of Personal Goals*. Wallingford, Pa.: Pendle Hill, 1959.

Roszak, Theodore. *The Making of a Counter Culture: Reflections on the Technocratic Society and Its Youthful Operation*. (Audion Books) New York: Doubleday, 1969.

Sexton, Patricia Cayo. *Spanish Harlem*. New York: Harper & Row, 1965.

Starke, Catherine Juanita. *Black Portraiture in American Fiction*. New York: Basic Books, 1971.

Steiner, Stan. *The New Indians*. New York: Harper & Row, 1968.

Textbooks and the American Indian. San Francisco: The Indian Historian Press, 1970.

Tinker, Miles A. *Legibility of Print*. Ames, Iowa: Iowa State University Press, 1963.

Valentine, Charles A. *Culture and Poverty: Critique and Counter-Proposals*. Chicago: University of Chicago, 1968.

Wakefield, Dan. *Island in the City: Puerto Ricans in New York*. New York: Corinth Books, 1957, 1958, 1959.

Witty, Paul A., editor. *The Educationally Retarded and Disadvantaged*. The Sixty-sixth Yearbook of the National Society for the Study of Education. Chicago: NSEE. University of Chicago Press, 1967.

Young, Whitney M., Jr. *To Be Equal*. New York: McGraw-Hill Book Co., 1964.

APPENDIXES

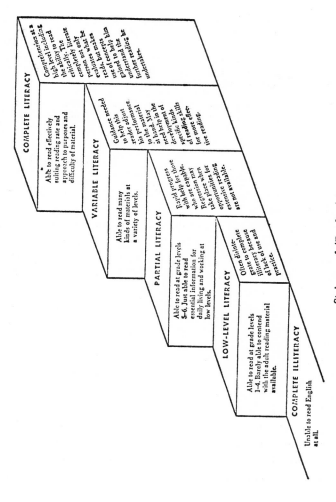

Stairway of (Reading) Literacy

From: Robinson, H. Alan. "Libraries: Active Agents in Adult Reading Improvement," *ALA Bulletin*, 57:417, May 1963. (Reprinted with permission.)

NATIONAL OPINION RESEARCH CENTER
University of Chicago

CONFIDENTIAL
Survey 4090
Nov., 1969

TIME BEGAN:	_____ AM PM

CASE NUMBER: _____

LIBRARY MATERIALS RESEARCH PROJECT
POPULATION STUDY QUESTIONNAIRE

BEGIN DECK 01

1. A. First, I want to read you a list of television programs. Please tell me if you <u>usually</u> or <u>regularly</u> watch any of them. (READ EACH ITEM AND CIRCLE APPROPRIATE CODE IN COLUMN A.)

   B. So you usually or regularly watch (NAMES OF PROGRAMS CODED YES IN A). Which <u>one</u> of those programs do you like best? (CODE ONLY ONE ITEM IN COLUMN B.)

	A. Usually Watch			B. Like Best (CODE ONE)	
	Yes	No			
(1) News and weather	1	2	10/0	01	28-29/00
(2) Let's Make a Deal.	3	4	11/0	02	
(3) Johnny Carson or Joey Bishop	5	6	12/0	03	
(4) Bonanza or Gunsmoke.	7	8	13/0	04	
(5) Black Journal.	1	2	14/0	05	
(6) Dean Martin or Johnny Cash Show. . . .	3	4	15/0	06	
(7) Movies	5	6	16/0	07	
(8) Mod Squad or Then Came Bronson	7	8	17/0	08	
(9) Sports	1	2	18/0	09	
(10) Cartoons.	3	4	19/0	10	
(11) Mayberry, RFD	5	6	20/0	11	
(12) Laugh-In or Hee Haw	7	8	21/0	12	
(13) As the World Turns.	1	2	22/0	13	
(14) Bill Cosby Show	3	4	23/0	14	
(15) Ironside or Dragnet	5	6	24/0	15	
(16) Mission Impossible.	7	8	25/0	16	
(17) Dark Shadows.	1	2	26/0	17	
(18) National Educational Television . . .	3	4	27/0	18	

2. When you have had free time during the last six months, did you do any of these things? (READ EACH ITEM AND CIRCLE APPROPRIATE CODE.)

	Yes	No			Yes	No	
(1) Visit with friends and relatives	1	2	30/0	(7) Practice judo or karate	5	6	36/0
(2) Listen to records	3	4	31/0	(8) Read a book or magazine	7	8	37/0
(3) Play cards, bingo or other games	5	6	32/0	(9) Play pool, baseball, or go bowling	1	2	38/0
(4) Go fishing	7	8	33/0	[ASK ITEM (10) ONLY IF R IS FEMALE]			
(5) Drive or walk around town	1	2	34/0	(10) Crochet, knit or sew	3	4	39/0
(6) Go to museums, concerts, exhibits	3	4	35/0				

3. How much do you enjoy watching sports? Would you say you enjoy watching sports a great deal, a little, or not at all?

A great deal 5   40/0

A little 6

Not at all 7

4. Do you ever get a chance to read a newspaper?

Yes . (ASK A-B & Q'S. 5-7) . . 1   41/0

No . . . (SKIP TO Q. 8). . . 2

IF YES:

A. What newspapers do you read? (Any other newspaper?)

42/
43/
44/
45/
46/
47/
48/
49/
50/
51/

B. Some people read newspapers more often than others. Do you read a newspaper every day, a few times a week, once a week, just on Sunday, or less often than that?

Every day 1   52/0

A few times a week . . . 2

About once a week . . . 3

Sundays only 4

573   Less often than that . . 5

5. In general, how interested are you in reading the advertisements in newspapers
    or magazines--a great deal, a little, or not at all?

                                          A great deal 3   10/0
                                          A little 4
                                          Not at all 5

---

6. A. When you read a newspaper, do you usually read each of these things or not?
        (READ EACH ITEM AND CIRCLE APPROPRIATE CODE IN COLUMN A.)

    B. If you didn't have a chance to read any newspaper for a few weeks, which
        one of those things you usually read would you miss the most? (READ
        ALL CODED YES IN A AND CODE ONLY ONE ITEM IN COLUMN B.)

	A. Usually Read			B. Miss Most
	Yes	No		(CODE ONE)
(1) News about world affairs	1	2	11/0	01 28-29/00
(2) Weather.	3	4	12/0	02
(3) Comics	5	6	13/0	03
(4) Sports	7	8	14/0	04
(5) Women's section.	1	2	15/0	05
(6) Editorials	3	4	16/0	06
(7) Letters to the editor.	5	6	17/0	07
(8) Stocks and bonds	7	8	18/0	08
(9) Advertisements (supermarket ads, other store ads, want ads)	1	2	19/0	09
(10) News about civil rights	3	4	20/0	10
(11) Death notices	5	6	21/0	11
(12) News about politics and government.	7	8	22/0	12
(13) Book reviews.	1	2	23/0	13
(14) Movie news.	3	4	24/0	14
(15) Your horoscope.	5	6	25/0	15
(16) Advice to the lovelorn.	7	8	26/0	16
(17) Television news	1	2	27/0	17

7. We are interested in where people read or glance through a newspaper. In the last six months, have you read or glanced through newspapers at any of these places? (READ EACH ITEM AND CIRCLE APPROPRIATE CODE.)

	Yes	No			Yes	No	
(1) At home	1	2	30/0	(7) At work	5	6	36/0
(2) At other people's homes	3	4	31/0	(8) At school	7	8	37/0
(3) In the library	5	6	32/0	(9) In coffee shops, bars, or restaurants	1	2	38/0
(4) At dentist's or doctor's office	7	8	33/0	(10) In drugstores, newstands or bookstores	3	4	39/0
(5) At barber shops or beauty shops	1	2	34/0	(11) In supermarkets, laundromats, or department stores	5	6	40/0
(6) On the bus, train, plane, streetcar, or at terminals or depots	3	4	35/0				

8. Do you ever listen to the radio?

Yes . . (ASK A) . . . 1   41/0

No . (GO TO Q. 9) . . 2

IF YES:

A. When you listen to the radio, do you usually or often listen to . . . (READ EACH ITEM AND CIRCLE APPROPRIATE CODE.)

	Yes	No			Yes	No	
(1) Music	3	4	42/0	(4) Religious programs	1	2	45/0
(2) News and weather	5	6	43/0	(5) Talk and interview programs	3	4	46/(
(3) Sports	7	8	44/0				

9. Now a question about music. Do you enjoy . . . (READ EACH ITEM AND CIRCLE APPROPRIATE CODE.)

	Yes	No			Yes	No	
(1) Country music	1	2	47/0	(5) Semi-classical or mood music	1	2	51/0
(2) Rock and roll	3	4	48/0	(6) Religious music	3	4	52/0
(3) Soul music	5	6	49/0	(7) Classical music	5	6	53/0
(4) Jazz	7	8	50/0	(8) Folk music	7	8	54/0

10. Do you ever read magazines?

Yes . . (ASK A-B & Q's. 11-12). 1   10/0

No . . . . . (SKIP TO Q. 13) . 2

IF YES:

A. What magazines do you read? Any others? (RECORD VERBATIM AND CODE AS MANY
APPLY. DO NOT USE CATEGORIES AS PROBES.)

(1) Life or Look 1   11/0

(2) Readers Digest 2   12/0

(3) Ebony or Jet 3   13/0

(4) News (i.e., Time, News Week, U.S. News & World Report) 4   14/0

(5) Women's (i.e., Ladies Home Journal, McCalls, Good Housekeeping,
Better Homes & Gardens) 5   15/0

(6) Women's Fashions (i.e., Glamour, Mademoiselle, Vogue). 6   16/0

(7) Men's (i.e., Playboy, Esquire, Argosy, True) 7   17/0

(8) Sports (i.e., Sports Illustrated, Field & Stream). 8   18/0

(9) Movie or Television (i.e., Modern Screen, Motion Screen,
Photo Play) 1   19/0

(10) Love & Romance (i.e., Modern Romance, True Stories, Tan) 2   20/0

(11) Religious (i.e., Sacred Heart Magazine, Catholic Digest,
Columbian 3   21/0

(12) Other Digests (i.e., Pageant, Coronet, Black Digest) 4   22/0

(13) Trade magazines (i.e., Mechanics Illustrated, Electronics
World). 5   23/0

(14) Other SPECIFY) 6   24/0

B. IF MORE THAN ONE READ: Which one of these magazines would you miss most
if you were unable to get it for several months?

25-2

11. Magazines have stories about many things. Do you usually read magazine stories about . . . (READ EACH ITEM AND CIRCLE APPROPRIATE CODE.)

	Yes	No			Yes	No	
(1) Crime and mystery .	1	2	27/0	(5) The lives of real people	1	2	31/0
(2) Space and science fiction	3	4	28/0	(6) Travel	3	4	32/0
(3) Love and romance .	5	6	29/0	(7) Sports	5	6	33/0
(4) War	7	8	30/0	(8) Adventure	7	8	34/0

12. We are interested in where people read or glance through magazines. In the last six months, have you read or glanced through magazines at any of these places? (READ EACH ITEM AND CIRCLE APPROPRIATE CODE.)

	Yes	No			Yes	No	
(1) At home	1	2	35/0	(7) At work.	5	6	41/0
(2) At other people's home	3	4	36/0	(8) At school.	7	8	42/0
(3) In the library . .	5	6	37/0	(9) In coffee shops, bars, or restaurants. . .	1	2	43/0
(4) At dentist's or doctor's office .	7	8	38/0	(10) In drugstores, news-stands, or book-stores.	3	4	44/0
(5) At barber shops or beauty shops . .	1	2	39/0	(11) In supermarkets, laundromats, or department stores.	5	6	45/0
(6) On the bus, train, plane, streetcar, or at terminals or depots	3	4	40/0				

13. When you have some free time, do you sometimes go to . . . (READ EACH ITEM AND CIRCLE APPROPRIATE CODE.)

	Yes	No			Yes	No	
(1) Dances	1	2	46/0	(5) The Y or YW	1	2	50/0
(2) The park or a zoo .	3	4	47/0	(6) A neighborhood center	3	4	51/0
(3) A bar, cocktail lounge, or tavern.	5	6	48/0	(7) Church, synagogue, mosque.	5	6	52/0
(4) The movies	7	8	49/0	(8) Pool hall or bowling alley	7	8	53/0

577

14. Have you ever gone to a public library?

                                          Yes . . (ASK A) . . . 1   54/0

                                          No   (GO TO Q. 15) . . . 2

A. IF YES: Within the past six months, have you gone to a public library . . .
             (READ EACH ITEM AND CIRCLE APPROPRIATE CODE.

	Yes	No			Yes	No	
(1) To meet friends.	1	2	55/0	(8) To see a movie .	7	8	62/0
(2) To take children there	3	4	56/0	(9) To borrow or listen to records	1	2	63/0
(3) To borrow books.	5	6	57/0	(10) To see an exhibit	3	4	64/0
(4) To ask for some information .	7	8	58/0	(11) To go to a lecture or program	5	6	65/0
(5) To read a magazine	1	2	59/0	(12) To tour the library	7	8	66/0
(6) To read a book.	3	4	60/0	(13) To study there . .	1	2	67/0
(7) To read a newspaper . . .	5	6	61/0				

                                                            BEGIN DECK 04

15. Do you ever read comic books?

                                          Yes . . . (ASK A) . . . 1   10/0

                                          No . . (GO TO Q. 16) . . 2

A. IF YES: Would you say you like comic books a great deal, a little,
             or not at all?

                                          Great deal 1   11/0

                                          A little 2

                                          Not at all 3

16. During the last six months, have you read any paperback or hard-cover books?

                                          Yes . (ASK A & Q'S. 17-18) . . . 1   12/0

                                          No . . . . . (SKIP TO Q. 19) . . 2

A. IF YES: About how many books have you read in the last six months?

                                          _____   13/
                                             (NUMBER)   14/

578

17. Thinking back over the last six months, could you name some of the books you have read completely or in part?

    (1) _____

    (2) _____

    (3) _____

    (4) _____

    (5) _____

    (6) _____

18. A. In choosing the books you've read or want to read, where do you usually see or hear about them? (CIRCLE AS MANY AS APPLY IN COLUMN A.)

    B. Thinking back over the last six months, where did you get the books you read? (CIRCLE AS MANY AS APPLY IN COLUMN B.)

	A. See or hear about		B. Get Books	
Friends	1	15/0	1	26/0
Member(s) of the family	2	16/0	2	27/0
Library	3	17/0	3	28/0
Book store	4	18/0	4	29/0
Drug store, grocery store, supermarket, 5 & 10 cent store	5	19/0	5	30/0
Newspapers or magazines	6	20/0	6	31/0
Radio or television	7	21/0	7	32/0
Newsstand or bookstand	8	22/0	8	33/0
School	1	23/0	1	34/0
Church	2	24/0	2	35/0
Other (SPECIFY)	3	25/0	3	36/0

19. Have you ever used books to help you with anything?

                                        Yes . (ASK A) . 1   37/0

                                        No (GO TO Q. 20) 2

A. IF YES: What things did they help you with? (RECORD VERBATIM AND CIRCLE
            AS MANY AS APPLY.)

Raising children, family relations (better mother and/or wife) . 1   38/0

School work, or school studies (tests in school, school sub-
    jects (science, geography, history, etc.) 2   39/0

Improving or learning English, reading ability and vocabulary . 3   40/0

Building, making or repairing things (carpentry, automobiles,
    machinery, welding, etc.) 4   41/0

Homemaking, nutrition, meal planning (sewing, interior decor-
    ating, planning economical meals) 5   42/0

Job placement or job improvement in present job or in another
    line of work 6   43/0

Other (SPECIFY) 7   44/0

---

20. Do you have any books of your own?   Yes . (ASK A) . 1   45/0

                                                   No (GO TO Q. 21) 2

A. IF YES: Are any of these books about . . . (READ EACH ITEM AND CIRCLE
            APPROPRIATE CODE.)

	Yes	No			Yes	No	
(1) Childcare	1	2	46/0	(11) Ways to better self (like how to get a better job)	5	6	56/0
(2) Health and nutrition	3	4	47/0				
(3) Love and romance .	5	6	48/0	(12) Building or making things	7	8	57/0
(4) Crime and mystery .	7	8	49/0				
(5) Science fiction . .	1	2	50/0	(13) Home decorating or furnishing . . .	1	2	58/0
(6) Black history or stories about black people . .	3	4	51/0	(14) Reference book, like a dictionary or encyclopedia . .	3	4	59/0
(7) Sports	5	6	52/0				
(8) Adventure	7	8	53/0	(15) Religious books, like the Bible .	5	6	60/0
(9) War	1	2	54/0				
(10) How to manage or budget money . .	3	4	55/0	[ASK ITEMS (16) & (17) ONLY IF R IS FE			
				(16) Sewing, knitting, or crocheting . .	7	8	61/0
				(17) Cooking	1	2	62/0

21. Here are some reasons people have for reading.   Are any of these true for you?
    (READ EACH ITEM AND CIRCLE APPROPRIATE CODE.)

		True	Not true	
A.	To help educate yourself	3	4	10/0
B.	To help with school work	5	6	11/0
C.	For employment	7	8	12/0
D.	To learn to do something	1	2	13/0
E.	For enjoyment	3	4	14/0

22. Comparing paperbacks to hard-cover books, would you say that you like paper-
    backs more, less, or about the same as hard-cover books?

More	 5	15/0
Less	 6	
Same	 7	
Don't know	 8	

581

23. ASK ALL PARTS FOR EACH BOOK BEFORE GOING ON TO NEXT.

A. Now I have the names of a few books. As I read each one, please tell me i you think it would be helpful, or not helpful to you. (CIRCLE CODE IN COLUMN A.)

B. Have you had a chance to read (NAME OF BOOK)? (CIRCLE CODE IN COLUMN B.)

C. IF YES TO B: How did you like (NAME OF BOOK)--very much, a little, or not at all? (CIRCLE CODE IN COLUMN C.)

	A. Helpful or not helpful	B. Read or not read	C. Did you like (NAME OF BOOK)?
(1) Write Your Own Letters: Simple Letters for Adults (by J. B. Rosenfeld & A.W. Cass)	Helpful . 1 16/0 Not helpful. 2 Don't know 3	Yes . 4 17/0 No . 5	Very much . 6 18/0 Little . . 7 Not at all. 8
(2) ABC's of Hand Tools (Public Relations Staff, GMC)	Helpful . 1 19/0 Not helpful. 2 Don't know 3	Yes . 4 20/0 No . 5	Very much . 6 21/0 Little . . 7 Not at all. 8
(3) Health in the Later Years (by Robert E. Rosenberg)	Helpful . 1 22/0 Not helpful. 2 Don't know 3	Yes . 4 23/0 No . 5	Very much . 6 24/* Little . . 7 Not at all. 8
(4) Get Your Money's Worth (by Aurelia Toyer)	Helpful . 1 25/0 Not helpful. 2 Don't know 3	Yes . 4 26/0 No . 5	Very much . 6 27/0 Little . . 7 Not at all. 8
(5) Baby and Child Care (by Dr. Benjamin Spock)	Helpful . 1 28/0 Not helpful. 2 Don't know 3	Yes . 4 29/0 No . 5	Very much . 6 30/* Little . . 7 Not at all. 8
(6) Getting and Holding a Job (by Bernard Schneider)	Helpful . 1 31/0 Not helpful. 2 Don't know 3	Yes . 4 32/0 No . 5	Very much . 6 33/* Little . . 7 Not at all. 8

582

4. How do you spend most of your time . . . working full time, part time,
looking for work, (going to school), (keeping house), or what?
(CIRCLE CODE THAT APPLIES.)

Working full time (35 hours or more) 1   34/0
Working part time . . . .
With a job but not at work because of (ASK A-E) 2
temporary illness, vacation, strike, etc. . 3

Unemployed (looking for work) 4
Retired . . . . (ASK F) . 5

Keeping house 6
In school . . . . (GO TO Q. 25) . 7
Other (SPECIFY) 8

IF CURRENTLY EMPLOYED (CODES 1, 2 OR 3), ASK A-E:

A. What kind of work do you do?

OCCUPATION: _____   35/
36/
INDUSTRY: _____   37/
38/
B. Have you done any special reading to prepare for your present work, 39/
or to improve yourself on this job?

Yes . (ASK C-D) . . 1   40/0
IF YES TO B: No . (GO TO D) . . 2
C. What reading have you done?

41/
42/

D. In connection with your work, is there any (other) special reading
you have to do?
Yes . (ASK E) . . . 3   43/0
No . (GO TO Q. 25) 4
E. IF YES TO D: What special reading do you have to do?

44/
45/

24. (Continued)

IF UNEMPLOYED OR RETIRED (CODES 4 OR 5), ASK F:

F.   What kind of work did you do on your last job?   46/
                                                                            47/
          OCCUPATION: _____   48/
                                                                            49/
          INDUSTRY: _____   50/

ASK EVERYONE BUT RETIREES:

25. Do you ever think about getting into some (other) kind of work?

                              Yes . . (ASK A) . . . 1   51/

                              No . (GO TO Q. 26) . . 2

     A.   IF YES: What type of work have you thought about getting into?
                    (BE SPECIFIC.)
                                                                  52/
                                                                  53/
                                                                  54/
                                                                  55/
                                                                  56/

---

26. In connection with your family and home life, is there any special reading
     you have done?
                              Yes . (ASK A) 1   57/
                              No . (GO TO Q. 27) . . 2

     IF YES:

     A.   What kind of things about your home life or relationships with family
          and children did you want to read about?   (RECORD VERBATIM AND CIRCLE
          ALL CODES THAT APPLY.)

                    Health 1   5/

                    Child care 2   5/

                    Budgeting 3   6/

                    Homemaking, cooking 4   6/

                    Family relationships 5   6/

                    Sex, hygiene 6   6/

                    Ethnic background (Black culture,
                       Spanish, etc.) 7   6/

                    Other (SPECIFY) 8   6/

27. We are interested in the kinds of clubs and organizations people belong to.
Are you a member of any club or group, or society or union?

                                   Yes . (ASK A-C). . .   1   10/0

                                   No   . (GO TO Q. 28) . 2

IF YES:

A. What clubs or organizations do you belong to? (CODE ALL THAT APPLY.)

         Labor union (local of some union) 1   11/0

         Religious group (men's club, Holy Name or Altar
            Rosary Society, Missionary Society) 2   12/0

         Fraternal organization or lodge (Masons, Knights
            of Columbus, Elks, Eastern Star) 3   13/0

         Veterans organizations (American Legion,
            Veterans of Foreign Wars 4   14/0

         Parent-Teacher Association   5   15/0

         Neighborhood Improvement Association, or
            neighborhood club   6   16/0

         Organization of people of the same nationality .
            background (Sons of Italy, B'nai Brith,
            Steuben Society)   7   17/0

         Sports or hobby club   8   18/0

         Political club or organization 1   19/0

         Civil rights group (SNCC, NAACP, CORE) 2   20/0

         Other (SPECIFY) 3   21/0

B. Within the last two years, have you been an officer of any of these
   clubs or organizations?

                                   Yes   3   22/0

                                   No   4

C. In connection with your club or group activities, have you used any
   special information or help from reading materials?

                                   Yes   5   23/0

                                   No   6

28. Within the last year, have you gone to any adult education classes or programs?

                                              Yes . (ASK A & B)   . . 7   24/0
                                              No . .(SKIP TO Q. 31). . 8

IF YES:

A. What were these classes or programs? (IF CLASS OR PROGRAM TITLE NOT GIVEN,
    GET FULL DESCRIPTION AND CODE ALL THAT APPLY.)

    Adult Basic Education 1   25/0

    Concentrated Employment Program   2   26/0

    Job Corps 3   27/0

    Laubach Literacy Program 4   28/0

    Manpower Development and Training (includes Skills
      Centers, On Job Training, and Education and
      Development Project) 5   29/0

    Neighborhood Youth Corps 6   30/0

    New Careers 7   31/0

    Opportunities Industrialization Centers (OIC) 8   32/0

    Special Impact 1   33/0

    Upward Bound 2   34/0

    Work Incentive Programs 3   35/0

    Public Library Programs or Reading Development
      Program 4   36/0

    Programs sponsored by private industry (i.e.,
      Project Tell by Telephone Co.) 5   37/0

    High School Equivalency Program   6   38/0

    Other (SPECIFY) 7   39/

28. Continued

   B. Specifically, what have you studied in this (these) class(es)?
      (CODE ALL THAT APPLY.)

English, reading, writing, spelling 1 40/0

Mathematics, arithmetic, bookkeeping 2 41/0

Science 3 42/0

American History 4 43/0

Child care, child psychology 5 44/0

Household skills (nutrition, cooking, sewing,
home management) 6 45/0

First aid, home nursing 7 46/0

Job training in basic office skills (typing,
filing, shorthand, business machines) . . . 8 47/0

Job training in manual skills (welding,
carpentry, machinery, electricity) 1 48/0

Other (SPECIFY) 2 49/0

---

29. Because of the things you learned in your class(es), did you go on to read any other things?

Yes 3 50/0
No   4

---

30. Because of the things you learned in your class(es), has your life changed in any way?

Yes . (ASK A) . 5 51/0
No (GO TO Q.31) 6

   A. IF YES: In what ways has it changed? (RECORD VERBATIM AND CIRCLE AS MANY CODES AS APPLY.)

Better relations or understanding of other people 1 52/0

Have more self-confidence, more mature, feel uplifted 2 53/0

Better job prospects 3 54/0

Better able to communicate with people (i.e., learned to read and write English, able to talk with all kinds of people) 4 55/0

Other (SPECIFY) 5 56/0

587

31. Have there been any periods in your life when you read very little or not
    at all?

                                    Yes . . (ASK A) . . . 1   57/0
                                    No   . (GO TO Q. 32) . . 2

    A. IF YES: When was this? Do you remember at what age? (CIRCLE APPROPRIATE
                 CODE.)
                                    Under 12 years of age . . 1   58/0
                                    12-16 years 2
                                    17-20 years 3
                                    21-29 years 4
                                    30-44 years 5
                                    45-64 years 6
                                    65 and over 7

32. At what times in your life have you read the most? (CIRCLE APPROPRIATE CODE.)
                                    Under 12 years of age . . 1   59/0
                                    12-16 years 2
                                    17-20 years 3
                                    21-29 years 4
                                    30-44 years 5
                                    45-64 years 6
                                    65 and over 7

33. Often when people are learning to read or try to improve their reading,
    they have problems of various kinds. Have you had any kind of reading
    problems that you had to overcome?

                                    Yes . (ASK A) . . . 1   60/0
                                    No (GO TO Q. 34) . 2

    A. IF YES: Did you overcome these problems?

                                    Yes 3   61/0
                                    No   4

34. A. What is the last year you completed in school?

                                   _____   10-11/99
                                   (LAST YEAR COMPLETED)

     B. What age were you when you left school?   _____   12-13/
                                                      (YEARS)

     C. What reasons did you have for leaving school?   (RECORD VERBATIM AND
         CODE AS MANY AS APPLY.)

             Was getting poor grades in school 1   14/0

             Expelled 2   15/0

             Trouble with teachers or school authorities . . . 3   16/0

             Disturbances in school 4   17/0

             Own illness 5   18/0

             Illness in family 6   19/0

             Other family problems 7   20/0

             Had to support self   8   21/0

             Had to support family 1   22/0

             Wanted to earn extra spending money 2   23/0

             Military service 3   24/0

             Married 4   25/0

             Pregnant 5   26/0

             Graduated 6   27/0

             Other (SPECIFY) 7   28/0

_____

35. What is your age now?

                                   _____   29-30/00
                                   (YEARS)

589

6. Some people have felt different about reading at different times in their life.

	A lot	A little	Not very interested
A. When you were a child--through the age of 12--how did you feel about reading? Would you say you liked to read a lot, a little, or you weren't very interested?	1	2	3 31/
B. Between the ages of 12 and 19, how did you feel about reading? Would you say you liked to read a lot, a little, or you weren't very interested?	4	5	6 32/
C. How about now? Would you say you like to read a lot, a little, or you're not very interested?	7	8	9 33/
D. IF APPLICABLE, ASK D (R IS OVER 20): During most of your adult years--between the ages of 20 and now, how did you feel about reading? Would you say you liked to read a lot, a little, or you weren't very interested?	1	2	3 34/

37. Now we are interested in how much you have read at different times in your life.

	A good deal	Some	Hardly any
A. When you were a child--through the age of 12--how much did you read? Would you say you read a good deal, you read some, or you hardly read at all?	4	5	6 35/
B. Between the ages of 12 and 19, how much did you read? Would you say you read a good deal, you read some, or you hardly read at all?	7	8	9 36/
C. What about now? Would you say you read a good deal, you read some, or you hardly read at all?	1	2	3 37/
D. IF APPLICABLE, ASK D (R IS OVER 20): During your adult years--between the ages of 20 and now, how much did you read? Would you say you read a good deal, you read some, or you hardly read at all?	4	5	6 38/

38. ASK ALL PARTS FOR EACH BOOK BEFORE GOING ON TO THE NEXT.

   A. Now I am going to read you the names of some more books. For each book,
   please tell me if you think you would like to read it or not. (CIRCLE
   CODE IN COLUMN A.)

   B. Have you had a chance to read (NAME OF BOOK)? (CIRCLE CODE IN COLUMN B.)

   C. IF YES TO B, ASK C: How did you like (NAME OF BOOK)--very much, a
   little, or not at all? (CIRCLE CODE IN COLUMN
   C.)

	A. Like to read or not	B. Read or not read	C. Did you like (NAME OF BOOK)?
(1) Call Them Heroes (by New York City Board of Education)	Yes . 1 39/0 No . 2	Yes . 3 40/0 No . 4	Very much 5 41/0 Little . . 6 Not at all 7
(2) Love and Sex in Plain Language by Eric Johnson)	Yes . 1 42/0 No . 2	Yes . 3 43/0 No . 2	Very much 5 44/0 Little . . 6 Not at all 7
(3) Reader's Digest Books	Yes . 1 45/0 No . 2	Yes . 3 46/0 No . 2	Very much 5 47/0 Little . . 6 Not at all 7
(4) Letters from Vietnam (by Bill Adler)	Yes . 1 48/0 No . 2	Yes . 3 49/0 No . 2	Very much 5 50/0 Little . . 6 Not at all 7
(5) People and Places (by Margaret Mead)	Yes . 1 51/0 No . 2	Yes . 3 52/0 No . 2	Very much 5 53/0 Little ... 6 Not at all 7
(6) The Holy Bible	Yes . 1 54/0 No . 2	Yes . 3 55/0 No . 4	Very much 5 56/0 Little . . 6 Not at all 7

591

39. Now I have a few background questions. How long have you lived in this city?

                                              _____   10-11/99

                                             (NUMBER OF YEARS)

                         All my life (SKIP TO Q. 42) . . . 88

---

40. A. Where did you go to grammar school?

            CITY/TOWN: _____   12/

            STATE: _____   13/

            IF NOT U.S., COUNTRY: _____

   B. Was that in the country, a small town or city, medium size city, suburb of a large city, or a large city?

                         Country 1   14/0

                         Small town/city (Under 25,000) 2

                         Medium size city (25,000-100,000) . . . 3

                         Suburb of a large city 4

                         Large city (100,000 or more) 5

---

41. A. Where did you go to high school?

            CITY/TOWN: _____   15/

            STATE: _____   16/

            IF NOT U.S., COUNTRY: _____

                         Didn't go (GO TO Q. 42) 17/R

   B. Was that in the country, a small town or city, medium size city, a suburb of a large city, or a large city?

                         Country 1   18/0

                         Small town/city (Under 25,000) 2

                         Medium size city (25,000-100,000) . . . 3

                         Suburb of a large city 4

                         Large city (100,000 or more) 5

42. From what country did most of your ancestors originally come?

England, Scotland, Wales, Canada, Australia . . . 01   19-20/0

Ireland 02

Germany, Austria, Switzerland 03

Scandinavia 04

Italy 05

France, Belgium 06

Poland 07

Russia, other Eastern European countries 08

Spain, Portugal 09

Africa 10

Mexico, Central America 11

Puerto Rico 12

Cuba, West Indies, Caribbean area 13

South America 14

China, Taiwan, Orient 15

Other (SPECIFY) 16

43. What languages do you speak? (CODE AS MANY AS APPLY.)

English 1   21/0
Spanish 2
Other (SPECIFY) . . 3

IF R SPEAKS MORE THAN ONE LANGUAGE, ASK A: 22/R

A. Which of these languages did you first learn to speak?

English 1   23/0
Spanish 2
Other (SPECIFY) . . 3

593

44. ASK ALL PARTS FOR EACH BOOK BEFORE GOING ON TO NEXT.

    A. Now I have the names of a few more books. For each book, please tell me if you think you would like to read it or not. (CIRCLE CODE IN COLUMN A.)

    B. Have you had a chance to read (NAME OF BOOK)? (CIRCLE CODE IN COLUMN B.)

    C. IF YES TO B: How did you like (NAME OF BOOK)--very much, a little, or not at all? (CIRCLE CODE IN COLUMN C.)

	A. Like to read or not	B. Read or not read	C. Did you like (NAME OF BOOK)?
(1) Up From Appalachia (by Charles Raymond)	Yes . 1 24/0 No . 2	Yes . 3 25/0 No . 4	Very much. 5 26/0 Little . . 6 Not at all 7
(2) The Autobiography of Malcom X	Yes . 1 27/0 No . 2	Yes . 3 28/0 No . 4	Very much. 5 29/0 Little . . 6 Not at all 7
(3) Perez and Martina, A Puerto Rican Folk Tale (by Pura Belpre)	Yes . 1 30/0 No . 2	Yes . 3 31/0 No . 4	Very much. 5 32/0 Little . . 6 Not at all 7
(4) Black Like Me (by John Griffin)	Yes . 1 33/0 No . 2	Yes . 3 34/0 No . 4	Very much. 5 35/0 Little . . 6 Not at all 7
(5) Selected Poetry (by Langston Hughes)	Yes . 1 36/0 No . 2	Yes . 3 37/0 No . 4	Very much. 5 38/0 Little . . 6 Not at all 7
(6) Profiles In Courage (by John F. Kennedy)	Yes . 1 39/0 No . 2	Yes . 3 40/0 No . 4	Very much. 5 41/0 Little . . 6 Not at all 7

594

5. Now I want to know how you feel about particular kinds of books. For example, poetry. Do you like to read poetry books very much, a little, or not at all? CIRCLE APPROPRIATE CODE. REPEAT FOR EACH ITEM BELOW.

		Very much	A little	Not at all	
A.	Poetry	1	2	3	42/0
B.	Plays	4	5	6	43/0
C.	Short stories	7	8	9	44/0
D.	Scientific writings	1	2	3	45/0
E.	Essays	4	5	6	46/0
F.	Novels	7	8	9	47/0
G.	Biography or autobiography (that is, the lives of people)	1	2	3	48/0
H.	Historical books	4	5	6	49/0

6. When you read, do you read more for pleasure and relaxation, or more for information?

Pleasure and relaxation . . . 1   50/0

Information 2

Both 3

Don't know 4

595

47. A. Here is the last list of book names. Again, for each book, will you tell me if you would like to read it or not? (CIRCLE CODE IN COLUMN A.)

B. Have you had a chance to read (NAME OF BOOK)? (CIRCLE CODE IN COLUMN B.)

C. IF YES TO B: How did you like (NAME OF BOOK)--very much, a little, or not at all?

	A. Like to read or not	B. Read or not read	C. Did you like (NAME OF BOOK)?
(1) Diane's New Love (by Betty Cavanna)	Yes . 1 51/0 No . 2	Yes . 3 52/0 No . 4	Very much . 5 53/0 Little . . 6 Not at all. 7
(2) James Bond Stories	Yes . 1 54/0 No . 2	Yes . 3 55/0 No . 4	Very much . 5 56/0 Little . . 6 Not at all. 7
(3) Hot Rod (by Henry Felsen)	Yes . 1 57/0 No . 2	Yes . 3 58/0 No . 4	Very much . 5 59/0 Little . . 6 Not at all. 7
(4) Shane (by Jack Schaefer)	Yes . 1 60/0 No . 2	Yes . 3 61/0 No . 4	Very much . 5 62/0 Little . . 6 Not at all. 7
(5) Perry Mason Mysteries (by Erle Stanley Gardner)	Yes . 1 63/0 No . 2	Yes . 3 64/0 No . 4	Very much . 5 65/0 Little . . 6 Not at all. 7
(6) Life with the Lucketts (by Phyllis Morris)	Yes . 1 66/0 No . 2	Yes . 3 67/0 No . 4	Very much . 5 68/0 Little . . 6 Not at all. 7

596

48. Now I would like to get some overall picture of your reading habits.

    A. What do you read most often--newspapers, magazines, or books? (CIRCLE ONE CODE IN COLUMN A.)

    B. And which do you read least often? (CIRCLE ONE CODE IN COLUMN B.)

	A. Read most often		B. Read least often	
Newspapers . . .	1	10/0	1	11/0
Magazines . . .	2		2	
Books	3		3	
Don't know . . .	4		4	

49. In your reading, do you ever read . . . (READ LIST AND CIRCLE CODE FOR EACH.)

	Yes	No	
The newspaper called News for You	1	2	12/0
A local neighborhood paper . . .	3	4	13/0
A church bulletin or newsletter .	5	6	14/0
A union paper	7	8	15/0
Club or organization bulletin or newsletter	1	2	16/0
Racing forms	3	4	17/0
Weekly Reader	5	6	18/0

50. Would you say that you read a great deal, some, a little, or hardly anything?

            A great deal 1   19/0

            Some 2

            A little 3

            Hardly anything 4

51. Would you say you are a good reader, a fair reader, or a poor reader?

            Good 5   20/0

            Fair 6

            Poor 7

            Don't know 8

52. When you were a child, did you read any books besides those in school?

            Yes   1   21/0

            No   2

53. When you were a child, did you have any close friends who read a lot?

Yes 3   22/0

No 4

Don't know 5

54. Do you recall your parents or other relatives reading to you at home when you were a child?

Yes . (ASK A) . . 1   23/0

No (GO TO Q. 55) . 2

A. IF YES: Would you say they read to you very often, fairly often, or only occasionally?

Very often 3   24/0

Fairly often 4

Only occasionally . . 5

55. When you were a teenager, did you read any books besides those for school?

Yes 1   25/0

No 2

56. Do you now have any close friends who read a lot?

Yes 3   26/0

No 4

Don't know 5

57. At the present time, would you say that you read more, less, or about the same as most of your friends do?

More 6   27/0

Less 7

Same 8

58. Would you say that you now read more, less, or about the same amount as your parents did?

More 1   28/0

Less 2

Same 3

Don't know 4

59. Would you say that you now read more, less, or about the same as the people who live with you?

More 5   29/0

Less 6

Same 7

Live alone 8

Don't know 9

60. Do you ever read aloud to other people?

                                            Yes . (ASK A) 1   30/0
                                            No   (GO TO Q. 61) . . 2

     A. IF YES: Who do you read to? (CODE ALL THAT APPLY.)

                                            Husband or wife 1   31/0
                                            Children 2   32/0
                                            Parents   3   33/0
                                            Other relatives 4   34/0
                                            Friends 5   35/0
                                            Other (SPECIFY) 6   36/0

61. Is there anything else you would like to tell me about your reading?

I have just a few final questions.

62. What was your total family income for the last twelve months, from
     all sources, such as wages, Social Security, or other payments?   37-41/

     $_____   IF R REFUSES OR DOESN'T
                                     KNOW, GIVE YOUR ESTIMATE: $_____   42/R

63. What was your own total individual income for the last twelve months,
     from all sources such as wages, Social Security, or other payments?   43-47/

     $_____   IF R REFUSES OR DOESN't
                                     KNOW, GIVE YOUR ESTIMATE: $_____   48/R

64. How many people live in this household,
     including yourself?   _____
                                                (NUMBER)   49-50/00

Thank you very much!

                              INTERVIEWER'S SIGNATURE: _____

┌─────────────────────────┐
│ TIME _____ AM   │   DATE OF INTERVIEW: _____ , 1969
│ ENDED: _____ PM   │   (Month)   (Day)
└─────────────────────────┘   51-52/00   53-54/00

TOTAL LENGTH OF INTERVIEW: _____
                           (Minutes)
                           55-57/000

                              599

INTERVIEWER REMARKS

FILL IN IMMEDIATELY AFTER LEAVING RESPONDENT'S HOME

A. Cooperativeness of respondent:

    Very cooperative . . . . 1　58/0

    Somewhat cooperative . . 2

    Not cooperative 3

B. Interest of respondent:

    Very interested . . . . 4　59/0

    Somewhat interested . . 5

    Not interested . . . 6

C. Respondent's race:

    White . . . . . 1　60/0

    Black 2

    Other (SPECIFY). 3

D. Respondent's sex:

    Male . . . . . 4　61/0

    Female 5

E. IF THERE WAS ANYTHING UNUSUAL ABOUT THE INTERVIEW SITUATION WHICH YOU THINK AFFECTED THE RESPONDENT'S ANSWERS, TELL US ABOUT IT HERE.

    Nothing unusual . . . 1　62/0

    Something unusual . . 2
      (DESCRIBE BELOW)

COMMENTS:

Appendix 4 Stratified Sample of Programs and Their Locations in National Adult Programs Study

Region	ABE 1	CEP 2	Job 3	Laub 4	MDTA 5	NYC 6	NC 7	OIC 8	UBP 9	VOC 10	WIN 11
Boston, Mass.	X			X	X	X		X	X		X
Hartford, Conn.	X	X		X	X	X	X			X	X
Providence, R.I.		X					X	X	X	X	
I. New York, N.Y.			X	X	X			X	X		X
Philadelphia, Pa.	X	X		X	X	X	X	X		X	
Pittsburgh, Pa.	X	X				X	X			X	
Drums, Pa.			X								
II. Washington, D.C.	X	X				X	X	X	X		X
Baltimore, Md.		X		X	X	X	X	X		X	
Louisville, Ky.	X			X		X	X	X		X	
Franklin, N.C.*			X								
Cherokee, N.C.*			X								
Atlanta, Ga.	X					X	X		X	2	2
Miami, Fla.		X		X	X			X		X	
Tamp-St. Pete, Fla.	X	X		X		X	X		X		
Bristol, Tenn.*			X								
Chicago, Ill.				X		X		X	X		
Detroit, Mich.	X	X			X		X				
Cleveland, Ohio	X	X			X	X	X	X	X	X	X
Golconda, Ill.*			X								
St. Louis, Mo.	X			X		X				X	
Minn.-St. Paul, Minn.		X	X				X	2	X		X
Kansas City, Mo.	X	X		X	X	X	X	X	X	X	X
Nemo, S. Dak.*			X								
Chadron, Nebr.*			X								

Programs[xx]

Region	ABE 1	CEP 2	Job 3	Laub 4	MDTA 5	NYC 6	NC 7	OIC 8	UPB 9	VOC 10	WIN 11
II. Houston, Tex.	X	X			X	X	X		X	X	X
Dallas Tex.				X	X	X	X	X	X	X	X
New Orleans, La.	X	X		X							
San Marcos, Tex.			X								
Albuquerque, N. Mex.*			X								
III. Denver, Colo.	X	X					X	X	X		X
Salt Lake City, Utah						X	X				X
Colorado Springs, Colo.	X						X				
Cottonwood, Idaho*			X								
Anaconda, Mont.*			X								
X. Los Angeles, Calif.	X	X		X	X	X	X			X	X
San Francisco/ Oakland, Calif.		X		X	X	X	X	X	X	X	X
Seattle, Wash.	X								X	X	
Astoria, Ore.*		X									
White Swan, Wash.*		X									

*Job Corps Programs are not in City

Region I: Conn., Me., Mass., N.H., R.I., Vt.
Region II: Del., N.J., N.Y., Pa.
Region III: D.C., Ky., Md., N.C., Va., W. Va.
Region IV: Ala., Fla., Ga., Miss., S.C., Tenn.
Region V: Ill., Ind., Mich., Ohio, Wis.
Region VI: Iowa, Kans., Mo., Minn., Nebr., N. Dak., S. Dak.
Region VII: Ark., La., N. Mex., Okla., Tex.
Region VIII: Colo., Idaho, Mont., Utah, Wyo.
Region IX: Ariz., Calif., Nev., Oreg., Wash.

1. Adult Basic Education (ABE) n=18
2. Concentrated Employment Program (CEP) n=17
3. Job Corps (Job) n=15
4. Laubach Literacy, Inc. (Laub) n=15
5. Manpower Development and Training Center (MDTA) n=14
6. Neighborhood Youth Corps (NYC) n=18
7. New Careers (NC) n=17
8. Opportunities Industrializatio Centers, Inc. (OIC) n=15
9. Upward Bound (UPB) n=17
10. Vocational Education (VOC) n=1
11. Work Incentive Program (WIN) n=18

total = 178

Appendix 7 : Sources of Adult New Reader Materials

Library Materials in Service   University of Wisconsin-Madison
to the Adult New Reader   Library School

AB---U.S. Office of Education, Adult Education Branch, Division of
     Adult Education and National University Extension Association,
     Bibliography Materials for the Adult Basic Education Student.
     May 1967.

AEC-- Ann Hayes, et al., *An Investigation of Materials and Methods
     for the Introductory Stage of Adult Literacy Education*
     (ED 014 629). Springfield, Ill., State Office of the Super-
     intendent of Public Instruction, 1967.

ASD--American Library Association, ASD Committee on Reading Improve-
     ment for Adults, "Books for Adults Beginning to Read, revised
     1967," *The Booklist and Subscription Books Bulletin,* 75 (Dec-
     ember 1, 1967), 426-37.

BA---Ibid.

BH---Robert F. Barnes and Andrew Hendrickson, *A Review and Apprai-
     sal of Adult Literacy Materials and Programs.* Ohio State
     University, Center for Adult Education, College of Education,
     1965.

BJC--Books/Jobs Project, *Core List.* Cleveland, Ohio, State Library
     of Ohio, 1968.

BJS--Books/Jobs Project, *Supplementary List.* Cleveland, Ohio, State
     Library of Ohio, 1968.

BO---Boston Public Library, The Committee on Easy-to-Read Materials,
     Materials for the Beginning Adult Reader. 1967.

BR---Don A. Brown and Anabel P. Newman, *Study Collection File for
     Research Project, A Literacy Program for Adult City Core
     Illiterates.* State University of New York at Buffalo, 1968.

CPL--Cleveland Public Library Adult Education Department, Reading
     Centers Project, *Suggested Books for Beginning Adult Readers.*
     1967.

CWU--Church Women United, National Program in Adult Basic Education,
     A Selected Bibliography for Volunteers in Adult Basic Education.
     1969.

DA---Louis A. D'Amico, Nicholas A. Fattu, and Lloyd S. Standlee,
     An Annotated Bibliography of Adult Literacy Training Materials
     (Bulletin of the Institute of Educational Research at Indiana
     University, vol. 1, no. 3), 1954.

DE---Denver Public Library, *Adult Basic Education Series*. n.d.

F1---Daniel N. Fader and Morton H. Shaevitz, *Hooked on Books*. New York, Berkley Publishing Corp., 1966.

F2---Daniel N. Fader and Elton B. McNeil, *Hooked on Books, Program and Proof*. New York, Berkley Publishing Corp., 1968.

FO---David Ford and Eunice Nicholson, *Adult Basic Reading in the U.S.* Newark, Delaware, International Reading Association, 1967.

K----Marion D. Spencer and Mary K. Chemerys, *Bibliography of Literacy Materials*. Kalamazoo Library System, Adult Reading Center, 1967.

LA---Los Angeles Public Library, *Report of Library Services and Construction Act*. 1966.

LN---Michigan State Library, Department of Education, *Adult Basic Education Program: High Interest - Low Difficulty Collection*. Lansing, Michigan, 1968.

MI---Milwaukee Public Library, *About People in A.B.E. Books*. 1967.

MI2--Milwaukee Public Library, *Adult Basic Education Books*. 1970.

PH---The Free Library of Philadelphia, *Reader Development Program Annotated Bibliography. January 1, 1971*. (This bibliography is a compilation of materials which appeared in *Pivot* during the period 1967-1971).

SM---Jeanette Smith, *Books for New Readers: A Bibliography*. Syracuse, New York, New Readers Press, 1964.

SU---Edward G. Summers, *Materials for Adult Basic Education: An Annotated Bibliography*. (Occasional papers in reading, v.1) Indiana University, School of Education, 1967.

VBK--National Book Committee, *Guidelines for VISTAS, for Use with VISTA Book Kits*. New York, VISTA, 1966.

WO---Wayne Otto and David Ford, "Materials for Teaching Adults to Read," in *Teaching Adults to Read*. New York, Houghton Mifflin, 1967, pp. 43-134.

LMRP STAFF, ADVISERS, CONSULTANTS, AND RESOURCE PERSONS

LMRP Staff

Helen Huguenor Lyman, project director

Orrilla Blackshear, materials analysis coordinator

Shirley Hall, field studies coordinator

Evelyn Levy, specialist in materials analysis

Lynn Lum, project specialist

Diane Wheeler Strauss, assistant materials analyst

Mary Hickey Teloh, materials analyst

Graduate Student Assistants

Robin Block	Renee Adler Mansheim
Joyce Bridge	Christine Moore
John Davidson	Veronica Murray
Yekutiel Deligdisch	Bonnie Prussin
Sandra Donovan	Anne Radtke
Jerilyn Dugan	Daniel Richards
Nancy Foth	Roger Rigterink
Prentiss Gillespie	Cheryl Sloan
David Grant	Nancy Sternback
Marguerite Hammett	Mary Hickey Teloh
Lawrence Hurlburt	Valerie Warren
Emil Levenson	Beacher Wiggins
Evelyn McQueen	Charles Wolfe
Ruth Mason	

LMRP Special Consultants

Helene Aqua, formerly associate director, Rural Family Development, University of Wisconsin-Madison, and El Centro Hispano, Milwaukee, Wisconsin

William F. Brazziel, director of general education, Norfolk Division, Virginia State College, Norfolk, Virginia

Don A. Brown, director of Reading Center Clinic, State University of New York at Buffalo

Philip H. Ennis, chairman, Department of Sociology, Wesleyan University, Middletown, Connecticut

Myron J. Lefcowitz, assistant director, Institute for Research on Poverty, and sociologist, University of Wisconsin-Madison

Margaret M. Miller, senior field supervisor, National Opinion Research Center, University of Chicago

Anabel P. Newman, Reading Center Clinic, State University of New York at Buffalo

Alice Norton, Alice Norton Public Relations, Ridgefield, Connecticut

Charles D. Palit, associate director, Survey Research Laboratory, University of Wisconsin-Madison

Jeffrey A. Raffel, project director, Study of Exemplary Public Library Programs, Barss, Retizel & Associates, Inc., Cambridge, Massachusetts

Harold H. Roeder, professor, Reading Center, New York State University College, Fredonia, New York

Paul B. Sheatsley, director, Survey Research Service, National Opinion Research Center, University of Chicago

Lynne Skenadore, librarian, Menominee County Library, Keshena, Wisconsin

Hardy R. Franklin, community field coordinator, Brooklyn Public
Library, and doctoral candidate at Rutgers University, School
of Library Services, New Brunswick

Annie T. Reid, faculty member, School of Library and Information
Services, University of Maryland, College Park

Harold H. Roeder, assistant professor, School of Education, New
York State University College, Fredonia, New York

LMRP Resource Persons in the Cooperating Public Libraries

Positions named are those in effect at the time of the study.

Boston Public Library
Kathleen B. Hegarty, coordinator of adult services

Brooklyn Public Library
Dorothy Nyren Curley, coordinator of adult services
John C. Frantz, director
Richard L. Keller, chief, Reading Improvement Division

Buffalo and Erie County Public Library
Diane Bockrath, assistant library-community coordinator
Barbara Foster, assistant library-community coordinator
Winifred Harper, deputy director
Lydia Hoffman, assistant library-community coordinator
William A. Miles, library-community coordinator, Inner City Project
  LEAP

Carnegie Library of Pittsburgh
Keith Doms, director
Kate Kolish, assistant director

Cleveland Public Library
Edward A. D'Alessandro, deputy director
Fern Long, associate director
Mary A. Springman, acting supervisor, Adult Education Department

Enoch Pratt Free Library
Edwin Castagna, director
Louise Leath, branch librarian, Pennsylvania Avenue Branch
Evelyn Levy, supervisor, library services, Community Action Program
Louise L. Litke, branch librarian, Dundalk Branch
Mary Logan, branch librarian, Walbrook Branch
Emily W. Reed, coordinator of adult services

The Free Library of Philadelphia

John A. Axam, head, Stations Department, Reader Development Program

Marie A. Davis, coordinator, Office of Work with Adults and Young Adults

Marilee Foglesong, field worker, Reader Development Program

Emerson Greenaway, director

Los Angeles Public Library

Marion K. Cobb, assistant to the dean for community and professional relations, Graduate School of Library Service, University of California at Los Angeles

Johanna G. Sutton, coordinator, Library Services Continuation Act Project

Madison Public Library

Ellen Ericksen, assistant director

Bernard Schwab, director

Milwaukee Public Library

Paul Gratke, coordinator, Service to Adults

Richard Krug, director, Milwaukee Public Library

Vivian Maddox, assistant city librarian, Milwaukee Public Library

Nolan Neds, supervisor, Neighborhood and Extension Service

New Haven Free Public Library

Meredith Bloss, city librarian

Eva Williams, director, Library Centers

The New York Public Library

Mary K. Conwell, children's librarian, South Bronx Project

Jean O. Godfrey, chief, branch libraries

Lillian Lopez, director, South Bronx Project

Bernice MacDonald, coordinator of adult services

Marian Phillips, adult specialist for the Bronx

Mary Lane Tacchi, first assistant, Kingsbridge Branch

Wendell Wray, director, North Manhatten Project

Prince Georges County Memorial Library

Elizabeth Abolin, coordinator of adult services

Anne A. Sweat, assistant coordinator of adult services

Norfolk Public Library

Arthur M. Kirkby, head librarian, Norfolk Public Library

William F. Brazziel, director of general education, Virginia State College

George C. Crawley, executive director, Southeastern Tidewater Opportunity Project

LMRP Resource Persons for the Population Study

Positions named are those in effect at the time of the study

Baltimore

C. Naomi Bauernfeind, specialist, Adult Division, Baltimore City Public
   Schools

Christine O. Coleman, counselor, Opportunities Industrialization
   Center, Inc.

Anna Curry, librarian, Hollins Payson Branch, Enoch Pratt Free Library

Fred W. Lane, 1st Street Branch, Enoch Pratt Free Library

Louise Leath, librarian, Pennsylvania Avenue Branch, Enoch Pratt Free
   Library

Evelyn Levy, supervisor, library services, Community Action Program,
   Enoch Pratt Free Library

Bill Streamer, librarian, Broadway Branch, Enoch Pratt Free Library

Brooklyn

Gladys Alesi, director, WIN, New York City Board of Education

Dorothy Nyren Curley, coordinator of adult services, Brooklyn
   Public Library

Mildred E. Hill, director, Neighborhood House of City of New York,
   Inc.

Cleveland

Corinne A. Allen, supervisor of assessment, Orientation Center,
   AIM-JOBS

Roger L. Crawford, executive director, Opportunities Industrialization Center, Inc.

Albert D. Cunningham, Jr., general manager, Woodland Job Center,
   Cleveland Board of Education

Louis J. Federico, supervisor, Manpower Training Center (Manpower
   Development and Training Program), Cleveland Board of Education

Miriam Grobsith, assistant director, Child Care Worker Training
   Program, Cleveland College Training Center

Ellsworth Harpole, director, Project PEACE Skill Center

Clarence H. Holmes, project director, AIM-JOBS

Peggy F. Hunter, Project PEACE Skill Center

Robert G. Keim, coordinator, Manpower Training Center, (Manpower
  Development and Training Program), Cleveland Board of Education

Fern Long, acting director, Cleveland Public Library

John L. McKenna, coordinator, Work-Study Program, Woodland Job
  Center, Cleveland Board of Education

Mary A. Springman, director, Books/Jobs Project, Cleveland Public
  Library

Nash Thompson, teacher, Opportunities Industrialization Center, Inc.

Ellen F. Wilde, Division of Adult Education, Cleveland Board of
  Education

Los Angeles

Faber K. Ames, principal, Abraham Lincoln Adult School

James S. Laster, vice-principal, Abraham Lincoln Adult School

Jean M. Lovell, head counselor, Watts Skill Center

John G. McCants, principal, Jefferson Community Adult School

Maurice McGehee, principal, Watts Skill Center

Clinton Rice, director, Community Skill Center

Robert W. Rupert, principal, Venice Community Adult School

Johanna G. Sutton, federal project coordinator, Los Angeles Public
  Library

Thomas G. Trusty, principal, Manual Arts Community Adult School

Milwaukee (pretest)

Helene Aqua, El Centro Hispano

Aldo W. Bertolas, assistant dean, Basic Education, Milwaukee
  Technical College

Vivian Harding, director, Laubach Literacy Center

Tom Holberg, Manpower Training Services

Thomas Newman, director, Manpower Training Services

Elaine E. Ong, Manpower Training Services

Philadelphia

Anthony J. Amico, supervisor, Operation Alphabet, Division of School Extension, Philadelphia Board of Education

Fletcher Amos, Opportunities Industrialization Center

John A. Axam, head, Stations Department, The Free Library of Philadelphia

Robert H. Coates, director, Division of School Extension, Philadelphia Board of Education

Marie A. Davis, coordinator, Office of Work with Adults and Young Adults, The Free Library of Philadelphia

Minerva Deame, Ernesto Ramos Antonini Development Center

Although the resource persons listed here made major contributions to the LMRP, many others, particularly teachers, contributed from time to time.